Morphologies of Faith

ÆR

American Academy of Religion
Studies in Religion

Editor
Lawrence S. Cunningham

Number 59
MORPHOLOGIES OF FAITH

edited by
Mary Gerhart
Anthony C. Yu

MORPHOLOGIES OF FAITH
Essays in Religion and Culture in Honor of Nathan A. Scott, Jr.

edited by
Mary Gerhart
Anthony C. Yu

Scholars Press
Atlanta, Georgia

MORPHOLOGIES OF FAITH

edited by
Mary Gerhart
Anthony C. Yu

© 1990
The American Academy of Religion

Library of Congress Cataloging in Publication Data

Morphologies of faith : essays in religion and culture in honor of
    Nathan A. Scott, Jr. / edited by Mary Gerhart, Anthony C. Yu.
    p. cm. -- (American Academy of Religion studies in religion :
    no. 59)
    Includes bibliographical references.
    ISBN 1-55540-509-6 (alk. paper). -- ISBN 1-55540-534-7 (pbk. :
    alk. paper)
    1. Theology. 2. Christianity and literature. I. Scott, Nathan
A. II. Gerhart, Mary. III. Yu, Anthony C., 1938- . IV. Series:
BR50.M657 1990
230--dc20   90-43164
                                                    CIP

Printed in the United States of America
on acid-free paper

Contents

II

✦═◉═✦

Genres and Types

III

✦═◉═✦

Studies of Individual Authors
and Texts

IV

-•➤═◉═◄•-

Bibliography of Nathan A. Scott, Jr.

V

-•➤═◉═◄•-

Contributors

Acknowledgments

A volume of this nature perforce owes its making to many hands. In addition to the contributors, several other persons should be mentioned. Mrs. Martha Morrow-Vojacek of The University of Chicago Divinity School has been tireless in the giving of time and energy for the preparation of the manuscript. Professors Lawrence S. Cunningham (Editor, *Studies in Religion Series*), Robert Detweiler (Chairperson, Committee on Publications, The American Academy of Religion), and Dennis Ford (Associate Director for Publications, Scholars Press) have all extended their crucial assistance at various stages to expedite the book's publication. They have the editors' lasting gratitude.

Nathan A. Scott, Jr.

Nathan A. Scott, Jr., An Appreciation

ANTHONY C. YU

-→=◎⊂=←-

By any account Nathan Scott must be reckoned one of the most extraordinary scholars and educators of twentieth-century America. Born in
Cleveland in 1925 but reared in Detroit, he won admission to the
University of Michigan at age 16 and took the B.A. in 1944. Two years
later he earned the B.D. from New York's Union Theological Seminary
and in 1949 the Ph.D. from Columbia University, where he studied with
such luminaries as John Herman Randall, Jacques Barzun, Lionel
Trilling, and Reinhold Niebuhr. Since then, over ten colleges and universities (including the University of Michigan in 1988) have recognized
his achievements with honorary doctorates.

His distinguished professional career began with his appointment as
dean of the chapel at Virginia Union University in 1946. From 1948 to
1955, he rose through the ranks from instructor to associate professor at
Howard University, where he also served as Director of the General
Education Program in the Humanities. Called to the University of
Chicago Divinity School in 1955, he became the Shailer Mathews
Professor of Theology and Literature in 1972 and concurrently was ap-
pointed Professor of English in the Division of Humanities. When he
joined the faculty of the University of Virginia in 1977, he first held the
Commonwealth Chair in Religious Studies and later the William R.
Kenan, Jr. Professorship along with membership in the English
Department. He is a Kent Fellow of the Society for Values in Higher
Education, a Fellow of the American Academy of Arts and Sciences, and
a past President of the American Academy of Religion.

A prolific author, Professor Scott has written and edited twenty-five
books, contributed essays to another forty volumes, and published

literally hundreds of articles and reviews. Specializing in the fields of modern theology, modern literature (Victorian and twentieth-century studies), and modern literary theory, he has pioneered (with Amos Wilder of Harvard, Preston Roberts of Chicago, and Stanley R. Hopper of Syracuse University) in the interdisciplinary study of literary figures, history, and theory in relation to the Christian tradition of the West. Since the earliest days of his career, students numbering in the hundreds from various academic departments have been the beneficiaries of his vigorous instruction in the classroom, his searching (and sometimes, even copious) notations on their papers, and his attentive and considerate counseling. More than forty students have taken their doctorates under his tutelage, and most of these are teaching in colleges and universities across the United States.

The importance of his career is not to be measured only by his extensive bibliography or the impressive number of students he has trained, but even more by the daring and incisiveness wherewith he has cleared a pathway in an uncharted region of scholarly inquiry. Since his first publications, Nathan Scott has always thought and written in the manner of "a tightrope walker" (as Scott's own mentor, Reinhold Niebuhr, once described his own professional stance), balancing with enormous intelligence, skill, and erudition the claims and counterclaims of two venerable disciplines. It is his success as an informed, judicious, and perceptive mediator that marks his permanent contribution to the academic study of religion and of literature.

His four decades of teaching, reflection, and writing all reveal a remarkable steadfastness of purpose and consistency of conviction. There seems never to have been any doubt in his own mind about the identity of his vocation: Nathan Scott has always considered himself first and foremost a Christian theologian. In addition to the study of the historical, liturgical, scriptural, or dogmatic heritage of the community of faith, his special mission, he has always believed, centers on the serious reckoning with certain cultural forms and materials of his time. It is not accidental, therefore, that the very first essay he published in 1949 focused on a subject of lifelong concern and reflection. Titled "A Neglected Aspect of the Theological Curriculum,"[1] the essay provides a succinct statement of what he conceived to be the proper task and content of the theological enterprise, a statement that was at the same time prophetic of his own aspirations for, and interests in, that enterprise.

---

[1]   In *Journal of Religious Thought* 7 (Aut/Wint, 1949-50): 38-46.

Distinguishing between the "kerygmatic theology" stemming from Continental Neo-orthodoxy and apologetic theology, Scott locates the curriculum for the latter kind of endeavor squarely within the university, thereby bestowing on it a public character decades before "public theology" became a fashionable epithet.[2] Inspired undoubtedly by Reinhold Niebuhr, of whom it was said that "theology broke into the world; theology was no longer quarantined, and men of letters, philosophers, sociologists, historians, even statesmen, began to listen,"[3] Scott rejects the notion of apologetics as merely the defense of a religious or theistic view of the world. The kind of apologetics he has in mind, rather, "'is concerned with the implications of the Christian revelation for the rational understanding of the world and our experience in it.'"[4]

If theology is to be "in conversation with the leading intellects of the age"[5] and thereby to monitor the pulse of its culture, it cannot focus alone on "the flux of contemporary political and economic movements"[6] and ignore other kinds of materials and analyses that more directly embody and address the "inner self-explorations" of an epoch. It is on this basis that Scott makes the following declaration:

> Surely it is hardly arguable that there is a dimension of our period that we can get at only through its cultural masterpieces—the visual discoveries in modern painting from Cézanne to Matisse, Rouault, Klee, and Picasso; the revolution in poetry, beginning with Baudelaire and Rimbaud, and extending through Laforgue and Mallarmé, Rilke and Claudel, Eliot and Auden; the purely formal and the metaphysical growth, too, of the novel, in the hands of James, Joyce, Kafka, and Mann; the music of Stravinsky and Schoenberg that is so adequate a vehicle for the spirit; and finally, the cinema of Chaplin and Cocteau, Eisenstein and Olivier. These are events which the church ought to understand and know how to evaluate "without special reference to organized religion . . . but with a decisive reference to the religious element which . . . is hidden" in them all, for "in all of them there is an

---

[2] The discussions on pp. 38-39 and cited documents (especially Footnote 2) of the essay situate the theological curriculum within the context of the university curriculum and educational reform. The University of Chicago, St. John's College, and colleges of Harvard and Columbia are named as centers exemplary of "the new thought and practice" in higher education.

[3] Emil Brunner, "Some Remarks on Reinhold Niebuhr's Work as a Christian Thinker," in *Reinhold Niebuhr: His Religious, Social, and Political Thought*, ed. Charles W. Kegley & Robert W. Bretall (New York: The Macmillan Company, 1956), p. 29.

[4] Scott, "Neglected Aspect," 41, citing Paul Tillich's definition in *The Protestant Era*, trans. James Luther Adams (Chicago: The University of Chicago Press, 1948), p. 223.

[5] Brunner, *loc. cit.*

ultimate, unconditional, and all-determining concern, something absolutely
serious and therefore holy, even if expressed in secular terms."[7]

I cite this passage at length because it provides an amazingly accurate prospectus of the kind of theological inquiry that Scott had yet to
take up and make it his own. The cultural materials that he would explore with such force and eloquence over the next four decades encompass a very large group of the masters of Western modernism. Although
that exploration will concentrate on canonical literary figures, it is also
one frequently informed by considerations of the other arts—especially
painting, music, and film.[8] The aim of such exploration is to help the
Christian community understand and evaluate the texts and events of its
own contemporary culture. The method is essentially one of excavation
and decipherment of meaning, for the assumption authorizing this activity is the Tillichian notion of the latent but pervasive religious character
of human culture.

It is again no accident that even at this early date Scott has turned to
the Tillich of *The Protestant Era* for the decisive principle guiding his theological analysis of culture. With respect to the by now all too familiar
maxim formulated by Tillich that "religion is the substance of culture
and culture the form of religion,"[9] what the quoted passage in Scott's article helps to clarify is the hidden character of this religious substance.
The substance (*Gehalt*) can only be comprehended in the content of an
expressive form. As Robert Scharlemann points out in his essay in this
volume, the theology of culture which Tillich envisions is not one *"about*
culture but a theology that is present *within,* or expressed by, the cultural
works themselves. . . . A cultural *theology* is possible to the extent that a
theological interpreter can identify and provide an interpretation of the
Gehalt that is being expressed in the works of a time."[10]

This view of Tillich's on the latent religious character of culture has
often been misunderstood, and those cultural critics who invoke such a
view as a guiding principle for their work have been susceptible to the
charge of religious imperialism. If one insists on discussing in religious
terms certain cultural forms or objects that seem manifestly secular in
content and spirit, is not this a blatant imposition of an ideology, an un-

---

[6] Scott, "Neglected Aspect," 42.

[7] *Ibid.,* 43.

[8] See the essay by Linda-Marie Delloff in the present volume.

[9] *The Protestant Era,* p. 57.

[10] See below, p. 110.

scrupulous act of colonization, a wilful feat of misreading and distortion?[11]

Although the performance of the individual scholar is, of course, always subject to critique, the attack on the unseemliness or inappropriateness of the very undertaking itself in this instance represents a serious misapprehension or ignorance of the ground for such activity. Tillich's definition of religion, in this regard, is avowedly not inductive in the sense that the understanding of the subject under consideration is not derived from empirical investigations of a particular tradition or system of rites and beliefs commonly regarded as religious. His approach was aprioristic, in a way like that of the late historian of religions, Mircea Eliade, who was inclined to conceive of religion as the revelation of the sacred. Religion in Tillich's and Eliade's understanding is unambiguously essentialist and substantive: it is a given, universal phenomenon with a variety of local manifestations.

According to Eliade, religion may be defined as hierophany, as "something sacred [showing] itself to us."[12] In such a conception the sacred as the Wholly Other does not vary from tribe to tribe, culture to culture, object to object; the modes and means of its manifestation do. Just as there may be different forms of hierophany, so also the media through which the sacred manifests itself can differ.[13] The most important feature

[11] Thus Theodore Ziolkowski characterizes such "intellectual imperialism" as that "which co-opts for 'religion' every cultural impulse," in "Religion and Literature in a Secular Age: The Critic's Dilemma," *Journal of Religion* 59/1 (January, 1979): 23. To be fair to Ziolkowski, I should point out that his remark here is not directed specifically against Tillich or Scott, but only against critics who, in his judgement, tend to misread literary texts because of indiscriminate use of theological categories. Ziolkowski himself, I should further note, has used Tillich directly in literary analysis. See his "An Ontology of Anxiety in the Dramas of Schiller, Goethe, and Kleist," in *Lebendige Form: Interpretationen zur deutschen Literatur. Festschrift für Heinrich E. K. Henel*, ed. Jeffrey Sammons and Ernst Schürer (München: W. Fink, 1970), pp. 121-45.

[12] Mircea Eliade, *Patterns in Comparative Religion* (New York: Sheed & Ward, 1958), pp. 7 ff.; cf. also *The Sacred and The Profane* (New York: Harcourt Brace Jovanovich, 1959), pp. 11 ff.; and his essay on "Hierophany" with Lawrence E. Sullivan in *The Encyclopedia of Religion*, ed. Mircea Eliade, 15 vols. (New York: Macmillan Publishing Company, 1987), 6, 313-16.

[13] To discuss both the unity and diversity of religious experience, Eliade appeals to a literary analogy that is interesting and revealing. His main purpose, he says, "is to bring out the specific characteristics of the religious experience, rather than to show its numerous variations and the differences caused by history. It is somewhat as if, in order to obtain a better grasp of the poetic phenomenon, we should have recourse to a mass of heterogeneous examples, and, side by side with Homer and Dante, quote

of such manifestation, however, is the paradox obtaining in the phenomenology of hierophany. "By manifesting the sacred, any object becomes *something else*, yet it continues to remain *itself*, for it continues to participate in its surrounding cosmic milieu. A *sacred* stone remains a *stone*; apparently (or, more precisely, from the profane point of view), nothing distinguishes it from all other stones. But for those to whom a stone reveals itself as sacred, its immediate reality is transmuted into a supernatural reality."[14] This "occultation" of the sacred not only points to its hidden character but also to the *skandalon* of its medium insofar as it exists as a profane object. Just as "the modern Occidental. . . finds it difficult to accept the fact that, for many human beings, the sacred can be manifested in stones or trees,"[15] so the same modern person may bristle at the Tillichian notion that a cultural artifact through study and interpretation can be rendered religiously significant even if the content of that artifact is patently irreligious or even anti-religious.

When Tillich's theology of culture is seen in this light, its attractiveness for Scott becomes readily apparent for at least two reasons. On the one hand, Tillich's claim about the presence of the religious in culture is indeed a totalizing claim. The religious is not one among many elements of culture; it is its very constitutive substance. It can, to be sure, manifest itself in contents and forms that are explicitly associated with, and enshrined in, various commonly recognized religious systems and traditions of the world. But religion, as Tillich is fond of declaring, is "more than a system of symbols, rites, and emotions directed toward a highest being."[16] The "concern" that is "ultimate, unconditional, and all-determining" and which Tillich regards as the essence of religion is also the defining characteristic of the human spirit. Thus religion, according to Scott's own interpretation of the Tillichian understanding, "does not pertain exclusively to any particular sphere of human life alongside other spheres or to any special psychic or cognitive function but . . . it has to

---

Hindu, Chinese, and Mexican poems; that is, should take into consideration not only poetics possessing a historical common denominator (Homer, Vergil, Dante) but also creations that are dependent upon other esthetics. From the point of view of literary history, such juxtapositions are to be viewed with suspicion; but they are valid if our object is to describe the poetic phenomenon as such, if we propose to show the essential difference between poetic language and the utilitarian language of everyday life." *Sacred and Profane*, p. 16. The stability and universality of "the poetic phenomenon" apparently finds its analogue in the ubiquity of "cosmic sacrality."

14   Eliade, *Sacred and Profane*, p. 12.
15   *Ibid.*, p. 11.
16   *The Protestant Era*, p. 56.

do, rather, with the direction of the human spirit—in all provinces of life and culture—toward that which concerns it *ultimately*."[17] Such a view of the relations between religion and culture, if one acknowledges its validity, provides a liberating basis for the activities of the theologian of culture, for there is no area or artifact of human culture that is not a legitimate object of reflection and inquiry. Cultural forms in such a view, to use the language of Mircea Eliade, become implicit "morphologies" of the sacred.

To the extent, however, that those morphologies are only implicit, that culture frequently masks or camouflages its religious substance, "a theological interpreter" of culture is always needed, as Scharlemann has observed, and this is, I believe, the second reason why Tillich's formulation holds such appeal for Scott. Not only does Tillich's conception of culture radically broaden the theologian's field of inquiry, it also at the same time enlarges the task of theology to include the interpretation—not just of history, scripture, ritual, and symbol—but of cultural materials, the arts and artifacts of human invention as well. Theology, as Tillich says, must respond to "the totality of man's creative self-interpretation in a special period."[18] This kind of hermeneutical undertaking directly involves the theologian in the analyses of such materials, much as any literary or art critic or intellectual and social historian who is also so engaged, but the goal of these analyses and the "set of systematic categories"[19] assumed by the theologian may be quite different. In Tillich's view, the theologian can never be merely a historian or a critic, just as the object under theological investigation is never merely a cultural object. "Pictures, poems, and music can become objects of theology, not from the point of view of their aesthetic form, but from the point of view of their power of expressing some aspects of that which concerns us ultimately in and through their aesthetic form."[20]

That Tillich's thought remains an abiding reference for, and a persistent stimulant to, the cardinal concerns of Scott's intellectual and academic career is everywhere evident.[21] To show how the theological cur-

---

[17] Nathan A. Scott, Jr., "Criticism and the Religious Horizon," in *Humanities, Religion, and the Arts Tomorrow*, ed. Howard Hunter (New York: Holt, Rinehart and Winston, Inc., 1972), p. 52.

[18] Paul Tillich, *Systematic Theology*, 3 vols. (Chicago: The University of Chicago Press, 1951-63), 1, 4.

[19] See Note 4 of Scharlemann's essay.

[20] Tillich, *Systematic Theology*, 1, 13.

[21] For a more recent essay in which Scott elaborates the Tillichian theology of the arts in the context of discussing postmodernist developments, see his "Tillich's

riculum may benefit from the addition of literary and cultural studies, Scott in several of his works has repeatedly set forth what may be termed the "diagnostic" aims of such studies. Regarding them as essentially similar to the notion of *Geistesgeschichte* descending from German Romanticism of the eighteenth century, Scott asserts that

> the literary imagination offers a peculiarly direct access to those deep interiorities of feeling that constitute a people's basic life-world. It is a kind of barometer that registers the deep currents of sensibility which give to a culture its distinctive tone and style; it brings to light what is inaccessible to the procedures of empirical study; it mirrors the age, in the subtlest nuances of its fears and aspirations, of its dreams and myths, of its hopes and nightmares. And thus, it is argued, the Christian enterprise, as it seeks to make contact with the living reality of its human environment, may find in literary art a most helpful resource. Art is viewed, in other words, in its capacity to document the Time-spirit, and, in this way, it is thought to offer churchmen an indispensable kind of index to the actual world to which the Christian Evangel is to be addressed.[22]

Reinforcing this apologetic concern for relating the Christian message to "the living reality" of the human world is Scott's conviction of what is to be the actual subject that theology must reckon with. "The sovereign intention of biblical faith (and hence of Christian theology)," he declares in another essay on pedagogical matters, "is that of addressing itself not to questions of metaphysics and ontology but to questions concerning the meaning of man's historical existence."[23] To be sure, Scott neither repudiates nor denigrates the discursive, philosophical forms in which Christian theology has expressed itself down through the centuries, for he has argued elsewhere, in fact, that those "conceptual forms" arose historically because "the stories which had constituted the original witness of faith" required "a systematic explication of the metaphysical claims and the Christology and the anthropology which these stories en-

---

Legacy and the New Scene in Literature," in *The Thought of Paul Tillich*, ed. James Luther Adams, Wilhelm Pauck, and Roger L. Shinn (San Francisco: Harper & Row, 1985), pp. 137-55.

[22] "On the Place of *Litterae Humaniores* in the Curriculum of Theological Studies," in *Negative Capability: Studies in the New Literature and the Religious Situation* (New Haven: Yale University Press, 1969), p. 163.

[23] "Introduction: Theology and the Literary Imagination," in *Adversity and Grace: Studies in Recent American Literature*, ed. Nathan A. Scott, Jr. (Chicago: The University of Chicago Press, 1968), p. 4.

tailed."[24] Although "the internal coherence" of the Christian faith and its ability to "speak most persuasively to its environing culture" both perennially make demand of "systematic" reason and reflection,[25] it is also apparent that for Scott, "the meaning of man's historical existence" cannot be fathomed sufficiently if that reflection is directed only at matter and materials canonically enclosed within scripture and tradition. What the community of faith must hear, in all its fullness and nuanced resonance, is the voice of the godless, secular world that has, in the words of Dietrich Bonhoeffer, "come of age." That is the lesson Scott draws for his theological community from the late writings by that German martyr.

This does not mean that the world asks the questions and the Christian gospel provides the answer, as the procedure is usually depicted in a caricature of Tillich's theology of correlation. "The Incarnation is best honored," says Scott, "not by derogating an autonomous secularity or by attempting to bully it into submission to some presumably sacrosanct authority of the Church's *kerygma* but, rather, by allowing the world to be itself."[26] Because he believes that the Word of God can be heard "not only in the scripture and proclamation and sacraments of the community of faith but also in all those intellectual and cultural forms which, as they arise out of man's deepest encounter with his world and his own humanity, are stamped by a self-authenticating genuineness and relevance,"[27] Scott can ascribe to literary art a function even weightier than that of cultural diagnostics. "In the quest of Christian theology for deepening of its own self-knowledge," literature "can also perform an important propaedeutic function"[28] through its affective potency to enact imagined existence. Because "what the poem wants to do is to convey, as it were, what it *feels* like to hold a given perspective, and what the existential consequences are in which the holding of it eventuates," an office of the literary imagination is thus always "to vitalize meditation on matters of ultimate concern by making concrete before the immediate gaze of the mind the real cost of a given life-orientation."[29]

---

[24] "The Rediscovery of Story in Recent Theology and the Refusal of Story in Recent Literature," in *Art/Literature/Religion: Life on the Borders*, ed. Robert Detweiler, JAAR Thematic Studies 49/2 (Chico, California: Scholars Press, 1983), p. 140.

[25] *Ibid.*, p. 141.

[26] "Theology and the Literary Imagination," p. 13.

[27] *Loc. cit.*

[28] "The Place of *Litterae Humaniores*," p. 164.

[29] *Ibid.*, p. 167.

This last declaration not only makes clear how imaginative literature will facilitate theological reflection, but the optical metaphor also reveals something of Scott's view of literature itself. Though writing in the heyday of New Criticism, Scott never subscribed unreservedly to its view of poetic language as a wholly reflexive symbolic system and its implied conception of verbal art as self-subsistent icon uncontaminated by either history or metaphysics. Assuredly, the work of art does possess a form of autonomy insofar as it exists, once it has been created, as an independent object. But that created object, as Scott is fond of saying, does not enjoy a full measure of "aseity" that Christian Scholastic theology once attributed to the deity. What is of interest for Scott is not so much the art object in itself as the decisive element that makes the object art in the first place. In Scott's view that element cannot be language alone. Rather, it must spring from the human act of willing, ordering, and making, which Western poetics from Aristotle to Romanticism has affirmed to be the fundamental source of artistic creation.

Drawing on thinkers as different as Jacques Maritain, Henry James, and Eliseo Vivas, Scott argues that "it is not language which brings meaning to birth and which enables the mind to order itself—not language but *vision*."[30] Vision thus conceived refers to an imaginative order—"a shape and a significance"—conferred by the artist on his materials and on the data of experience. The artist, says Scott,

> wants to contain the rich plenitude of experience within a pattern that will illumine and give meaning to its multifarious detail and its bewildering contingency. He cannot, of course, discover such a pattern unless he has a vantage point from which to view experience and by means of which his insights may be given order and proportion. Which is to say that he can transmute the viscous stuff of existential reality into the order of significant form only in accordance with what are his most fundamental beliefs about what is radically significant in life, and these beliefs he will have arrived at as a result of all the dealings that he has had with the religious, philosophical, moral, and social issues that the adventure of living has brought his way.[31]

If such assertions bring him perilously close to the position of elevating the artist above art, Scott is too astute a student of literary theory to allow himself to be mistaken for an advocate of biographical criticism

[30] "Criticism and Theology—The Terms of the Engagement," in *Negative Capability*, p. 126.
[31] *Ibid., loc. cit.*

tout simple. Admittedly, the known author of any work of art must be, at one time, a living, historical person, and to that extent biography cannot but be a relevant context for interpretation. Nonetheless, the "vision" and "fundamental beliefs" posited for any particular work are to be detected primarily through investigation of the work. "Whatever it is . . . that concerns the poet ultimately, that constitutes his 'ruling passion' and the substance of his vision, is something to which the critic can be attentive only as it is discoverable in the work."[32]

The selection of the word, ultimately, in this assertion is manifestly deliberate, for the projected faith of the artist so understood forges the crucial link between Tillich's conception of religion and Scott's poetics. It is the point of correlation which allows Scott to stake his claim incisively: what he means by "the religious dimension of literary art" need not refer to "any special iconic materials stemming from a tradition of orthodoxy which may or may not appear in a given work." Since the creation of any work of literary art must perforce presuppose the artist's vision, "the religious dimension is something intrinsic to and constitutive of the nature of literature as such."[33]

Enabled by this understanding of the relations between religion and literature, Scott over the span of four decades of writing has covered a very large landscape encompassing different cultural subjects, issues, and figures. When one works through his formidably large bibliography, several centers of recurrent interests and emphases are evident. There are capacious but intensely focussed studies, in the form of book chapters or published essays, of individual writers who, in the earlier period of his career, are largely though not exclusively novelists. These include such familiar figures of the canon as Kafka, Silone, Lawrence, Camus, Beckett, Hemingway, Dostoievsky, Hardy, Bellow, Graham Greene, Flannery O'Connor, Norman Mailer, George Orwell, and Andre Malraux. Building on his lifelong devotion to Eliot and Auden, Scott has also written on Roethke and Gerard Manley Hopkins. More recently, the poets and philosophers who have received his attentive scrutiny include Coleridge, Arnold, Pater, Santayana, Heidegger, Stevens, Elizabeth Bishop, A. R. Ammons, Robert Penn Warren, and Richard Wilbur. As befits the creed of Scott's own poetics, these studies combine searching

---

[32] *Ibid.*, p. 129.

[33] *Ibid.*, p. 132. Scott has maintained this view steadfastly throughout his career. Cf. his article on "Religious Dimensions of Modern Literature" in *The Encyclopedia of Religion*, 8, 569-74.

textual analysis with provocative explorations of the writer's vision or belief.

Perhaps less well-known to his wide circle of colleagues and friends is Scott's judicious and discerning criticism of Black artists. From his prolific pen have come illuminating discussions of Richard Wright, James Baldwin, Ralph Ellison, and Romare Bearden. The long, informative chapter on "Black Literature" in *The Harvard Guide to Contemporary American Writing* (1979) is a profound and moving gift to his readers, as revelatory of himself as it is of his assessment of the subject.

Although this brief rehearsal clearly establishes the ease and erudition with which Scott has trafficked in the world of literary art, it by no means delimits the range of his learning or intellectual interests. The sustained effort to explore the intricate relations between the study of literature and the study of religion, for him, is not to be confined to the critical inspection of individual artists, however much such an effort may remain as one of fundamental importance in his teaching and research. With characteristic and exemplary originality, Scott throughout his career has sought to probe for new openings or points of contact between the two disciplines, to examine certain theoretical issues in different light, and to raise new questions even as he seeks solutions for old problems.

The essays gathered in his book of 1966, *The Broken Center: Studies in the Theological Horizon of Modern Literature*, may perhaps best illustrate the scope of his concerns, for they comprise diverse chapters on period styles, generic implications of comedy and tragedy, disparate topics such as mimesis and time and society and self in modern literature, and the "New Theology" of the Death-of-God theologians of the sixties. In addition one must mention a host of different studies that testify to the astonishing breadth of Scott's theological and philosophical knowledge. Among the numerous titles that can be cited are two books on existentialism, a widely acclaimed monograph on Reinhold Niebuhr, essays on Tillich, and a penetrating account of recent theologians and novelists who maintain conflictive attitudes toward narrative.

Because Tillich enjoys unambiguous prominence in Scott's own thinking, and because of the latter's steadfast commitment to engage literature in theological terms, Scott's writings can invite the occasional criticism that they are too overtly theological. An essay title such as *"Sola Gratia*—The Principle of Bellow's Fiction"[34] may startle and perhaps even

---

[34] *Adversity and Grace*, p. 27.

mislead, until the complete perusal of the essay itself makes one realize
that the critic has absolutely no intention of dubbing the novelist, as it
were, a cryptic Lutheran. The diction of both Christian and Jewish spirituality is invoked to chart and gauge "the fundamental orientation or
posture of the human spirit towards reality" evident in Bellow's novels.
In a subsequent chapter on this same author, in fact, Scott has moved beyond either the language of Christian ritual or even "a denominational
tag" like Hasidic Judaism and turned, however briefly, to names and
texts of other religious traditions for comparison with some of Bellow's
heroes and their characteristic achievement in life and self-acceptance.[35]

That chapter's allusion to the *Bhagavad-Gita* and Lao-Tse is fleeting,
and I am not aware of any instance in Scott's writings where he makes
extensive use of religious texts or ideas outside the Western Christian
tradition.[36] Nonetheless, even these brief moments may point to a problem of such importance that any program of theological criticism as the
one Scott has envisioned must sooner or later confront: namely, how
does one fulfill in practice the Tillichian ideals of apologetic theology?

We have seen that the desideratum of theological analysis of culture
is to translate what is hidden into the manifestly religious. This project,
as authorized by Tillich's method and agenda, has the twofold purpose
of interpreting the world to the religious community (thus deepening
Christian theology's self-knowledge) and of interpreting the Christian
message to the world in terms relevant to a specific temporal situation. In
both directions of this reciprocal movement of theology, one crucial
problem must be finding the language that is appropriate to such a task
of semantic transaction.

[35] "Bellow's Vision of the 'Axial Lines'," in Nathan A. Scott, Jr., *Three American Moralists: Mailer, Bellow, Trilling* (Notre Dame: University of Notre Dame Press, 1973), pp. 124-25: "in the life that is lived at the Center of life there is no straining, no muscular effort, but only a certain kind of strict attentiveness and (as Gabriel Marcel terms it) *invocation*. There, at the Center, we consent to take our hands off our lives and simply to wait—for the stroke of Grace: it is something like this that is said in the *Bhagavad-Gita* and by Lao-Tse, in the Hasidism of the Baal-Shem-Tov and by Meister Eckhart. 'Damn braces, bless relaxes.' And it is also a kind of *falling*-into Peace which seems to be the essential reality being dramatized in the late work of Saul Bellow."
[36] On one other occasion, Scott refers to *The Mustard Seed Garden Manual* (*Chieh-tzu-yuan hua-chuan*), an instructional manual for painting compiled in the Ch'ing dynasty, and lifts up the harmonious vision of man and nature ostensibly pervasive of traditional Chinese art and contrasts that spirit with the forlorn and desolate universe appearing in Camus' *L'Étranger*. See *The Broken Center*, pp. 150-51.

   Tillich's discussion of the history of Christian thought and the "theological circle" has made it clear that every generation of theological thinkers must make use of "the conceptual tools" of their period for re-stating the Christian message. "Since language is the basic and all-pervasive expression of every situation, theology cannot escape the problem of the 'situation',"[37] which is the problem of language. Just as Scholastic Theology appropriated the re-discovered vocabulary of Aristotelian philosophy for its systematic articulation, so a modern theologian like Tillich has turned to the languages of Existentialism, depth-psychology, and the philosophy of ontology for his own constructive elaboration. Tillich himself can assert that "ultimate concern is the abstract *translation* of the great commandment"[38] precisely because this form of linguistic substitution and paraphrase of Mark 12:29 is deemed necessary to make the biblical injunction understandable and meaningful. Indeed, his *Systematic Theology* is arguably the most consistent and thorough attempt since Schleiermacher's *Glaubenslehre* to translate systematically the categories and structures of Christian dogmatics into the conceptual idioms of a specific epoch.

   On the other hand, if theology is to investigate the ordinary, common activities and artifacts of secular culture, what kind of discourse can the theologian employ to name and interpret them as objects of theology: that is, to acknowledge and assess "their power of expressing some aspects of that which concerns us ultimately"? If religionless modernity tends to isolate our writing artists and forces them to discover and create for themselves the fundamental principles of meaning (and thus they must become their own priests, their own Vergil and guide),[39] with what frame of verbal expression can the critic enclose such highly individualistic visions so as to render them meaningful to a larger public? If the products of culture are in want of "any special iconic materials" that relate them to any specific religious tradition, what is the appropriate language of interpretive translation? And finally, is the language of Christian theology the most appropriate language, or is there another kind of language that, without also being tied to a specific tradition or community, may better serve to denominate and elucidate the manifold meanings of the religious?[40]

---

37 *Systematic Theology*, 1, 7.
38 *Ibid.*, 1, 11 (emphasis mine).
39 *The Broken Center*, p. 8.
40 These last two questions have also been the preoccupations of theologian Langdon Gilkey. As indicated in its title, *Naming the Whirlwind: The Renewal of God-*

Considerations such as these, I suspect, have prompted Scott to turn increasingly to the thought of Martin Heidegger for the kind of philosophical and linguistic resource he seeks. As Scott declares in *The Wild Prayer of Longing* (1971), he wants to try to articulate "a sacramental vision of reality" without the baggage of supernaturalism.[41] The problem, to put it in the simplest of terms, is how to reformulate the Platonic question of appearance and reality without giving the impression of advocating the construction of a two-storied universe.[42] The language of Heidegger, saturated as it is with his life-long meditation on the Being of beings—the differences of different beings and the onefoldness of their identity—and on the relationship between being and language, seems particularly helpful to Scott in his attempt to express a new kind of sacramentalism of world and art. Thus the Heideggerian notion of Being as that which permits and enables the things of earth to "come-to-presence" suggests to Scott "a profoundly religious outlook," because though not to be identified with the tenets of classical theism, this notion nonetheless can be taken to affirm both Being as "steadfast," "trustworthy," and "gracious," and the universe as its transparent sign and embodiment.[43] Moreover, the emphasis of Heidegger on the thinker as poet and on the alethetic nature of poetic language (truth as disclosure and unconcealment) has special resonance as well. Commenting on Heidegger's famous discussion of a Van Gogh's painting, Scott gives us this summation:

Language (Indianapolis: The Bobbs-Merrill Company, Inc., 1969) is a sustained attempt to come to terms with the many ramifications of these problems of the form and validity of religious language in a secular culture, and of the possibility of detecting religious meanings in non-religious discourses. See esp. pp. 247 ff. For a more recent discussion of the problem of language in relation to theological discourse, see David Tracy, *Plurality and Ambiguity: Hermeneutics, Religion, Hope* (New York: Harper & Row, 1987), pp. 47-65.

[41] See pp. 59-60 of the book.

[42] Tillich has stated this problem succinctly in his *Systematic Theology*, 1, 20: "What is the relation of signs, symbols, or logical operations to reality? Every answer to this question says something about the structure of being. It is ontological. . . . Ontology is not a speculative-fantastic attempt to establish a world behind the world; it is an analysis of those structures of being which we encounter in every meeting with reality. This was also the original meaning of metaphysics; but the preposition *meta* now has the irremediable connotation of pointing to a duplication of this world by a transcendent realm of beings. Therefore it is perhaps less misleading to speak of ontology instead of metaphysics." Tillich's indebtedness here to Heidegger seems obvious.

[43] *The Wild Prayer of Longing*, pp. 71-73.

So poetic art, because it renders us alert to the concrete realities of the world in the dimension of presence, brings us into the region of Being, since Being itself is nothing other than Presence. In performing this kind of function, however, poetry is for Heidegger but the crucial instance of language in general, since, as he says in the *Holzwege*, the primary task of language is not merely to be a technique of signification but "to bring beings as such for the first time into the Open." Indeed, man does not have a "world," does not have any sort of unified matrix of meanings and relations in which to dwell, unless he has a language, a way of declaring what things "appear to be as they come into the Open." This, one imagines, is the insight that he takes to be implicit in the saying of Hölderlin for which he has such a great liking, that "poetically,/Man dwells upon the earth." Man dwells upon the earth— in a really human way—only in so far as he transforms "earth" into "world," and he can have a world only if he has language, only if he has a way of being open to Being and of naming the things of earth in which Being resides: which is to say that he can have a world only as he manages in some manner to be a "poet."[44]

Given such a view of being and presence, of poetry and language, it is not surprising to find Scott deeply troubled in recent years by the practitioners of *nouvelle critique*.[45] For the kind of skepticism championed by post-structuralist theorists in regard to textual meaning, as all students of Foucault and Derrida have come to recognize, represents finally a direct assault on the possibility of asserting any sort of "presence" evoked by language. The problem of the meaning of meaning, as George Steiner has pointed out in his latest book, is indeed "a transcendent postulate,"[46] but the raging debate in the academy these days ultimately boils down to the question that has occupied Western civilization for

---

[44] *The Poetics of Belief*, pp. 159-60. Scott's reading of Heidegger here retains echoes of Tillich. Cf. the latter's *Systematic Theology*, 3, 58: "In language, communication becomes mutual participation in a universe of meanings. Man has the power of such communication because he has a world in correlation to a completely developed self. . . . He experiences world in everything concrete, something universal in everything particular. Man has language because he has a world, and he has a world because he has language."

[45] Scott has vented his irritation and misgivings in several pieces, but the most concentrated expression is to be found in "The New *Trahison des Clercs*: Reflections on the Present Crisis in Humanistic Studies," *The Virginia Quarterly Review* 62 (Summer, 1986): 402-21.

[46] George Steiner, *Real Presences* (Chicago: The University of Chicago Press, 1989), p. 216.

more than two thousand years: is meaning possible only because being is sayable?

Scott is justifiably disturbed by the contemporary cultural scene, for the high tide of linguistic nominalism flooding the guild threatens to sweep away not only theologians and theological critics but poets as well, committed as they both must be to the service of *Logos*. If the function of language is always merely reflexive and never ostensive, if its nature is ever grammatological and hardly referential, and if there can never be any final coherence of signs and signifieds, how could one talk about the artistic treatment of reality, let alone ultimate reality? When the poet speaks of the "candor" in things (Wallace Stevens), or of "God's Grandeur" with which the world is charged (G. M. Hopkins), or of the "radiance, that. . . does not withhold/itself but pours its abundance without selection into every/nook and cranny not overhung or hidden" (A. R. Ammons), has he erected by means of language a true "house of Being" or only its chimerical abode?

The crisis brought on by such a view of language and reality is far more severe than the challenges to religious faith and understanding posed by the apostles of high modernism. Whereas those apostles in the persons of a Kafka, a Joyce, and an early Eliot present us with a universe seemingly devoid of belief and presumptuous of God's death, it is never a universe devoid of meaning. The devastation wrought by post-structuralism lies precisely in its radical insistence on the death of meaning, on the abrogation of any transcendental signified as a guarantor of meaning.

Can any remedy be found in linguistics or literary theory to counter this determined "annulment of the *Logos*," this programmatic abolition of "the contract between word and world"? Steiner, for one, is exceedingly pessimistic about any such possibility.[47] Because the premise of deconstructionism on its own terms and planes of argument is "irrefutable," the only possible gambit in face of its challenge is a wager on meaning, on the semantic "pay off" that we must regard as forthcoming when we encounter a work of art in the painstaking, expectant labor of philology and textual analysis. To what end do we work to receive a poem, a painting, or a musical composition if it is not to deny that it is "a tale/told by an idiot . . . signifying nothing"?[48]

---

[47] *Real Presences*, pp. 132-33.
[48] This is Steiner's entire line of argument, brilliantly developed, in *Real Presences*.

The magnitude of Nathan Scott's contribution to scholarship is to be measured precisely by the intensity and scope of this kind of labor, by the persistence of his efforts, and by the steadiness of his vision. He has never tired of wrestling with the great texts and figures of our turbulent modernity, and the resultant "pay off" continues to reward and stimulate. The *élan* and deepest impulses of his writings can worthily be compared with what he himself has indicated as "that in which the greatness and the glory of modern literature in its finest moments consist: namely, its determination to *cope* with 'the human condition' and to find new stratagems for 'giving a shape and a signficance to the immense panorama' of confusion and disquiet that continues to surround the days of our years."[49]

For the many of us who have known Nathan Scott beyond the office and the classroom, to speak more personally, his and his wife Charlotte's home is a haven of the warmest hospitality. To be in their presence is to know the meaning of graciousness, beauty, and good will without measure. The books, the art works, the elegant appointments, and the mellifluous strains of Elgar or Mahler that greet the visitor all bespeak their deep and abiding love for things of the spirit. The bountiful table that they provide for their guests is an eloquent extension of themselves: their boundless generosity and loyalty to their friends. And on the occasions when those gathering around the table include the entire family—Alex and Carol, Leslie and Sam, and their children—the convivial joyousness of their company is itself a feast.

Students who acquire their first knowledge of Nathan Scott from the lecture hall would likely marvel—as do his old friends and colleagues constantly—at the sheer energy of delivery, the passion of speech, and the seemingly endless flow of immense erudition. Those who advance sufficiently to sit through an oral examination in Scott's presence are not apt to forget this bracing rite of passage. Beneath the imposing gaze of silent, distinguished witnesses (in the form of mounted photographs of Faulkner, Camus, Sartre, Lawrence, Joyce, Niebuhr, and Tillich hung in his office), the questions precise and probing come in rapid succession. The interrogation, never mean or opprobrious, nonetheless bores in to uncover what the candidates know of the subject at hand, or what they should have known. And those who finally managed to turn in chapters of their dissertations might discover, perhaps with some chagrin, that the

---

[49] Scott, "Tillich's Legacy," p. 153

scrutiny they had received during the qualifying examinations could reach a new level of intensity. Here the discerning scholar and the master editor unite so that few details of errant style or inconsequential substance can escape the keen eyes and the querulous pen.

Yet, for those who have taken their final degrees with Scott as their thesis director, the picture of the stern, exacting schoolmaster fades with the years, yielding to a knowledge of someone enormously kind, genial, and trustworthy. If the mentor is demanding without compromise, he is even more generous in his self-giving as friend and colleague. Ever loyal and supportive, ever sensitive to the aspirations and wants of his friends, Nathan Scott is quick to provide a word of testimony when opportunity beckons, to lavish praise in the moment of triumph, or to offer comfort and assistance in the hour of need. Impatient with indolence (for he holds himself to the highest standards of dedication and diligence), he is nevertheless gentle with his despondent comrades, always ready to cheer them on. No stranger to bigotry or prejudice, he remains magnanimous and swift to forgive. "A teacher," Thomas Mann once wrote, "is the personified conscience of the pupil, confirming him in his doubt, explaining his dissatisfactions, stimulating his urge to improve." It is a description entirely worthy of the man whom this volume of essays seeks to honor.

It is most fitting as well that the unifying impulse of these essays is to be found in both spirit and example of Scott's scholarship: section one examines intersecting concerns of theology, literary criticism, and aesthetics, section two treats certain problems relative to genres and types, and section three addresses the religious and philosophical issues provoked by individual texts and authors.

I

Criticism, Aesthetics, and Theology

Shelley, Rahner, and the Religious Imagination

J. ROBERT BARTH, S.J.

English Romantic poet Percy Bysshe Shelley and German theologian Karl Rahner might at first be thought of as an odd couple. One is tempted to say that all they have in common is the brilliance of their vision and the obscurity of their language. However, both have written about the human imagination with a depth of feeling and a perceptiveness that may shed light on the relationships between literature and religion.

As a professed agnostic, Shelley may seem a curious choice. It might be, however, that the claims made by Shelley for the human imagination—in his famous *Defense of Poetry*—could bring home with special force how universal are these claims. First of all, he insists, the working of the imagination, as "a principle within the human being" by which we order our experience, is instinctive and universal: "In the youth of the world, men dance and sing and imitate natural objects, observing in these actions . . . a certain rhythm or order."[1] This is not, however, a merely subjective ordering of the world, for the poet (and here Shelley uses the term in its broadest sense of any "artist" or "maker") is able to perceive and imitate the universal and objective laws that govern the world, and thus has access not only to the present but the future: "For he not only beholds intensely the present as it is, and discovers those laws according to which present things ought to be ordered, but he beholds the future in the present, and his thoughts are the germs of the flower and the fruit of latest time" (p. 31). Hence poetry acts for the good of society, "to produce the moral improvement of man" (p.39), because it awakens and enlarges the mind itself by rendering it the receptacle of a

---

[1] Percy Bysshe Shelley, *A Defence of Poetry*, ed. John E. Jordan, The Library of Liberal Arts (Indianapolis: Bobbs-Merrill, 1965), p. 28.

thousand unapprehended combinations of thought. Poetry lifts the veil from the hidden beauty of the world, and makes familiar objects as if they were not familiar" (pp. 39-40). This is something science alone cannot do, Shelley claims: "The cultivation of those sciences which have enlarged the limits of the empire of man over the external world, has, for want of the poetical faculty, proportionately circumscribed those of the internal world; and man, having enslaved the elements, himself remains a slave" (p. 69). What poetry can offer, Shelley believes, is a light on the universe: "it is ever still the light of life, the source of whatever of beautiful or generous or true can have place in an evil time" (p.50). And its object is indeed universal, so much so that all poetry is ultimately one—representing one truth, one beauty. All the beauty mankind has made or represented throughout history is somehow true—"episodes to that great poem, which all poets, like the co-operating thoughts of one great mind, have built up since the beginning of the world" (p. 51). The great works of art are like the "sacred links" of a great chain, "which descending through the minds of many men is attached to those great minds, whence as from a magnet the invisible effluence is sent forth, which at once connects, animates and sustains the life of all" (p. 50).

Finally, central to Shelley's whole analysis of poetry is love. Speaking of the close link between poetry and morality, Shelley writes: "The great secret of morals is love; or a going out of our own nature, and an identification of ourselves with the beautiful which exists in thought, action, or person, not our own. A man, to be greatly good, must imagine intensely and comprehensively; he must put himself in the place of another and of many others; the pains and pleasures of his species must become his own. The great instrument of moral good is the imagination. . ."(p. 40).

In turning to the work of Karl Rahner—specifically his magisterial essay "Poetry and the Christian"—we turn our attention from an agnostic poet to a Christian theologian. Perhaps I should offer some apology for appealing to a theologian so professedly Christian in his analysis of literary art and imagination, but I feel it is best for me to speak out of my own tradition, in the hope that my words may evoke suggestive echoes and resonances for those of other religious traditions.

Rahner begins with the assumption that Christianity, as a religion of "the word proclaimed, of faith which hears and of a sacred scripture, has a special intrinsic relationship to the *word* and hence cannot be without such a special relationship to the *poetic* word."² Needless to say, of course, Christianity is not the only religion in which a sacred scripture has a central role, and much of what Rahner says of the Christian will have deep resonances for those of any religion in which the spoken or written word is important.

For Rahner, it is important that the hearing of the word of God is not "different in kind" (to use the Coleridgean phrase) from our hearing of the poetic word; the grace of God is at work not only in the message of the gospel but in every work of humankind. "The grace of God," he writes, "does not only start to work for the first time, when the word of the gospel reaches man through the official preaching. It precedes this word, it prepares the heart for this word by every experience of existence which takes place in the heart of man. It is . . . secretly and powerfully active in what we call human culture" (p. 358).

There are four requisites, Rahner suggests, for the proper hearing of the gospel, and these requisites involve skills which can be learned through our hearing of the poetic word. The first is the ability to hear through the word the "silent mystery" of God, for "only the *word* has the power of naming the nameless." Words define and designate, to be sure, but they also evoke "the silent, mystic presence of the nameless" (p. 358). In the very process of "putting individual things in order," the word "points to a fundamental background order which cannot itself be ordered but remains the perpetual *a priori* antecedent to all order," for "the small, limited region of the determinative word lies within the vast, silent desert of the godhead. But it is this nameless being that words try to name when they speak of things that have a name." Through words "God's incomprehensibility" reaches out to us, to "draw us on into his superluminous darkness," to "call us out of the little house of our homely, close-hugged truths into the strangeness of the night that is our real home"(p. 359).

In short, whoever would hear the words of the gospel, must learn through the evocative words of poetry to "have ears for the word where the silent mystery makes itself unmistakably heard as the foundation of existence" (pp. 359-60). As Wordsworth expresses it in "Tintern Abbey," "I have felt . . ./ A sense of something far more deeply interfused, / Whose dwelling is the light of setting suns, / And the round ocean and the living air, / And the blue sky, and in the mind of man" (ll. 93-99).

---

² Karl Rahner, "Poetry and the Christian," *Theological Investigations* IV, trans. Kevin Smyth (Baltimore: Helicon, 1967), p. 357.

The second requisite for the proper hearing of the gospel is "the power to hear words which reach the *heart*, the centre of man." The words to which one listens are not simply "rational words of the intellect, since this can be understood merely as the faculty which grasps and masters the comprehensible," but they are words which appeal to "the primordial faculty which allows itself to be gripped and overwhelmed by the incomprehensible mystery" (p. 360). What is required here is a kind of humility before the word, a willingness to make oneself vulnerable to the word that can strike like a lance, opening up our "inmost depths"—so that we hear (in Wordsworth's eloquent phrase) "the still, sad music of humanity."

The third requisite is what Rahner calls "the power of hearing the word which *unites*" (p. 360). Such words "reconcile," Rahner says: "they free the individual from the isolation of his loneliness, they make the whole present in each one; they speak of *one* death and we taste the death of all; they voice one joy and joy itself penetrates our heart; they tell of one man and we have learned to know all men" (p. 361). The authentic word speaks "only of one thing, the mystery of love." How similar this is to Shelley's insistence that "a man, to be greatly good, must imagine intensely and comprehensively; he must put himself in the place of another and of many others; the pains and pleasures of his species must become his own" (p. 40); or to Wordsworth's deep belief that to know a thing truly we must first love it.

The fourth and final requisite Rahner sets down for the hearing of the word of God is a willingness to hear the *individuality* of every word that is spoken, because "in the region encompassed by the human word, infinity has built itself a tent, infinity itself is there in the finite." Because the Logos became flesh, with all the individuality that entails, the human word is not simply a pointer, "pointing away from itself to the mystery." Rather, "in every word, the gracious incarnation of God's own abiding Word and so of God himself can take place, and all true hearers of the word are really listening to the inmost depths of every word, to know if it becomes suddenly the word of eternal love by the very fact that it expresses man and his world." The mystery of the infinite is grounded for us in the mystery of the finite individual. As Rahner puts it, "one must have courage for what is clear and definite, in order to become aware of the inexpressible, one must bear and love the candour of what is close at hand, to be able to reach what is far away" (p. 362).

What common notes can we discern in these two very different thinkers? I suggest at least the three following for our consideration. (1)

First of all, the poetic word—the product of the imagination—has a *universal* value. While it has value in itself, it also points beyond itself and beyond the finite reality it represents, to (in Shelley's phrase) "the universal and objective laws that govern the world," to (in Rahner's terms) the "fundamental background order which cannot itself be ordered but remains the perpetual *a priori* antecedent to all order." (2) The aesthetic beauty expressed by the imagination is on some deep level ultimately *one*: for Shelley, all works of art are "episodes to that great poem, which all poets . . . have built up since the beginning of the world; for Rahner, poetic words "make the whole present in each one." (3) The act of the imagination is at bottom—for both Shelley and Rahner—an act of *love*, by which the poet opens himself to the finite world around him and, through that finite world, to the larger universe beyond—giving himself in loving service to mysteries, both finite and infinite, which he does not fully comprehend.

I find, too, one further implication that can be drawn from these two analyses—a reflection that, in fact, gives the lie to the title I first gave to this paper: "Literature and the Religious Imagination." Implicit in both Shelly and Rahner is the belief that there is not a "literary imagination" and a "religious imagination." There is only "imagination"—a single human faculty which unites the secular and the sacred, the finite and the infinite—which comprehends the symbolic language of religion as well as the symbolic utterances of art. This is, in fact, precisely what another great Romantic writer, Samuel Taylor Coleridge—who was himself both poet and theologian—believed about imagination. Perhaps Coleridge's *Statesman's Manual* may shed further light on our subject here. Coleridge is careful to distinguish there, as elsewhere, between the mechanical work of the Understanding—whose characteristic is "Clearness without Depth" and which "contemplates the unity of things in their *limits* only"—and the Imagination, "the completing power which unites clearness with depth, the plenitude of the sense with the comprehensibility of the understanding." Such is the power of imagination that when understanding is "impregnated" with imagination, understanding itself becomes "intuitive, and a living power."[3] Indeed, it is imagination which produces the very Scripture itself, for the scriptural histories are, Coleridge says, "the living *educts* of the Imagination; of that reconciling and mediatory power, which incorporating the Reason in Images of the

---

[3] Samuel Taylor Coleridge, *The Statesman's Manual*, in *Lay Sermons*, ed. R. J. White, in *The Collected Works of Samuel Taylor Coleridge*, ed. Kathleen Coburn, Bollingen Series LXXV (London: Routledge & Kegan Paul, 1972), p. 69.

Sense, and organizing (as it were) the flux of the Senses by the permanence and self-circling energies of the Reason, gives birth to a system of
symbols, harmonious in themselves, and consubstantial with the truths,
of which they are the *conductors*. These are the Wheels," he goes on,
"which Ezekiel beheld, when the hand of the Lord was upon him, and he
saw visions of God as he sat among the captives by the river of Chebar"
(p. 29). The work of the imagination is precisely to create symbols, which
reveal eternity through the works of time, which show forth the infinite
in and through the finite. As Coleridge continues in the same paragraph,
a symbol "is characterized . . . above all by the translucence of the Eternal
in and through the Temporal. It always partakes of the Reality which it
renders intelligible; and while it enunciates the whole, abides itself as a
living part in that Unity, of which it is the representative" (p. 30). For
Coleridge there is not, nor can there be, a distinction between a literary
imagination and a religious imagination. The literary imagination is itself
of its very nature religious, for it is the symbol-making faculty as well as
the faculty of perceiving symbols; it is the faculty without which we can
neither conceive nor know either God or eternity or even our own immortal spirit. In his classic definition of imagination in the *Biographia
Literaria* Coleridge goes even farther, when he claims for the human
imagination a share in the divine act of creation: "The primary
IMAGINATION I hold to be the living Power and prime Agent of all
human Perception, and as a repetition in the finite mind of the eternal act
of creation in the infinite I AM. The secondary I consider as an echo of
the former, co-existing with the conscious will. . . ."[4] The very act of
imagination, then, whether of the secondary imagination in the creation
of a symbol or of the primary imagination by which we perceive
symbols, is for Coleridge itself a religious act—both in its origin, since it
is empowered by God, and in its effect, since it allows us to perceive the
eternal revealed in and through temporal reality.

We who study the works of the human imagination, therefore, may
have something important to offer the theologians who study the word
of God; and it is no surprise that theologians like Rahner have begun to
interest themselves more and more in literature and the ways of the
imagination. In the Coleridgean conception, the imaginative symbol both
expresses temporal reality in all the richness of its individuality and di-

---

[4] Samuel Taylor Coleridge, *Biographia Literaria*, ed. James Engell and W. Jackson
Bate, in *The Collected Works*, ed. Coburn (Princeton: Princeton University Press, 1983),
I: 304.

versity and at the same time remains open to the transcendent. For, as theologian James Cutsinger has remarked in the *Harvard Theological Review*, "through the transformation of his vision, Coleridge had glimpsed a world translucent to deity. He had found, in short, that revisioning one's world could mean the very en-visioning of God."[5] The word "translucent" is crucial here, for it is only through the exercise of imagination and the perception or creation of symbol that such an envisioning of the divine can be achieved. As Coleridge has written, "a symbol is characterized . . . above all by the translucence of the Eternal through and in the Temporal. It always partakes of the Reality which it renders intelligible." The two realities, temporal and eternal, are "translucent" to one another: the same light shines through both, allowing the reality of both to be glimpsed in a single vision. And this is so precisely because the temporal "partakes of the Reality" of the eternal. The assumption here is that there is, as Coleridge wrote in "The Eolian Harp," "one Life, within us and abroad," that all reality is (to use the consecrated phrase Coleridge borrowed from Christian theology) "consubstantial." Underpinning Coleridge's entire conception of symbol is an acceptance of the notions common throughout the Platonic Christian tradition of "analogy" and "participation": because all reality is analogous, legitimate predication can be made between visible and unseen reality (it is meaningful to say, for example, both "I love" and "God is love"); and it is "participation"—by which we actually share in the love which God possesses in its fullness—that grounds such analogous predication.

The value of the imaginative symbol is two-fold, however. It includes not only the "vertical" dimension by which the transcendent world can, in however limited a way, be apprehended and expressed, but also a "horizontal" dimension, open to the movement of time and therefore capable of growth. For the imaginative symbol is not static, fixed and limited to one or even several meanings. It is not primarily denotative but connotative—taking its significance not only from historical usage at a point in time, but comprehending in its resonances all its past uses, the pressure of its present context, and still open to new uses in fresh and changing contexts in the future. Thus the symbol is singularly apt for the expression of religious experience, for not only is our experience of the divine necessarily open because of the very nature of infinitude—we can

---

[5] James S. Cutsinger, "Coleridgean Polarity and Theological Vision," *Harvard Theological Review* 76 (1983): 93.

catch glimpses of infinity but never fully comprehend it—but also because of the nature of human knowledge, which is essentially cumulative
and time-bound. Human symbols, therefore, are of their nature organic,
taking on new meanings and emotional resonances from the pressure of
new contexts, enclosing fresh insights and experiences both of temporal
reality and of the divine—and remaining always, as Coleridge insists,
"translucent," so that eternal reality is perceived in the "light" of what
we see and hear, while the spirit of the eternal within us remains (in
Wordsworth's phrase from his "Ode: Intimations of Immortality") the
"master light of all our seeing" (l. 153).

There are two concerns in particular of contemporary theology
which, it seems to me, can be enlightened by the study of literature and
the imagination. The first is the concern that the experience of religion
not remain an abstraction, that there be an "encounter" between the worshipper and God—a personal experience of commitment and of love.
Since it is capable of encompassing both the universal and the profoundly individual, both infinite and finite, eternal and temporal—and
because it can evoke both a range and a depth of emotional resonance—
the imagination and its symbols can be a privileged *locus* for the encounter between humanity and God, making present some aspect of the
divine reality and calling the creature to a loving relationship with its
Creator.

A second concern of theologians today is the issue of process. The
human experience of religion is not seen as simply a "given," a more or
less fixed state by which one is either committed in faith or not. It is
rather conceived of as a journey of discovery which is never finished, in
which God continues to reveal God's self to us throughout our lives—so
that our work of self-discovery goes hand-in-hand with our continuing
discovery of God. It is perhaps for some such reason that so-called
"narrative theology" has come to the fore in recent years. Each of us lives
in a "story," it has been said—as did Adam and Moses and Abraham—
and God is part of our story, as God was of theirs. The works of
imagination, whether in the Bible or in so-called secular literature, can
shed light on our own stories—so that our way may be lit for the
continuation of our journeys. Our journey is through time, and it is the
imagination—reconciling temporal and eternal—that can at once encompass the passage of time in our journey and keep us in touch with
the eternal source of light.

This realization is echoed in the words of a poet who, while standing within the Christian tradition, was able to hear the voice of God in the traditions of the East as well: T. S. Eliot.

> . . . to apprehend
> The point of intersection of the timeless
> With time, is an occupation for the saint—
> No occupation either, but something given
> And taken, in a lifetime's death in love,
> Ardour and selflessness and self-surrender.
> For most of us, there is only the unattended
> Moment, the moment in and out of time,
> The distraction fit, lost in a shaft of sunlight,
> The wild thyme unseen, or the winter lightning
> Or the waterfall, or music heard so deeply
> That it is not heard at all, but you are the music
> While the music lasts. These are only hints and guesses
> Hints followed by guesses; and the rest
> Is prayer, observance, discipline, thought and action.
> The hint half guessed, the gift half understood, is Incarnation.
>   ("Dry Salvages")

This is what we are about, I suggest, when we speak of the relationship between religion and the human imagination: Incarnation—the incarnation of God in the word the artist speaks. To "apprehend / The point of intersection of the timeless / With time" is an occupation not only for the saint, but for the artist as well—and for us who follow after in the artist's footsteps. It may be only in "hints and guesses," it may be a gift only "half understood," but it is truly "incarnation"—God reaching out to touch us, sometimes even to walk with us, on our journey.

Varieties of Religious Aesthetic Experience*
FRANK BURCH BROWN

I. Religious and Aesthetic Variety

Like the adjectives "artistic" and "aesthetic," the term "religious" applies to a wide range of heterogeneous phenomena. The extent of the variety within what has been called religious is so great, in fact, that it cannot possibly be encompassed by any one theory or inquiry. Even William James in his classic study *The Varieties of Religious Experience* (1902) ends up discussing mainly varieties of personal spirituality, and of these mostly the Western, modern, and vaguely mystical.

The present essay, in any case, makes no claim to be comprehensive. On the contrary, it focuses on but one religious tradition—the Christian—and on no more than a few of the major modes of Christian religious experience, showing how each comes to be shaped and expressed aesthetically. Yet even so restricted a study in religious aesthetics may be sufficient to suggest that some varieties of what can be termed aesthetica[1] (including some kinds of art) are not just *related to* religion, or attached to it as ornaments, but are actually a vital *part of* religion and its many varieties, Christian and non-Christian alike.

Of course some people might hesitate to speak at all of a genuinely and integrally *religious* aesthetic experience, since it has commonly been thought that one of the points in calling something aesthetic is to say that

---

[1] The English language has no general term for aesthetic objects or phenomena (which certainly are not all "beauties," for instance). On the basis of the Greek *aesthetika*—meaning, literally, "perceptibles"—yet also relying on connotations of the word "aesthetic" that have been present ever since Alexander Baumgarten's work in the 18th century, I have coined the term "aesthetica" (singular: "aestheticon") in order to fill this gap.

in this respect it is *not* religious or moral (or practical or cognitive) but rather is valued sheerly "for its own sake." And certainly it must be acknowledged that there can be religious experiences that have little immediate aesthetic interest, and also moments of *aesthesis* that have no immediate religious significance. One can be glad for divine forgiveness without enjoying it aesthetically, and one can take delight in the beautiful geometric design of a snowflake without finding it religiously meaningful.

Nevertheless, contrary to what purist approaches to aesthetics would have us believe, the realm of what we label "the aesthetic" is itself quite varied; and aesthetic predicates such as "graceful," "sublime," or "beautiful" are never actually reserved only for what pleases apart from any cognitive, moral, or religious appeal. Indeed the more complex and rewarding varieties of what we think of as aesthetic satisfaction often reflect and affect religious or moral concerns. Thus, in one's response to Chartres Cathedral, perceptions of aesthetic style, form, and medium normally influence—and are influenced by—perceptions of religious content, substance, and message. A Disneyland replica of Chartres, no matter how exact, would look less "sublime," aesthetically speaking, than does the religious edifice; and a cathedral without any of the formal aesthetic excellence visible even in the replica would not have the same sort of religious stature and power as Chartres.

Having clarified these theoretical premises, we can begin to inquire into both the expression and experience of religion in its aesthetic varieties. Although the focus of our discussion will be on the Christian tradition alone, at least it can be said that Christianity as a whole has never been accused of lacking variety. Indeed, so great is its variety that we will only be able to hint at the range of aesthetic expression that is in keeping with various aspects of the tradition. Even so, our analysis should give some indication of what it means for one religious tradition—one "variety" of religion—to be in itself variously expressed by aesthetic means.

At the outset, however, we must confront the fact that frequently it is not variety that leaps to mind when people think of Christian aesthetic values; it is monotony—a monotonously pristine, ethereal, "angelic," or perhaps even ascetic approach to aesthetic expression. We therefore begin with several observations about this way of picturing Christian aesthetic experience.

II. Imagining Christianity Aesthetically

One of the most highly regarded dance critics of the nineteenth century, Théophile Gautier, once contrasted two dancers in the following way:

Mlle. Taglioni is a Christian dancer, if one may make use of such an expression in regard to an art proscribed by the Catholic faith: she flies like a spirit in the midst of transparent clouds of white muslin with which she loves to surround herself; she resembles a happy angel who scarcely bends the petals of celestial flowers with the tips of her pink toes. Fanny [Elssler] is a quite pagan dancer; she reminds one of the muse Terpsichore, tambourine in hand, her tunic, exposing her thigh, caught up with a golden clasp; when she bends freely from the hips, throwing back her swooning, voluptuous arms, we seem to see one of those beautiful figures from Herculaneum or Pompeii. . . .[2]

It is interesting to set alongside this characterization of a "Christian" versus a "pagan" style the complaints that John of Salisbury, writing in the twelfth century, lodged against what he clearly took to be an unchristian style of singing in Christian worship:

Music [now] sullies the Divine Service, for in the very sight of God, in the sacred recesses of the sanctuary itself, the singers attempt, with the lewdness of a lascivious singing voice and a singularly foppish manner, to feminize all their spellbound little followers with the girlish way they render the notes and end the phrases. . . . Indeed, such is their glibness in running up and down the scale . . . —[and] to such an extent are the high or even the highest notes mixed together with the low or lowest ones—that the ears are almost completely divested of their critical power, and the intellect, which pleasurableness of so much sweetness has caressed insensate, is impotent to judge the merits of the things heard. Indeed, when such practices go too far, they can more easily occasion titillation between the legs than a sense of devotion in the brain.[3]

Even allowing for the likelihood that various issues are being addressed and possibly confused in this condemnation of a manner of sing-

---

[2] Théophile Gautier, "Fanny Elssler in 'La Tempete,'" in Roger Copeland and Marshall Cohen, eds., *What Is Dance?: Readings in Theory and Criticism* (Oxford: Oxford University Press, 1983), p. 431.

[3] From John of Salisbury, *Policratus* (1159), quoted in Piero Weiss and Richard Taruskin, eds., *Music in the Western World: A History in Documents* (New York: Schirmer, 1984), p. 62.

ing, it is clear that John of Salisbury shares at least one major assumption in common with Gautier and countless other people—the assumption that properly Christian aesthetic expression has to do with what is "higher" and indeed transcendent and therefore cannot or should not appeal too much to feelings that are emphatically bodily and particularly sexual.

"Transcendence"—in the sense of something far different from what ordinarily is experienced as real or possible—is indeed a major Christian motif, being especially ascribed to God. Furthermore, because transcendence when translated into experience always entails a change in perception and in the perceiver, it gives rise to the companion motif of transformation, or conversion. The etherealized spirituality or "angelism" implicit in the views of Christianity just now cited, however, gives us but one rendition of these Christian themes. Our aim now is to show something of the genuine variety within Christian aesthetic experience by analyzing in the next two sections four different forms of the aesthetic expression of divine transcendence, all of which a fuller analysis could show to be correlated with different varieties of human transformation. This exploration will enable us to see how aesthetic expressions and perceptions contribute to the kind of variety in religious experience that is common to Christian life and practice in general and also generative and symptomatic of sectarian differences.

III. Christian Aesthesis and Divine Transcendence (1)

To transcend is literally to climb across— not to ascend or descend, but to cross over and go beyond. From what we already have said about the Christian tradition, it should be clear that the one supremely transcendent reality envisioned in Christian thought and experience is God. But what does God cross over? In what way and to what extent does God go beyond? And how can this be expressed and experienced by creatures whose own capacity for transcendence is limited both by their finitude and by their persistent failing/falling?

Christian theology suggests that divine transcendence occurs in numerous different modes—in relation to time, place, knowledge, morality, and so forth. Here we will propose that it also appears in at least four major forms, which we will term negative transcendence, radical transcendence, proximate transcendence, and immanent transcendence. As we will see, each of these forms of transcendence is expressed and experienced in some ways that are markedly aesthetic and that potentially make for new possibilities of transcendence or transformation within human life. In this section we examine the aesthetic expression of negative and then radical transcendence.

Most Christian theologians are inclined to say that divine transcendence actually exists not only in many modes but in all possible modes, because God as maker of all things visible and invisible is essentially and infinitely beyond anything we know or experience, including time, place, materiality, and thought. But if God is totally beyond us, then God may be "experienced" by us chiefly as a kind of Holy Void. When this perception predominates in one's response to the divine, one is on the route of negative theology and is entering the way of darkness, silence, and emptiness in religious experience.

The sense of God's transcendence as Infinite Difference, Hiddenness, and Darkness rarely occupies the center of Christian devotion or worship and certainly cannot be restricted to any one Christian group. One reason, perhaps, is that such transcendence is literally unimaginable and inexpressible. And yet at least its possibility can be expressed, as well as something of its import. Furthermore, it appears that much that is expressed with respect to this negatively experienced transcendence may take significantly aesthetic form. For the language eliciting acknowledgement of and response to the literally Inexpressible and Incomprehensible Other must in large part be that of paradox and catachresis, the meaning of which is felt or intuited aesthetically rather that strictly thought out. Such is the figurative language of Pseudo-Dionysius when he speaks of the luminous, "superessential darkness" that is God, and of Meister Eckhart when he preaches: "The final goal of being is the darkness or the unknowability of the hidden divinity, which is that light that shines 'but the darkness has not comprehended it.'"[4]

Beyond such figures of speech per se, the aesthetic forms that can serve to call to human awareness the One that can never literally be called to mind include dark, vacant cells for meditation and rugged, forbidding terrain such as that surrounding the monastery of St.-Martin-du-Canigou in France. They also include numbingly repetitive chants, or amazingly lengthy and logically redundant catalogs of what God is *not*, such as are found in apophatic mysticism. Likewise great Stillness or Otherness may be pointed to through music that borders on silence or chaos, as in passages of Penderecki's *Magnificat* (1974) and *Requiem* (1987). Then there is painting of the sort encountered in Anselm Kiefer's

---

[4] Matthew Fox, *Breakthrough: Meister Eckhart's Creation Spirituality in New Translation* (Garden City, N.Y.: Doubleday-Image), p. 169.

enormous and controversial *Osiris and Isis* (1985-87, San Francisco Museum of Modern Art)—a work that presents us with the charred remnants of sacred and political power. Here a vast pyramid, strangely surmounted by a burnt-out circuit board from which copper wiring extends in every direction, appears in its ravaged condition to be neither safe nor amenable to any ordinary means of restoration of demolition. Through such aesthetica (whether explicitly Christian or not), positive religious perceptions can be challenged, the world made to appear as nothing inherently holy and abiding, and something More nonetheless signalled by what is seen to be only a sign and neither presence nor genuine mediator.

It is scarcely surprising that Christians for whom the experience of negative transcendence is compelling or predominant often resonate with modern Jewish works such as Arnold Schoenberg's great unfinished opera *Moses and Aaron*, in which one hears the strange and alienating half-singing (*Sprechgesang*) of Moses as he strives without success to utter the truth of the infinite, unperceived, inconceivable God. Significantly, Moses's "truth" of the Incomprehensible One largely goes unheeded. Meanwhile Aaron (a tenor) sings in a relatively lyrical *bel canto* style as he caters to the popular demand for palpable, accessible gods. The arts of unutterable transcendence are seldom popular.

We should note, last, that in our day it is not uncommon for the *via negativa* and its aesthetic expression to pass over into the outright negation of theology and of the supposed reality of God as well. At such times the experience of transcendence becomes an experience of God's eclipse, absence, or death. That it could remain religious at all may seem strange; yet those on this tortuous path suggest that the deconstruction of Logos and God may leave a trace of something beyond even God— something that always is on the other side of what can be said or seen and that is evoked aesthetically in absurd play and parody, in redoubled paradox, and in carnivalesque transgression of the ordinary.[5] We have testimony that such a vision of negative or paradoxical transcendence can be evoked through the parables of Borges. That it could claim to find itself sparked or inspired by the paradoxical parables of Jesus as well may seem strange, yet also is true.[6]

---

[5] See Mark C. Taylor, *Erring: A Postmodern A/theology* (Chicago: University of Chicago Press, 1984); and Charles E. Winquist, *Epiphanies of Darkness: Deconstruction in Theology* (Philadelphia: Fortress Press, 1986).

[6] See John Dominic Crossan, *Cliffs of Fall: Paradox and Polyvalence in the Parables of Jesus* (New York: Crossroad-Seabury Western, 1980).

Having considered the aesthetic expression of the Christian and Post-Christian response in which divine transcendence is experienced chiefly as that which is Divine Negation, Otherness, or even finally Absence, we now can reflect on expression and experience in which transcendence seems a step closer to the world we humanly know. This is a transcendence that is radical and yet communicative, as though it were an electric charge that could arc across an infinite gulf between heaven and earth.

The conviction that God can in some way be known and experienced positively is not, of course, unusual among Christians. Indeed the majority of Christian theologians assert that, although God as known to God's own self must be essentially unknown and incomprehensible to human beings, God chooses in acts and events of self-communication, and especially in the Incarnation, to relate to humanity truly and trustably, and in some manner appropriate to our limitations. Just how transcendent God continues to be even after such self-revelation is, however, a matter about which Christians differ greatly both in theory and experience. And in fact the God revealed in Christ and Scripture remains in other ways and at most times radically transcendent for many Christians. Although every tradition or denomination at some points recognizes experientially and aesthetically more than one form of transcendence, those in the Reformed line (mainly Calvinist) are among those in whose experience radical transcendence predominates.

For that branch of Reformation piety and theology known as the Reformed, it seems the case that religious awareness, though not consigned to silence and darkness, is most often confronted by a God of Unlikeness before whom one stands struck, if not by awe, then by a sense of the incapacity of anything finite to bear or contain the infinite. To be sure, one still may believe that certain things of divine import and all things necessary for salvation are made plain in Christ, in Holy Writ, and by the testimony of the Spirit. Yet even in the more rationalist Reformed churches, it is widely acknowledged that God's ways and truths are far from rational by our standards; God's infinite goodness, moreover, is deemed quite unapproachable from our side.

Yet when a radically transcendent God wills to be encountered, it will come to pass. And in the eyes of the Reformed tradition God is able to make use of aesthetic forms, among others, to mediate or prepare for divine self-disclosure. In seventeenth-century England, for instance, Anglicans influenced deeply by Calvinism formulated expressly biblical poetics that repeatedly affirmed that in the Bible one has exemplary art, and art with the overwhelming capacity to reveal God's providential power, law, judgment, love, and grace. The Holy Spirit is seen, in short, as a transcendently magnificent poet. And though God is supposedly a "direct" God, as John Donne says, and frequently would be understood literally, God also is "a figurative, a metaphoricall God too" whose tropes and allegories put profane authors to shame.[7]

Of course when human beings themselves seek to employ the rich rhetorical resources of scripture in their own writing and preaching there is, from a Reformed viewpoint, a distinct danger of conceit—in the usual sense rather than the rhetorical one. The Puritan and early Calvinist sermon tended therefore to be plain and sober despite achieving at times a remarkable degree of rhetorical appeal.[8] And the Baroque style of the English metaphysical poets, many Calvinist in theology, was of religious value because it had the capacity ultimately to reveal its own incapacity, thereby potentially functioning—paradoxically—as a vehicle of religious receptivity. Thus the early Anglican lyric of the seventeenth century exists by and large as what has been called a "self-consuming artifact": a work that, "by conveying those who experience it to a point where they are beyond the aid that discursive or rational forms can offer," becomes "the vehicle of its own abandonment," and potentially of the corresponding abandonment of self to the action of grace necessary for salvation.[9]

Self-effacement, if not self-abasement, is even more evident in the aesthetics of the Puritan meeting house in New England. Such a building makes visible the conviction that human effort cannot bring the divine closer. The very plainness and simplicity of form testifies that these (and other) Calvinist houses really are not meant to be "houses of God"; that nothing made with hands can house divinity or can properly become a focus of God's presence. For we ourselves, as Calvin insisted and as the poetry of George Herbert reiterates, are made to be the real Temple of God, and we have nothing to offer of our own but our impoverishment. At the same time, the physical barrenness of the interior of the building, typically devoid of images of any kind, has the value of permitting one to

---

[7] See Barbara Kiefer Lewalski, *Protestant Poetics and the Seventeenth-Century Religious Lyric* (Princeton: Princeton University Press, 1979). Quotation on p. 85.

[8] See ibid.; and Terrence Erdt, *Jonathan Edwards: Art and the Sense of the Heart* (Amherst: University of Massachusetts Press, 1980), pp. 63-77.

[9] See Stanley E. Fish, *Self-Consuming Artifacts: The Experience of Seventeenth-Century Literature* (Berkeley: University of California Press, 1972), p. 3. Fish makes it plain that artifacts that self-consume are not all of one religious persuasion—Anglican or Puritan, for instance. Many are indeed Calvinist, however.

attend chiefly to the divine Word, with the gathered people themselves as the true Church.

It is indeed the Word, delivered literally from on high, that dominates the aesthetics of communication within the traditional setting of Reformed worship. Certainly there is no dance or drama. Nor is there great interest in what is seen (or tasted) in communion now that "Real Presence" is spiritualized or even converted into Zwinglian memorialism. In any event, communion is celebrated less frequently and ceremoniously than in Catholic, Lutheran, or later Anglican traditions.

Traditionally the one sensuous art that the Reformed tradition employs extensively is also aural and thus intangible—namely music, the physical medium of which conveniently self-destructs rather than remaining as a potential distraction and temptation. The religious significance attached to this art should not be underestimated. George Herbert spoke for many Calvinists in and out of the Church of England when he commented that the times when he felt closest to heaven were during prayer and while hearing the music in Salisbury Cathedral.[10] Many a Calvinist could say with Luther: "After theology I give music the highest place and highest honor."[11] Even so, much more than Lutherans, Calvinists typically insist here too on an art of "less" rather than "more"; of poverty rather than abundance. Whereas Luther borrowed secular melodies, unwilling—as he said—to let the Devil have all the good tunes, Calvinist songs (ordinarily Psalms) were from the beginning sober and unmistakably "sacred" in style: originally sung in union and unaccompanied.

Finally, we must stress that when the Reformed religious aesthetic sensibility extends beyond the church itself, it continues to acknowledge and proclaim the radical transcendence of God. The Calvinist typically sees nature and its orderly beauty as directly subject to God's will, as providing a proper theatre for divine action, and as declaring the glory of the Creator—possibly even supplying, as Jonathan Edwards thought, images and shadows of divine things. But this God, while working through nature for providential purposes as well as for purposes of chastisement, is not present *in* nature, but "above" it. Nature serves mainly as the stage for history, which turns out to be sacred drama at its highest: the comedy of salvation, with the tragic sub-plot of damnation.

---

[10] Quoted in C. John Sommerville, "The Religious Music of the Twentieth and Twenty-First Centuries," *Religion* 14 (July 1984): 245-67.
[11] Quoted in Friedrich Blume, ed., *Protestant Church Music* (New York: Norton, 1975), p. 10.

Mindful of this grand plot, Reformed Christians seek to organize life as a whole, creating orderly social structures, works, and habitations. This aesthetic impulse seems to assume a divine will-to-order, possibly anticipating the Great Housecleaning of the Last Judgment.

Thus, above all, Reformed piety affirms the power and activity of a radically transcendent God. This is a God who graciously chooses to communicate through particular forms—even aesthetic. Although in principle reserving the right to grace and bless everything equally, the God of radical transcendence makes most use of what is plain, humble, and pure in sense, form, and imagination.

Up to now we have concentrated on kinds of Christian religiosity frequently regarded as alien either to the definite experience of transcendence, as in the case of negative theology, or to the truly aesthetic expression and proclamation of transcendence, as in much of Reformed Christianity. Having seen that in actuality there is in each case, after all, such experience, expression, or proclamation (and hence an aesthetic befitting transcendence or its shadow) we can turn to the rather more obvious possibilities of aesthetic expression afforded by divine transcendence experienced as proximate and as immanent.

IV. Christian Aesthesis and Divine Transcendence (2)

Any form of Christianity that extends across different epochs and cultures is bound to exhibit considerable internal variety, as do the religious predilections of individual Christians within any given tradition and at any given moment in time. It must again be emphasized, therefore, that every tradition is in some way and to some degree open to various of the forms of religious experience we are examining. Yet the balance and emphasis differs among traditions. Just as we can say that the theology and experience of the Reformed tradition tends to place special emphasis upon a sense of God's radical transcendence, so can we also say that the pervasive sacramentalism of Catholicism, including that of the Orthodox and Anglo-Catholic traditions, fosters an especially keen sense of what we will call proximate or "near" transcendence. As we will see, an equally proximate but quite different sort of transcendence is experienced in the kind of Evangelical Christianity exemplified in much of the worship of Black Free Church and Pentecostal congregations in the United States. In both contexts the experience of transcendence by its very nature calls for and is shaped by distinctive kinds of aesthetic expression.

Hardly anyone would deny that in Catholicism there is a commitment to preserving a sense of the transcendence and mystery of God,
whose essential unknowability is emphasized by theologians from
Augustine through Thomas Aquinas to Karl Rahner. Yet this is a transcendence that draws near to us in a number of ways. It supports and illuminates our God-given capacity for reason, so that reason itself, while
unable to understand the inner nature of God, can show that God exists.
And through grace it precedes, meets, and uplifts our efforts at goodness, so that righteousness is not merely "imputed" to us, as Luther
thought, but is also actualized in us. Moreover, in this understanding of
the Transcendent, it is susceptible to being described and represented
truthfully, albeit not univocally, in the language and art of analogy.

Equally important from the standpoint of aesthetics, the Incarnation
is here typically taken to mean that bodily, physical mediation of the
holy is not to be scorned. The Orthodox theologian John of Damascus
speaks for a significant part of the entire Catholic tradition when, in responding to any and all iconoclasts, he declares: "Perhaps you are sublime and able to transcend what is material . . . , but I, since I am a human
being and bear a body, want to deal with holy things and behold them in
a bodily manner."[12]

Not surprisingly, in the Catholic understanding of proximate transcendence there is great emphasis on the sacraments. What is significant
about this is not just that Christ is affirmed to be really present in the
consecrated elements of the Eucharist, which Lutherans (among others)
also would affirm. It is also that the sacraments as such are greater in
number and more diverse in function than among Protestants. Even
more, it is the fact that there is a general sense of sacramentality that extends to other things of this world whereby God's presence is mediated.[13]

It is to be expected, therefore, that the Catholic liturgy of the
Eucharist would regularly make use of abundant aesthetic means of mediation: bells and incense, gestures and processions, poetic or (formerly)
archaic language, vocal and instrumental music, and often impressive architecture. Even if many of these aesthetica never draw attention to
themselves individually, they collectively and cumulatively create a rich

---

[12] Quoted in Jaroslav Pelikan, *The Christian Tradition*, vol. 2: *The Spirit of Eastern Christendom, (600-1700)* (Chicago: University of Chicago Press, 1974), p. 122.

[13] On the principle of sacramentality see Richard P. McBrien, *Catholicism* (Minneapolis: Winston, 1981).

sensory and imaginative milieu that contributes to one's awareness of sacramental presence.

One may claim, of course, that none of this counts except the Eucharist itself and that Christ's presence depends not at all on the incense and music and lofty space. Yet, as even a theology of objective Real Presence will admit, Christ's presence is not efficacious for the partaker unless one is properly receptive. If the prospective communicant despairs of ever approaching God, communion may be declined; if the communicant is proud or alienated from the larger community of the Church, the heart may be hardened. The aesthetic milieu of the Mass works against these attitudes. God must be very great and awe-inspiring to warrant such extraordinary art and ceremony; one therefore is humbled in God's presence. Yet the rank upon rank of significantly aesthetic forms associated with the Eucharist creates the sense that approach is indeed possible from both sides—God's and ours—and in many ways, and from varying degrees of distance, all in community.

Beyond this, we would argue that the whole range of religious mediation recognized by the Catholic tradition—mediation accomplished not only by liturgical acts but also by a host of saints and angels, by the Blessed Virgin, by the persons of the Trinity, by the clergy and the sacraments they administer, and implicitly by all of sacred history—this mediation is itself in significant measure *aesthetically* mediated to the believer and worshipper. That is to say: In the experience of the devout the reality and value of acknowledged religious mediators, visible and invisible, are to a significant extent made more proximate and "immediate" by means of aesthetic modes of expression—sounds and sights, smells and colors, shapes and rhythms, stories and metaphors, images and spaces.

This suggests that, whereas in its theoretical statements the Western church generally has justified its arts on pedagogical grounds, pointing out their usefulness for the poor, the uneducated, and the spiritually immature, the truth seems to be that in practice the arts (broadly conceived) have helped grant to all the faithful, in varying degrees, access to the Church at its very heart, and to a God who would approach and be approached.

Of course not all Catholic aesthetica that serve this function do so in the same way. Even within monasticism there is both art that purges and pares away and art that fills up and spills over—the Cistercian versus the Cluniac, for instance. Likewise there is accessible art such as a folk-like "Alleluia" from Taizé and difficult art such as a highly melismatic twelfth-century "Alleluia" from Notre Dame de Paris. Then, too, there is "chaste" art of the sort clearly preferred by John of Salisbury; and there is the worldly, corporeal religiosity of Rubens and much of the Baroque. Throughout, however, the sense of sacramentality and of the potential proximity of the divine persists to a remarkable extent.

Nevertheless, it is characteristic of Eastern Catholicism that the greatest possible tension is created and sustained between utmost transcendence and utmost proximity. Among the Orthodox the liturgical singing, for instance, is traditionally austere in that it often has restricted itself to chant; and yet the chant as sung is frequently ecstatic and voluminous, lifting one into the very presence of the Most High and reminding one that in this tradition we ourselves are to be transfigured and ultimately divinized.

Again, in Orthodox churches the cosmic, majestic Christ—impassive emperor of the universe—typically stares out from mosaics where he appears as the awesome yet inescapable Presence of the God declared not later than the fourth century to be incomprehensible, glorious, and fearful. And in the liturgy the laity, having been excluded from the offertory procession, look on as spectators in what is described as a theatre wherein the holiest of dramas takes place. At the crucial point in this drama they look not into the sanctuary itself, nor upon the acts of consecration, but upon the Iconostasis, which screens off the sanctuary per se. Nevertheless, the numinous and awe-inspiring comes close. In the rite the Bishop processes in plain view, "acting the part" of Christ. Above, the usual dome stands as the image of heaven, yet plainly resting on architectural members that connect it with "earth." The Eucharistic elements— the very body and blood of Christ—finally are indeed shared. And by then the icons of Mary, the Saints, and Christ—although stiff, hieratic, and "un-natural" in appearance—have long since been kissed and venerated by the faithful. The holiest of the holy comes nearer than near through the power of God and the art of vision and enactment.[14]

We observe, last, that in Catholicism as a whole the aesthetic acknowledgement and expression of divine proximity and presence extends to the realm of nature. Although the natural world itself is in no part God, it perpetually participates in the being of God; for nothing can so much as exist without deriving its principle of existence from the divine source of all being. By the same token—especially in the neo-

---

[14] See Otto G. von Simson, *Sacred Fortress: Byzantine Art and Statecraft in Ravenna*, 1948; reprint ed. (Princeton: Princeton University Press, 1987); and Pelikan, *Eastern Christendom*, pp. 91-145.

Platonic strains of Catholicism—all light and all beauty in nature as well as in art share in some way (sometimes said to be literal, sometimes analogical) in the light and beauty of God. Thus, however dimly, they reflect God's glory and point beyond themselves to the Invisible Light and Beauty that can be seen directly only in the spiritual Beatific Vision.

As we noted early on, however, this is not the only form of religiosity in which the Transcendent becomes proximate. Quite different theological assumptions and religious experiences of transcendence are apparently at work within Evangelical Protestantism, and especially in lower-income Black churches in America that clergy in the Black community often describe as being "mass" rather than "class" in character.[15] Three features of this tradition stand out as important to note in relation to questions of transcendence and aesthetic form.

First, proximate transcendence experienced in the context of such African American churches is not so connected with the mediating status and apparatus of the institutional church per se as it is with a sense of the power of the Holy Spirit and of the Living Christ to operate freely, outside existing human structures of power and legitimation. The peculiar authority of the Black church is thus in part the authority to allow spiritual and aesthetic freedom—within definite bounds—and so to let the Spirit move as it wills:

(All)   Every time I feel the spirit
           Moving in my heart I will pray.
           Every time I feel the spirit
           Moving in my heart I will pray.

(Solo)   Upon the mountain my Lord spoke
           Out of His mouth came fire and smoke.
           In the valley on my knees,
           Asked my Lord, Have mercy, please.

This spirit-filled freedom does not always lead to modes of singing or expression that would be judged decent and decorous by standards of other communities, particularly the White (and sometimes the Black) middle and upper class. Charles Wesley's fifth rule for singing hymns, of which he and his brother John wrote almost six thousand, was this: "Sing

---

[15] See Wyatt Tee Walker, *"Somebody's Calling My Name": Black Sacred Music and Social Change* (Valley Forge, Pa.: Judson Press, 1979), pp. 91-145.

modestly. Do not bawl." Methodists in the main, however, have not been afraid of lively tunes drawn from secular sources, with dotted notes and springy rhythms. And many Black Methodists, especially, have not been afraid to "bawl" when the Spirit moves them. The fact is that the large measure of uninhibited, spirit-moved improvisation found in jazz, for example, finds its way naturally into most aspects of this worship, from the loose "order of worship" to the spontaneous congregational responses of "Amen!" and "Praise the Lord!" Preaching itself becomes a venture into territory not entirely charted ahead of time even by the Good Book.[16] Frequently improvisatory, it is marked by striking and often colloquial images, vivid narratives, powerful cadences, and a tone charged with emotion. The God celebrated in this religious aesthetic is the One who liberates and saves, delivering Daniel from the fiery furnace, Israel from Egypt's land, and prayer and praise from the shackles of rigid propriety.

The second point we would make is that the transcendent God experienced in this tradition is usually not just proximate but also participative and quite anthropomorphic: jubilant, angry, passionate, tender. It is fitting, therefore, that here the differences separating sacred style from secular can be narrow indeed, with God's love and the love shown to God both seeming close to human love in general. In short, "our" style and "God's" style are not radically different. One dresses differently for church and keeps certain kinds of language and behavior out of places of worship. It is not a question of being irreverent. Yet in contemporary Black gospel music, for example, there are virtually no musical instruments automatically ruled out. Aretha Franklin, the "Queen of Soul," sings in much the same style whether in church or in concert. From the point of view of many of her churchly listeners (though by no means all), it would seem that a God who frowned on this would be a God unwilling to get divine hands dirty by working alongside human beings frequently sweaty and downtrodden. Instead of staying "above it all," this God comes as the Jesus who eats and mixes with sinners; who even as Lord and Christ suffers with and for his servants. No wonder the aesthetic styles suitable to this sort of transcendence tend to be earthy, eclectic, and generally uninhibited.

The third point is presumed by what we already have said: The aesthetic predominant in a great many African American churches is largely

---

[16] See James H. Cone, *The Spirituals and the Blues* (New York: Seabury, 1972), pp. 40-41.

popular and egalitarian. This does not mean that there are no standards of quality. Good singers, like good preachers, are recognized and praised; their gifts are counted as gifts from God. It does mean, however, that here aesthetica expressive of God's close way of being transcendent have an immediacy and accessibility that is itself a vehicle and sign of the immediacy and accessibility of God's own saving power and grace.

Even so, relatively few Christians in this tradition go so far as to regard the human and the earthly as always and already in some sense divine. This outlook is more characteristic of those responsive to our fourth and final variety of transcendence—namely, immanent transcendence. Among such Christians, who give voice to a recurrent but subordinate motif with many different Christian traditions, God is primarily experienced not as a reality near or present *to* us but as the extraordinary and miraculous reality ever present and immanent *in* us and in all other things, which intimately share in the very life of God. Even here, however, it is not claimed that anything on earth can contain the divine completely; rather, there is a sense that all things both contain and are contained by what always is more than merely finite and temporal.

In Martin Luther's writings this sense occasionally is expressed with great passion (and perplexity):

> God is substantially present everywhere, in and through all creatures, in all their parts and places, so that the world is full of God and He fills all, but without His being encompassed and surrounded by it. . . . These are all exceedingly incomprehensible matters; yet they are articles of our faith and are attended clearly and mightily in Holy Writ. . . . For how can reason tolerate it that the Divine majesty is so small that it can be substantially present in a grain, on a grain, over a grain, through a grain, within and without, and that, although it is a single majesty, it nevertheless is entirely in each grain separately? . . . And that the same Majesty is so large that neither this world nor a thousand worlds can encompass it and say: "Behold, there it is!"[17]

The references to God's substantial presence in, on, over, and through a grain recall Luther's insistence that in the sacrament Christ's body and blood are present in, with, and under the elements. But now, if only implicitly, it is the whole world that is the sacrament. Transcendent immanentalism of this kind is really sacramentalism pushed to the limit. But in contrast to much neo-Platonic sacramentalism, there is no hint that in the created order we see just a vestige or imprint of God's presence;

---

[17] Quoted in Heinrich Bornkamm, *Luther's World of Thought*, trans. Martin H. Bertram (St. Louis: Concordia, 1958), p. 189.

and in contrast to Thomas's views, there is no suggestion that God's governance of and presence in the world proceeds through an immense hierarchy of beings and powers.

In the modern period, as influences from the Orient, from Western Romanticism, from the new physics, and from process theologies and philosophies all combine in new ways, the immanental side of the transcendent comes to the fore in much Christian spirituality, thought, and worship. God is experienced as being related to us and the world as we are to our bodies. Or God becomes the Christ within. This experience, which normally stops short of pantheism, finds itself often embracing what has been called panentheism.[18]

The Catholic poet Gerard Manley Hopkins expresses something of this sense of immanent transcendence in the sonnet that opens with the declaration: "The world is charged with the grandeur of God"—a perception related to Hopkin's assertion elsewhere that "All things are charged with love, are charged with God and if we know how to touch them give off sparks and take fire, yield drops and flow, ring and tell of him."[19] It is characteristic of the aesthetic of immanent transcendence to discover the radically extraordinary within the ordinary—as Sylvia Plath does in her lyric "Black Rook in Rainy Weather," or as others do in natural phenomena seen as beautiful, sublime, or perhaps (to our minds) terrible. Thus one also proceeds to find the supernatural within the natural, as in much of Wordsworth and in the fierce, rugged poetry of the American Robinson Jeffers. Musically the *Missa Gaia*, or *Earth Mass* (1981), of Paul Winter and his consort follows such a path by blending Franciscan piety with a renewed sense of the earth as itself holy.

As we already have indicated, however, immanent transcendence does not have only to do with nature. The photography in the classic yet popular collection *The Family of Man* is so arranged as to suggest to many viewers that the human too is somehow holy in its very acts of love, work, and strife. In a quite different vein, moreover, there is art that, moving within one mode such as the proximate, suddenly breaks into this one. In the *Sanctus* of Bach's *Mass in B Minor* the contrapuntal setting of the phrase "Heaven and Earth are Full of Your Glory" can become a

---

[18] The works of Alfred North Whitehead, Charles Hartshorne, and John Cobb exemplify this understanding of the relation between God and world. Teilhard de Chardin develops a more mystical form of this vision.

[19] Quoted in W. H. Gardner, *Gerard Manley Hopkins*, vol. 2 (London: Secker and Warburg, 1949), p. 230.

veritable epiphany of divine plenitude as heaven and earth seem to converge, revealing their ultimate union/communion.

So it is that transcendence in its immanent form, as in the others we have examined, inevitably is connected with transformation. Any aesthetic mediation of a sense of the transcendent constitutes, in fact, a transfiguration of ordinary perception. It amplifies or diminishes, gives more than what is expected or undercuts all expectations, radically affirms or radically negates. In these diverse ways it changes those it addresses and engages.

Our study of religious aesthetic experience therefore leads back to the observation that religious aesthetica are concerned not only with divine transcendence but with human transformation. In each tradition the characteristic aesthetic strategies for expressing something of the transcendent reality of the divine depend partly on how that tradition assumes human beings need to be altered so as to respond appropriately to what in some sense transcends themselves. The Calvinist, for example, typically looks for aesthetic strategies that will make us conscious of our inherent inadequacy in contrast with God's glory, which nonetheless condescends to us in grace. Eastern Orthodoxy especially cultivates arts that will usher us into the presence of numinous mystery and move us toward our own transfiguration in the image of God. The process panentheist (of whatever affiliation) cherishes aesthetica that can open us to new possibilities for cooperating with God to create a future in which we can truly though limitedly share, thanks to that One in whom we live and move and have our being. In all these ways religious *aesthesis* reflects, contributes to, and alters the variety and the commonality of human existence, which for Christians is always an existence lived out before and in relation to the transcendent reality of God.

* This essay is a substantially shortened and modified version of Chapter 5 of Frank Burch Brown, *Religious Aesthetics: A Theological Study of Making and Meaning* (London and Princeton: Macmillan Press Ltd. and Princeton University Press, 1989). Permission to reprint has kindly been granted by the publishers.

The Crisis of Christianity in North America: Its Implications for China

LANGDON GILKEY

That there is a crisis of Christianity in the West, all agree. What that crisis is, and what its deeper causes may be, is another matter; diagnoses and suggested cures alike diverge radically. The reason is that such analyses of large historical shifts or movements, especially contemporary ones, are, while hopefully informed, woefully speculative in character and certainly not easily verifiable. This is one such precarious diagnosis; it makes sense to me, but its status is that only of a *proposal* for the reflection of others. I shall confine my attention to North America; the situation there at present appears to be significantly different than in Europe and in South America, and in any case the former is "home ground" for me.

My analysis has two stages or tiers: one, the encounter of modern scientific, technological and democratic culture with religion (especially Christianity) and all the effects and surprises that encounter has entailed. The, second, the quite recent but deeper problems or travail which have beset that modern secular culture itself. In the first, our gaze is especially on religion (Christianity) in the West as it has faced (since roughly 1800) the strong, powerful, luring forces of modern scientific rationality, historical consciousness and democratic idealism. In the second, we shift to look at the secular culture of the West to see the perhaps even more fundamental crisis into which it is now passing. Quite deliberately I will seek to evoke "echoes" of unexpectedly parallel crisis and reaction to crisis in China's spiritual history in the same period.

I. The Encounter of Religion with Modern Culture:
The Spiritual Crisis of Religion

The dominant issue for Christianity (and perhaps later for Judaism) has been "What shall we do with the modern world?" This "world" began to develop powerfully in the seventeenth century with the exploration of the whole earth, the rise of science, the appearance of mechanical technology and so industry, and the slow development of democratic, liberal and capitalistic ideals. This rapidly expanded and transformed culture became full-blown by the eighteenth century; and it has in ever new forms dominated not only the West ever since but also, till 1945, the entire rest of the world. At the start this culture was, to be sure, "Christian," and it remained so until roughly 1900 to 1918. It certainly seemed to represent a unified "Christian West" to other invaded cultures. However, from the eighteenth century on a serious split was occurring. The intellectual and moral *heart* of the Enlightenment was rationalist and humanist; it believed in the identity of Nature and Reason, and in the *autonomy* of the rational and moral human being. It was on the whole anti-traditional, anti-metaphysical and anti-religious. Certainly there appeared liberal Christian and liberal Jewish forms of this culture, but as the nineteenth century developed, the intellectual classes slowly moved away from these religious institutions. More and more they became "secular," possibly agnostic, atheist, anti-religious or humanistic. The intelligentsia on the whole felt well represented by Feuerbach, Marx, Nietzsche, Darwin, Huxley, Freud, Dewey, and A. J. Ayer.

Strange as it may seem, this encounter was almost as traumatic for Western religion as was the appearance of the scientific, technological, industrial and democratic West on the horizon of nineteenth-century traditional Chinese spirituality. For both the question, "What do we do with this powerful invader of our spiritual home?" became uppermost. And to take a simplified view—even more clearly than in China, the forces of religion in the West slowly divided themselves into two increasingly distinct groups: a) the "orthodox" who resisted many of the *general* ideals of the modern West (its *Weltanschauung*) in order to retain intact their orthodox *doctrinal* interpretations of God, world, human being and history; and b) the "liberals" who accepted (i.e., "believed in") the results of science, the possibilities of technology and industry, and the deals of democracy, and sought to reinterpret Christian doctrines in the light of modern experience and modern thought. (Incidentally, both groups swarmed into China in the late nineteenth and early twentieth centuries, represented respectively, let us say, by the CIM and the American Board!)

It should be noted that the relations to secular culture, to so-called "modernity" or "modern culture," by these groups are by no means simple—namely, a mere matter of the repudiation of the culture by the orthodox and its acceptance by the liberals. The orthodox had no discernable qualms about capitalistic industry and commerce, about private property, even fewer about class, and none at all about nationalism and imperialism; these powerful forces of the modern West they not only accepted but encouraged, usually without criticism. Correspondingly, the liberals challenged much of modern culture: its "materialistic" concern for property in capitalism, its virulent nationalism, its slavery (prior to 1864), its disdain for the poor, its racism and its militarism. They were enthusiastic about modernity's ideas and prophetically horrified at its social realities. It was liberal, not orthodox, missionaries who railed against Western imperialism in China and frequently pled the cause of the "colonies" against their own country's power when they returned home. Like the most creative of the Chinese reactions to the West, the Christian liberals (and the Jewish Reformed) mounted this criticism on the basis of their own deeper spiritual tradition: the value of person, the love and goodness of God, and the possibilities in history of universal brotherhood, namely the Kingdom. In any case, fundamentalism appears out of this split, as the increasingly conservative reaction of the orthodox to the onset of liberalism and modernism. Horrified at the so-called Christians who "adapted pagan ideas"—evolution, historical criticism and social democracy—many of the orthodox shifted radically to the right and began to defend "fundamentals": verbal inspiration of the Bible, a six-day creation, the Virgin Birth, the Blood Atonement, the Bodily Resurrection, and the Approaching End.

In the second half of the nineteenth century and the first half of the twentieth, it was widely assumed among the intellectual classes of the West, perhaps after 1918, especially in the United States, that this liberal culture developed in the eighteenth century—"modernity," as it was called—would only increase in scope, influence and dominance. As a boy I can recall vividly how this vision was taken for granted by most everyone in academic and liberal Protestant circles in the '20s and the '30s. Correspondingly, it was to everyone certain that orthodoxy and fundamentalism would slowly die out as scientific knowledge, technical rationality and industrial competence increased; and in time the world beyond the Western middle classes would be converted to this enlight-

enment; and with that conversion the myths and fears and fanaticisms—
the "superstitions"—of past religious history would vanish.
Fundamentalism in America was seen by liberals as a traditional, "old
fashioned" carryover of rural, pre-scientific, pre-technical society and
thus soon destined to die out. Ironically this same view of Progress led
the secular among the elite to see liberal religion itself as on its own way
out; in the end, like the archaic religions of Asia, all religion, liberal and
orthodox alike, would give way to modern secular forms of society, as
history's outmoded absolutist politics and its hierarchical social forms
would slowly give way everywhere to democratic and liberal social ideals. As science would become the universal form of *inquiry* and of *consciousness*, so liberal democracy would become the universal form of *social structure* and of *morals* alike. Finally, for those who stubbornly remained religious, at home or on the mission station, liberal, free-church,
Protestant Christianity would provide the model for the universal forms
of religious and moral consciousness: tolerant, congregational, autonomous, egalitarian, and above all, humanitarian.

In sum, Marx saw the industrial proletariat as determined by history
to become the universal class of humanity, slowly extinguishing injustice
and replacing religion, so, strangely, the Western bourgeoisie—and their
intellectuals—saw their own middle-classes as forming the center and
the model for the universal secular civilization to come. *This* was
Progress, the culmination of history's developments from the very beginning; and Progress was the symbol dominant in elite religion, in education, in politics and in social activities alike.

The first level of the crisis, then, and one of the first signs that this
vision of Progress was in fact an illusion, is the sharp falsification of this
prediction of the coming dominance of liberal religion, in fact an almost
complete reversal of this entire set of historical predictions. *Their* future
in 1910 is now *our* present in 1988; and 1988 defies in fact almost all they
had foretold—except steady advances in science and technology. Instead
of being the wave of the religious future, liberal Protestantism has since,
say, 1930, steadily declined in prominence and influence everywhere in
the West. Churches remain relatively full, to be sure, in the U.S. and
Canada; but neither their belief systems nor their public moral pronouncements—socially daring and even radical as they may be—are noticed, except where (as with race and Vietnam) they partly joined and
partly led a wider political protest movement. Catholic episcopal pronouncements (on nuclear arms, capitalistic exploitation, and sexism),
equally daring and radical, attract more attention. Catholics agree that it

is the lingering shadow of traditional episcopal authority that accounts
for this (as well as the intellectual and moral excellence of the statements); but most add that in time that authority too will wane.
Catholicism in North America has since 1964 joined "the modern scene";
in that sense it is liberal and at one with the liberal Protestant churches.
Altogether, however, their influence, even in ecumenical unity, has dramatically receded even in the last sixty years. This decline could be documented in any number of ways. So far, the secular critics of religion
seem to be correct: in a scientific, technological and democratic culture,
liberal religion is as inexorably if gradually eclipsed as is orthodox religion.

Why has this happened? Why have weakness, irrelevance, almost
"invisibility" become the apparent fate of precisely those churches in
modern culture that sought to be modern: to make accommodations to
science, to democracy, to autonomy, psychoanalysis, or reform politics?

1. Certainly the rise of the "secular option" is at work here; more and
more (since, say, 1900) the lure, the advantages, the sheer possibility of
being secular, unreligious and unchurched, has spread among all classes.
This tendency toward secularity is by no means universal; the core of
present churches, especially in the cities, is constituted by persons who
have "tried" that option and found it lacking, and are in church through
deliberate and eager intellectual and spiritual decision. For many of these
a more "biblical faith," "neo-orthodoxy"—modern and yet also traditional—represents by and large the appropriate theological center.
Clearly these are a minority now, though the churches represent large
sections of the larger population.

2. The union with modern science and historical consciousness has
inexorably *relativized* any particular statements of religious faith; the
older certainty and exclusiveness is, fortunately, gone; and an irenic, co-
operative, ecumenical and tolerant spirit reigns. Inescapably, however,
there is a bill to pay: why relate in commitment to a *perspective*; why give
your soul to a view and a community that is tolerant of other views and
inclusive even of its own opposites? Is there anything here that can break
open the bondage of sin, conquer the anxiety of Fate, dispel the fear and
grief of Death?—or heal the exploited? If not, why be religious?

3. All of these "mainline" churches, Protestant and now Catholic
alike, have precisely by their responsible acceptance of science, social
science, psychoanalysis and liberal politics associated themselves with
the classes who are the *bearers* of those functions in society, i.e., the middle-classes. Inescapably, despite the predominantly leftish ("liberal")

character of their clergy ("social gospelers"), these churches have more and more become *bourgeois* churches supported, financed and populated by the professional and managerial elements of society. Like *Time*, a college education, and the station wagon, these represent a part of successful corporate, even suburban America—despite their liberal, "protesting" leadership. Their clients like and seem to need church, even though they disagree with their minister's "naive liberalism."

In the meantime, however, the "WASP" (white, Anglo-Saxon, Protestant) component of the middle classes has dramatically shrunk, from an unequivocal dominance to perhaps a third or a quarter, as Jews, Catholics, the unchurched, the orthodox, Asians and Blacks have moved into the bourgeoisie. Thus the membership of the mainline Protestant churches is no longer, as it once was, identical with the dominant portion of the managers, the owners, the professionals, the academics of North America. It represents a minority at best.

Finally, this association with mainstream, bourgeois America—its industry and commerce, its science, technology and academia—means that if anyone becomes spiritually "alienated" from that ambiguous world and protests religious against it, such a one will find some other religious home than in the mainline churches—and hence the vast number of "cults," some imported, some homegrown, that have arisen among precisely the children of the bourgeoisie since 1960. In short, a vast new *pluralism* has become realized in America. A wide variety of ethnic groups (East Asian, Indian, Hispanic, Southern and Eastern European, Jewish and Arabic) and of religious groups and communities now move in and out of mainstream American life; their numbers are slowly entering the business, commercial and academic communities. Only the Black population, which is also entering the mainstream, retains its concern for and loyalty to its Protestant churches. Although the churches are in this way bourgeois, the day of the Protestant and even of Christian dominance of this class is over. The Christian voice is heard, but it is one among many, and thus it is far more muted than it once was. Liberal Christianity encountered modernity, accepted much of it—and now, instead of inspiring, directing and renewing modernity, Christianity has almost disappeared within it.

The gradual waning of liberal religion was one surprise. A far greater surprise has been the sudden and even accelerating rise of fundamentalist religion. It is the juxtaposition of these two that represents what I am suggesting to be the first tier or first level of the spiritual crisis of the West—unless, of course, one assumes that empowered fundamentalism represents a renewal and not a crisis! For almost three decades it has been clear that very conservative Protestant communities (conservative Baptist, Assemblies of God, Pentecostal, and so on) represented the fastest growing segments of Christianity, as Mormonism (also conservative religion) was the most expansive single group.

Then about two decades ago, the immense popularity of TV evangelists—Oral Roberts, Pat Robertson, the Bakkers, Jimmy Swaggert and so on—became evident to all, as did the even vaster amounts of money they were collecting—not to mention the estates and commercial enterprises they were purchasing, and the universities, institutes for research, and vacation resorts they were establishing. Associated groups were concurrently seeking changes in local and state laws to foster and to "establish" in the wider society their beliefs and their morals, particularly the *Creationists* who sought to ban the teaching of evolution.

Finally, with the Republican Convention of 1980, at which the fundamentalist "Evangelicals" played an important role, it became clear that already they represented a powerful *political* force. Many spoke now of the aim of dominating the Republican party; many important fundamentalist leaders (e.g., Jerry Falwell and Pat Robertson) began to call the country "back" to its foundations as a "Christian nation governed only by committee Christians." Without exception, they all represented the most right-wing political and economic views at home and the most militaristic and imperialistic anti-communism abroad. The alliances the fundamentalist could "trust" were those with the world's remaining dictatorial regimes: Marcos, Pinochet, Noriega, and of course the government of South Africa. In 1988, one of them sought to run—unsuccessfully, to be sure—as the Republican nominee for president.

Fundamentalism has become a powerful religious, moral, and now political force. Its aim is openly nationalistic and theocratic: to glorify America, to return American to its purported Christian beginnings and thus to restore its moral and religious authority in the world and its moral values at home. To those who fear it, it has racist potentialities; and certainly like all theocracies, it can easily move in a repressive, totalitarian direction. Fortunately, the pluralism and the secularism that are eating away at the cultural and economic dominance of the *liberal* churches "from above" also prevent this new *theocentric* mode of dominance "from below."

Nevertheless, the growth of fundamentalism is a crisis: it represents a threat for liberal religion, for free and open education, for rational and irenic international policy, and for a humane domestic economic and social policy. To everyone's surprise, the "illiberal" religion that seemed adamantly to resist the world now appears to be almost winning the world; and even the atheists are astonished that, far from an innocuous and waning epiphenomenon in a scientific age, religion has shown itself—as it has in Islam—to be a powerful, effective and dangerous modern force. Similar associations of "fundamentalist" religion with modern technical, modern scientific and contemporary life have appeared in Canada and Australia, in important segments of Judaism, in Sikhism, Hinduism, and in Japan, and of course in Islam. If ours began as a "secular" century, it is certainly ending as a "religious" one!

The contemporary relation of resurgent fundamentalism to the modern world is even more complex than was that of the orthodox and/or the older fundamentalism that preceded it in the first decades of this century. There is no question that these groups—e.g., the Creationists—deny crucial *general* ideas associated with modern science and modern culture: the immense age of the universe, the fundamental changes that have taken place in all its aspects, the changes of forms of life and of species, the relativity of all historical expressions to their time and place (including religious scriptures), the uniform working of "natural law" in nature and of strictly historical causes in history. The liberal ethical and democratic political ethos of modern culture—tolerance of other ideas, concern for economic and social justice, for peace and for individual liberties—all of this the fundamentalist leaders repudiate; social reform, civil rights, and freedom of ideas and of speech seem to them unchristian and even communistic.

For them, the scriptures are verbally infallible, the creation a recent (ten to twenty thousand years) six-day sequence of events, the biblical history of Eden, of Noah and of the patriarchs more authentic than the secular history of hunting, gathering and early urban societies—and so on. To them also the Bible is a repository of scientific and historical facts, of theological doctrines, specific laws and particular commandments which, properly interpreted, can give utterly authoritative guidance for any sort of theoretical question or moral dilemma raised in the course of ordinary life.

All this seems—and for good reason—to hark back to at least well before the eighteenth century in Europe and the early nineteenth century in North America. Are these, then, not *pre-modern* groups antithetical across the board to all of contemporary civilization and not merely to its science? So it seems, and so most members of the academic and the scientific communities view them.

A closer look reveals something else, in fact another set of surprises. First of all, socially and economically these groups do not represent rural "backwaters" on the periphery of contemporary commercial, technological and even educational culture. On the contrary, they own, manage and participate in large-scale commercial enterprises; they own, manage and staff nationwide, even worldwide, TV chains and programs; they have easy access to more wealth and property than most of the mainline churches; they operate schools, colleges and some universities; they are effectively organized politically at every relevant level; and finally they study science, participate in technology, engineering, medicine and law—and to cap it all, they now claim that *their* world view represents "true science!"

At the Scopes trial in 1925, the fundamentalist movement repudiated completely any relation at all with science, technology and commerce, with what they called "urban, Wall Street, university and scientific paganism." More concretely, the present leaders and authors of the works of "creation science" possess Ph.D.'s in natural science from such recognized universities as Berkeley, MIT, Ohio State, University of Pittsburgh; and creationists are visibly present on the scientific faculties of many reputable scientific universities: Purdue, Carnegie Tech, Iowa State, and in the many research laboratories of large industrial concerns. As we have noted, resurgent fundamentalism has moved powerfully into the political and commercial worlds.

Without question, therefore, these groups have accepted the economic, political and social structures of modern civilization (capitalistic, nationalistic, technological and scientific), and the more "worldly" of its goals (monetary rewards, financial success, political and cultural power). What they have *not* accepted are its world view on the one hand and its deeper personal and social moral ideals (democratic reform, individual rights, cooperation and peace among cultures and religions). They are, in other words, fully as much modern as they are traditional, and they cannot be understood except in this dual light.

It might be interesting to note further that they are one example of the adoption of only the "material" level of Western culture, i.e., only its science (in part), its technology, its industrial, commercial and organizational assets; having, then, repudiated the best of the spiritual traditions of the West, they seek to combine this material and technological side of the West with their own traditional and so virtually unchanged religious and moralistic viewpoint. If this is in fact what they are, then some of the suggestions among nineteenth-century Chinese intellectuals that "only the material capabilities, the science and the technology of the West be adopted" might look more ambiguous now than they did then. Here an uncritical and unrevised form of traditional Christianity reappears powerfully in contemporary life armed now with the science, the technology, the industrial and commercial potencies of modern culture. Many in the West feel that this union of unrevised religion with the material powers of modern culture is frightening.

Once we are enabled to understand contemporary fundamentalism as in fact a *union*, however unexpected, of fundamentalist religion with modern culture, even a "supernatural" religion with science, then we see how false and misleading were several of the widely held assumptions of liberal culture about religion. I refer, first, to the assumption that modern scientific culture is antithetical to orthodox faith, even to fanatical faith; and second, to the assumption that science always separates itself from, in fact actively repels, religious and ideological fervor. And when one sees those points, a new view of the twentieth century becomes possible; at last we can now understand some of the bizarre "marriages" of science with religious ideology in our time as more than merely inexplicable anomalies. For there are several of these cases which, in fact, dominate the landscape in the twentieth century. Two facts seem certain about contemporary cultures: one is that all intend to become scientific, technological and industrial as quickly as possible, and another is that they intend to do this on their *own* terms, e.g., in union with their own religious and/or ideological stance.

First, there was the union of science, technology and industrial power with Shinto religion in the Japan of the '20s, '30s, and '40s. Next, there was the undoubted coopting of the immense German scientific and technological establishment by Nazi ideology in the '30s and '40s; the effects of this union on the human sciences of anthropology, cultural history, psychology and sociology were disastrous. Concurrently, there was the uneasy marriage of Stalinism with science and technology in Russia, whose effects on biology as well as on cultural history, economics, sociology and political theory are widely recognized. Next in line—but never able to become actual—would have been the union of powerful ideology with science and industrial technology projected by Maoism. And finally, there is Iran with the prospect of a Shi'ite science, technology and industrial establishment. Hundreds of Iranians are being trained at present in science and engineering in the United States; most will return to Iran, and all who return there will perforce adapt the science and the technology they have learned here to the self-understanding of the Shi'ite religion and the stern Sharia (law) of that Islamic community.

None of these versions represents the "science" of the American Association for the Advancement of Science, either in method or in the content of their theories. Are they, then, "science" or not? this is a question not easy to answer, as the question, What is "real Christianity" or "real Confucianism"? is never easy to answer.

In any case, let us note (1) that the question of the relation of the modern scientific, technological and industrial culture (developed in the West but now not confined there) to traditional religions and to religious ideologies remains perhaps the dominant question of our century. Further, (2) that a wide variety of unexpected and bizarre "marriages" of that modern culture with religion and with ideological matrices has occurred, despite the seeming impossibility of any such rapprochement. And (3) that all this reminds us of the long debated issue in China: "How are we to accept the valid elements of modern culture without losing our own identity, in fact without losing our souls?" "How are we to unite modern science and technology to traditional Chinese religion, philosophy and social viewpoints?" Finally, (4) let us not forget that this same question, and the crisis it has precipitated, has forced itself on Western Christians—only over a much longer stretch of time—much as it has disturbed Chinese Confucianists.

II. The Spiritual Crisis of Modern Western Culture and Its Effects on Religion

We now turn our gaze in another direction, looking not so much at religious institutions and movements as at the career of Western culture itself. For as yet we have left quite unexplicated the causes or sources of the unexpected resurgence of fundamentalism: Why has supra-orthodox religion suddenly reappeared with great power when fifty years ago every sign seemed to promise its steady decline?

We must not be fooled by the words "spiritual crisis." Of course this phrase can refer to crises of "religious belief," doubts whether there is a God, a next life or an immortal souls—and generally that is what the phrase does mean. But "spiritual crisis" can, and most importantly does, refer as well to states of deep anxiety, of not-at-homeness or alienation in the world, of lostness or uprootedness, of meaninglessness and emptiness in life, of futility and despair about the future. These represent the *crisis* referred to when loss of faith in God appears.

Loss of belief in God can surely cause such a crisis, but so can other apparently "unspiritual" matters, for example, changes in wider history that effect the quality or security of life. Times of social upheaval—or the threat of it—are themselves also times of deep anxiety. In turn, anxiety signals the most important and often dangerous of spiritual situations; out of such situations of anxiety, if courage, confidence and self-control do not appear, can emerge radical sin and its consequence, injustice.[1]

Every important social structure has its spiritual reflection: a creative structure is reflected in spiritual symbols that in turn support, invigorate and direct the common life (e.g., those of Confucian China and of democracy). A structure in disarray is reflected in the spiritual situation of anxiety, thus possibly in radical fanaticism or radical despair, and in the end, a kind of blind paranoia: "ate," madness. Thus when we speak of the contemporary political, economic and social "time of troubles" besetting Western culture, we are not looking *away* from spiritual crisis—away, for example, from the deeper causes of fundamentalist and fanatical religion—but precisely at the sort of situation or condition that engenders crises of the spirit and thus the disarray of religious institutions.

I have mentioned already some of the possible so-called "religious" causes of the fundamentalist renewal. Certainly the relativization of scriptural authority, of treasured doctrines and of moral rules has encouraged a conservative reaction. Certainly also there is the sense, also accurate, that the traditional values of our culture: sexual continence, the stability of marriage, parental authority and responsibility, hard work and honesty, self-control (to name a few) are slipping badly, as they are, in contemporary life. Again the reaction is to depend on and stress an oppressive religious legalism. There has been also the clear loss, already referred to, of the predominantly *Christian* character of American life, and so the conviction that the spiritual bases of society are seriously evaporating. (Is this an "echo" of the earlier sense of the loss in China of the *Confucian* character of its common life?)

Finally, in school, in public discourse, and via the media, much of the population has become conscious for virtually the first time of the *secular* character of modern civilization. Many people literally had no idea that the autos, TVs, consumer goods and airplanes they had learned to depend on and rejoice in were themselves directly and inherently depen-

---

[1] For the most perceptive of the analyses of the relation of anxiety, sin and social injustice, cf. Reinhold Niebuhr, *Nature and Destiny of Man*, 2 vols. (New York: Charles Scribner and Sons, 1941), 1: chaps. 7-9.

dent on a science and a technology whose naturalistic and at best agnostic world view challenged their own spiritual assumptions. Such a secular ("atheistic") vision of reality thus appears to them to be a recent intruder into American life, a kind of foreign conspiracy of Satan or of communism, a set of "heresies" quite separable from the science and the technology they admire as "American" to the core, a conspiracy generated by such notorious, if as yet unread, heretics as Marx and Darwin.

Present fundamentalism understands itself as a reaction to the modern "godless culture" rampant in public schools, in secular universities, and in mainline churches—*not* to science, technology and industrialism; and it sees itself as the one bulwark against the moral decay evident in promiscuity, abortion, divorce and drugs. Not unlike the consciousness of many of the Islamic and Communist countries, its own self-consciousness is that it is counteracting—while the other churches are encouraging—the religious and moral laxity of present American life.

Deeper than all of this, however, lie cultural stresses and strains which equally disturb the spirit; at least that is my thesis. And it is here that the most interesting parallel with familiar "spiritual" problems in China's encounter with the West appear. I have spoken of the "time of troubles" of Western culture, a phrase Arnold Toynbee used to describe a period in a culture's life when breakdown or decline first become possible, though never necessary, and consequently when awareness of the fragility of both security and meaning in life tends to become both sharper and more painful. I shall refer to this "time of troubles" on two different levels: the *social* bases, on the one hand, and their *spiritual* consequences, on the other. In such periods of significant social disarray (e.g., the late Hellenistic era and the Late Medieval period) religion, both fanatical and profound, bizarre and traditional, tends to increase in scope and intensity—as the profusion of new cults in the late Roman Empire illustrates.

In describing the "time of troubles" facing Western culture as a whole, the place to start, so I believe, is the precipitous loss of dominance by the West in the last four decades. From the mid-sixteenth century the dominance of the Western nations over the rest of the world steadily increased; it was a dominance more and more unchallenged by any non-European power. By the mid-nineteenth century, Western nations enjoyed a sovereign control over nearly the entire globe, ruling in fact whatever they did not own—as the Chinese are well aware.

Four hundred years is an incredible length of time; a sense of what we might call a "natural right" to sovereignty, of superiority of intellect, of power, or even of virtue and of religion, inevitably appears and becomes habitual, taken for granted (e.g., recall the film *Passage to India*). Such ruling communities feel incredibly secure until they begin to cease to rule, until that rule is challenged.

In our present, that rule has suddenly *vanished*; the empires are gone, and with them the monopoly of dominance has fled. America has inherited what is left of the West's power—but the sovereignty over the entire globe that Europe once possessed, *that* America has not inherited. Other powers outside the West: some of them present allies of the West, some alien and opposed, and some even neutral, all significantly *different*, have appeared and will only increase in economic, political and military strength. The Boxer Rebellion at the start of this century was quelled in two short weeks by a small European force; seventy-five years later, no amount of American power could even rescue the hostages in Teheran.

This fast change is *good* for the world, for justice, humanity and peace. But at the same time, this change represents an utterly new role in the world for the West: the world's present barely remains "Western," the future almost certainly will be non-Western. As a consequence, the sense of security that an assumed dominance breeds is much more vulnerable, and an anxiety about the shape of the future is manifest all over the West. Not many leaders articulate these realities; most of them are not, I believe, fully aware of them (most Europeans and Americans mistakenly think America has simply replaced Europe as the world's leader). But this slippage of sovereignty, of security, of superiority, of the proud sense of the universality—yes, even of the "eternity" of their culture—is deeply *felt*. And the result is anxiety and the need for "roots," for deeper structures of courage, confidence and meaning.

Toynbee describes a "time of troubles" as appearing in connection with the fundamental institutions of a culture—those institutions on which the security, creativity, power and so growth of the culture had depended. At some point, because of important historical changes, these institutions get, so to speak, out of sync, start to misfunction; and at this point these essential institutions, instead of resolving fundamental problems, begin to cause ever further and deeper problems. Such was the ultimate fate of the feudal system in Europe; creative of necessary order in the chaos of seventh- to eleventh-century life, the feudal aristocracy became an oppressive burden by the sixteenth and seventeenth centuries—and only radical revolutions could open Europe up for a new creative phase.

Unquestionably, those institutions on which the astounding growth and predominant power of the modern West have depended have been science, technology and industrialism. In our lifetime, however, each of these has undergone an unexpected and disorienting metamorphosis. From an apparently unqualified blessing each has changed into an exceedingly ambiguous social reality, bearing in itself a threat as well as a promise, a curse rather than its opposite. Advances in science now frighten us as much as they excite us;[2] technological developments threaten our existence and our humanity in ever new ways; industrial expansion seems to have destroyed beauty and quality of life everywhere—and, finally, science, technology and industrialism together threaten the natural harmonies and resources upon which our common life depends. Civilization as developed by the West has become *zweideutig*, ambiguous, able to destroy us more quickly and surely than it can secure us. The dramatic symbol of this terrible ambiguity is, of course, the bomb, symbol of science and yet also of death. We are aware, moreover, that with that self-induced destruction appears the possibility, also new, of the virtual end of humanity, of nature and so of history itself. Who could have thought that *this* was a possibility in 1910, or even in 1930?

Again, this unconditional danger consequent on an unconditional power is more felt than articulated, but it surely is widely felt. Ironically and surprisingly, such a worldly Apocalypse, in the hands of humans, poses an ultimate threat and nurtures an ultimate anxiety. Emotionally and imaginatively, it seems to call for a corresponding divine Apocalypse and divine rescue to introduce back some hope. No wonder supernatural religion flourishes because of the advances of science, technology and industrialism rather than despite them!

As our most recent points have made clear, important military, political, economic and social changes—and the threats they may well contain for the sense of security and meaning among those long accustomed to both—engender spiritual crises, crises of the soul. In such times religion tends to prosper, especially supernatural religion which promises to bring in from elsewhere permanent rescue from beyond the obvious, "empirical" confusion and disarray of the present.

Empiricism in a time of decay, let us recall, generates not optimism but despair, not a sense of freedom but of fatedness, not confidence but

---

[2] Cf., for example, the new book, *Nuclear Fear: A History of Images* (Cambridge: Howard, 1988), written by Spencer R. Weart.

the loss of confidence. Even more, such social catastrophes—or the threat of them—can represent a direct threat to the religious beliefs themselves of those suffering from the catastrophe. When a city or a country is overwhelmed by the superior force of a conqueror, the "gods" of the victims, themselves suffering defeat, tend to lose status and glory—and their devotees may well look elsewhere for help. (The notable exception was of course Yahweh on the occasion of the exile and then later the demolition of the temple.) Something like this, let me suggest, has been happening to the "gods" of the West in the twentieth century.

Many people in the West, and perhaps especially in North America, are genuinely Christian or deeply Jewish. Nevertheless, as we have noted, the West had in a significant part become spiritually secular or quasi-secular; and the major religious groups of the West have identified themselves at very deep spiritual levels with the modern culture in which they have found themselves. The beliefs, even of religious groups, that motivated and empowered most persons, secular and religious alike, were therefore beliefs that characterized the culture as a whole; most forms of religion were spiritually as well as economically, politically and socially acculturated.

It has, moreover, been almost uniquely characteristic of the modern West that what it believed in was *itself*; that is to say, in its own creative achievements, in its science, its technology, its democratic ideals, its freedoms, and its predominant modes of being human. Most Westerners, and perhaps especially most Americans, were convinced that in the various facets of Western civilization human kind had reached its apogee, its supreme level, its classic excellence. In Western civilization all other civilizations had reached their fulfillment. During the long processes of historical change, culture had gradually developed and improved: in knowledge, in technical capacities, in organized skills, in social institutions and in moral sensibility. Slowly these developments on all fronts had reached their modern form: in empirical science, in mathematics, in democratic politics and ideals, in Western (Christian) morals, in Western social institutions. Now they stood at their highest point.

This confidence in development towards the ideal was precisely what they meant by *Progress*, and everyone who regarded themselves as "modern" took such Progress, ending with the achievements of modern civilizations, quite for granted. I am sure the Chinese were well aware of the presence among Westerners of this assumption of superiority; and strangely, to almost all, Western and non-Western alike, this assumption seemed strongly credible—for the dominance remained unchallenged.

As Vice President Lyndon Johnson said in 1959 (I heard him say it), "Everyone on the globe wants to be an American—and for good reason—it is the natural way of being human!"

Nature and history have combined to produce, over centuries of struggle, modern Western civilization. History here has reached its highest point, and America especially represents that present culmination. Having come this far, history will continue to develop this model and so continue in ever new forms to develop these Western modes of excellence. Time is increasingly *sacred*, increasingly fulfilled by the development of civilization in the West; and the sacred *space* where this wonder is now placed is in the West, particularly in the northern hemisphere. Such was the common faith, the "religious substance," of most of modern Western culture.

Those familiar with the sacred connotations in classical Chinese culture of China as the Central Kingdom at the center of the universe, and of *jen* as the fulfillment of humanity itself in relation to the cosmic Tao, will feel a parallel, however surprising, in these notions of Western superiority. Perhaps they will understand, therefore, how such an apparently *incredible* view of itself was possible for the West and for America. And perhaps the main difference in these visions was the shift from the center of cosmological *space* to the fulfillment of *time* as constituting the central axis according to which ultimate meaning became concrete on earth.

This belief in Progress and in Western civilization as its embodiment and bearer represents the "spiritual substance" or the "religious substance" of Western culture. That culture proved more powerful in spreading *this* substance than Christianity, the "official" religion which it proclaimed. This pseudo-religion appeared among intellectuals and authors usually in secular form as evolutionary and historical progress; it appeared in religious form in liberal Christian theology and Reformed Judaism as a doctrine of divine immanence in history; and it inserted itself as the worldly aspects of the faith of most Orthodox Christians and even Jews in the West. Few denied this sense of the progress of civilization and history, and few there were who did not associate the meaning of their own lives, the tasks of their country and the career of their local community with that faith.

As is obvious, Marxism represents another, socialist, form of this belief in historical development as fulfilling itself in the gradual creation of an ideal community. Again, social community, the developmental progress of civilization and of meaning, and the processes of the whole of history combine in what can only be called a "religious" belief or myth.

Now the point is that the social "time of troubles," described above, has directly challenged this spiritual or religious set of beliefs about history and its meaning. In fact, the process of the *falsification*, if I may use that strong term, of the hypothesis of progress has been growing in intensity. The former bases of confidence in Progress have been eroded; the dominance by the West of the globe has gone; the advances of science and technology and the spread of industry have created many more lethal problems than they have resolved; and social suffering, if not on the increase, seems as much the lot of humanity as before. Above all, history itself seems to have lost its one clear thread of meaning. The West finds itself not only in serious internal self-contradiction but suddenly displaced from the center—and the future appears now radically uncertain, even scary.

If all this is so, what, then, is the human story all about? Is it about *nothing*; is it going *nowhere* at all; is there *no* center to space and no direction to time? These questions—again posed on the feeling level if not yet articulated—signal a "death" of the "gods" of the West, and the consequent need for some new, more deeply grounded faith. The present and future appear in disarray, out of touch with order, with *Tao*. Fundamentalism is, I think, one alternative answer, and a powerful one, to this deeply felt anxiety.

One further point. As the West has developed, its sense of confidence in rational autonomy and in its ability to know and control the world expanded. It became enamored with the *external* control its knowledge gave it rather than with its inner awareness of its roots in the depth of being and in authentic humanity. With that expansion of self-confidence, seemingly objectively confirmed by the expansion of Western political dominance over the world, by technical dominance over nature, and by industrial control of human wants, came a disdain for mystery of any sort: the mystery of the self, of history, of social community, of reality itself. Questions that can be answered by empirical inquiry became the only legitimate questions. Problems of technical competence became the only questions for common debate.

To the empirical and pragmatic mind of the West, symbols and myths no longer spoke to real spiritual needs but reflected only the ignorance and weakness of pre-modern human being. Even rational reflection on the nature of reality, of truth and of the good became "meaningless." In short, the mind of the West moved itself radically and exclusively towards concentration on the surface of life and evacuated life's depths. Thought concerned only means and not ends; it dealt alone with successful practice and not reality; its sole purpose was to fulfill our immediate wishes rather than to criticize, control or ground them.

Such a mindset, long at ease in a time process of developing Progress, and long at home in the sacred space of the West, was ill-prepared for the sudden appearance of radical evil, of triumphant evil, and so of the inexorable return of the tragic, of "mysteries" that could neither be solved nor removed. It had cut itself off from its own deepest roots, those symbols and concepts which could disclose to us universal reality, all encompassing truth, and ultimate good. For it is only through such symbols associated with mystery that what is *permanent* and what is *healing* can be glimpsed, approached and grasped even within the shadow and the terror of the tragic.

The West had been founded on such symbols and concepts, such "myths" one might say. Greek, Judaic, Christian, and Enlightenment symbols had long fed its spirit and made its creative development possible. It had powerful roots, expressible in religious myths, theological symbols, philosophical concepts and normative judgments, a deep symbolic structure that undergirded the human elements in its ethics and political theory. In fact, on these bases depended its empirical science, its democracy and its socialism, its humanitarian legal and social developments.

These symbolic foundations, however, were progressively ignored, scorned, even ridiculed in an increasingly positivistic and pragmatic culture. Natural and social science, technical and organizational rationality alone remained as legitimate activities of "mind." But this restricted scope of reason or spirit provides poor defenses indeed when the religious substance of the culture falls apart, and when the deeper questions concerning reality, truth, and not least of the grounds in cosmos and history of values, push themselves brutally forward in consciousness. Again, it is no wonder that naive but unassailable dogmas, identifying ultimate reality and traditional values, and so providing answers to these now looming questions, and above all promising security and meaning to spare, appear powerfully on the scene.

It is not only interesting but surprising to find that this situation, with all its dangers of spiritual superficiality accompanying radical irrationality, parallels the problems in Chinese culture seen so clearly by Hsiung Shih-li in the first half of this century. As Tu Wei-ming has made plain,[3] Hsiung feared above all that Chinese intellectuals would adopt "surface" skills of the West: science, technology and industrialism, without establishing them in correlation with China's own deeper moral, ontological and even religious roots, i.e., abstracting its *yung* from the profound *t'i* on which every *yung* is necessarily founded.

As Hsiung realized, Western skills *themselves* rested on a profound symbolic ontological and moral base reaching back into the intellectual and spiritual traditions of the West. This was, however, not the way the West presented itself (e.g., in Dewey), nor the way most Chinese intellectuals wished to receive it and adapt to it. Only, however, if China reexamined and rethought its own spiritual foundations could it accept these new modes of knowing and doing, in correlation with those foundations, without disaster.

As our analysis has sought to show, this is not only a Chinese problem in relation to the West. It is a modern Western problem in relation to the modern scientific and technical culture that the West has itself developed. For the loss of the West's own ontological, moral and religious roots has resulted in an excessive spiritual vulnerability in the face of the crises and dilemmas of a culture in travail, and in *essential* travail. This is the deepest level, I believe, of its spiritual crisis, one it surely shares with China, if for different reasons. And it is this crisis within modern culture itself which more than anything else gives us insight into the sources of the fundamentalism that has suddenly appeared all around us.

[3] Tu Wei-ming, *Humanity and Self-Cultivation* (Berkeley: Asia Humanities Press, 1979), pp. 229-40.

On New Uses of the "Secular" and the "Religious" in Contemporary Criticism: Edward Said, George Steiner, and the Counter-Example of Eric Heller

GILES GUNN

> As a teacher [the humanist] is involved in a task which would appear impossible by the standards of the scientific laboratory: to teach what, strictly speaking, cannot be taught, but only "caught," like a passion, a vice or a virtue. This "impossibility" is the inspiration of his work. There are no methods that comprehend his subject; only methods, perhaps, that produce the intellectual pressure and temperature in which perception crystallizes into conviction and learning into a sense of value.
>
> *The Disinherited Mind*, ix.

In his moving and important book on *The World, the Text, and the Critic*, Edward Said has attempted to revive, with what seems to me to be unfortunate consequences, the venerable distinction in critical theory between the "religious" and the "secular." Indeed, so influential is Said's work and so authoritative his example that this distinction has now reachieved something bordering on canonical status. My own view is that the distinction between the "religious" and the "secular" is, as Said employs it, doubly misleading. Not only does it simplify the relations between these two terms by treating almost as ontological a set of abstractions that since the Renaissance can only be understood when historicized; it thereby tends to deform as well as to mask what is philosophically if not theologically problematic about the distinction itself.

By religious criticism Said, of course, means a good deal more than criticism that operates within the intellectual shelter of some traditional religious orthodoxy; he means all criticism that defers rhetorically, if not also politically and morally, to what is conceived of as, in his terms, "transhuman authority." Hence evidence of the "religious" in this sense is to be found not only in the eruption of theological fundamentalism all over the world but also in the increased role which the "Manichean theologizing of 'the Other'" now plays in contemporary intellectual discourse.[1] This theologizing of "the Other" can be found wherever one comes upon references to such vague and semi-sacred abstractions as the Orient, the Feminine, History, Terrorism, the West, Blackness, the Third World, logocentricity, Communism, America, God, and now, liberalism, and wherever one encounters frequent methodological recourse to forms of undecidability, the unthinkable, paradox, nothingness, and silence, on the one side, or appeals to magic, divine necessity, or the spiritually esoteric, on the other. In addition to reflecting what Said describes as the terrible need in our time for a kind of human assuagement that only the largest and crudest metaphysical generalizations can provide, such appeals promote what he views as a dangerous sort of "uncriticality" that shares in common with most other religious discourse an interest in premature closure, in metanarrative, and in pious subservience to transcendence.[2]

By contrast, "secular criticism," as Said defines it, is worldly, skeptical, and radically iconoclastic. The very opposite of what he calls "organized dogma," secular criticism is suspicious of all totalizing concepts, impatient of all reifications, and discontent with all professional "guilds, special interests, imperialized fiefdoms, and orthodox habits of mind." Opposed in principle to every form of intellectual and emotional tyranny, "secular criticism" seeks to advance what Said describes as "noncoercive knowledge produced in the interests of human freedom."[3]

"Secular criticism" is therefore, to use the term similarly employed by Jonathan Culler, "oppositional." The function of such oppositional criticism, as they construe it, is to challenge and, where possible, to deconstruct all the forms in which literary study, whether intentionally or not, has collaborated in the maintenance of cultural (which is to say, religio-humanistic) piety, and both associate the possibility for such oppositional thinking with a criticism that is, at its best, emphatically comparative and intransigently adversarial. Indeed, Said and Culler both come very close to identifying such criticism with the field or specializa-

---

[1] *The World, the Text, and the Critic* (Cambridge, Mass.: Harvard University Press, 1983), p. 291.

[2] *Ibid.*, p. 290.

[3] *Ibid.*, p. 29.

tion of comparative literature itself, and they define comparative literary study, by which they really mean comparative cultural criticism, as essentially a critique of religion, or, rather, the critique of possible collusion, if not conspiracy, between organized religion and the critical defense of the Western literary tradition that is implied, so they hold, by the titles of such recent and widely known books of criticism as Frank Kermode's *The Genesis of Secrecy,* Northrop Frye's *The Great Code,* Harold Bloom's *Kaballah and Criticism,* Rene Girard's *Violence and the Sacred,* or, for all I know, Nathan Scott's *The Wild Prayer of Longing* or *The Poetics of Belief.*[4]

Such fears will sound excessive only if one fails to attend to the arguments of traditional humanists who, like the deservingly admired George Steiner, are frequently disposed to turn criticism in the direction of theological apologetics. In is 1985 Leslie Stephen Memorial lecture, for example, Steiner not only urges a restoration of ethical standards in literary criticism but also a revival of the notion of religious transcendence on which he thinks they were formerly based.[5] Such a recovery of the concept of transcendence will not only encourage an attitude of intellectual humility among literary and cultural critics, Steiner believes, but possibly induce in their readers an appropriate sense of piety towards it.

It is comparatively easy to take exception to Steiner's recommendation—I have already done so in another context—because his view of transcendence is premised on supernaturalist conceptions about religion that have been unacceptable to most people who think seriously about

---

[4] Said's position is most fully adumbrated in the two chapters of *The World, the Text, and the Critic* entitled, "Secular Criticism" and "Religious Criticism," pp. 1-30, 190-92; Culler's in an article entitled, "Comparative Literature and the Pieties," in *Profession 86,* pp. 30-32. Of the two, Said's seems the more moderate. At times he speaks as though "secularity" involves little more than a skeptical, self-consciously situated criticism "reflectively open to its own failings" and by no means value-free. At other times, however, he speaks of "secular" or "oppositional" criticism as one which is not only suspicious of all totalizing, reifying, dominating habits of mind but also wholly defined by its incomparability with any other intellectual practice. The more the identity of this kind of criticism is based upon a self-consciously maintained difference from every other mental activity or form, the more it succumbs, because of its wholly oppositional nature, to a totalization of its own.

[5] George Steiner, "Viewpoint: A New Meaning of Meaning," *Times Literary Supplement,* November 8, 1985, pp. 1262, 1275-76. This position has now been elaborated at greater length in Steiner's *Real Presences* (Chicago: University of Chicago Press, 1989), particularly pp. 137-232.

religious and theological issues for well over a century.[6] Here, however, I want to take issue with Steiner's proposal on somewhat different grounds: because in addition to proposing what I take to be a specious view of transcendence, he misleadingly allies that idea of transcendence with the humanistic canon of Western literature itself. Steiner writes in this essay, as he and so many others have elsewhere, as though the literary canon of Western humanism carried with it a kind of religious warrant, as though its deepest spiritual intention had always been to bring those individuals critically capable of achieving a satisfactory appreciation of it into a new understanding of the divine, into a more stable and comprehensive relation with whatever is regarded as sacred in the past.

To put this differently, Steiner turns to criticism, and by extension its disciplinary counterpart, the humanities, into a special scene of spiritual crisis. This scene is defined by a distinctive relationship between religion and literature in which each takes on a new theological importance for the other. On their deepest levels of cultural interrelation, where they contribute to our image of the human, to our notion of humanity itself, both religion and literature are assumed to be at once crucially at stake and also deeply complicit. They are crucially at stake because Steiner assumes that the humanities—which amounts, as I said, to the same thing as the canon of Western classics—encompass a body of learning or a repository of values that, like one half of T. S. Eliot's notion of tradition, is not only invulnerable to time but perennially relevant. They are complicit because Steiner's way of "privileging" the humanities, and the canon of texts that represents them, only serves to valorize a kind of criticism that views literature and religion as intimately related, that construes literature *as* a species of religion (or, in Northrup Frye's formulation, as secular scripture) and religion *as* a species of art (or mode of inspired expression where culture consummates itself through the creation of acts or forms that in effect transcend its own categories or horizons of meaning).

To "religious" critics like Steiner, the chief value of all interpretive or hermeneutic activity—of the effort, as Clifford Geertz says somewhere, "to translate the idioms of one people into the metaphors of another"—is to reveal or disclose or uncover that fundamental oneness of human

---

[6] See Giles Gunn, *The Culture of Criticism and the Criticism of Culture* (New York: Oxford University Press, 1987), ix-x. The present paragraph and several others in this essay are drawn from various sections of this book and my *The Interpretation of Otherness: Literature, Religion, and the American Imagination* (New York: Oxford University Press, 1979).

identity that underlies the otherwise superficial differences that separate human selves and societies. To "secular" critics like Said or Culler, or, for that matter, like Geertz as well, this humanistic enterprise too often effaces the singular and often discrepant characteristics of the very humanity it is attempting to understand. Having lost faith in anything like a single or common human nature, they have also ceased to believe in the existence of some universal wisdom that is supposedly locked within the covers of the world's best books. Thus "secular" critics, or at least some of their more self-conscious representatives, are inclined to believe that all the residual temptations to regard imaginative literature as a medium of revealed truth, however heterodox, should be dismissed as expressions of nostalgic regression, and all attempts to keep alive a sense of literature's canonical authority by defending the concept of the humanistic classic should be regarded as morally suspect.

But there are problems with both these critical positions, with both the "religious" and the "secular," because of the way the difference between them has been framed. Each has a tendency to turn the virtue of their position into a kind of vice. Thus while Steiner, for example, is surely correct in holding to the impossibility of dissociating the history of literary expression in the West, or anywhere else for that matter, from the stuff of religion, he and other so-called "religious" critics like him are clearly mistaken in assuming that the humanities do, or necessarily should, valorize a specific view of the transcendent. And while Culler and Said are equally as justified in believing that the real religious question about the humanities is rather with how, or whether, the humanities can transcend various forms of valorization, they are at the same time quite mistaken in concluding, along with many other "secular" critics, that every intellectual attempt to explore the meaning of this process of critical transcendence in religious terms is ethically questionable.

"Religious" critics like Steiner, who tend to assume that the past speaks in some univocal voice, or that its traditions rest on some externally fixed Archimedean standpoint, however deeply buried, simply do not appreciate what "secular" critics have been pointing out for almost two centuries: that the voice of the past is not singular but plural, that Archimedean standpoints are not discovered but fabricated. By the same token, "secular" critics like Culler and Said, who deduce from this that modern culture has somehow been—or in any case should be—inoculated against religious interpretation, because religion invariably works to subvert all awareness of human distinctiveness and cultural plurality, seem to have forgotten that when religion gave up its priority of place in the modern period to the domain of art, the problem of belief was simply transformed, as Nietzsche was the first to note, into the problem of values, and particularly into the question of the value of life itself.

Thus from a critical perspective, the difficulty with the stance both of "religious" critics of the Steiner variety and of "secular" critics of the Culler or Said variety is that hey each tend to conceive of religion in substantialist terms and thus to construe the question of religion's relation to literature as a question of contents. Hence what the Steiners of this world want is simply what the Saids and Cullers apparently don't want: that literature should conduce to the same view of the world, or the same way of acting in the world, as religion traditionally, or at least potentially, proposes. What both kinds of critics fail to grasp is that the nature of the attraction between literature and religion, and hence the basis of their relationship in the present scene of crisis in the humanities, is principally morphological and pragmatic rather than thematic or prescriptive. It is not a question of essences so much as of homologies: the issue at the center of their relationship has far more to do with the processes they serve than with the propositions they assert.

To speak more plainly, religion isn't so much about deities, duties, or ritual divinizations as it is about how to make sense of experience when for a variety of reasons—because of the erosion of meaning, or the eruption of evil, or the breakdown of justice—experience becomes radically problematic. One makes religious sense of such radically problematic experience by devising a mode of living *within it* that feels congruent with what seems to be the underlying or overarching structure *of it*. To speak of religion in this way is inevitably to suggest that religion differs from other cultural formations not because it is made up of different materials—they, too, can presumably concern themselves with gods, codes, and rites—but because it possesses different aims which it seeks to realize through the creation of a specific structure. Religious structures attempt to secure a measure of existential confidence in the face of circumstances that are always threatening to undermine them, and they do so by constructing an image of the way the world is put together that bears a structural, if not formal, analogy to the way one is supposed to dispose him- or herself towards that understanding of the world. John Dewey captured this morphological and meliorist understanding of the distinctiveness of religion, and the basis of its comparison with other kinds of cultural forms, when he noted that "the deepest problem in modern life" is how to restore integration and cooperation between [our] beliefs about the world in which [we] live and [our] beliefs about the values and purposes that should direct [our] conduct.[7]

The terms "religious" and "secular" thus turn out to be too unstable as well as imprecise to mark the critical distinction at issue. If "religious" criticism as here defined often amounts to little more than a technique for effacing otherness through Manichean idealizations of the Other, "secular" criticism too easily risks fetishizing opposition by assuming that criticism can constitute itself solely through what Said calls "its differences from other cultural activities and from systems of thought [and] method."[8] Of the first, one might say with Kenneth Burke, it doesn't understand it own "fundamental kinship with the enemy."[9] Of the second, one might add that it doesn't know how, in Burke's terms, "to get off before the end of the line."[10] Both could use William James's reminder that "the only *real* guarantee we have against licentious thinking [in any field] is the circumpressure of experience itself, which gets us sick of concrete errors, whether there be a transempirical reality or not."[11]

To be more specific, the humanities need not, as Steiner thinks they should, induce in us a sense of piety toward their institutional canonizations, nor need they direct the whole of their critical energies, as Said and Culler assume they must (at least when they are viewed comparatively), toward the exposure of religion's complicit relation with them. In a number of textual instances, the humanities as a discipline, no less than humanism as a critical stance, enables the religious task, contra Said and Culler, to be seen as the deconstruction or displacement of the canonical truths of the classic literary heritage, and in others the humanities as a discipline, and humanism as a critical stance, also permits the literary task, contra Steiner and others like him, to be viewed as the revaluation, and even the transvaluation, of religion itself.

One of the more interesting examples of this double perspective is to be found in the criticism of Eric Heller. Heller is the author of numerous studies of modern European literature and thought, but his major work remains the often-expanded but still insufficiently appreciated mono-

---

[7] John Dewey, *The Quest for Certainty* (New York: Capricorn Books, 1960), p. 255.

[8] Said, p. 29.

[9] Quoted, Stanley Edgar Hyman, *The Armed Vision* (New York: Vintage Books, 1955), p. 380.

[10] Quoted, *ibid.*, p. 381.

[11] William James, *Pragmatism and Other Essays*, (New York: Washington Square Press, 1963), p. 172.

graph he first published in 1952 under the title, *The Disinherited Mind*.[12]
Part of the reason for the book's neglect may derive from the fact that it
appears from the outside to be a quintessential example of what a
"secular" critic would call "religious" criticism. Its orientation is
Eurocentric, its bias anti-positivist, its view of culture metaphysical, and
its own discursive practice relentlessly ontological.

Viewed from within, on the other hand, the book presents another
story. For if *The Disinherited Mind* centers its attention on the modern
culture of the West, it does so only for the sake of disclosing how
severely the notion of the Western or European mind has been decentered through the disintegration of certain of its foundational assumptions. If it tends to view culture metaphysically in terms of the beliefs by
which culture is constituted, its interest is less in those overt beliefs on
which people purportedly agree than on those covert beliefs that determine their sense of what is disputable. If it challenges the positivism of
the scientific establishment on the grounds that such a mentality typically effaces important questions of value, it does so not in behalf of
proposing another standard of value to take its place but only in the interests of showing how processes of valuing or valuation are ingredient
in all mental processes. And, finally, if *The Disinherited Mind* insists that
axiological reflection inevitably leads to fundamental thinking about the
nature of being itself, Heller's conception of the nature of being is anything but essentialist or foundationalist. In each of these ways, then, *The
Disinherited Mind* exposes itself to the strictures of "religious" and
"secular" criticism alike only to elude them both.

A study of modern German literature and thought, *The Disinherited
Mind* is everywhere characterized by the assumption that modern writers
and thinkers have been confronted with a spiritual crisis that is historically unprecedented. It is the crisis of finding oneself living in a world
whose intellectual and symbolic constructs no longer house or nourish
one's deepest feelings. The superstructure of belief no longer bears any
relation to the substructure of feeling. What Goethe once termed the
"Age of Prose"—when people feel compelled, as he said, "to drag into
the vulgar light of day the ancient heritage of a noble past, and destroy

[12] Heller's other books include *The Ironic German: A Study of Thomas Mann*
(London: Secker and Warburg, 1958), *The Artist's Journey into the Interior* (New York:
Random House, 1968), *Franz Kafka* (London: Fontana Books, 1974), *The Poet's Self and
the Poem* (London: Althone Press, 1976), *In the Age of Prose* (New York: Cambridge
University Press, 1984), and *The Importance of Nietzsche* (Chicago: University of
Chicago Press, 1988).

not only the capacity for profound feeling and the beliefs of peoples and priests, but even that belief of reason which divines meaningful coherence behind the strangeness and seeming disorder"[13]—is therefore, Heller believes, still upon us. We now live in the grip of what he calls "the Creed of Ontological Invalidity." This is the modern dogma that dismisses apriori all assertions about being or ontology, and deprecates the faculty of mind which, "grasping their intelligence, responds positively to questions about *what* the world is."[14] It accepts as real, or given with Nature, only that which science can empirically verify, and agrees with science that the experimental method is the corrective to all ontological reflection.

The problems with this view seem comparatively obvious. On the one side, it reduces the question of Truth to "a plebicite of facts" by indulging the belief, so dear to modern educationalists, that "any kind of knowledge, as long as it supplies us with correctly ascertained facts, is worth teaching and learning, and that the more such correct facts we accumulate, the nearer we come to Truth."[15] On the other, it evades Werner Heisenberg's warning that experimentation may only lead us away from the Truth rather than toward it, "for our complicated experiments have no longer anything to do with nature in her own right, but with nature changed and transformed by our own cognitive activity."[16]

Heller's skepticism about the achievements of the scientific method stems from two sources. The first is his suspicion that much of what modern science has discovered as true may not, in fact, be worth knowing at all. The second is a conviction that all scientific discovery depends upon underlying assumptions about the nature of reality that are rarely acknowledged, much less scrutinized. He credits this latter perception as one of Goethe's greatest discoveries about the history of science: "that every scientific theory is merely the surface rationalization of a metaphysical substratum of beliefs, conscious or unconscious, about the nature of the world."[17] As Heller realizes, this is not merely, or even mainly, to say that theories are based upon world views; it is rather to

---

[13] Quoted, *The Disinherited Mind: Essays in Modern German Literature and Thought* (Cleveland and New York: Meridian Books; The World Publishing Company, 1959), p. 96.

[14] *Ibid.,* p. 16.

[15] *Ibid.,* p. 19.

[16] Quoted, *ibid.,* p. 33.

[17] *Ibid.,* p. 26.

claim that our perception of the world, at least as we perceive it, is the results of what is now called "theorizing." Heller puts it as follows:

> One usually assumes that the beliefs or unbeliefs of modern man originate in the scientific discoveries made in the seventeenth century; it may be equally correct to say that the scientific discoveries of the seventeenth century could not have been made without the vision of reality, held by man, having previously undergone a radical change. There is perhaps a direct line linking the minds of the Reformers of the sixteenth century, invoking the authority of the Bible against the tradition of the Church, to the mind of Francis Bacon claiming the authority of nature against the tenets of scholastic philosophy; from Luther's biblical pragmatism to Bacon's natural pragmatism, and from Rome being discredited as the focus of Christendom to the earth being dislodged from its central position in the universe.[18]

But Heller is convinced that "the Creed of Ontological Invalidity" contains within it still greater difficulties. By declaring all thinking about the nature and meaning of Being an irrelevance, it has turned modern spirituality into a kind of invalid. With the Church reduced in much of the world to little more than an outpatient clinic, the human capacity "to respond creatively to the ontological mystery ha[s] been stunted into something that produce[s] merely an irritated state of mystification."[19] In this diminished condition, human beings are thrown back upon themselves precariously suspended between one of two convictions: either that they are nothing in the vastness of all that is, or that they are all that is and the rest is nothing. In the first instance, as Pascal discerned in the *Pensees*, despair engulfs the self; in the second, as Conrad portrayed in *The Heart of Darkness*, the self engulfs the world.

Heller's response is to turn for guidance to those intellectuals and artists in the modern German tradition who have attempted to think their way through this crisis from different directions—Goethe from the philosophy of science, Burckhardt and Spengler from the philosophy of history, Nietzsche from ethics and the theory of tragedy, Rilke and Yeats from the theory of poetry and poetics, Kafka and Karl Kraus from the theory and practice of prose. What they have shared in common is simply a sense of the desperateness of their own spiritual disinheritance. Cut off from the past, to paraphrase Heller, by their conviction that the framework of belief which once gave significance and order to human experience has now been shattered; alienated from the rest of the human

---

[18] *Ibid.*, p. 27.
[19] *Ibid.*, p. 17.

community by their commitment to see through and beyond this crisis to implications following form it that have never been contemplated or willed before; subjected during the course of these reflections to the most terrible self-doubt and emotional agony by virtue of their awareness that in willing what they believe to be true but also know to be terrible they must somehow transmute the pain and sorrow of a world without God into a source of joy instead of despair, all in the very act of willing it; and, finally, racked with skepticism and guilt about whether it will ever be possible to create a new order, or a new idea of order, which is not achieved, as they are convinced all former spiritual orders have been achieved, at the expense of the fullness of life itself—these intellectuals and artists have persevered to the end, and, in Nietzsche's case, beyond the end, in the conviction that when the spiritual framework or thought-mold of one's world no longer springs from the deepest levels of personal experience, then the creative person must engage in a kind of fundamental thinking, must, in effect, do *all* the thinking for him- or herself.

No matter what their field, this crisis has transformed each of these thinkers and writers into, as Wallace Stevens described the modern poet, "a metaphysician in the dark." As metaphysicians they are still charged with the task of ferreting out the meaning or reason of things in the being of things, but now they are reduced to pursuing it by, as Stevens' continues in "Of Modern Poetry," "twanging

> An instrument, twanging a wiry string that gives
> Sounds passing through sudden rightness, wholly
> Containing the mind, below which it cannot descend,
> Beyond which it has no will to rise.[20]

Moreover, all of them have suffered that peculiar form of metaphysical disappointment long made familiar to moderns by philosophers from Heidegger and Nietzsche back through Kierkegaard to Pascal himself. This is the disappointment that ensues when the relationship between immanence and transcendence, between the profane and the sacred, breaks down under the weight of its frustrated achievement. As Heller put it, every experience of immanence is bordered with the realization of a sphere of existence that seems to invite, and yet simultaneously to discourage, every attempt at transcendence. Hence the striking resemblance among these different figures: despite the various course of their spiri-

---

[20]   *The Collected Poems of Wallace Stevens* (New York: Alfred A. Knopf, 1964), p. 240.

tual odysseys, they all nevertheless possess a similar potential
destination.

In Heller's reconstruction of this odyssey, they are in quest of a "true
order" of experience which matches, in its profoundest emotional regis-
ters, the terms of their own need for it. Though radically religious, this
quest is undertaken wholly within the terms of secular or profane experience. Its pursuit is predicated on the assumption that there should be
some congruence, however obscure, between the geology of human
feeling and the architecture of truth; that between our felt need as human
beings to believe and the ultimate order of the believeable, there should
be some at least fragile structure of correspondence.

In some of the subjects of Heller's study—in Burckhardt and
Schopenhauer, for example—this search for a "true order" precipitated a
realization that, while Christianity still offers the best interpretation of
human pathology, the Christian redemptive scheme—the fall from grace,
the iniquity of sin, the need for repentance, and the promise of deliverance and new life—was incapable of earning their own personal cre-
dence. All they could do was admire the aptness of the diagnosis and accept their disbelief in the form of the prescription. On the other hand,
when the world failed to satisfy Nietzsche's rage for the same sense of
order, he was forced to conclude that the rage itself was to blame, that
the desire for "true order" was itself the disease from which humankind
must be delivered. Hence his concept of the Superman, joyfully
accepting the eternal recurrence of senselessness, as the cure. Yet still
others—Rilke comes to mind and, with another side of himself,
Nietzsche again—turned this quest for "true order" into what Heller
describes as a kind of *religion intransitiva*. Though scarcely to be confused
with a fixed faith, Heller thinks that this religion "on the way" may one
day be acknowledged as the most distinctive religious achievement of
modern Europe, a Continental analogue to Wallace Stevens's more
American-sounding quest for a belief without belief "beyond belief."[21]

Culler and Said might well reply that any quest for "true order," or
an "idea of order" conceived as "true," is, no matter how theologically
deracinated its participants, either a form of wishful thinking or simply a
throwback to theological supernaturalism. In either case, they would no
doubt view it as a clear expression of "religious" criticism that, in Said's
words, "expresses an ultimate preference for the secure protection of systems of belief (however peculiar those may be) and not for critical activ-

---

[21] Wallace Stevens, *Opus Posthumous* (London: Faber and Faber Ltd., 1957), p. 202.

ity or consciousness."[22] But Heller appears to have addressed it explicitly in the "Postscript" to the chapter that in one edition closed *The Disinherited Mind*, the chapter entitled, "The Hazard of Modern Poetry."

The "Postscript" turns on the possibility that Heller's position is "obscurantist" and "reactionary."[23] This possibility appears the more likely just because any position that associates itself with the claim that human beings no longer possess a widely shared, or shareable, system of symbols in which to vest their deepest feelings sounds like an apology for "religious cliches" and incidentally betrays a lack of faith in the creativity of literature itself. And when Heller continues by agreeing with Rilke that the time for spiritual wandering may be over and the time for "homecoming" may have arrived—"we have assimilated as many terrors as we can without being destroyed"[24]—his argument begins to sound, at least to his "Listener," positively medieval. Never mind Heller's warning that "too many terrors dull the mind, too many riches impoverish the imagination"; or that poetry, literature, art are not omniscient, hence cannot "for much longer continue to be everywhere and above everything," since beyond the aesthetic everywhere "may be yet another nowhere"—his auditor is unable to consider the prospect that art's "offer of illimitable freedom is deceptive" and "soon exhausted."[25]

Heller's sense of caution here results from his suspicion that the "fair" may be over, that the targets may have already been packed into boxes, the last ball thrown may never return because the empty wall of canvas will give, and then—as once before when "the big showman packed the targets into boxes" and "the canvas gave" and "the ball was not returned"—the people, "having spent their last exploratory sixpence," will "cast creativity to the winds and follow another showman who promise[s] them targets and hits."[26] To Heller's "Listener" this all sounds like madness or mysticism. What is it but madness to ask for meaning from what has been described by so many modern writers as a meaningless universe? This metaphysical nostalgia, Heller's Listener suggests, may be a function of no more than the excess of intelligence granted us by a whimsical Nature to cope with the rigors of existence, an intellectual excess that is now left to expend itself asking questions that are superfluous. And if it is not madness, then it is the sort of sheer mys-

22 Said, p. 292.
23 Heller, p. 297.
24 *Ibid.*, p. 291.
25 *Ibid.*
26 *Ibid.*

ticism that wants to crawl back again "to the single-minded symbolic order of the Middle Ages."[27]

Heller's response is circumspect. If it makes little sense to credit excess intelligence with asking foolish questions, so, too, it seems absurd to respond to the present by retreating into the past. "But from this," Heller reasons, "it does not follow that we must rush forward. The order is neither behind us nor before us. It is, or it is not. The sensible movement," Heller avers, "is in another dimension."[28] But does this response answer the real question or merely beg it? Heller remains equivocal; or, better, turns equivocality in the direction of this new dimension, when he counters the Listener's, "I wonder," with an admission that he does, too; and then adds: "Maybe we differ only in degrees of wonder."[29]

What Heller is here alluding to is an experiential dimension that derives from our spiritual capacity for wonder but refuses to attach that capacity to any reified image of wonder itself. Curiously enough, this is a dimension of experience to which, by his own admission, Heller gained access not so much through an investigation of the study of nature but from study of history. As he notes, historical study continually presented him with the paradoxical spectacle of many things that once were regarded as true but are now discounted as such. From this he eventually concluded that if the candidates for truth are always being displaced, the one thing that may remain constant is uncertainty about just what the truth is—not, he goes one to remark, because people keep discovering new things to be true but simply because they decide from time to time to experience differently, or at least to describe their experience of truth in different vocabularies.

Heller's position on truth is virtually identical with that of pragmatists like James and Dewey. Truth has ceased to be a function of the relation between our statements and some unchanging essence intrinsic to the things they describe and has become instead a function of the relations between our statements and the perspectives on things they afford. What Heller resists is the conclusion that contemporary neopragmatists like Richard Rorty draw from this that truth must thereby be a function of the relations of our sentences with themselves. For Heller, truth is neither in our sentences alone nor in some substance that lies wholly beyond them; it is rather a function of understanding what our failures to

---

[27] *Ibid.*, p. 295.
[28] *Ibid.*, pp. 295-96.
[29] *Ibid.*, p. 296.

formulate a permanently satisfactory or acceptable conception of their relationship means.

This conviction could—and for many critics both "secular" and "religious" all too often does—merely furnish an argument for relativism, or cynicism, or even nihilism. In Heller's case, however, there are two reasons why it does not. The first is that he finds despair to be as much of an evasion of the truth that "uncertainty alone is ineluctably real" as the opposite tendency to regard as "true" only that which can be verified empirically.[30] The second derives from his conviction that uncertainty as such cannot be accepted as the only ultimate truth without, as Heller adds rather puckishly, a particular kind of faith and, in addition, love and hope as well. The question then becomes: what conception of order, or idea of order, can keep alive our sense of wonder while at the same time accommodating the view that uncertainty about the true or the real may be the only truth, the only reality, there is? And can such a notion of "true order," as Heller calls it, resist becoming just another hypostasizable, transcendent content, another reifiable absolute?

To answer either of these questions, Heller must first of all dispose of the association we are all to likely to make between the notion of order and the notion of rational system. As he puts it,

> Truth is likely to be untidy, the *enfant terrible* in the systematic household. For the last three centuries the intellectual life of Europe has been dominated by a passion for rational tidiness, critical analysis and constructed systems. The results seem often little more than the logical guise of a constant hankering after trivialities. That which is systematic in a system is merely the trivial aspect of true order.[31]

Thus the only conception or image of "true order" that can embrace the possibility that uncertainty about the true or the real is our only real truth, our only true reality, is one, as he says, "that embodies the incalculable and unpredictable transcending our rational grasp precisely where it meets the reasons of the heart."[32] This is therefore an idea of order that in its mystery and undecidability can only be grasped by the imagination rather than by the reasoning mind, and can only be embraced as "true" because the imagination responds, in the famous Pascalian formula, to the sorts of reasons of which the reasoning mind does not know—in

[30] *Ibid.*, p. 288.
[31] *Ibid.*, p. 292.
[32] *Ibid.*, p. 295.

short, to the logic of the heart rather than the logic of the head, the logic of the affections, not the logic of concepts.

However, Heller adds one caveat to this formulation. Such an idea of order is accessible only to the art of the symbol. "The symbol is the body of that which transcends, the measure of the immeasurable and the visible logic of the heart's reasoning."[33] As such, the symbol, like the sense of order it is capable of mediating, resists reductionism or reification because it depends for its meaning neither on a set of ideas nor on a set of feelings but only on the kind of figuration that is possible when they are brought into imaginative conjunction. But this belief in the symbol entails a series of historical acknowledgments:

> That the great experiment of separating meaning from reality, and symbol from fact, has ended in failure. That our passion for 'reality' has rendered absurd our desire for meaning. That our insistence on 'fact' has given the lie to truth. That our love of 'truth' has begotten an unlovable world. We have become prisoners of our intellectual freedom, an amorphous mass of victims to our sense of rational order. We are the chaos inhabiting the tidiest of all worlds. We calculate splendidly, but our calculations show that we have not enough to live by; we predict infallibly—even unpredictability is merely a factor within high statistical probability—but what we predict is not worth living for.[34]

Heller can thus argue that it is not in where they "came out" that Goethe, Nietzsche, Rilke, Burckhardt, and the others were religious, so much as in where, as it were, they "got in" and with what tenacious logic they followed it through. Referring to Goethe in words that apply to them all, Heller asserts: ". . . it is neither his opinions nor their inconsistencies that matter in this context. What matters is the level on which his convictions are formed, or the pressure of spiritual energy by which they are sustained."[35] This is not to say that Heller is indifferent to their conclusions; only that he finds those conclusions unintelligible apart from a sympathetic understanding of the spiritual courage and relentlessness and honesty with which these writers struggled toward them, and the way those conclusions were revealed most clearly as they were brought to bear on a critique of the age. Their work was united not only in an acknowledgment that "the great experiment of separating meaning from reality, and symbol from fact, has ended in failure," but in their refusal of

[33] *Ibid.*
[34] *Ibid.*
[35] *Ibid.*, p. 97.

the comforts of some new facile synthesis, some easy reconciliation.[36] The "true order" for which they sought and of which Heller speaks is an order that is "transcendent" only in its resistance to all metaphysical efforts to essentialize, to become foundational, to in any way restrict the sphere of the real.

Heller's conception of the relation between literature and religion, between art and faith, thus tends to frustrate "religious" and "secular" critics alike, or at least to frustrate the distinctions by which they try to differentiate themselves from one another. Both kinds of critics tend to work from the premise that the purpose of literature should be either to lead us toward a better religion or toward no religion at all. To put this differently, both kinds of critics suppose that in literature as in everything else, religion inevitably conduces to one and only one version of the universe, that religion is an affair of absolutes. But this is to confuse what seems to have universally been sought in experience with what has historically been achieved by experience. What convinces a religious agnostic like Heller, no less that a religious skeptic like Schopenhauer, that human beings deserve to be described as the *animal metaphysicum* is not that all human beings do, or even should, believe in one and the same idea of "true order," but that the universality of their need to order their life in relation to some such putative "idea" seems the one attribute they all share in common as human beings. Hence Heller, like Schopenhauer before him, can concede the infinite variation in what men and women take to be ultimately real and still argue that history nevertheless tends to confirm that they have always been surprisingly consistent, even obstinate, in their desire to search out and lay claim to some version of it, and that no conception of what a "true order" might be can fail to take account of this fact.

The humanities, as we call them, are simply one of our best records of this paradox. But they will remain so only if we refuse to reduce their interpretation either to self-valorization or to self-deprecation. Borrowing some words of Fredric Jameson's, Haydon White has furnished one of the most arresting definitions of their "theological" meaning by describing them as "instantiations of the human capacity to endow lived contradictions with intimations of their possible transcendence."[37] While this may not be the only way to describe the humanities—or, rather, to describe those texts that seem to represent them most adequately—it is

---

[36] *Ibid.*, p. 295.
[37] Haydon White, *The Content of the Form* (Baltimore: The Johns Hopkins Press, 1987), p. 157.

fully consistent with Heller's view that whatever else they do, the humanities compel us to reconceptualize our understanding of the relations between literature and religion just insofar as they can be said to confront and engage the spiritual possibilities that transcend reason with the kinds of reasons that reason doesn't know.

Thomas Hardy and the Limits of Modernism
WESLEY A. KORT

"It is a happy custom that we have in the academic community of periodically arranging to notice in a formal way"[1] the contribution to our
common life that one from among us has made and of doing that by presenting a suitable volume to which, as in this case, colleagues, friends,
and former students are asked to contribute. Such moments are both retrospective and constructive, for they require comment on the contribution of the person so to be recognized and on the place of that contribution in the larger, on-going scholarly context in which the honoree has a
role.

The difficulty of such a task is enlarged in this particular instance by
the size of Nathan A. Scott's contribution to literary, cultural and theological studies. Detailing that contribution and its consequences would
be a daunting task, and placing it in the present, complex scholarly scene
presents an even greater challenge. Neither job—not to speak of both—
could be accomplished in the limits of a brief essay. But within the confines of these few pages, I would like, nonetheless, to address some matters both retrospective and constructive.

For my text, I shall turn to Professor Scott's essay, "Hardy and the
Victorian Malaise," a work to which, by my opening sentence, I have already referred. I choose this piece because it helps to reveal the kind of
literary, cultural, and theological investments that support "Religion and

---

[1] The complete opening sentence of Nathan A. Scott's "Hardy and the Victorian
Malaise," in *Craters of the Spirit: Studies in the Modern Novel* (Washington: Corpus
Books, 1968), reads as follows: "It is a happy custom that we have in the academic
community of periodically arranging to notice in a formal way some of the great
milestones of cultural history" (p. 45).

Literature" so conceived and prosecuted. I address the essay not so much
from an interest in Hardy or the Victorian period as from the question of
what kind of project it indicates and what continuity it may have with
work that will begin more and more, it seems to me, to shape the field.

I.

There is in this essay, as in all of Nathan Scott's work, a largeness of
perspective and an inclusiveness of issues that grant it, as much as does
anything else, its power and significance. One form this expansiveness
takes is the attempt to bring the Victorian period under the Modernist
heading. There is something non-Modernist about that attempt and the
attitude it suggests, for the emphasis on continuity and inclusion counters the stress on discontinuity with previous generations that generally
characterizes Modernist styles. However, the way in which Professor
Scott manages to extend the period of literary Modernism well back into
the Victorian age is characteristically Modernist. He projects a continuity
of problematic between ourselves and the Victorians. We share with
them a culture of stress and uncertainty. His principal goal, then, is to
clarify a ground that we and they have in common, namely, a world that
has become highly problematical.

The terms of the problem are not so much social or psychological as
they are ontological. A radical change occurred in and for Victorian culture during the formative years of Thomas Hardy's life, namely, the disorienting consequences for the sense of human location and significance
produced by the publication of Charles Darwin's *The Origin of Species*
(1859) and *Essays and Reviews* (1860). These publications mark the end of
a world-view in which the human was taken to be central to the cosmic
situation and one in which Christianity was taken to be central to the human. What Darwin's book subverted in the sense of the centrality and
uniqueness of human life in its physical and biological context, *Essays
and Reviews* managed to subvert in the minds of sensitive and intelligent
Christians about their own particular religious history and identity. Scott
argues that these "are, perhaps above all others, the two texts, especially
when taken together, which lead us into the very center of what was
problematic in the spiritual situation of the English-speaking world a
hundred years ago."[2] The argument has two steps. First, the Victorian
period is described as a troubled and uncertain one, different as a consequence from what we sometimes think it to have been, and, second, the

---

[2] *Ibid.*, p. 54.

disorientation created at that time not only continues to affect us today but places us in the same episteme with them. Hence, late Victorians like Hardy should be read as citizens with us of the Modernist period.

Having established this continuity of cultural distress, Professor Scott draws a line from the mid-nineteenth to the mid-twentieth centuries and attaches to it an array of writers and thinkers who in many ways are very much unlike one another, from Ruskin, Carlyle, Arnold, and Pater to Kafka, T. S. Eliot, Malraux, Camus, Hemingway, and Robert Penn Warren.[3] However unlike one another, they are all instances of a single story—one in which the culture has become problematic because it has been disoriented and decentered by the dissolution of the distinctiveness of human life in the larger ontological situation and by the dissolution of spiritual traditions in the larger historical, human context.

Scott's literary and theological methods depend directly on this general cultural assessment; indeed, the assessment may be determined by these methods. The theological interest Scott brings to this and much of his work reflects Paul Tillich's correlation paradigm. That paradigm is explicit in this essay through the reference to Tillich in the essay's penultimate paragraph and affirms the accuracy of the human problematic as revealed or documented in cultural artifacts. The problematic is addressed with an ontology commodious enough to comprehend the negation articulated by the artifacts within an ultimate affirmation that finds its fullest expression in Christian faith and theology. The literary method, then, is to allow the text, this time primarily Hardy's *The Return of the Native*, to testify to disorientation—to the human enterprise in trouble because it has lost its sense of place and purpose. The novel is not expected to resolve this situation. Indeed, Hardy

> seems to have had this kind of skittishness about committing himself to strict, measured statement on the ultimate quandaries that baffle human thought, and about all he could to was to acknowledge his own inability to see as final anything other than "crass Casualty" and "purblind Doomsters"—which is to say that Hardy would have agreed with Melville, that "Though in many of its aspects this visible world seems formed in love, the invisible spheres were formed in fright."[4]

The theological and the literary methods reinforce one another.

The reading of Hardy in general and of *The Return of the Native* in particular is, therefore, "existentialist," if one word can be called on to

[3] *Ibid.*, pp. 55, 68-69.
[4] *Ibid.*, p. 60.

do. The heath stands, as the plague does in the novel by Camus, as symbolic of the conditions under which humans find themselves forced to live.[5] These conditions make of life little more than something to be put up with, and the characters, while called on to be instances of "resolution," "energy," or fortitude, cannot maintain themselves against such conditions, so harsh and pervasive are they. The heath becomes, then, Hardy's image "of what life in the modern world is like," of "that blind, massive inertia in things whose indifference to all the great aspirations of the human spirit is the proof of the frailty and impotence of man. . . ."[6] Having read the novel in this way, Scott can draw a direct line from it to Sartre's *La Nausée* and Camus' *L'Étranger*, further "rehearsals of discomposure" or additional chapters in the one story.

If there are, as Roland Barthes contends, people who read many texts in the same way and people who read few texts in differing ways, one would be justified in placing Nathan Scott in the first group. And it is this that accounts, at least in part, for the power and significance of his work; he can take diverse and unrelated texts and position them as voices in a single statement. Texts so constituted reflect and amplify one another, like the mirror effects on one another of Modernist skyscrapers, in a mutual corroboration and reinforcement. Texts, method, and meta-narrative become versions of one another. The power and significance of the effect is formidable.

It is not my intention to question this project. In fact, I see no way to do so, since the only adequate challenge to it would be a differing meta-narrative of equal size and plausibility, and I am not at all certain that one could be told. Rather, I would like only to identify the project as Modernist, to acknowledge its worth, and to go on, now, to ask what relation it may have to "Religion and Literature" work in a time that appears increasingly to be non- or post-Modernist.

II.

Characteristics of the present context for "Religion and Literature" require a closer look at interests represented by such a project as this. For example, the assumption that a particular story is a part or a version of some larger story, such as Nathan Scott's existentialist paradigm, has come increasingly under pressure. What is questioned is the essentialism or Idealism implicit in such methods: namely, that particular texts draw

---

[5] *Ibid.*, p. 63.
[6] *Ibid.*, p. 65.

their meaning from some larger, inclusive whole which no text by itself incorporates but that all texts serve to reveal. Modernist methods lead to reading texts that same way, as instances of some larger plot, pattern, or structure that validates particular texts but is not wholly available in any one.

A second point of the essay that may not now so easily be assumed is that our culture is joined, even unified, by a common problematic, a common threat, crisis, or illness thought to join people who otherwise have little in common. It would go too far, perhaps, to suggest that the purpose, conscious or not, of describing a general, shared problematic is to create thereby a negative form of community, of people joined by a common plight, but it certainly can be said that the sense of a shared problem and a sense of a unified culture have much to do with one another for the Modernist. But the notion that we are all in the same boat, that underneath differences there is a more important unity or continuity, comes under question both in and through an emphasis on differences and a suspicion that claims of unity conceal differences in privilege and opportunity. In addition, a case could be made that the language of crisis and problem now competes with an emphasis on consumption, play, and comfort. The problematic cannot, now, be taken for granted in the post-Reagan era.

A third assumption of the essay that stands apart from current interests is that behind texts are the minds and imaginations of great individuals—authors who become heroes and representative men. Hardy's novels in the essay have authority because they come from a man who lived on the frontier of new and disorienting ideas. This position gives to *The Return of the Native* its weight, because the novel, when read right, is really about the author and his own heroic position in "that trauma in the nineteenth century out of which the modern existentialist imagination was born. . . ."[7] This originating and authoring role of the writer is no invention of Nathan Scott; Modernist attitudes emphasize one's own position as unprecedented and problematic, a position that requires something bold, if not heroic. In contrast to this construction of authorship, originality, and heroism, we find now an orientation to social systems and inter-textuality. In such discourses writers become products or sites, and texts, no longer autonomous or directly tied to their authors' imaginations, now derive their positions by their relations to one another.

[7] *Ibid.*, p. 68.

Another characteristic of the essay is its foundationalism. The essay describes the Modernist period as determining the conditions of life negatively in relation to human needs, desires, and well-being. Nevertheless, in Modernism those conditions have a reality, stability, and continuity that grant to the culture an assurance of being in contact with an actual state of affairs. Richard Rorty calls this interest of the entire Modern period a quest not so much for foundations as for certainty.[8] Scott's essay is marked by certainty or a desire for it. However bleak the reports of the situation in which we find ourselves, we can take comfort at least in the certainty that these reports give us the situation as it actually is. In fact, there is a close tie between the paradigm of the hero or the courageous and bold individual and a willingness and an ability to accept these reports as accurate. Work of this kind, then, looks for readers who stand ready to have the curtain of illusion and comfort lifted to reveal the world as it is in its harsh, unpredictable, and uncentered actuality.

A fifth characteristic of work of this kind, one that also comes under pressure from the present scholarly context, is its construction of history as a single story, what Jean-François Lyotard calls a "meta-narrative."[9] The idea of a single story comes under pressure for several reasons, some of which have already been suggested. Primarily, though, the questions raised concern authority and exclusivism, as though there is not only one reality but also only one story about it. Actually, that about which the story or history is told has been constituted before the story or history, so that the story or history is a justification or legitimation of what has been constituted.

Finally, the essay's focus on the single story, while alluding to other works, reveals a Modernist interest in compactness and simplification. A few years ago, Ihab Hassan distinguished two styles by their differing ways of approaching silence. One style moves towards silence by expansion, inclusion, and explosion and the other by exclusion and reduction.[10] It may be fair to say that Modernist styles work for exclusion and simplification. Remarking on the matter of style in architecture, Robert Venturi points out that Modernist styles streamline and universalize

---

[8] Richard Rorty, *Philosophy and the Mirror of Nature* (Princeton: Princeton University Press, 1979), p. 228.

[9] Jean-François Lyotard, *The Post-Modern Condition: A Report on Knowledge*, trans. by Geoff Bennington and Brian Mussumi (Minneapolis: University of Minnesota Press, 1984), pp. 34-37.

[10] Ihab Hassan, *The Literature of Silence: Henry Miller and Samuel Beckett* (New York: Alfred A. Knopf, 1967).

while postmodernist styles include.[11] Linda Hutcheon points out that Modernist styles work toward conclusion while postmodernist create "both/and" situations.[12] And Fredric Jameson characterizes the post-modernist style as one in which "difference relates."[13]

III.

The dissonance between Nathan Scott's essay and scholarly interests and emphases that seem to shape the present situation means that those of us in the field are in a period of transition and exchange. I am not certain of the final issue, but I would like to return to Thomas Hardy and to *The Return of the Native* in particular in order to adumbrate some possible mutations for "Religion and Literature" work.

The first thing that should be said about the novel is that the narrator, while certainly understanding himself as standing in a situation that previous generations did not share, does not think of this situation as revealed for the first time. Indeed, he tries to create as many parallels and connections with the past as possible. He and his contemporaries now experience, for example, affronts to expectations about life that Aeschylus once depicted. People now are more like contemporaries of the ancient Greeks than like their own immediate ancestors. The difference is one of degree perhaps. Now children will begin to recognize what only some astute adults knew in ancient times. The narrator and his contemporaries have more in common with Aeschylus than with their immediate ancestors because the grand Christian interim has ended. The narrator turns his attention to the heaths of Southern England and their inhabitants because these people in that location seem largely to have been unaffected by that interim and to carry on in their rituals and attitudes practices and beliefs of a pre-Christian kind. This gives them a certain authority; they have not been distracted by the protections of Christian institutions and beliefs. They have authority also because they live in the North. Southern regions tend, he thinks, to lull people into inattentiveness to their situation. The North is a beachhead or a place of exposure where vigilance and adaptation are required. Eustacia, along with whatever else is wrong with her, is linked to Southern Europe, and

---

[11] Robert Venturi, *Learning from Las Vegas: The Forgotten Symbolism of Architectural Form* (Cambridge, Mass.: The MIT Press, 1977), p. 52.
[12] Linda Hutcheon, *A Postmodernist Poetics: History, Theory, Fiction* (New York and London: Routledge, 1988), p. 49.
[13] Fredric Jameson, "Postmodernism or the Cultural Logic of Late Capitalism," *New Left Review*, No. 146 (July–August, 1984), p. 75.

her desire always for a different, better world is consistent with her orientation to gentler and easier locales. Although the characters of the
novel stand temporally a generation earlier than the narrator, we can
turn to them, even return to them, to find out what we should make of a
world revealed now by the ending of the Christian interim, a world they
knew because Christian England had never quite taken control in the regions of Egdon heath.

A second observation that seems worth making about the narrator is
that he does not seem to side with the characters against the conditions
established by the heath. It is not that he and the characters are allied
against a situation that is opposed to their common interests. Rather, the
narrator seems to side with, or at least to be particularly and primarily
interested in, the situation and its conditions. And he does not describe
them always in a negative mode. There is an affirmation of and an admiration for the heath and the conditions it creates as well. It is certainly
valued over other places, especially cities. The heath, while it imposes
limits and has at times a negative impact on the lives of characters, bears
also, by its vastness and the exposure it grants, positive consequences. Its
vastness grants an expansiveness of perspective, for example. The narrator has this perspective, and it shows in his ability to appreciate the setting and its implications for human life. The environment, which the narrator describes before introducing characters, is large, various, and
forceful; it grants to human life a capacious as well as an unpredictable
context. It provides a counterweight and an inclusiveness that will be
welcomed by the "mind adrift on change, and harassed by the irrepressible New."[14]

A third observation concerning the narrator's attitude toward the
heath is that he does not employ it as a negative principle by which a
positive contrary—the unity created among people by their common
plight, for example—is established. The heath is more likely to separate
and isolate people than to force them into groups. The principal interest
of the narrator is in the heath and its characteristics; it is not for the sake
of human beings and its possible effects on them that he is interested in
the heath or in the conditions of life the heath represents.

The narrator's orientation to the environment and its determination
of the conditions of life is particularly piqued by times of transition. We
find this already on the first page of the novel: at the "transitional point

---

[14] Thomas Hardy, *The Return of the Native*, ed. by George Woodcock (Penguin
Books, 1978), p. 56.

of its nightly roll into darkness the great and particular glory of the Edgon waste began, and nobody could be said to understand the heath who had not been there at such a time."[15] The exchange of one state for another—day for night, fall for winter, winter for spring—creates a place between states, one Victor Turner would call "liminal," and the narrator is particularly arrested by those between times of transition. They are times of "dubiousness."

Corresponding to betwixt and between situations created by the diurnal and seasonal changes on the heath are the transitions in the lives of the characters. They live at a time that is ending because railroads are beginning to approach them. They are also between a pre-literate and literate period. And the major characters are all themselves unsettled or in transition. It can be said that the narrator seems to be arrested and fascinated by transition. He finds in-betweeness itself to be a real and revealing state. Uncertainty and an unresolved state become not a passing but a permanent or constant disposition. It seems suited to the conditions of life as they are revealed by the heath. What characterizes other attitudes and unsuits them for these conditions—attitudes Christian, Romantic, or nationalistic—is their permanence or concealment of transition.

As in other of Hardy's novels, so here, the narrator, having established the situation, context, or environment in which he is primarily interested, places characters in it to reveal types of human responses to it, most of them inappropriate or inadequate. The characters in *The Return of the Native*, rather than of primary importance, stand in for types of responses that the narrator is in the business of judging. The judgments are not in any case wholly positive because it is the narrator's own position or attitude toward the conditions of life that is being advocated by the novel. While some of the characters stand closer to it than others, none is so appropriate or adequate as that of the narrator himself.

There are, then, three main types of characters. The first is represented by the rustics who live close to their environment, know it well, and are adjusted to it. Since these characters are often dismissed as "flat" or as mere props on the stage, we should recognize that they are valued in the economy of the book. They bear a resemblance to more highly favored characters such as Venn, who, like them, knows the heath and moves easily about on it, and Clym, who is admired by them and is willing to work alongside them. The rustics have their own culture and

---

[15] *Ibid.*, p. 53.

language, one suited to their environment. We can call this group "the innocent."

In the second group, we find Mrs. Yeobright, who differs from the rustics because of her discontent and self-pity. She wants something better for her children, and she looks beyond the wilderness like a Moses from Mt. Nebo.[16] A curate's daughter, she may have brought to her life expectations that create discontent. She wants better than Venn and Wildeve for Thomasin, living vicariously an escape from her conditions that she cannot herself effect. Wildeve is a more developed example of this type. He hates the heath and longs for the far. He is a man of sentiment. Impulsive and restless, he easily falls under the power of Eustacia. And she, Eustacia, is the most developed along these lines. She resists and resents the heath and longs to be delivered from it by some great love. So intent is she on altering her state that she subjects all other interests to this goal. She is manipulative and whimsical. She actually disdains other people as much as she does nature.[17] She ends resenting the whole world and thinking of herself as Heaven's victim,[18] although she is primarily only a victim of her own discontent and ambition. Let us call characters of the second type people of "knowledge."

The third group, like the first, has a more positive attitude toward the heath than those in the second group. Thomasin is the first and least developed of them. She is, like the rustics, a trusting, uncomplaining, and sober woman. She is different from the rustics in being more self-conscious, more aware of her environment than they, but, unlike those in the second group, she does not long for some other place. She is a peaceful woman, a person of integrity and constancy. Venn shares with her and all in this group an affinity with, knowledge of, and appreciation for the heath. He can travel on it with ease, even in the dark. It seems to have produced in him a patience and self-disinterestedness that grants him moral stature but that Eustacia thinks of as "absurd."[19] He is a wanderer, a kind of border figure, a hurt man who tries to help others, a liaison figure, a good Samaritan in devil's dress. Finally, Clym should be put into this group. His life is most closely tied to the heath: "He was permeated with its scenes, with its substance, and with its odors."[20] He finds the

---

[16]   *Ibid.*, p. 83.
[17]   *Ibid.*, p. 244.
[18]   *Ibid.*, p. 421.
[19]   *Ibid.*, p. 209.
[20]   *Ibid.*, p. 231.

place "exhilarating," "strengthening," and "soothing."[21] He is willing to forgo personal interests for the sake of others, and he has no consuming self-pity, no matter how difficult his lot becomes. And he has a strong reputation as artist and scholar. With the others in this group, he has the "knowledge" of the heath and its differences from other places that those in the second group have, but he is identified with the heath as fully as those in the "innocent" group. We could call this combination of innocence and knowledge "wisdom."

In addition to these interests of the narrator—the setting, environment, or conditions of life and types of human responses to them—we should also mention his use of other texts. The novel is rich in references and allusions to a wide range of material, especially classical and biblical. But I would like to select from among these moments the interest of the narrator in biblical wisdom, because I think that interest is substantial and pivotal. We can start with Clym.

First, we have Clym's judgment that the life he observed in Paris was marked by vanity. He recognized the pretensions and illusions of the culture from his position in the diamond trade. He returns to the heath to find a more valid way of life and a more rewarding vocation. He wants to promulgate Utopian ideas, but his experiences on the heath divest him of such ambitions. He gradually becomes a teacher, and his message is " . . . knowledge of a sort which brings wisdom rather than affluence,"[22] ennoblement rather than repentance. Later, his plan is to instill "high knowledge into empty minds without first cramming them with what has to be uncrammed again before true study begins."[23] Also, he learns in his personal life not to make distinctions and evaluations others seem so ready to make: "But the more I see of life the more do I perceive that there is nothing particularly great in its greatest walks, and therefore nothing particularly small in mine of furze-cutting."[24] He compares himself to Job: "In the words of Job, 'I have made a covenant with mine eye; why then should I think upon a maid?'"[25] Finally, at the very end of the novel, he has chosen for the text of his message a passage from I Kings that depicts Solomon, whom Hardy would regard as the patron of and contributor to biblical wisdom, with his mother, Bathsheba.

[21] *Ibid.*, p. 245.
[22] *Ibid.*, p. 230.
[23] *Ibid.*, p. 233.
[24] *Ibid.*, p. 315.
[25] *Ibid.*, p. 464.

The narrator, I think, uses biblical wisdom not only to articulate the position of Clym but to develop his own. It is material well suited to his interests. By granting authority to experience and observation rather than to institutions or written codes, the wisdom literature directs attention to the complexities and harshness of life as well as to its joys and beauties. The reader or hearer is taught that life is more complicated and more difficult than one expects it to be. Caution, restraint, humility, and integrity are attitudes most appropriate to life so understood. While experience is disillusioning, it also produces respect for life, a sense of what is and what is not important, and an appreciation for the magnitude and complexity of the world in which we find ourselves.

In my opinion, the narrator does not advocate the position of any of his characters or some general human position as much as he does his own. While those in the "wisdom" group are preferred to the others, they do not have the standing, the range, and the sophistication that the narrator himself possesses and that he expects from his readers. His own position outstrips that of his characters in range, sympathy, and appreciation. He is himself the kind of artist and thinker that Clym, in his haphazard way, is struggling to become. He is himself a teacher, and when he chooses texts for his lessons, they are most fully drawn from biblical wisdom literature.

By emphasizing motifs of biblical wisdom in this novel—and a case could be made for the importance of these texts in his other novels as well—I do not intend to offer an explanation of Hardy's work, to discount his use of other texts and prototypes, or to grant his work some kind of legitimacy it would otherwise lack. I want only to point out that the situation Hardy found himself in and the change that he underwent was textual. Indeed, wisdom texts have several characteristics relevant to Hardy's needs, some of which I have already mentioned: an emphasis on experience as teacher, a curiosity about the nature of the world we live in and about how people behave in it, an orientation to the mysteries of the general order of things, and an understanding of cosmology as the residence of numinous power. The view of life as both predictable and unpredictable, ennobling and disillusioning, and its emphasis on both the importance and the unimportance of human life in the whole design of things—such aspects of biblical wisdom are applicable to the transitional and ambiguous position the novel reveals and addresses.

This means that Hardy did not so much exchange a Christian understanding of things for a non-religious one, but rather that he exchanged an ecclesiastically centered biblical orientation for a position indebted, among other things, to biblical wisdom texts. In his novels, the conditions of life are either or both malignant and beneficent, and the world seems always to be more and different from what characters expect it to be. But all of this does not melt into a doctrine of God. Indeed, if there is anything of primacy in power and being, it is the conditions of life themselves, fascinating and frightening, malignant and inspiring, generative and destructive. The conditions of life themselves deserve regard as well as caution, fear as well as respect.

IV.

I find Nathan Scott's essay relevant to the present situation not only because it reveals "Religion and Literature" as a Modernist project, thereby allowing the gaps between this kind of work and present attitudes to appear, but also because his essay on the beginnings of Modernism can be used to address the present situation. What presently prevails is a sense of the ending of Modernist styles and a renewed sense of transition and uncertainty such as that which Nathan Scott so effectively identified as a mark of Hardy's times and which I tried to implant more deeply in *The Return of the Native* itself. What are some of the possibilities associated with this sense of transition?

First of all, I think that it is necessary to recognize "Religion and Literature," as so beautifully exemplified in the essay by Nathan Scott, as a Modernist project. This means that there is no possibility of simply carrying on, of straight continuity with it. An assessment of the present context is required, one that can be called, for lack of a better term, postmodern. I do not mean by this a wholesale and uncritical adoption of all that goes on under that heading. But questions raised for the field by the present foment cannot be ignored or avoided. The task that lies ahead is to articulate "Religion and Literature" as a project free from assumptions that have become questionable and as not confined by modernist styles. This effort will, I think, prove far from fruitless precisely because of the kind of work "Religion and Literature" inherits from Nathan Scott and people like him. The combination of literary, religious, and cultural studies that we have seen in this essay and that flesh all his work position those who inherit its burdens in a complex and promising situation. No field will, it seems to me, so quickly and so thoroughly suffer the effects of a postmodernist critique, but just as much is there no field so able to recover from and to thrive on the present complexities and the trauma of destabilization. I say this because, in this field, "Religion and Literature" are not names for some essentialized realities but for complex cultural productions with particular historical, institutional, and social factors.

This means, for example, that there are no longer general stories to which many, if not all, narrative texts can be subjected or that they can be forced to serve. We need no longer use a Hardy novel to footnote a chapter in a larger story. Conversely, we can recognize limited and particular stories as potentially and actually expansive and inclusive. That is, we should not only recognize the limited, conditional status of "universal" stories but also the "universal" potential of particular stories. This means both that *The Return of the Native* does not derive its significance from some larger story to which is can be referred and that it is itself a fully adequate, large story. It has within it, along with its particularity, it own language of "universality."

The second point has to do with transition, with uncertainty. The narrator of *The Return of the Native* is particularly attentive to transition and to the dubious state it creates. What I would suggest is that this novel (like all discourse) is also about itself. That is, it is not only a narrative about transition; it is also a narrative about the unsteadiness of narrative. We do not have here a fixed narrative about the unfixed; we have an unfixed narrative as well. Narrative is itself uncertain and dubious. As I have tried to point out in other places, the variability of narrative is not superficial but constitutive. Narrative is variable, I argue, because narratives are inadequate responses to issues that defy the coherence which particular narratives require. The house of fiction (and of historical narrative as well), therefore, is built not on rock but on sand.

The third point has to do with place and space. Of the many things I like about Hardy's novel and Nathan Scott's essay is that they are attentive to location, place, and environment. But the novel narrativizes place, while Scott, like most Modernists, wants to exclude place, space, and environment from narrative. Place for him has a general, non-textual, and permanent status. Place quickly becomes that negative reality about or against which narratives are drawn, that stands before us as a monolithic, forbidding, and unyielding end ontologized as a present fact. Why is it so easy to free space from narrative?

First, it is so easy because as Modernists we tend to think of narrative as primarily (for some, exclusively) temporal. Many theorists—Frank Kermode, Gérard Genette, Paul Ricoeur, and many more—have encoded in different ways the assumption that narrative is removed from, is above, space, place, and environment. Hardy did not think so. His novels are first of all narratives of place, situation, and atmosphere.

The second reason is that place and space are not narrativized because they are owned. Time, in contrast, belongs—or so we think—to
nobody or everybody. But places and spaces are different. There is no
place free from political, economic, or social claims. How much more is
involved when we are "put in our place" than when we are "put in our
time." The narrativization of place means the involvement of narratives
and the reading of them in questions of power, ownership, and privilege,
even when, as in *The Return of the Native*, the place is unincorporated by
the dynamics of possession. To take place seriously is to grant "Religion
and Literature" a critical turn.

Ernesto Buonaiuti—Forgotten Modernist

NORMAN PITTENGER

So far as I know, Nathan Scott—in whose honour this, like the other essays in this book, is being written—has never concerned himself with the Modernist movement in the Roman Catholic Church. That movement, whose dates are the last decade of the nineteenth century and the first two decades of the twentieth century, had it adherents in Britain, on the continent of Europe and in the United States. In Britain and Europe it had a considerable following; in the United States a rather smaller one, although some of the American Modernist were important Roman Catholic clergy and laymen.

But why should it seem appropriate to write an essay about a leading and now largely forgotten European Modernist, to be included in a volume in honour of Nathan Scott, an American Episcopalian scholar and teacher? There are two reasons for my doing this. The first is that Buonaiuti himself, Italian though he was, might well be called a man of such breadth of interest and one who had such an affectionate following in Italy, quite apart from his scholarly attainments, that he deserves to be remembered; and, alas, he has been largely forgotten save in some few Italian circles; and this is an injustice which needs correction. The second reason for writing about him in the present context is that in certain respects, as the material which follows will perhaps show, Buonaiuti represented in his time a breadth of intellectual interests and a capacity to win the affection of those who studied under him or were influenced by him, which are also to be found in Nathan Scott himself. Nathan Scott is a man of extraordinary learning, a man who has won the affection of hundreds of his students, and is himself a devout Christian believer; he is like Buonaiuti in these respects. Although I am not sure that he would agree with and have sympathy for much of the work of the Italian priest and scholar, so far as the latter's theological orientation is concerned, I do find that the two somehow belong together in my own thinking—although fortunately Nathan Scott has not suffered the dismal fate of Buonaiuti and the latter's rejection by the officials of the *ecclesia* of which he was a devoted (if critical) representative.

I.

Ernesto Buonaiuti, leading figure among Italian Modernists during the tempestuous days in the Catholic Church in the early part of this century, was a man of many parts. He was a distinguished historian; he was a devout Christian and, in this respect, an interesting combination of simple piety and radical thought. He was a brilliant lecturer, a devoted and beloved teacher, a fearless fighter for causes in which he believed, yet a humble and modest man in his personal life. He was an open and friendly personality adored by his students, a writer of what an Italian critic has recently called "the most beautiful, tightly-packed Italian of the last fifty years." And he was a man who was hounded and persecuted by official Vatican Council authority, to an extent that to us today seems incredible—despite the recent actions against many scholars and thinkers. Yet he never doubted his love for the Church of his birth and he sought by every honourable device to be re-instated in the exercise of his priesthood even after he had been excommunicated *vitandus*.

His biography *Pellegrino di Roma* was published shortly before his death at the age of sixty-four. It has never been translated into English. It is very much more than an autobiography, however. It is a confession of his personal faith, a summary of his considered thought, and a painstaking and careful account of the Modernist Movement in Italy as seen by one who was at its very heart. It is also his portrayal of what he believed to be the essence of the Christian message. At the same time it gives an honest account of the historical studies which brought him to get at, and to state, that essence in a way that could hardly be pleasing to ecclesiastical authority at the time. But it is even more; for it is a record of events in Italy during the first half of the century, with attention to the intellectual and cultural currents, the political intrigues which culminated in the rise of Fascism and its ultimate collapse, and the social issues that were so much to the fore in Italy during those years. Finally, it is the story of what its author called "the generation of the Exodus" to which he felt he belonged: those who were not able, or not permitted, to remain in the "old ways" and who, therefore, were forced to make an exhausting pilgrimage towards some new "promised land," whose existence and promise Buonaiuti never doubted, even in his most despairing moments. Besides all this, it is written in a moving style and from his very heart and soul. A reader would perhaps catch some hint of this in translation, although it is extraordinarily difficult to convey it in English, not least because of his ability to play on words in a manner possible only in Italian, and by frequent inversion of word order to give peculiar effect to the expression of an idea.

All this makes Buonaiuti an exciting person. But it does not explain why even today his name remains important to many Italians, so much so that as recently as 1964 a new edition of his autobiography was necessary to meet popular demand. The reason for this continuing concern is that it was Buonaiuti who, as a professor at the University of Rome, became the hero of the young non-Fascists of his time, whether students or men and women of culture, after he had categorically refused to take the oath of allegiance to the Fascist regime, an oath which was imposed on all professors in State universities in 1927. Plainly and publicly he said why he refused. He tells about the incident in his autobiography; but doubtless he would have been astonished to know that more than twenty years later, when I asked an Italian bookshop for a book written by Buonaiuti, the face of the owner, a man then in his fifties, lighted up and he said, "Ah, Buonaiuti! He was the hero of our youth. He dared to defy Mussolini." The bookseller then went on to add his own personal conviction, that Buonaiuti's treatment by the Church's Holy Office had been responsible for alienating numbers of young men and women of his generation from the Catholic Church. "They, the Church, did not see what a great man he was; it did not see that he had made Christianity possible for us," he said; and he concluded, "It was a tragedy, a terrible tragedy."

In this essay I shall first give a brief sketch of Buonaiuti's life and the Modernist Movement as a whole, with which Buonaiuti's name will always be associated. Then I shall summarize his own position, religiously speaking. Finally, I shall say something about the possibility that views such as his have had their continuing influence in the Catholic Church, despite all that was done to suppress them, and how those views may be reflected to some degree in Vatican Council II and some of its results despite the new conservatism of Pope John Paul II.

II.

Ernesto Buonaiuti was born in the Ripetta section of Rome, not far from the Piazza del Popolo, on June 25, 1881. His father, Leopoldo, owned and operated a small and not too successful tobacconist's shop in the neighborhood; he was of a Florentine family, perhaps with some Jewish blood. His mother had come to Rome with her parents after her father had suffered reverses in his business of cattle-dealer in the country between Tuscany and Romagna. Leopoldo and his wife had seven children, all of whom pre-deceased Ernesto. The father died when Ernesto was a child, leaving Signora Buonaiuti to run the business and to provide for her family. One of Ernesto's brothers, Alfredo, the oldest of the children, became a priest and was for a time the *parroco* or parish priest of Settecamini in Via Tiburtina in Rome. As a young boy Ernesto himself had a moving experience one evening in the parish church of San Rocco, near his home; it was this experience, recounted at length in the autobiography, which decided him on the priesthood. He was helped by the local parish clergyman and by some others who recognized his spiritual and intellectual promise; hence he was able to go to a school for intending clerics and later to the great college and seminary of Sant'Apollinare, its name coming from its location at the time in the Piazza di Sant'Apollinare, although officially it was (and is) the Roman Pontifical Seminary with lower schools attached.

Buonaiuti was a brilliant student. He proceeded through the college and seminary with highest honours, and after ordination to the priesthood at the Chiesa Nuova in the Corso Vittorio Emmanuele, he was nominated by two of his former professors to teach both philosophy and history in the very place where he had been trained. It was while teaching there that he had as one of his students a young man from Bergamo called Angelo Roncalli who later became Pope John XXIII. It may be worth noting that one day, when Pope John had a visit from an Italian journalist who had removed to the United States, he remarked (after the conversation had got round to a discussion of the journalist's schooldays in Rome and his study at the college under Buonaiuti) that he too had been a student there and then added, "I learned a great deal from Don Ernesto and I always pray for him." Furthermore, a year or two before that experience of Buonaiuti's teaching Pope John had been chosen a *compagno di seminario* (or fellow-student) of his teacher for some six months in 1901.

It was while Ernesto was a young teacher that his troubles with ecclesiastical authority began. He had written some articles which were much disliked by certain clerics and his name had been sent to the Holy Office. As a result he was removed from his post and given an insignificant secretarial job in the ecclesiastical office which administered funds for Masses to be said for the legators or their relations. It is not necessary to give here the whole story of his ecclesiastical vicissitudes; suffice it to say that after a series of condemnations and restorations, he was finally—many years after most of the other Modernists—excommunicated *vitandus* (to be avoided by all the faithful) on January 25, 1926. By this time he was Professor of Church History in the Royal University of Rome—one of the very few religious Chairs which remained in State institutions after the establishment of the Italian national state. He continued at the University until 1931, although for some years he was forbidden to teach and engaged only in scholarly research. This ban was imposed because in the negotiations for the Lateran Pact, bringing Church and State into agreement and establishing Vatican City as an independent "nation," the Vatican insisted that no priest, under major excommunication, was to be allowed to continue teaching "in matters of religion." In 1931, excommunicated, he refused to take the Fascist oath and was ousted from his Chair.

During the years that followed, he supported himself by lecturing in many of the cities in Italy, by teaching in the Wesleyan (Methodist) seminary in Rome, and by acting as part-time professor (without permanent official status) at the University of Lausanne from 1931 to 1939. He declined to become an adherent of the National Church of the Canton of Vaud, a pre-requisite to such permanent official appointment at Lausanne; hence he could not be given the Chair there with a full-time appointment. His reason for declining adherence to the National Church of Vaud was his desire to be loyal to "my mother the Catholic Church of Rome" in which he had been brought up, which he dearly loved, and to which he longed to be re-admitted if this could be done without sacrifice of conscience. Later, the Fascist Italian government refused to renew his passport and he could not continue even his part-time work in Switzerland.

During the Second World War, he lived in a small villa in what was then one of the outskirts of Rome. He watched with increasing horror the cruelty associated with the occupation of the city by the Germans; but he could not fail to recognize that what happened was a just penalty for the Fascists' willingness to throw in their lot with Nazism. In 1945, when the War was over, he was at last restored to his professorship in the University; but once again he was not permitted to teach—the documents in the case indicated that again there was ecclesiastical pressure on the new Italian government. He continued his writing—certainly there have been very few more prolific scholars—but his health was broken.

He had undergone a surgical operation many years before and had never completely recovered from the surgery. On Saturday in Holy Week, April 20, 1946, he died of myocarditis, after the hour when the bells of all the churches in Rome were ringing their Easter welcome to the risen Christ after the customary three days of silence. He was buried in the cemetery next to the Basilica of San Lorenzo ad Veranum. On the slab marking his grave, as he had desired and requested in his "last testament" (which will be reproduced at the end of this essay), there was a cut what he there styled "the symbol of the eternal Christian priesthood, the Chalice and the Host," and his name.

So much for a bare outline of Ernesto Buonaiuti's life.

III.

The papal encyclical of 1907, *Pascendi gregis*, which condemned Modernism and inaugurated a witch-hunt of those who were supposed to be Modernists, spoke of Modernism as if it were a unitary movement with a specific programme and with agreement (among those influenced by it) about objectives as well as about basic assumptions. The fact, however, is that there was never any such thing as Modernism *per se* nor was there any unitary Modernist movement. The slightest acquaintance with the relevant literature makes this abundantly clear. There were only *modernists*; that is to say, there were individuals, each with a personal slant, a personal interest, and a personal hope for the Church. The one thing that brought them together in what very loosely may be called a "movement" was their agreed conviction that unless there was what Buonaiuti himself called a "renewal" or an "updating" of the Catholic Church, its future was very dark indeed. All those who were in any way associated with what was condemned in the words of the encyclical as "the synthesis of all heresies" had a realistic understanding of the contemporary world, its changed outlook, its respect for scientific method, its new democratic concerns, and everything else that was at the poles from the fixed position of the *ecclesia* as this was represented by the official theologians and rulers of the Church. All of them desired that in some fashion or other there should be an *aggiornamento* in the Church, so that it could meet this new questioning and the problems of a new age with something better than obstinate opposition. They desired an understanding of, but not necessarily an agreement with, what was going on in the world at large. They believed with all their hearts that Catholic Christianity had a message of supreme value for the world; that it was the central, if not the only, channel for Christ's work among men and women; and that its rich tradition, as Buonaiuti liked to say, was the patrimony of the present as well as the remembrance of the past.

There were four main types of Modernism; and even then, not all the Modernists quite fitted into any of these, precisely because of their individual ways of looking at things. But let us say something about each of the broad four types.

First and most obviously, there were those whose major concern was with historical matters. Sometimes these were centred in questions of Biblical research. They were distressed to see that officialdom had neither awareness of nor anxiety about the developments in this field in Protestant and secular circles. Everywhere else in the world of scholarship a new approach was being taken to ancient documents. There was the study of source-material, seeking to get back to the most primitive forms; there was the enquiry into the way in which ancient writings had been emended, edited, and modified in the course of their transmission; there was lively interest in the influences which had played upon belief and practice and moral opinion, as these were reflected in the documents and especially as these were influenced from non-Jewish and non-Christian sources. But the official Church and its authorized teachers of Scripture seemed to be unaware of all this.

Modernists of this type sought to awaken Catholic Christians to the new methods, the new approach, and the possible new conclusions. In particular, most of them were keenly conscious of the eschatological element in the New Testament. They felt that unless due account was taken of this element, there was no hope of getting at the teaching of Jesus, his view of himself, how his disciples regarded him, and the way in which primitive Christianity made its initial impact on the Graeco-Roman world.

There were other historically-minded Modernists whose field was the history of the Christian tradition. They realized the changes in doctrine and in worship during the course of the centuries. They were not afraid to acknowledge these changes, for they believed that truth must be honoured above all else. But neither they, nor the Biblical scholars, felt that recognition of the actual primitive factual data and the obvious reality of change in interpretation and practice, invalidated the essential Catholic reality. Indeed, one of their basic contentions was that a living organism, a vital tradition, is bound to change with the passage of time; while their loyalty to the Catholic Church led them to insist equally on a continuous quality, a deep identity, between the first preaching about Jesus, as the Messiah who would come to bring in the Kingdom, and the conciliar affirmation that this same Jesus was somehow, for faith, both divine and human. So also with the other great points of Catholic faith and practice—as for example, the Eucharist. In its development from a meal in the Upper Room, anticipating the coming Kingdom, to the Mass as celebrated in the humblest parish or in St. Peter's in Rome, there was a genuine continuity and an underlying identity, since in the whole development the Lord's sacrificial presence and power were made known to those called to be members of his mystical Body the Church.

So much for a brief notice of the historically-minded Modernists. There were also those whose major concern was with philosophical and theological matters. These scholars had great respect for St. Thomas Aquinas and the scholastic tradition; but they knew that despite the revival of Thomism under Leo XIII, this kind of philosophical approach and this kind of metaphysical position could no longer readily command acceptance by contemporary thinkers. Hence they sought to work out a new Christian apologetic and a new way of stating the theological convictions of the Church which would be open to the newer philosophies and which took very seriously the fact of evolution in all its phases, the stress on God's immanent operation in the world, and the possibility of an approach to the transcendent God through the "way of immanence."

Their belief was that if one analyzed what it means to be human, in all its finitude, limitation, and boundless yearning, one would be led to see that a God who transcended both the world and human existence was required if sense were to be made of the human situation. If dogma were no longer regarded as absolutely fixed for all eternity, but as the best humanly devised statement of the deepest deliverances in experience as human beings responded to the impact of the transcendent One upon them, then the Church's traditional beliefs could be seen in a new light. No longer would they be fetters upon freedom of thought, but they would serve as arrows of direction towards the richest and fullest knowledge and service of God as God had willed to be revealed to us. Men like LeRoy and Tyrrell urged that "the rule of praying" was the key to the "rule of believing," that *lex orandi* and *lex crendendi* belong together. Dogma, then, was not an arid propositional statement but a guide to prayer and attitude. Yet they did not stop there, for they also insisted that what thus guided prayer and attitude was also in genuine contact with how things *really are*, in God, the world, humanity, and in their relationships.

In the third place, there were Modernists who were especially impressed by the democratic and liberal movements in the secular world of the time. Should not the Church be open to them, listening to what they had to say and seeing in them a sort of secularized version of Christian teaching about human relationships, human equality, and the inalienable freedom of the human agent? They thought that it was a fatal mistake to condemn—if not that, at least to sneer at—these manifestations of human yearning for a better world where there would be wider sharing and greater justice. After all, Christianity had a word to say to the new political, economic, and social movements of the day; and that word was simply that unless such efforts were inspired and empowered by a spiritual energy given form God they were likely to end up in mere economic levelling, political manipulation by those who gained power among the masses, and the kind of socialism which was nothing but disguised materialism. Therefore, they sought to win the Church to a more friendly attitude to the newer social movements, because unless there was such an assurance of sympathetic understanding the Christian message, so necessary for them, would never be heard.

Finally, to complete this brief notice of varieties of Modernists, there were the many ordinary clergypersons and laypersons who wished to change the spirit of the historical Christian institution from an assumption of dictatorial, even tyrannical, control over human beings, to a pastoral and parental concern for them. They were convinced that the pomp and glory (nowadays we would say the "triumphalism') of many in the upper reaches of the hierarchy and above all in the Roman curia itself, did not fit very well with the humble Carpenter of Nazareth who had no place to lay his head. They were sure that an authoritarian approach to people *de haut en bas* did not accord with the loving and compassionate concern that Carpenter had felt for those who needed his care. Let the Church be simpler in organization, more parental in attitude, more pastoral in approach, more charitable and compassionate in all its ways and works. Then the common people would listen; they would be attracted by the spirit they saw in their religious leaders; they would respond with a new allegiance and devotion.

Of this last type of Modernist the central character in Fogazzaro's novel *Il Santo* is the supreme example. Simple in spirit, humble in manner, convinced in faith, open to others' needs, always ready and available to help: this was the model for the true pastor of souls. This was what was needed at every level of the Church's organized life. Priests who thought and felt like this were the least vocal of all the Modernists, but once we begin to penetrate into the life of the period and understand its real motivations, we can see that they were numbered in the thousands.

And there were thousands of lay people who like these priests had the vision of what today we should style "the servant Church."

IV.

But the whole movement in all its aspects was pitilessly crushed. There were many reasons for this. First, there was the intransigence of official rulers and teachers. Second, there was the apparent threat to what those in authority regarded as the unchanging nature of the Christian tradition. Third, there was a very human resentment at people who dared to call in question those who were set over them, and who ventured to look with suspicion at many of the things the hierarchy said and did. Doubtless most of the leaders who condemned Modernism in one or other, or in all, of its aspects, had a conscientious belief that these Modernists were wrong. Many of the "oppressors" were very good men—it makes one think of Pascal's saying that a man never sins so ardently as when he does it with a good conscience.

For the absolute and uncompromising suppression of Modernism *was* a sin. Buonaiuti himself calls it an instance of "the sin against the Holy Ghost" because it was a denial of truth staring one straight in the face. However we may think of his way of putting it, we can say that the suppression was a sin because it was accomplished by sheer assertion of ecclesiastical power, without any opportunity offered for explanation or defence on the part of those condemned. They were hounded and harried; they were forced either to take an oath which to many of them was an outrage to their conscience, or to leave their cures, their professorships, their office and work. They were spied upon, informed against, and miserably misrepresented by those who took action against them.

If this last paragraph seems too harsh, one need only read Buonaiuti's objective account, written with a passion that he cannot conceal, of the treatment which he and his friends received. Probably it could not happen how, although the behaviour of the Holy Office towards Hans Küng and others makes one hesitate in saying this; but it did happen once—and it was a terrible moment in the history of Catholic Christianity. Perhaps others will feel that something should be said on the other side. Doubtless it should. But one does not need to agree with the opinions expressed by the various Modernists to feel that this was no way to treat persons whose only real fault, if it was a fault, was their probably excessive confidence that the hardened minds of those in authority could be softened and that what seemed in so many respects a dead tradition could quickly become a living and vital movement in human history. Perhaps only the cynical Alfred Loisy was able to see, in his jaundiced way, that under the circumstances of the time of Modernism, in all its forms, was bound to be a lost cause. That may be why he took his final dismissal from the Church in such an apparently light, not to say relieved, fashion. Yet even in his case, we must remember that in his *Memoires*, with all their cynicism, he tells us how his heart was broken by the way some of his superiors, including Pope Pius X himself, treated his plea that he might remain within the visible body of the faithful: "something broke in my heart."

V.

Looking back now, at a distance of much more than half-a-century, we ourselves can make criticisms of Modernist ideas. We can see that often for instance there was a too ready acceptance of the latest developments in Biblical and historical study. But was not that typical of almost scholars of the time, who had not yet come to realize the enormous complexity of the issues, the great variety of possible interpretation, and the relativity that attaches to all so-called "historical" findings? We can recognize that in their zeal for a new kind of apologetic and a new conception of the nature of dogma, they overlooked problems that dog us to this day. Despite their firm Catholic convictions they were too cheerful about human possibilities and too optimistic about the response which would come to a new approach. in the social field, Buonaiuti himself was prescient enough in his very early days to warn his friend Don Murri of the problems which a Christian version of modern democracy must face. There is fascinating material in his autobiography on the disagreement between the two men. It may even be the case that the priests who wanted a simpler and more pastoral Church had not reckoned with the need of common people for a voice which speaks with definite authority and sure conviction.

And yet, with all these criticisms, no fair judge today can help feeling respect for those who risked everything for a renewal of the Catholic tradition in its every area—risked everything, and lost: lost their cures, their positions, their means of livelihood, everything that mattered save their self-respect. Or, if they did not suffer in this fashion, they were obliged to submit to an oath which needs only to be read to see its antiquated and outrageous spirit. The way to have met the Modernists was through better argument, wiser counsel, deeper understanding, paternal treatment. Some of us feel that the great achievement of a man like Pope John XXIII—who although never a Modernist was yet suspected of it by the Holy Office, and who when Pope examined some old documents and found that this suspicion of him was explicitly stated in one of them— was to serve as the instrument for the Holy Spirit of God in the ancient Catholic tradition, teaching that tradition that love is better than hate, compassion better than rejection, humility better than pride of authority and position, and earnest devotion to truth better than zealous maintenance of accepted positions. Angelo Roncalli, speaking to the Italian-American journalist and saying that he had "learned much from Don Ernesto," did not specify what it was that he had learned. May it not have been the spirit of love, faith, hope, and the sheer goodness which shines through the whole life of this leading figure in the Italian Modernist movement?

VI.

We turn now to a sketch of Buonaiuti's own position as a Modernist. To present this is not quite so easy as it might appear. Buonaiuti himself was in many ways a very simple man of faith, but there was a certain complexity in his philosophical and theological ideas that makes a straightforward statement about his views extremely difficult. Yet there is one point that can be make at once. Buonaiuti was utterly convinced of the reality of the transcendent God and at the same time he insisted that this transcendent One is our "heavenly Father" who loves and cares for us, providentially guides us, and never leaves us comfortless or alone.

But having said this, we must go on to notice that he had little if any use for an approach to this God by way of the usual "proofs." Faith for him was in what he often called the "subconscious depths" of human experience, where humans are thirsty for the infinite which will fulfill their being. In one sense, then, God is the projection or this enormous human exigency. But such a statement must not be misunderstood. Buonaiuti did not think for a moment that the reality or the existence of the heavenly Father depended upon such a projection; on the contrary, the projection (although this is not a word which he himself used) is *evoked* from us by the continual pressure upon us of transcendent realities (about which we must speak in a moment) that are inescapable and that give us tidings of a being greater than, more than, and exalted high above, the world of creaturely experience however important and profound that experience might be.

Over and over again Buonaiuti claimed that he had never departed in any essentials from the general Aristotelian-Scholastic vision of the world. Certainly he disliked the later developments of this view and thought that the arid and formalized statement of it in the textbooks used in seminaries was appalling and mistaken—it succeeded in alienating those who were unable to penetrate through it to the basic elements in the Scholastic vision. But the vision itself was for him nothing but the truth. He believed in the genuine reality of the finite world, as against all idealistic efforts to interpret it as merely "mental" or as insignificant in comparison with "mind." He accepted the Scholastic position that through sensible things we are brought to know invisible ones, through temporality to eternity, and through finitude to the infinite. The world round us, as well as our human existence within it, are not to be explained away by any philosophy which contemptuously dismisses it as merely "an appearance." That world, and we ourselves in it, must be seen as *there*.

At the same time, he accepted an essentially social view of the world. Subjectivism, especially when it centres all its attention on human internal thought and thinking processes, was his great enemy. His Catholic spirit, with its utter devotion to the Church as a community, and his Latin mind, with its unfailing conviction of the community or society of men and women, made him sure that anything which would treat men and women as if they were the central theme in the nature of things, was not only un-Christian and un-Catholic but false to the deliverances of common human experience.

His philosophical realism, his awareness of corporate human life, and his own very deep sacramental sense, nurtured as he was in what he called "the charismatic life of the sacraments in the Catholic Church," doubtless explain his strong dislike of philosophical idealism, especially the variety associated with the name of Hegel. He regarded its Italian representatives as traitors to the whole "Mediterranean civilization and culture," as he often put it. In attacking German idealism and in tracing its history, one must think that he overstated his case. He thought that Luther's centering of attention on individual salvation had been so subjective that in effect it made the human need for "justification" more important even than God, whose principal significance was that only God could supply the answer to this human need. Buonaiuti traced from Luther onwards growing subjectivism in German thought which, in his view, led inevitably to an overwhelming emphasis on inner human experience. When with this had been associated a variety of philosophy which made the real nothing but the "rational," the world of material stuff and corporeal existence was done away. Furthermore, he regarded Kant's critical philosophy as far too rational, unable to take account of the (to Buonaiuti obvious) fact that we live by symbols, by "myths" (by this word he did not mean falsehoods but pictures of reality grasped in terms other than conceptual), and by our vision of values which cannot be captured in any form of words but speak to the depths of human life and evoke a response of wonder, gratitude, and love. And Kant's ethical theories he could not accept, since for him they were too "formal," without specific content, and hence drove us back to acceptance of the imposed requirements of human society in its finitude, especially to the laws set up by the civil authority.

Now all of this is surely a biased interpretation of the development of German idealism. On the other hand, we can readily see how a man of deep piety and mystical sense, with a strong feeling for the fellowship of the brethren in and under the *charisma* of the sacraments and with an awareness of mutual sharing with others in a life touched by eternity, would react negatively to an approach (and to conclusions) which were so rational, so individualistic, and at the same time so damaging to the sense of personal participation in a realm of "eternal values" and "divine ideals."

What makes Buonaiuti's position seem almost self-contradictory is that at the same time that he attacked idealism, he was himself deeply aware of those "values" and "ideals" to which we have just referred. Indeed his references to them, with the use of just those words, can become a little wearying for a reader. But it is clear that he did not mean by them some aery region in the skies where "ideals" or "values" dwell in a sort of eternal limbo. He was really talking about the Kingdom of God, constantly impinging upon the world, judging the world's inadequacy, failure, and wrong, and promising redemption from these into the abiding realm of God's kingly rule.

The reference just made to the Kingdom of God provides us with a starting point for Buonaiuti's specifically Christian religious position. He believed that the world is a battle-field where two forces are ceaselessly struggling. One of these forces is the evil or wickedness which we know so well and which he called "Satan" or "the Malignant One"; the other is the sheer goodness, love, and righteousness which are from God the Father who himself is all love and goodness and righteousness. This moral dualism runs straight through all of Buonaiuti's thinking and explains why any and every sort of monism, which might threaten a denial of what to him was a patent fact of experience, was simply anathema. It also explains why he could entertain such a high opinion of the insight of the half-mystical Iranian prophet Zoroaster, with his conception of two powers in the world, good and evil, in conflict with one another.

Buonaiuti believed that much of this Iranian view had been taken into late Judaism, by channels which are but dimly known. Thus the eschatological picture, in which God's Kingdom is to come as the triumph of the forces of goodness over everything wrong and hateful, was for him a highly pictorial, vivid, and compelling portrayer of the real human and cosmic situation. The only way in which we can grasp the unfailing pressure upon us and upon our world of the abiding reality of God, of what Buonaiuti styled the "values" of the Kingdom, is by seeing it as coming upon us, into our world, in a crowning event which will make all things new. If we do not picture it in some such fashion, but instead try to think abstractly about a realm of values always related to the temporal and spatial world, we shall find ourselves emotionally unmoved and altogether too content so that we speak in vague and even smooth language about concepts. We need *pictures*; or as Buonaiuti insisted again and again, we need "myths." In this sense, then, the "myth" of the Kingdom is one of the most important contributions of the Judaic-Christian faith to the tradition of the Church.

Jesus came preaching the approaching advent of that Kingdom. He was concerned to prepare and make ready the way, so that when it came humans would respond to it. In that very preaching, as well as in the initiation of a preliminary response, the Kingdom was *already present*, by anticipation. Here we have a view which resembles more recent scholarly talk of the "inaugurated" eschatology said to be found in the Gospels. When Jesus said, "the Kingdom of God is among you [or in your midst]," this was his point.

Jesus himself was central to the preaching and preparation. Whatever he might have thought about his own person, his mission was plain: it was he who had been sent by God to do just this preaching and thus to "inaugurate" the way for the coming of the Kingdom, and in himself to represent in the world of men and things that Kingdom and the Father-God who was its sovereign. Hence the Church was entirely correct in its further interpretation of Jesus' person and work, although inevitably it stated this in language drawn from the prevalent concepts of the day and in the Hellenistic philosophical idiom which was familiar at the time. Buonaiuti never doubted that Jesus must be understood as a genuine Man of his time and place; but he was also never in doubt that in and through that Man, God was both present and at work in such a fashion that Jesus Christ was to be adored and obeyed as One who had been called the "Man-God."

Yet this knowledge of Jesus, his preaching, and the specific way he portrayed the coming Kingdom, was available, in the fullest sense, only within the Catholic Christian tradition which had faithfully conveyed it through the centuries. Thus the Church was the divinely established field for the knowledge of Christ and for the love and service of God in the way in which Christ had taught it. What is more, in the life of the Church there was a living and present awareness of Christ as the Son of God— chiefly, but not exclusively, through the sacraments which it celebrated. The Church was truly the mystical Body of the living Christ, organized and ordered in such a way that as a community in the world it had continuity and identity with itself. Here we have Buonaiuti's case for the Catholic Church and its absolute necessity. For only in the Catholic tradition do we see the genuine continuity and identity of which we have just made mention.

In later years, he was more friendly towards the Evangelical Churches, especially after his experience at the University of Lausanne and the welcome the Evangelical community in that city gave him, not to mention the friendliness of the Methodists in Rome and the extraordinary hospitality shown him for many years by the Roman headquarters of the Young Men's Christian Association and its American secretary, Dr. Claud Nelson, who was a dear personal friend of Buonaiuti's (and, it may be added, of the writer of this essay), and the branches of that association in other Italian cities and provincial towns. Nonetheless, he never wavered in his loyalty to the Catholic tradition and he yearned for the day when that tradition would realize its vital and dynamic nature and give up its too zealous adherence to the doctrinal formularies and the details of administration which it had inherited from its past. Precisely because the Catholic Church was what he loved to call "the visible organism of the faithful who constitute the mystical Body of Christ," it should constantly be open to change, like any healthy living organism—and only through such change could it maintain and concretely demonstrate to the world its genuine self-identity through the centuries.

Buonaiuti was convinced that the Church, in this exalted sense, must never be confused with existing political, social, or economic parties or platforms or positions. If it permitted itself thus to be confused with worldly patterns, it would be salt which had lost its savour; it would no longer be able to witness to the eternal values of the Kingdom of God, to stand in judgment on human wickedness in high places and in low, and to provide the charismatic strength necessary if any human pattern is not to collapse into the struggle for power, a grasping for place, or merely materialistic concerns. At the same time, Buonaiuti was vividly conscious of the sinfulness of human nature—indeed on occasion he put this in extreme terms, perhaps because of his great admiration for the thought of St. Augustine, to which he had devoted much study. He was no cheerful optimist who thought that human existence was on the whole very good and only required a little more instruction and encouragement to become perfect. On the contrary, it needed to be redeemed from its wrongness into the rightness which alone could make it *truly* human—that is, into the divine intention for it. Buonaiuti was sure that Christian faith offered just such salvation and that the means of grace found in the Catholic tradition are the effective way of bringing this home to every faithful member of the Body of Christ.

VII.

Finally, some brief remarks on the possible influence of Modernism in its various forms, and of Buonaiuti's own views, on the Catholic Church in the years preparing for and succeeding Vatican Council II.

Some have felt that this influence has been practically non-existent. For example, Dr. Jemolo (who writes the introduction to the new Italian edition of the *Pellegrino*, published in 1964) says flatly that Modernism, killed or at least driven underground by the condemnations, *could* not have been influential. Indeed, he says that the various changes and reforms which have happened with and since Vatican II were bound to occur in any case. But he is mistaken in his judgment not least because he has also to admit that Modernism or at least the Modernists, despite condemnation, did continue, in however enfeebled a fashion, after those tragic events. And if the changes and alterations which he admits have taken place were not simply bolts from the blue, they must have had some background and context. Just here, some of us think, is where the Modernist movement had its part to play.

There was no *direct* and acknowledged influence. But ideas are strange things. Once they are in the air, it is almost impossible to kill them. They may be suppressed, condemned, or rejected; yet somehow they persist. Furthermore, when those ideas are so much in accord with the deepest spirit of an age, they have an even greater capacity for survival. Then, when the right moment occurs, they have their chance. So it was with Modernist views.

Had Buonaiuti been present at Vatican II, he would have heard distinguished bishops and archbishops, cardinals, and other high dignitaries, express in their own words much for which he had contended. The conception of tradition as vital and dynamic was defended as against a more static idea, and it won the day. The Church as a servant Church was presented as opposed to the Church in a "triumphalist" mode, and it won the day. The view of the Eucharist as an action in which what happens to and with the sacramental elements is always and necessarily in the context of the Church as a human society, a family in Christ, was urged upon the Fathers of the Council, and it won the day. Here are places where victory went to those whose position was practically identical with that taken by those who were condemned and excommunicated in the first two decades of the century. So also unfettered Biblical study, already hinted at by Pope Pius XII in his encyclical *Humani generis*, come into its own. A friendly and welcoming attitude to non-Catholics, even to the point of allowing them to attend the sessions of the Council and serve as expert witnesses for some of the commissions, replaced the older suspicion, if not contempt, for religious bodies which were not explicitly part of the visible Catholic Church. Religious freedom was asserted as an inalienable right—and not in purely human liberal terms, but because with freedom Christ has made men and women free. These too were Modernist ideas.

Although Pope John XXIII had been a fellow seminarian with, and later a student of, Buonaiuti's, it would be a mistake to believe, with one Italian newspaper at the time of the Council, that much of what he said he hoped for from the Council was nothing other than an acceptance of views which his old friend and teacher had advanced many years before. There *is* a possibility that the word *aggiornamento* which he used so frequently was adopted from Buonaiuti—the latter uses the word several times, although more often he speaks of *svecchiando* (renewing or rejuvenating the old, renewal) and the like. But then *aggiornamento* is a fairly common word in Italian usage: the latest dictionaries translate is as meaning "bringing up to date." It is indeed true that in at least one respect Pope John was very like the Modernists of our fourth group, wishing to simplify the organization and customs of the institution, concerned for a pastoral, rather than a dictatorial, ministry and anxious to reach out to people of all kinds, whether practicing Christians or nominal Christians or no Christians at all, so that they might hear the Gospel of God's love in Christ. But all this does not quite add up to the notion that he was doing what in the days of the Council the conservative Italian journal (mentioned above) thought and regretted: reviving Modernism in its Buonaiuti version.

We must also observe that many of the outstanding theologians of the progressive school in the Church have disavowed interest in or even influence by what they have read or heard about the Modernist movement. Karl Rahner told an acquaintance of this writer that he was aware of no connection whatsoever between his way of stating the doctrine of Christ and some of the things said by Modernist writers sixty years before. On the other hand, one of the Dutch scholars active in progressive Catholic theological work today has devoted a considerable section of one of his books to a discussion of Modernist ideas, in which he criticizes them as being inchoate and vague, but acknowledges that they had value in their own time and are suggestive even today.

In one sphere most of the Modernists were themselves rather "old-fashioned." They had little if any interest in liturgical changes and were content with the conventional missal, ritual, and ceremonial. They were often more devout and precise in their manner of saying Mass than many other priests of the time. A friend of Buonaiuti's has remarked that instead of rushing through the service in twenty minutes or less, he celebrated with great attention and concentration, every act and word being done or said deliberately and reverently. But in his writings he says nothing about liturgical reform: his one concern in respect to the Eucharist is to emphasize that the "real presence" in it can only be given proper meaning when it is seen in the context of the living presence of the Lord in the fellowship of the faithful as they share together in the breaking of bread and the offering of the eucharistic sacrifice. His view might be styled a theology of Christ's eucharistic presence in the context of Christ's real social presence in the Church which is his Body; and he defended this interpretation by a careful analysis of what St. Paul had to say on the matter in his first letter to the Corinthian Christians.

In summary, we may conclude that there has been a certain underground persistence of ideas for which Modernists risked their positions and their ministry, but that this has not been an *obvious* influence. It has been much more a matter of the way in which, as I have said, ideas once expressed have a certain enduring and pervasive quality. On the other hand, there can be no doubt that certain Modernist principles, in a general sense, have revived in recent years: the recognition of the necessity and duty of studying the Scriptures historically as well as using them for theological purposes; the conception of the Church as a living organism and not as a communication of propositions, ideas, or doctrines; the conviction that there must be a simplifying of ecclesiastical government and organization; the vision of the Church as the servant of God and God's people; and an openness to new social, economic, and political movements. Finally, despite recent oppressive measures by the Holy Office, there has been a notable advance in granting a certain measure of freedom for expression of opinion, as well as freedom in research and enquiry. Whether all this would have taken place had Modernism never existed is a question which cannot be answered. Probably it would have come eventually since (as Buonaiuti used to say) the Spirit is likely to work against the wishes and actions of persons of narrow mind, as well as through the dreams and aspirations of those with more liberal outlook.

Some have thought that the "new springtime" of Pope John's day was replaced by a more conservative attitude under the leadership of his successor. That may be to do an injustice at least to "Papa Montini." It may be more just to say that Pope Paul VI inherited a renewing movement which he felt was going too fast and without sufficient thought; hence he "braked" the speed of change but did not entirely stop it. One must regret his "new creed" and his position on contraception and certain other matters. But in one respect at least he carried on the reforming work, simplifying the administration of the Church, opening the door to some measure (however slight) of collegiality in sharing his supreme office with the world episcopate, and appointing to high office men who if not themselves marked as progressives were at least not the old warhorses of traditional "triumphalism." Pope John Paul II, however, has certainly been much more conservative and has allowed the Holy Office to engage in quite oppressive measures and actions.

The Church has changed; and the changes have been on the whole in the direction that Buonaiuti and his fellow-Modernists hoped would be taken, even if not all that they desired has been conceded. Perhaps some of the things they longed for, or contended for, ought *not* to be conceded. But Buonaiuti himself said, in writing his "balance-sheet" of Modernism (in his little study *Il Modernismo cattolico*) that the movement at the time of its suppression was far too much a young child who had not grown sufficiently to give adequate expression of his deepest and most mature yearnings. It was inchoate, often confused, he said, and never had had a simple and single agreed programme.

As we end this essay we come back to the point made earlier. Modernism was never a unitary movement but a general attitude. It was a longing for the Church's renewal in all aspects of its life excepting the liturgical one, about which (as we have indicated) its representatives had little to say. A Christian believer, who would see the life of the Church as being (like everything else in the world) under God's providential care, might say that Modernism played its part, did its work, and suffered suppression; and that it was a genuine expression of God's Spirit at work in the lives of men and women and in the institution which they loved and tried to serve. What that providence will formally make of it, and how God will use it in the future, is hidden from us.

I close this essay by translating in full one of the most moving things Buonaiuti ever wrote. Just before his death he entrusted to some dear friends a single page. It was what he called his "testament," written, during his last illness, on the night of March 18, 1946. It reads as follows:

> One ideal has sustained me throughout my life, that of reviving all the genuine Christian values and of contributing to their transfusion into the new ecumenical civilization, of which my suffering generation may see the first signs upon the far-away horizon. I may have been mistaken, but I do not find in the substance of my teaching anything that I should now repudiate or retract. In this peaceful consciousness I face the oncoming mystery of death. All those—and they are legion—who have raised obstacles to the normal development of my public activities, even resorting to unnatural alliances, I humbly forgive. It was God's will that what came to be called Modernism (inappropriately, since it was only intended to be a revival of the pure evangelical ideals of the gospel, should meet with the harshest and most disloyal opposition that any spiritual movement has ever encountered. Perhaps this is the infallible sign of its ultimate success. My manifold experiences have taught me a lesson to which I here bear witness—I feel myself to be a partaker in home and communion with the new ecumenical Church as part of which I have also seen the Evangelical denominations, which are vivified by an authentic sense of brotherhood, peace, and charismatic life, at work in this sorrowful world. I owe a word of fraternal gratitude to the representatives of these ecumenical movements whose cordial solidarity I have had the privilege of enjoying, through the providence of the heavenly Father. In harmony with the spirit of my great brother, George Tyrrell, I wish that the symbol of the eternal Christian priesthood, the Chalice and the Host, be engraved on my funeral slab.

BOOKS WRITTEN BY ERNESTO BUONAIUTI

(A complete bibliography, including his hundreds of articles in various learned and popular journals, has been compiled by Marcella Rava, published in Florence in 1951 under the title *Bibliografia degli scritti de Ernesto Buonaiuti*. The list below included only his published books. It may not be entirely complete, since there are some indications of one or two others books, or duplicated sheets, written by him.)

Il Programma dei modernisti. Rome, 1907, and Turin, 1911.

Lo Gnosticismo. Rome, 1907.

Lettere di un prete modernista. Rome, 1980.

Saggi di Filologia e Storia del Nuovo Testamento. Rome, 1910.

L'Isola di Smeraldo (with N. Turchi). Turin, 1914.

Il Christianoesimo medioevale. Citta de Castello, 1916.

La genesi della dottrina agostiniana intorno al peccato originale. Rome, 1916.

Sant'Agostino. Rome, 1917.

L'Essenza del cristianesimo. Rome, 1922.

Escursioni spirituali. Rome, 1922.

Sant'Ambrogio. Rome, 1923.

San Girolamo. Rome, 1923.

Voci cristiane. Rome, 1923.

Apologia del cristianesimo. Rome, 1923.

Tommaso d'Aquino. Rome, 1924.

San Paulo. Rome, 1925.

Saggi sul cristianesimo primitivo. Rome, 1925.

Une fede e una disciplina. Foligno, 1925.

Gesu il Cristo. Rome, 1925.

Translation of Rudolf Otto's "Idea of the Holy," under title *Il Sacro*. Bologna, 1926.

Maurizio Blondel. Milan, 1926.

Tertulliano. Milan, 1926.

Le piu belle pagine di Fra Paolo Sarpi (edited by E.B.). Milan, 1926.

Lutero e la Riforma in Germania. Bologna, 1926.

Verso la luce (Saggio di apologetica religiosa). Foligno, 1027.

Giansenio. Milan, 1927.

Il modernismo cattolico. Modena, 1927. (French edition, *Le Modernisme catolique*. Paris, 1927.)

Le origini dell'ascetismo cristiano. Foligno, 1928.

Il misticismo medioevale. Foligno, 1928.

Giocchono da Flora: I Tempi, La Vita, Il Messagio. Rome, 1931.

La Chiesa romana. Milan, 1933.

Dante come profeta. Modena, 1936.

Gesu dice. Modena, 1938.

Amore e morte nei tragici greci. Rome, 1938.

Storia del cristianesimo (three volumes). Milan, 1942-43.

La fede dei nostri padri. Modena, 1944.

Pellegrino di Roma. Rome, 1945. (New edition, edited by Mario Niccoli, with notes; and with introduction by Arturo Carlo Jemolo. Bari, 1964.)

Transcendental and Poietic Imagination in a Theology of Culture

ROBERT P. SCHARLEMANN

There are more routes than one along which a theology of culture can be pursued. Still, it is owing largely to Tillich's essay "On the Idea of a Theology of Culture" (1919) that the notion of theological analyses of culture has become part of the contemporary world, and in that sense his essay may be regarded as foundational. It is in that essay, too, that we find what is still the most precise formula for a method of interpreting culture theologically. The precision in Tillich's terminology is, of course, systematic rather than lexical. That is to say, the concepts are precise because each has an exact place among the systematic categories. Only if one is familiar with the systematic edifice can one see what Tillich envisaged as the method of analyzing culture theologically. The formula reads: "Der Gehalt wird an einem Inhalt mittelst der Form ergriffen und zum Ausdruck gebracht" (The *Gehalt* is grasped in a content by means of the form and brought to expression).[1]

---

[1] In the English translations, the clarity of the formulation suffers somewhat. The standard translation is this: "Substance or import is grasped by means of a form and given expression in a content." This is the reading in Paul Tillich, *What Is Religion?*, ed. James Luther Adams (New York: Harper & Row, 1969), p. 165, as translated by William Baillie Green. This translation, besides forcing the syntax of the sentence, appears to me to miss the point Tillich is making. Victor Nuovo's more recent translation, in *Visionary Science: A Translation of Tillich's "On the Idea of a Theology of Culture" with an Interpretive Essay* (Detroit: Wayne State University Press, 1987), is different, but it too seems to me to miss the point: "substance is caught up into content by means of form and brought to expression" (p. 27). The most normal translation seems to be the one that makes most clear Tillich's point—that in order to know what the

What is this *Gehalt*, which can be translated as "substance" or "import" or "depth-content" or "substantial meaning"? The word refers to the "third dimension" which, along with form and content, constitutes the reality of real things. That much is clear. Everything, and particularly every work, which can be analyzed from the point of view of its form or of its content, can also be viewed from its *Gehalt*. Culture theology, in contrast to ecclesiastical theology, depends upon the recognition of this dimension. A theology of culture is not a theology *about* culture but a theology that is present *within*, or expressed by, the cultural works themselves—"of culture" is a subjective genitive. A cultural *theology* is possible to the extent that a theological interpreter can identify and provide an interpretation of the *Gehalt* that is being expressed in the works of a time. For the theology that is in a cultural work is to be found in the way the *content* of a work shows how *Gehalt* is breaking into the *form* of the reality. Thus, a landscape painted in an expressionistic style shows the disruption of the natural forms of the trees, the brooks, and other things by a depth-content, a *Gehalt*, that shows through the everyday content by the way the forms are disrupted. The disruption itself is not formless; rather, it has the form of breaking through the content-forms. As soon as we say what the meaning of the disruption is, we are interpreting the cultural work theologically, because such an interpretation amounts to grasping the *Gehalt* in the work. Tillich sketched such an interpretation in the 1919 essay and provided a more complete account some years later in *Die religiöse Lage der Gegenwart* (1926).[2] In this latter work, he formulated the theological theme as a revolt against capitalist society, that is, a self-transcendence taking the form of a testimony against the spirit of self-sufficient finitude (*in sich ruhende Endlichkeit*).

This is a simplified account of what Tillich proposed as a cultural theology to be developed alongside ecclesiastical theology. It has been pointed out that the formula for its execution is more suited to an analysis of painting than it is to literature or even to music.[3] One would have

---

substance (or import) is we must see it in the content, but we can see it in the content only by what is happening to the form (of the content).

[2] Now in Paul Tillich, *Main Works/Hauptwerke*, vol. 5: *Writings in Religion/Religiöse Schriften* (Berlin and New York: De Gruyter-Evangelisches Verlagswerk, 1988). The English translation is by H. Richard Niebuhr, *The Religious Situation* (New York: Living Age Books, 1956).

[3] It can even be granted that, as John Dillenberger has noted, *abstract* expressionism, in contrast to the German and French expressionism with which Tillich was most familiar, cannot adequately be analyzed by the same formula. "Here [in Abstract Expressionism] was an art," Dillenberger writes in his "Introduction" to

to grant, too, that Tillich's own interpretations of culture given in his writings over the years depended as much upon the sureness of his intuitions as it did upon a strict method.[4] But the idea of a theology of culture served to reopen the possibility of understanding culture itself as bearing a theological meaning—it reopened the possibility envisaged on a grand scale by the nineteenth-century Hegelian theologian Richard Rothe. Although no one today would think it possible to carry out such a project in the manner of Rothe's speculative idealism, since we have become too acutely aware that the gap between the ideal and the real cannot be bridged from the side of thought alone, Tillich's appeal to the reciprocity between cultural and ecclesiastical theology opened a new path for theology of culture which did not require speculative pretensions.

All of that seems clear about the intention in Tillich's guideline that *Gehalt*, the religious dimension of a work, is to be sought in the content by means of the form of a work. But the guideline is indifferent to a distinction that was of paramount importance in the systematics of the later Tillich—the distinction between the ontological and the theological. What is ontological and what is theological in *Gehalt* as such? This question, which emerges in another fashion in the hermeneutical discussions of recent years, can be answered, I think, only—or best—by a detour through the imagination. Specifically, the problem is one of distinguishing the transcendental imagination, which appears in nature and in myth, from the poietic, which appears in art. The thesis to be pursued can be put thus: The creations of poietic imagination are syntheses of reality and meaning, adding *meanings* to the realities of the natural and *realities* to the meanings of the mythical syntheses, which are the work of the transcendental imagination.

I. The Schemata of the Transcendental Imagination

The concept of the transcendental imagination is Kantian in origin. It is the concept of an agency, an a priori imagination, that has always al-

---

Paul Tillich, *On Art and Architecture* (ed. John Dillenberger and Jane Dillenberger [New York: Crossroad, 1987]), "in which the subject matter was not necessarily disrupted, a qualification so central to Tillich's view of expressionistic art" (xxi).

[4] That Tillich's analyses of art often agreed very little with what art critics said about the same works does not seem to me to tell against Tillich's analyses. Art critics work with a different set of systematic categories, seldom explicated as such, and the question whether those categories serve a purpose different from Tillich's or whether art criticism has adequate categories for its own purposes is a matter that needs to be made explicit before fruitful comparisons or reciprocal criticisms can be made among different kinds of analyses.

ready done its work even in our everyday understanding of the world. The "schematism" that is its work is, as Kant put it in his *Critique of Pure Reason*, "an art concealed in the depths of the human soul, whose real modes of activity nature is hardly likely ever to allow us to discover" (A141/B180). Imagination as such is the synthesizer of sense and thought, or of the phenomenal and the noumenal, or of an object as it is perceived with the senses and the same object as it is abstractly conceived. The transcendental imagination produces the schemata by which to connect the percept and the concept of any given object, such as—to use one of Kant's examples—the generalized image of a dog which is not a picture of any real dog but which has something in common with the generality of the concept and the concreteness of the empirical perception.[5] This work is one of the conditions of the possibility of knowledge at all. For we could not know some perceived thing *as* a conceived thing if we did not have, besides our capacities to perceive and to conceive, the capacity to produce schemata of the connection. It is "transcendental," rather than empirical, because we cannot introspect the act of imagining as we can the acts of perceiving and of abstractly conceiving; we know of it only by uncovering it as the condition of the possibility of our knowing anything at all. Critical philosophy rests on the distinction between sense and thought, since "knowledge" exists only where both sensation and thought are involved, but also upon the work of the imagination in bridging the gap between the two.[6] The transcendental imagination harbors the rules for connecting the perceptible and the conceivable.

---

[5] "The concept 'dog,'" Kant writes in the *Critique of Pure Reason* (A141/B180), "signifies a rule according to which imagination can delineate the figure of a four-footed animal in a general manner, without limitation to any single determinate figure such as experience, or any possible image that I can represent *in concreto*, actually presents." There are schemata of empirical concepts (such as dogs) but also of "pure" concepts (such as "reality" and "substance"); of the former we can also form pictures but not of the latter—we could sketch a picture of a dog-schema but not of a substance-schema.

[6] It is frequently said that, according to Kant's epistemology, we can "know" only the phenomena but not the noumena. But that is a misleading way of putting the matter (even though one can find formulations very close to it in Kant's *Critique of Pure Reason* itself). The more precise statement is that we cannot "know" either a phenomenon *or* a noumenon; we can "know" a thing only when there is a unity, a synthesis, of the phenomenal and the noumenal. Thus, we can "know" whether a leaf is green only if, besides understanding what the concepts of leaf and green mean (in other words, relating ourselves to the green leaf as a thought-thing, a noumenon), we can also see, or otherwise sensibly perceive (that is, relate ourselves to a sensed-thing,

This imagination enters as the mediator between sensation and thought in epistemology. But it also enters hermeneutics, because it has to do with the *being* of an object, in contrast to the object's concrete particularity or abstract generality. Critical epistemology is for that reason but one aspect of the whole of our understanding of being. The connection between the two—the critical and the hermeneutical—is most visible, I think, in Paul Ricoeur's *Fallible Man*.[7] Not only does this book follow the pattern of the three Kantian critiques in analyzing reason as theoretical, practical, and affective; what it identifies as the "objectivity" of the object (which is constituted by the synthesis of finite perspective and infinite meaning in knowledge), the "humanity" of the person (which is constituted by the synthesis of finite character and infinite happiness in practice), and the "conflict" or "primordial discord" suffered by the "heart" (in trying to constitute existence between *bios* and *logos* in feeling) is, in a triple division, the understanding of the *being* of human existence. Ricoeur has, in other words, followed Heidegger in making explicit the way in which Kant's epistemology opens upon an existential hermeneutics.

But the transcendental is not the poietic imagination, and the difference between the two is essential for showing how culture can be interpreted ontologically and theologically. The synthesis that the transcendental has always already performed in our everyday understanding of being is not the same as the synthesis of empirical and intelligible that is made when cultural works are created. Unlike the transcendental imagination, which has always already done its work when we try to get it into view and whose work is never displayed as such but only as the condition of understanding being, the poietic imagination produces works which enter the empirical world and are as real as the objects of nature. A statue or a written work is no less empirical a thing than is a tree, a melody no less so than the wind in the trees. Yet there is a difference between the necessity of the transcendental and the freedom of the poietic.

An illustration will help to make the difference clear. If, while walking in a forest, we come upon a painting of the forest hanging on one of the trees or upon a sign attached to a tree and bearing the legend, "This is a tree," such a painting or sign would obviously have a meaning that is

---

a phenomenon), something as a green leaf. "Knowledge" is always of a noumenon *as* a phenomenon or of a phenomenon *as* a noumenon.

[7] Paul Ricoeur, *Fallible Man*, trans. Charles Kelbley (Chicago: Henry Regnery, 1965).

different from the trees themselves.[8] This difference between a natural and a cultural object does not alter the fact that both of them are real things in space and time, but it is a difference we recognize and one that is related to the transcendental and poietic. Transcendental imagination has no works other than the objects already there in the world; poietic imagination adds real objects to a world of objects that is always already constituted as a world by the transcendental imagination. That is why the empiricality of nature and art differs. The difference and the connection can be formulated in this way: poietic works provide existent *meaning* for the *reality* of natural things. The juxtaposition of meaning-bearing works and real things is what initially makes an ontological or theological interpretation of reality possible by occasioning another kind of synthesis.

Before explicating this relation of the poietic and the natural, however, we must take up the question of myth because the status of mythical figures is also at issue. Are mythical figures the work of poietic or the work of transcendental imagination—or of some agency different from both? Was the Orphic story of Dionysus as he was devoured by the Titans, who were in turn reduced to ashes by the lightning bolt of Zeus, ashes from which the human race was then born, a poietic or a transcendental work? The myth itself, the *palaios logos* to which Plato referred for his understanding of the soul and body, cannot be documented as such. As a tale it exists only since the time of the Neoplatonists. But this fact does not tell us whether such a myth is transcendental or poietic in origin. Ricoeur's hermeneutics seems to suggest that myths are poietic in origin—a myth *donne à penser*, it provokes an effort to understand, it does not represent an understanding already accomplished. But is that the case with myth? Is the interpretation of myth like the interpretation of art or is it like the interpretation of everyday understanding?

Hermeneutics is concerned with understanding what we (always already) understand. In philosophical existentialism, the means for doing

---

[8] This illustration is adapted from a suggestion in Robert Sokolowski, "Referring" (*The Review of Metaphysics* XLII, 1 [September 1988], 27-49). Sokolowski begins his essay by illustrating how words "interrupt the dense continuity of things." "Pictures do as well," he continues, "but in a different way. . . . I can go from the table to the rug to the chair to the lamp and to the wall [when looking over the objects in a room]. But if at some point I come to a picture, this plain sequence is broken, . . . it is interrupted by the picture. When I hit the picture, I am no longer just with what is immediately there. I am with the depicted as well as with what is itself there. It is as though a fourth spatial dimension suddenly came into play, not effacing but being added to the three that were there all along" (27).

so is to grasp in reflective concepts the understanding that is prereflec-
tively expressed in everyday talk. A well-known illustration is the interpretation of the phenomenon of death given in Heidegger's *Sein und Zeit*.
The phenomenon is already understood and expressed in the way people
talk about death. Hermeneutics makes explicit what that understanding
is by putting it into such existentialist concepts as *vorlaufende
Entschlossenheit* (precursive resolute openness). Ricoeur's hermeneutical
project in *Fallible Man* represents the same kind of undertaking. Indeed, it
goes the early Heidegger one better by recognizing where a shift in direction has to be made. As Ricoeur indicates at the end of *Fallible Man*, reflective concepts make it possible to grasp the fallibility, or the possibility
of falling, that human existence displays, but they cannot grasp the actual falling or having fallen. In other words, the analysis of theory, practice, and feeling as involving a synthesis of finite and infinite elements
shows how we *can* but does not explain why we *do* fail or why we have
always already in some way failed or fallen. We *can* fail because we are a
synthesis of opposites and the connection in the synthesis can always be
missed. The root or the possibility lies, in other words, in the synthetic
work of the transcendental imagination. But that we *do* fail is not thereby
explained. To interpret the transition from fallibility to fault requires a
different method, one which is explicitly hermeneutical and hermeneutical in a different sense—not the conceptual grasping of the prereflective
language of understanding but, rather, the thinking that is provoked by
symbols of the fall. We express an "understanding" directly in the way
we talk about anything. This understanding can be grasped in reflective
concepts, so that, hermeneutically, we can also understand what we understand. But we do not "understand" the act of failing or fall itself. Of
that act we speak indirectly or symbolically. We cannot elevate symbols
to intelligible concepts by reflection; we can only interpret the meaning
of symbols according to the way in which they make us think.

Reflective understanding is based upon what Kant called a rational
idea, a *Vernunftidee*, that is, a concept for which there can never be an intuition; interpretation of symbols, on the other hand, is based upon an
"aesthetic idea," that is, an intuition which can never be exhausted by a
concept.[9] According to the Kantian critiques, as we all know, there are

---

[9] An "aesthetic idea," Kant wrote in the third critique (*Kritik der Urteilskraft*
A190/B192), is that *Vorstellung* of the imagination (*Einbildungskraft*) which "viel zu
denken veranlaßt, ohne daß ihr doch irgendein bestimmter Gedanke, d.i. Begriff
adäquat sein kann, die folglich keine Sprache völlig erreicht und verständlich
machen kann" (makes us think a lot without, however, the possibility that any defi-

three rational ideas: the I (as free), the world (as a whole), and God (as absolute). Nothing we perceive can ever be said to be the I, the world, or God. In that sense, the ideas can never be empirically exhibited and there is, therefore, no "knowledge" connected with them. Pure *practical* reason does have access to the ideas as realities, but only in practice itself. *In the act* of heeding the moral imperative—when we do what is right for no other reason than that we can do so—we do indeed have "knowledge" of real freedom. Along with this knowledge of freedom, which we have directly (but only in the act itself), we have, indirectly, a knowledge of God, for only the idea of God can make moral practice intelligible. Thus, although we can have no theoretical knowledge of the self (in its freedom) or the world (in its totality) or God (in absoluteness), we can know freedom practically. There is a knowledge of the self in its freedom directly. There is also, indirectly, a knowledge of God (because the idea of God is the only idea that, along with the idea of an intelligible world, makes moral freedom possible). Hermeneutically, we can say that the Kantian critiques show how we do always already understand the being of nature theoretically and the being of freedom practically. These same critiques raise the question, however, which is also raised by Ricoeur's shift at the end of *Fallible Man*, whether myths, too, belong to the work of transcendental imagination.

The *pathétique* and rhetoric that serve as Ricoeur's starting points are, in his account, the direct language of prereflective understanding, which can be grasped in reflective concepts. Myths and symbols of the fall are, by contrast, an indirect language. They require a different hermeneutical approach. Does that mean they are the result of poietic imagination rather than transcendental imagination? The answer is not clear in Ricoeur, since he does not pose the question in that fashion. But let me propose here that mythical figures (and stories about them) are *not* the work of poietic reason, or the aesthetic imagination, but the work of transcendental imagination—that they are not, therefore, aesthetic ideas (in Kant's sense) or religious symbols but rather a second part of the work of transcendental imagination. The proposal is, in other words, that mythical figures are syntheses of a percept and a concept, syntheses of an intuition and a thought; they do not add to the world of natural objects (as do works of art) but are given parts of that world. We *find* them, but we

---

nite thought, that is, concept, can be adequate to the idea, an idea which, consequently, no language fully reaches or can make intelligible). Such an idea is the opposite of a *Vernunftidee*, or an *intellektuelle Idee*, that is, "a concept to which no intuition (representation of the imagination) can be adequate."

cannot create them. I shall develop this proposal not directly, by citing qualities of myth that seem to align it with natural objects, but indirectly, by explicating what follows for the ontological and theological interpretation of culture if myth is transcendental rather than poietic in origin.

II. Myth and Art

The starting point for our discussion here is the assumption that myths and symbols, that is, the events and the objects contained in the mythological world, are data in the same way that empirical perceptions of the physical world are data, even if they involve no external perceptibility. Schelling's notion that myths arise through a necessary process within the human consciousness is, according to this assumption, at least on the right track. For the notion implies that there is a givenness about the mythological gods and deeds which is comparable to the givenness of objects in the empirical world. Poetry is free production; myth is necessary production. Art works are contingent products; mythical figures are necessary products. The necessity of the mythological figures refers to their arising within consciousness not as the result of fabrication or creative work but rather in a manner similar to the way in which perceptions of physical reality arise in our mind. When we are looking at a stone, we perceive the qualities of the stone whether we choose to do so or not. There is a constraint upon what we can sensibly perceive that originates in the object of perception itself. To the extent that we are aware of ourselves as perceiving what is there on its own, we must perceive a stone as a stone, a flower as a flower, and so on, because that is how they show themselves to be. (This is, of course, not the same as saying that the name and the object are essentially or naturally connected with each other.) When we are in the presence of an object and intend to perceive it as it is on its own, we are not free to perceive it in an arbitrary way. The situation is similar with mythological figures. They, unlike the creations of poietic imagination, arise and present themselves to our mind independently of what we might choose to be seeing. Hence, the necessity that is connected with them is comparable to the constraint imposed upon our mind by actual physical perception.

If this is so about myths—and our working assumption is that it is so—then mythical figures are as much data for our consciousness as are the perceptions that we have of the physical world by means of our outward senses. In other words, we intuit ("see") mythical figures, we do not create them as we create works of art. When we read a novel, our imagination makes visible by a creative act, by an act of poiesis, the world that is being portrayed in the words of the novel. If we did not have the capacity for imagining the world that is being described by the words of the novel, we could not behold or otherwise know that world. In a mythical tale, however, it is not an act of imagination which enables me to see the mythical figures but rather an act of direct, though interior, intuition. Seeing a mythical god—let us say the god Dionysus—is comparable to seeing a physical object despite there being no outward perception. Mythical images, like dream images, are the result not of our making but of a direct presentation. They present themselves *to* us. They are, furthermore, part of the same world as nature, not of art, even though they appear to consciousness only with an inward necessity and not through outward physical perception.

If myth is in this way part of the given world and has its origin, as does our empirical knowledge, in the transcendental imagination—which produces the schemata for synthesizing particular and general—what does poiesis add to it? The transcendental imagination is the one that is at work in the understanding of being to which we give expression in the way that we talk about things in everyday language as well as in our scientific cognition of the world. Poietic reason adds works to these natural objects. Its works not only are "things-there," like the things of nature, but also "things-with-meanings." Similarly, there is an understanding of being in the myths we tell. Poietic reason adds empirically real gods to the mythical gods. The movement from transcendental to poietic imagination is, thus, a movement from an understanding of being which is always already there to an understanding of being that is added to the given world of nature and myth. Of course, there is an understanding of being, that is, a synthesis of perception and conception, in any work of art, just as there is in our everyday talk of things, but it is a new being. Similarly, poietic reason adds to the mythical gods real gods. Mythical gods are gods who have meaning but no physical reality because they are inwardly, though necessarily, perceived. Natural objects have physical reality but no inward meaning. Poietic works are either physical objects with meaning or they are mythical gods with reality. In its creative capacity, imagination synthesizes things and meaning in one of two directions. It creates natural things that also bear meanings or it creates gods which also have reality. The being of works of art is a "new" being over against myth and nature because it is a unity of meaning and reality built upon, or added to, the unity of sense and thought that is always already there.

But we need to introduce one more distinction before taking up the matter of a theology of culture. Transcendental imagination produces the syntheses of nature and myth. If we call the one synthesis, in a hermeneutical context, the *understanding of being*, we can call the other synthesis *the trusting in God*. These designate the two original, synthetic capacities of the transcendental imagination. The one capacity is that of the understanding of being. We give expression to it whenever we recognize something *as* something. We do not understand being *as being*, but we understand the being *of things*, and have always already done so. The other synthetic capacity of the transcendental imagination is the trusting in God that we have always already done in the myths we tell. But just as we do not naturally understand being as being, so we do not mythically trust God *as God*. We trust God *in the gods* but not *as God*. This is not to suggest that understanding being and trusting God are unmixed with misunderstanding and mistrust but only that it is understanding and trust that are always already accomplished in the data of nature and myth.

In other words, when we come to consciousness or self-consciousness, we find ourselves (that is, in Heidegger's language, our *Befindlichkeit*) as always already having understood being, though not *as being*, and trusted God, though not *as God*. In the synthetic work of the transcendental imagination these are two equally original accomplishments, which we can never get behind because they are always already there.

III. Ontology and Theology of Culture

How do poietic works in conjunction with myth and nature make an ontology and theology of culture possible? We have already hinted at the reply. The understanding of being that is always already accomplished is of the being of things but not of being as being, and the trust is in God in the gods but not in God as God. Culture is ontologically and theologically interpretable when its works add a meaning to understanding and a reality to trust that point in the direction of the meaning of being as being and the reality of trust in God as God. An ontology and theology of culture draws an arc from the transcendental to the poietic in the direction of a goal that can always be pointed to but never actually pointed out—the understanding of being as being and the trust in God as God. Drawing the arc from our natural understanding of objects in the world to the understanding of being as being, which can be signified in works of art, is the ontological side of the task. Drawing an arc from the mythi-

cal trust in the necessary gods to the trust in God as God, which poietic
works can express, is the theological side of it. The synthesis of the transcendental and the poietic, of reality with meaning and meaning with
reality, is a synthesis always in the making but never completed. Because
it is so, it is a synthesis that signifies.

Two examples can serve to illustrate what is involved here. One example is a painting, van Gogh's *Starry Night*. It is an object added to the
objects of nature. There are starry nights in natural fact and not only by
poietic creation. But if we look at van Gogh's *Starry Night* and try to
draw an arc—I shall leave unspecified what kind of drawing this is—
from the natural understanding of the being of things that is contained in
our recognition of something as a starry night to the meaning contained
in van Gogh's portrait of a starry night, then we see a meaning of being
that points in the direction of the meaning of being as being. Tillich's
analysis is that we see the disruption of natural form by the breaking in
of a *Gehalt*, which is seeking a form but has not found a form adequate to
it. In other words, what we see as "being" in the starry night is being-
itself, the negation and affirmation of the finite forms of being that we
call a starry night. This is, we should note, an ontological, not a theological, interpretation of the painting. It points our understanding toward
being as being by the synthesis of a natural understanding with a graphic
meaning. What the painting calls upon us to do, according to this interpretation, is understand the depth of being that appears through the
forms of finite being. We can read the work of art from the standpoint of
the question, "What does it signify about being as being by the meaning
of the being of the night that is entitled *Starry Night*?" Poietic works add
to the understanding of the being of things that is always already accomplished the possibility of understanding being as being. Being *west an*,
"spooks around," in the painting as creative and disruptive of the being
of things.

The second example is a classical work. In Bach's *Passion according to
St. Matthew*, there is, between two tenor recitatives, a short, two-measure
choral setting (no. 73) for the words, "Wahrlich, dieser ist Gottes Sohn
gewesen [Truly, this was God's son]," with which the captain and those
with him who were guarding Jesus responded to the earthquake. In the
recorded performance of this passion by the Bach Choir of Munich under
the direction of Karl Richter, the tempo and the volume are so exactly
modulated as to have an astonishing effect. The sudden slowing of the
tempo, after the recitative, the gradual crescendo through the words
"Dieser ist Gottes Sohn," and the decrescendo in which the tone lingers

on the long vowel of the syllable "we-" in *gewesen* until it comes to rest in the short "-sen" just before the silence create an image both acoustic and visual. If there is any piece of music which conveys the dawn of understanding and trust in a sonance that conjures a visual image, and does so in connection with mythological language, then this is it. The effect is as though the sun has gradually broken through the clouds of a violent storm and brought a momentary tranquility. The words say, "gewesen," "was," as though it were "We come too late, but can trust even so."

I cite these two examples in order to illustrate the way in which an ontology and theology of culture might draw an arc from the understanding of the being of things, which is the work of transcendental imagination that we have always already accomplished in our knowledge of the world, to the understanding of being *as being* which is signified in the poietic work and which requires an act of interpretation, and another arc from the trusting of God in the gods, which is implicit in our necessary myths, in the direction of trusting God *as God* which is made real in the poietic work. The poietic work makes the mythical meaning real, just as it makes the natural reality meaningful. If the added meaning and reality point toward the meaning of being as such and the reality of God as God, then the cultural work can be interpreted ontologically and theologically. An ontology and theology of culture investigates, it analyzes, it interprets works. It does so with the intention of showing how, by reference to the understanding of the being of things, understanding of being as being is in the cultural work. Similarly, it looks to cultural works in order to compare the real gods who are there with the mythical gods who are the data of everyday. But doing so constitutes an ontology and theology of culture only if we can see in some works of art not just an understanding of the being of things but also an understanding of being as being and not only another real god added to the necessary, mythical gods but also a believing in God *as God*. This is a different formulation from the one that Tillich gave in his essay of 1919 on the theology of culture. But I think what he meant by the *Gehalt* in artistic works, in contrast to their form and content, is specifiable as the understanding of being qua being that may be in a work of art and also the believing God qua God that may be in the work.

What remains unanswered here is the question whether there is yet another unity: the synthesis of the *understanding* of being with the *trusting* in God. Is there an act perhaps exceeding the work of all imagination in which understanding being as being and trusting God as God are synthesized in an acknowledgement of the being of God and the godliness of being?

Charity, Obscurity, Clarity: Augustine's Search For a True Rhetoric

DAVID TRACY

I. Introduction: Puzzles and Paradoxes

It would be difficult to name a more rhetorically informed contemporary theologian than Nathan A. Scott, Jr. His contributions to the discipline of "theology and culture" are without equal. And those theological contributions are always rendered in a style that fits the mature reflections of a theologian who unites content and style. Scott's Anglican heritage, united to the more Reformed tonalities of his mentors, Paul Tillich and Reinhold Niebuhr, have given his theology a deeply Augustinian cast. But, unlike Tillich and Niebuhr and more like the classic Anglican tradition from the Caroline divines through T. S. Eliot, Nathan Scott has appropriated not only Augustine's profound theological vision but also his concern with rhetorical practice and theory.

Any theologian who writes as well as Augustine did and as Scott does is, ironically, always in danger of being misunderstood by theological practitioners of the "plain style" of what the ancients named dialectics. Not until the recent revival of rhetorical theory and hermeneutics have the limitations of dialectic and the persuasive power of rhetoric been readmitted to the more usual conversations of philosophers and theologians. To the purely dialectical mind, a rhetoricized theology can seem a half-way house to "true" theology. This dialectical self-deception belies both the rhetoric in all dialectical arguments and the argumentative force of all good rhetoric.

Augustine, the greatest of rhetorical theologians, is often the first victim of this widespread prejudice. Indeed, Augustine never explicated his full rhetorical theory. But he did leave us his great text *De Doctrina Christiana*. That text, I fear, is too often hurried through by many theologians anxious to move on to Augustine's more speculative (*On the Trinity*) and more anti-Pelagian writings. However, as Nathan A. Scott's remarkable *oeuvre* and as the recent revival of interest in rhetoric demonstrate, this will not do.

For only in *De Doctrina Christiana* does one find Augustine's clearest statement of his hermeneutics and what he left us of his rhetorical theory. Too often Augustine's theory has been read through the neo-Aristotelian eyes of many modern rhetoricians as concerned solely or, at least, principally, with style rather than with content, i.e., with the need for *inventio* as discovery of true arguments and topics.[1] This reading, however familiar, is, I fear, a serious misreading. Augustine, to be sure, is deeply concerned with style. But he is equally concerned with a rhetoric of *inventio*. However, the Augustinian understanding of *inventio* can only be understood in his theological terms and not in purely philosophical terms. Augustine continues to persuade, i.e., to "instruct, delight, and move," because he has also developed hermeneutical and theological principles of discovery or *inventio* by means of which he could instruct and move his readers. On the welcome occasion of a *Festschrift* for Nathan A. Scott, Jr.—a theologian who has so instructed, delighted, and moved us all over the years of his remarkable career—it seems fitting to return to Augustine, the first great rhetorical theologian, and to his classic rhetorical text, *De Doctrina Christiana*. There one may find both a classic formulation of "theology and culture" as well as a rhetoric of both discovery and communication.

Before interpreting Augustine's text, however, there are three background issues worth noting: the first two suggest possible difficulties with the text itself; the third with the history of its interpretation. All three issues demand attention if an interpreter is to explicate the partly explicit, partly implicit, theory of Christian hermeneutics and rhetoric in this text of a former professor of rhetoric in the cosmopolitan capitals of

---

[1] On the discussion of the relationships of Augustine's rhetoric to Greek and Roman models, see James J. Murphy, *Rhetoric in the Middle Ages: A History of Rhetorical Theory from St. Augustine to the Renaissance* (Berkeley: University of California Press, 1974); Richard McKeon, "Rhetoric in the Middle Ages," *Speculum* I (1926): 1-32; Maurice Festard, *St. Augustine et Ciceron*, 2 vols., *Etudes Augustiniennes* (Paris: Aubier, 1958). For the Greek and Roman models, see George Kennedy, *The Art of Persuasion in Greece* (Princeton: Princeton University Press, 1963); idem, *The Art of Rhetoric in the Roman World* (Princeton: Princeton University Press, 1972).

Milan and Rome turned Christian bishop-rhetorician in the provincial city of Hippo.

1) The first issue is both the most obvious and, hermeneutically, the most central: the strange combination of simplicity and complexity of *De Doctrina Christiana*. On the one hand, this influential text of Augustine seems far less complex in its analysis of rhetoric than the texts of either Plato or Aristotle or even Augustine's own major mentor, Cicero. *De Doctrina* is also far less complex a text than other texts of Augustine himself: not only the *Confessions, The City of God, On the Trinity,* but also some of his great commentaries on Genesis, the Gospel of John, and the Psalms. On the other hand, as I hope to show, *De Doctrina Christiana* (henceforth *DDC*) remains a quintessential Augustinian text which can illumine all his more "complex" texts and is illuminated by them. For the hermeneutical and rhetorical theory on the relationship of theology and culture in *DDC* is often a central clue for reading other Augustinian texts.

2) The problem of the text is further complicated by the question of whether it is, in fact, a "whole." The circumstances of *DDC*'s origins and completion over a twenty-year period are not without interest here. It seems reasonably clear that after Augustine resigned as professor of rhetoric following his Christian conversion, he desired to remain a contemplative (more exactly a Christian Platonist contemplative) in the company of a few like-minded friends. He hoped to produce dialogues like those at Cassiciacum (*De Dialectica, De Musica, De Magistro, De Ordine,* etc.). It is important to recall that Augustine's Christian conversion is the final conversion in a prolonged journey of conversion. The first conversion was to philosophy itself as the search for true wisdom via Cicero's now lost *Hortensius*. The second conversion was to the realm of the "invisible," the "intelligible," the "spiritual" via "some writings of the Platonists."[2]

In his early years as Christian convert, priest, and even bishop, Augustine never lost sight of the importance of these first two moments in his long journey to Christian conversion. Like his rhetorical mentor, Cicero, Augustine tried to be faithful to the search for both wisdom and eloquence. Like his Platonist contemporaries and against his own earlier materialist instincts, Augustine wanted, above all, to contemplate the truths of Christianity "spiritually." To Augustine, the great example of the preaching of Ambrose in Milan demonstrated that this ideal could be

[2] Robert O'Connell, *St. Augustine's Confessions: The Odyssey of Soul* (Cambridge, Mass.: Harvard University Press, 1969); idem, *St. Augustine's Early Theory of Man, A. D. 386-391* (Cambridge, Mass.: Harvard University Press, 1968).

made actual: a spiritual ("Platonist") reading of the Scriptures and all Christian doctrine which could "teach, delight, and move" other like-minded searchers for wisdom and eloquence. Christian theology, as, philosophically, the true wisdom and, rhetorically, the true eloquence, was the now available goal of the search of all true seekers for wisdom and happiness. With this goal in mind, Augustine intended to write reflections on all the "liberal arts" by dialogues with his small group of Platonist friends—but except for *De Musica* and certain parts of his *De Dialectica* these texts are now lost. The extant dialogues of that early period (especially *De Ordine* and *De Magistro*) show the promise of that desired life of communal contemplation—a life which was not to be.

Why Augustine returned to North Africa—and especially the "tough" provincial town of Hippo—remains something of a mystery to his biographers. But whatever else that attempt to "go home again" meant, Augustine still wanted to continue the *otium liberale* with a small circle of friends in order to understand what he had come to believe. The famous medieval motto—an ideal which shaped Western Christian thought for centuries—finds its roots in Augustine's use of both dialectic and rhetoric throughout his life: "Believe in order to understand; understand in order to believe."

The ideal remained. But these early hopes for the *otium liberale* proved illusory dreams. For Augustine was elected (forced seems the more exact verb) by the acclamation of the people to become, first, priest, and then, bishop, of Hippo. As bishop of an often unruly people, he found himself with a whole new set of problems. Augustine was too keen a rhetorician not to realize that he now had a very different audience: the remarkably diverse congregation of Hippo rather than the little group of like-minded contemplative friends living the *otium liberale*.

This shift of audiences is a major impetus behind the emergence of *DDC*. Augustine began to write this text shortly after he became bishop in 396. But then—*our* problems with this text increase. For Augustine ceased writing *DDC* in 397 at Book III, paragraph 35 (i.e., in the midst of his discussion of the "rules for interpretation of the Scriptures by Tyconius"). The difficulties of interpretation of *DDC* increase when we realize that Augustine was also writing the *Confessions*—the great rhetoric of conversion—at this same period. Is this merely an historical accident of a prolific and deeply occasional writer? Or does this suggest that Augustine needed both the *Confessions* and *De Doctrina Christiana* to express his full rhetorical theology at this crucial moment of transition in his life—the transition from being a member of fellow contemplatives to

becoming a bishop responsible for a congregation that, although it included the educated, was comprised principally of the uneducated? The
rest of the text of *DDC*, moreover, was not completed until 427, i.e., after
Augustine's famous struggles and writings against, first, the Donatists
and then, the Pelagians. Where, then, in the post-427 additions to *DDC*
can one find the famously pessimistic Augustinian vision of the human
situation: the new theological vision which emerged from the anti-
Pelagian struggles, that troubled vision which has seemed to many
commentators (including Pelagius and Julian of Eclanum) effectively to
cancel out the relative optimism (especially on free will) of his earlier,
more Platonist, dialogues?

Given the shifts from pre-Hippo Augustine to post-Hippo
Augustine, it is amazing that this text (*DDC*) does form so clear a whole.
In fact, there are very few references in the remainder of Book III and
Book IV to the Augustinian anti-Pelagian bleaker vision of human perversity. Nor in his famous *Retractions* at the end of his life does
Augustine find it necessary to call into question the relative optimism on
"pagan culture" to be found in *De Doctrina Christiana*. But the question
recurs: should he have done so? In another context and on other theological questions, my claim would be the strong claim that *DDC* is a mature,
indeed central, text of Augustine. For this exemplary hermeneutical text
articulates the central theological vision (viz., *caritas*) that pervades
Augustine's entire thought through all its remarkable twists and turns,
its revisions, intensifications, exaggerations, and retractions up to and
including the final bleak, even tormented, vision of the human condition
surfacing in his anti-Pelagian writings. That strong claim, I admit, would
be difficult to maintain given the "family quarrels" over the interpretation of the theology of Augustine in Western Christianity: Thomas vs.
Niebuhr and Paul Tillich vs. the "Liberals," etc.

However, for the present question of how to read the complex text of
DDC, my more modest claim is less controversial but, given the difficulties of the text, must also be tentative (which is to say it is also controversial). The claim is this: despite the significant interruption in the writing,
the text of *DDC* nonetheless constitutes an authentic whole. *DDC* thereby
discloses what we can know of Augustine's unwritten rhetorical theory
even as it explicitly discloses his basic position on both biblical
hermeneutics and the relationships of theology and culture. What the
text of *DDC* is not fundamentally about, I believe, includes two other
central Augustinian rhetorical exercises: first, although *DDC* includes
apologetic elements, it is not rhetoric of Christian apologetics (here

Augustine's earlier dialogues seem the more appropriate candidates); second, *DDC* is also not a rhetoric of conversion. Here his *Confessions*—which, to repeat, he was writing both before and after he broke off the writing of *DDC*—remains the central text in his extraordinary *oeuvre*. Indeed, some commentators have suggested that, in the course of writing *DDC* Augustine discovered that he needed a rhetoric of conversion in order to complete his Christian rhetorical essay—hence the *Confessions*. This hypothesis seems to me a fruitful guess. But even if a fuller Augustinian theory of religious (here Christian) rhetoric does also need an explicit rhetoric of conversion-confession, that fact only suggests the incompleteness of *DDC* as a theological- rhetorical theory, not the incorrectness of the theological-rhetorical theory actually rendered there. But this is to get a bit ahead of the story. We need first to see the final hermeneutical complication for any interpretation of the text *DDC* before risking an interpretation of this seemingly straight-forward text.

3) The third complication is, indeed, the complex and conflictual history of effects of *De Doctrina Christiana*. Bluntly stated, given the actual conflict of readings, *DDC* might as well have been two texts, not one. As modern hermeneutics argues, the "history of the effects" of a classic text (i.e., its history of interpretations or readings) cannot be separated neatly from our present reading of the text itself.[3] Any later reading must, therefore, also address this "history of effects" problem as not simply an external problem to any good reading. In one sense, any Western Christian thinker (and a good number of post-Christian secular thinkers) are a part of the history of effects of the texts of Augustine. Indeed, one need only read any Eastern, i.e., non-Augustinian, Christian thinker (e.g., Mircea Eliade) to understand the profoundly Augustinian character in all the family quarrels of Western Christians: Catholic vs. Protestant and liberal vs. neo-orthodox.

If we attend to the history of readings of *DDC*, the problem of the unity of the text occurs on new grounds. The fact is that *DDC* has had such different readings that it almost seems to suggest that we have not one but two influential texts. The first text (Books I-III) is one of the crucial texts in Western biblical hermeneutics—i.e., the text that employs Eastern allegorical methods in a Western anthropocentric (not Eastern cosmocentric) manner. This text gave the major impetus to Western theo-

---

[3] Hans Georg Gadamer, *Truth and Method* (New York: Crossroad, 1976).

logical figurative readings of the Christian classics, the scriptures.[4] In more general cultural terms, this first text also provided the major impetus to a defense of "obscurity" as an intellectual value. For the medieval Augustinians (e.g., Bonaventure), a defense of "obscurity" was largely a defense of symbolic-religious texts. For moderns, since Petrarch, Erasmus, and Boccaccio through the Romantics and the Modernists to the hermeneutical theories of our own period, a defense of "obscurity" became a claim to the priority of the poetic and symbolic over the conceptual, the propositional, and, in that limited sense, the "literal."

It is not, of course, as if Augustine was simply an Alexandrian with a strong (indeed, too strong) emphasis on the "allegorical" sense of Scripture. Indeed, in *DDC* and elsewhere Augustine provides one of the great defenses of the "literal" sense of scripture. This is the case even if a modern reader suspects that Augustine's heart (i.e., his Christian Platonist heart) is elsewhere: with his equally strong defense of the spiritual, allegorical sense of scripture, Augustine, to be sure, does not strictly argue for the primacy of the "literal" sense in the manner of his later and very different admirers, Aquinas and Luther. Rather, Augustine's rhetorical sense of the importance and value of "obscurity" in *both* the literal and the spiritual senses of the scriptures led him to employ the New Testament tradition of typological reading in a manner that could, in principle, honor both the "literal" and the "spiritual" senses of the scriptural texts. As Hans Frei justly argues, Augustine did envisage the world as formed by the history-like and realistic narratives rendered in the biblical stories as the "history of salvation."[5] In that post-Augustinian sense, Augustine could be said to accord a certain priority to the "literal" sense: i.e., as "plain sense of the Christian community." At the same time, Augustine's further rhetorical and theological interests lay elsewhere: assuming the plain sense of scriptures and assuming the traditional typological mode of readings, how can a Christian interpreter honor and control the reading of both the "literal" and the "spiritual" senses of the text whenever the "obscurity" of the text itself demanded such further reflections—as, for Augustine, the Bible often did? Here the history of the readings of Books I-III fruitfully shows that Augustine's joint defense of both obscurity in the text allied to a necessary plurality of readings is the

---

[4] James Preus, *From Shadow to Promise: Old Testament Interpretation from Augustine to Young Luther* (Cambridge, Mass: Belknap Press of Harvard University Press, 1969); Henri de Lubac, *Exégèse Médiévale*, 3 vols. (Paris: Aubier, 1968).

[5] Hans Frei, *The Eclipse of Biblical Narrative: A Study of Eighteenth- and Nineteenth-Century Hermeneutics* (New Haven: Yale University Press, 1974), pp. 1-3.

one sure clue to the heart of Augustinian biblical and cultural hermeneutics. This will also prove central to his rhetorical theory.

The second "text" (Book IV) is often cited by historians of rhetoric as a major influence of a different sort: viz., the narrowing of Western rhetorical interests to concerns of style alone. On that reading, Book IV and its profound influence on Christian preaching and rhetoric is charged with no little of the blame for the removal of philosophical *inventio* from the rhetorical tradition in favor of an overconcern with style—an overconcern which is always in danger of sliding into "mere rhetoric." A strange charge to post to the door of the Ciceronian professor of rhetoric of Milan and Rome; or even, as I shall try to show, to post on the door of the beleaguered bishop of Hippo!

But the charge would basically hold if all we could learn from *DDC* on the rhetoric is found in Book IV. But what if the text really constitutes a whole? What if Books I-III effectively (if largely implicitly) give Augustine's new suggestions for Christian theological *inventio*? What if the hermeneutical concerns of Books I-III constitute a new form of philosophical-theological *inventio* suggesting new topics and new forms of argument for the new Christian reading of both the old classics (the liberal arts) and the new classics (the scriptures)? Then what is really involved in Augustinian *inventio* is a new model for the relationship of Christianity and culture. That Augustinian model formed medieval and Renaissance culture and continues to inform much contemporary Christian theology, including the magisterial and here clearly Augustinian new principles for *inventio* in the *oeuvre* of Nathan A. Scott, Jr. On this reading, the text of *De Doctrina Christiana* must be read as a whole. On this reading, moreover, the Augustine of *DDC* never suffered the nightmare of his contemporary Jerome who dreamt that at the Last Judgment he declared himself a Christian only to have Christ condemn him as a "Ciceronian." Nor did the Augustine of *DDC* share the belief of his North African forensic rhetorician predecessor, Tertullian, that the question "What has Athens to do with Jerusalem" was a "merely" rhetorical question to which the implied answer is, of course, "nothing." In one contemporary language, the question of *DDC* is: what has a hermeneutics of *inventio* to do with a rhetoric of style? In Augustine's own context the question is: what have Books I-III to do with Book IV? Or even, what does the Ciceronian professor of rhetoric of Milan and Rome have to do with the bishop of Hippo?

II. Inventio *as Hermeneutics: Book I*

There are two things necessary to the treatment of the Scriptures: a way of discovering those things which are to be understood, and a way of teaching what we have learned. We shall speak first of discovery and second of teaching (I, 1).[6]

In one sense, Augustine places the reader *in media res* in a pursuit of principles of discovery (*inventio*) for interpreting the scriptures. More exactly, we are quickly informed that in order to understand the scriptures we must pay attention to two related realities: things (*res*) and signs (*signa*). There follow brief examples of this distinction; for example, the thing "stone" in contrast to the "stone" on which Jacob placed his head. The latter is both a "thing" and a "sign," i.e., "a thing used to signify something else." As influential and complex as Augustine's theory of signs will prove to be, however, here in Book I we principally find his characteristic insistence that in order to understand signs at all, we must first understand things.

But this typical move leads just as swiftly to another famous Augustinian distinction: between *frui* (to enjoy) and *uti* (to use). Both of these realities, in turn, are quickly related to our loves and desires. What is going on here? As the next chapters (III to XXXIV) suggest by their frequent if abbreviated Augustinian excursions into dialectic and rhetoric (many of the chapters are, in fact, capsule summaries of arguments from his earlier dialogues), what we find in Book I, in the most general terms, is the fundamental "discovery" (and "method of discovery") informing Augustine's entire thought: the reality of love (*caritas*). Simultaneously, we find that Augustine, the Christian convert-rhetor, has not and will not abandon his first two "conversions" (to philosophy as the search for wisdom and to the realm of the intelligible, invisible, immutable, spiritual) after his Christian conversion—even after his forced assumption of duties as bishop-preacher at Hippo.

---

[6] Saint Augustine, *On Christian Doctrine*, trans. D. W. Robertson, Jr. (Indianapolis, Ind.: Bobbs-Merrill, 1958). The translations throughout are Robertson's. I have used the Book, chapter (I, 1) in the text itself to facilitate use of both Robertson's fine English translation and the original Latin. The latter may be found in J. B. Migne, ed., *Patrological cursus completus. Series Latina* (Paris, vol. 34.1, and in *S. Aurelei, Augustini de doctrina christiana libros quatuor*, ed. H. J. Vogels, *Floridegium Patristicum*, Fasc. XXIV (Bonn, 1930). The necessary citations are, therefore, in the text of this essay rather than in the footnotes.

To return, then, to the distinction between *frui* and *uti*. The distinction itself is clear: "To enjoy something is to cling to it with love for its own sake. To use something, however, is to employ it in obtaining that which you love, provided it is worthy of love" (I,IV). In the next chapter this distinction is quickly linked with the search for true things (*res*): "The things which are to be enjoyed are the Father, the Son, and the Holy Spirit, a single Trinity, a certain supreme thing common to all who enjoy it, if, indeed, it is a thing and not rather the cause of all things, or both a thing and a cause" (V).

This all seems clear enough, save, as Augustine knows, how are *we* to know God, the "supreme reality?" Augustine does not hesitate to insist that God could be discovered by us only if God gave the grace (gift-power) for the discovery. A finely Augustinian paradox ensues: God must give us the grace to discover God, and yet we are inexorably driven and called to that discovery both before and after grace comes as pure gift. *DDC* is presumably written for an audience who is already in some sense "converted" yet still needs to discover the ways to understand the supreme reality who converted them and thereby allowed them to find new principles of *inventio* ("Believe *in order* to understand").

At the same time, one cannot help noticing that another audience also seems to surface in the speculations and arguments of Book I: those not converted to Christianity as well as the always present "unconverted" aspects of converted Christians—i.e., all those who need to "understand in order to believe." What any rhetorical thinker with that kind of intellectual problem most needs is some new form of ancient rhetorical *inventio* by means of which to discover the places (*topoi*) where true arguments can be found. To provide a full rhetorical theory, Augustine's principle of rhetorical *inventio* must also prove a matter of transformational *ethos*. That *ethos* will, in the Augustinian vision, necessarily be a complex one, at one and the same time respecting our desire (*eros*) for wisdom and happiness while honoring, above all, the fact that only God (the "supreme reality") can give us the living gift of grace (*agape*) to turn us around (*conversio*) to see the truth of things and thereby to transform both our understanding and our wills by reordering both rightly. Contrary to many readings of Augustine, he does develop a rhetoric of *inventio*. But his notion of *inventio* is necessarily neither Platonic nor Aristotelian nor even Ciceronian. Augustinian *inventio* is necessarily Christian theological (which includes, but cannot be confined to, philosophical *inventio*). His principal audiences are Christian interpreters who wish to know how to interpret the scriptures correctly. A proper hermeneutics here is, therefore, simultaneously a rhetoric of discovery or *inventio*. For only that kind of *inventio* will allow Christians to know how to find the new true topics revealed by the "supreme reality," God, in the true "signs" of the scriptures.

Nor does Augustine disappoint his readers. Unlike some of his later writings (think of the *massa damnata* motif of the anti-Pelagian writings on sin and grace, or even *The City of God* on the "virtues" of the pagans become "splendid vices" and the Empire itself become a "robber-band writ large"), grace in *DDC* does not simply confront nature to make us recognize our perversity, habits, sins. Rather, even the occasional references to such perversity and the allusions to our human, willful genius at trapping ourselves by our habits seems to function in *DDC* as unsettling but not finally incoherent moments in a larger theologically transformational context.

That key to a true interpretation is *caritas*: the transformation of our *eros* by God's *agape* of grace.[7] This alone frees us to discover both the true wisdom of all our inexorable desires and strivings for wisdom and happiness and to discover the true way to interpret (and thereby argue from) the signs of scriptures, the new "classics" of the converted ones. In Augustine's mature theological understanding, the fall caused a rupture between our knowledge of reality and our use of signs. Even in his earlier theories on "signs" and "things," it is clear for the rhetorical thought of Augustine that we can only read "signs" correctly if we somehow already understand the "realities" to which they refer. Hermeneutically construed, Augustine's principle can be stated clearly: we must have some pre-understanding of the subject-matter in order to interpret the "signs" in texts correctly. On this reading, therefore, Augustine's position in Book I is not dependent on either his implicit philosophical position on "sense" and "reference" or on his theological reading of the Fall as causing the rupture of "signs" from "things" that he believed he found in his own lifelong convalescence. As important as these principles are for the implications of Augustine's fuller theory of "signs" and "things," they do not determine the fundamental hermeneutics of *inventio* of Book I. For that, we need only understand initially that we must have some understanding of the *res* (the subject-matter) if we are to understand "signs" at all. But how can we have a true understanding? That is Augustine's problem in Book I.

---

[7] The best modern study of *caritas* is John Burnaby, *"Amor Dei": A Study of the Religion of St. Augustine* (London: Hodder and Staughton, 1938).

The highly abbreviated reflections of Book I can be considered, therefore, both dialectically and rhetorically. They are rhetorical and dialectical arguments on why God alone (as true *res*) can be truly enjoyed and can only be truly enjoyed by one who has been given the grace from the same God to enjoy "that supreme thing." These arguments (most of them, to repeat, summaries of the dialectical and rhetorical arguments of his earlier Dialogues) take up familiar Christian Platonist themes. The drive to true wisdom is the drive to enjoy the invisible and the immutable and is only fulfilled if the immutable discloses itself. The drive to true happiness for our highly mutable wills meets two chief obstacles: the multiplicity (and thereby internal conflict) of our desires and the traps we set for ourselves by allowing our habits to congeal into the perversity of enjoying what we should use (all mutable things, especially ourselves) and using what we should enjoy (especially the immutable, the invisible, the eternal supreme reality, God).

These two drives to wisdom and happiness constitute the fundamental *eros* that at once impels us and traps us. Only through the gift of the self-revelation of the immutable in incarnation become grace for us could *we* discover true wisdom and true happiness. For only then could we enjoy what is to be enjoyed (viz., God) and love all else by using it for the sake of that love-enjoyment of God. For Augustine, even the neighbor is to be loved as "used," i.e., for the sake of God: recall Nygren's anger at Augustine's interpretation of Christian neighbor-love as *caritas*.[8]

But faith and hope for the converted render possible a transformation of the self which allows for a new search for the true discovery of wisdom and happiness. That transformation is *caritas*: since God's grace-*agape* is sheerly given, it frees the *eros* of our necessary drive to wisdom and happiness to the new synthesis of *caritas* and, therefore, new possibilities for the discovery of true wisdom and true happiness. This transformational principle of *caritas* would seem to suggest that, for Augustine, rhetorical discovery (*inventio*) is entirely a matter of the proper *ethos*. But even aside from the notorious (or, at least, anti-Quintillian) problem of the preacher who does not, alas, practice what is preached (Book IV), this strictly *ethos* reading does not seem to hit the mark on how *caritas* also transforms the *logos* of the Christian rhetorician for the discovery of true understanding.

[8] Anders Nygren, *Agape and Eros* (New York: Harper & Row, 1969), pp. 449-563, especially pp. 539-43.

Caritas is needed, to be sure, to transform the *ethos* of the rhetor. But *caritas* is also another kind of clue, and one more related to *logos* and thereby *inventio*. For *caritas*, formulated as the principle of "love of God and love of neighbor," becomes the means by which new wisdom is born. "Faith" for Augustine can now be understood as a "wisdom born of *caritas*" (B. Lonergan). *Caritas*, formulated as a transformational principle, transforms both *ethos* and *logos*. *Caritas* becomes the means to discover the true meaning (and thereby the true arguments) from the new "classics"—the scriptures. Yet, however new these biblical classics may be for the educated of antiquity,[9] they will be classic only because they are the authoritative "signs" of the self-manifestation of the true *res*, "the supreme thing," or "cause of all things," God. These signs, as Books II and III will show, will yield their true meaning (and their new topics) only to the one who has grasped (or, more accurately, been grasped by) the true *res*—i.e., to the one who knows that divine reality by knowing that the central topic of both the whole scriptures and all our desires must be "the love of God and love of neighbor." The *caritas* principle of Augustine, moreover, is clearly christomorphic but still more clearly radically theocentric.

So much is this the case that Augustine does not hesitate to state what would upset many a biblical Christian even today: "Thus a man supported by faith, hope, and charity, with an unspoken hold upon them, does not need the Scriptures except for the instruction of others. And many live by these things in solitude without books" (XXXIX). So central is the *res* of God for both *ethos* and *logos* that true Christians could live without the *signa* (the words of scripture). And yet we have these "signs" and they will help us to discover true wisdom provided we keep clearly in mind the fundamental principle of Augustine: the love of God and love of neighbor. *Caritas*, then, as both *ethos* and *logos*, will prove to be the central hermeneutical new principle of discovery (*inventio*) for both the signs of *eros* in the search for true wisdom in the classics of the pagans and the signs of *agape* in the new classics, the scriptures. As a transformative (and not purely confrontational) principle, moreover, Augustinian *caritas* will allow the Christian rhetor to continue to learn

---

[9] The classic study is Henri-Arenee Marrou, *Saint Augustin et La Fin de La Culture Antique* (Paris: De Boccard, 1949); see also, Ragnar Holte, *Béatitude et Sagesse: St. Augustin et le problème de la fin l'homme dans la philosophie ancienne* (Paris: Etudes Augustiniennes, 1962). These works should be read in conjunction with the fine biography by Peter Brown, *Augustine of Hippo: A Biography* (Berkeley: University of California Press, 1969).

from the wisdom of the pagan classics even while interpreting the new wisdom of the new classics of the scriptures. Athens (and Milan and Rome), it seems, still have a good deal to do with Jerusalem (and Hippo). For theology and culture are reunited rhetorically under the new principle of *inventio*, love of God and love of neighbor.

III. On Discerning the Signs of the New Classics: A Defense of Obscurity and Plurality (Books II and III)

Book I, therefore, has been concerned with "things," especially the supreme thing, God, and the principle (as both *ethos* and *logos*) by means of which Christian interpreters can find principles of discovery for true wisdom and true happiness (*caritas*). But God, we have also been informed, has revealed Godself through certain "signs." The supreme "sign" of that self-revelation (viz., the "incarnation") is mentioned in Book I. Curiously, however, Augustine does not dwell upon the incarnation when he comes to reflect upon "signs" themselves. But perhaps this strange silence is lessened if we remember that the *caritas* principle is, for Augustine, precisely what the incarnation as sign reveals about what has happened to us through incarnation. Indeed, the principle of love of God and love of neighbor is what Augustine consistently employs when he does a Christian typological (and, in that sense, christological) reading of the figurative signs of the Old Testament.

It does no injustice to Augustine's relative silence on the incarnation as the "supreme sign" of the "supreme *res*" to suggest that his fundamental theological presupposition on signs in *DDC* and elsewhere can be restated in modern theological-hermeneutical terms. That presupposition is this: for the Jew and the Christian (the Muslim is, significantly, i.e., hermeneutically, different here), the relationship of the "texts" of the scriptures and the "events" to which those texts bear authoritative (i.e., canonical) witness is this—the revelation occurs in events of divine self-disclosure (e.g., Sinai or the incarnation) to which the biblical texts witness.[10] The "events" are both historical (e.g., Jesus of Nazareth) and trans-historical (i.e., the divine self-disclosure in Jesus the Christ). The texts, the scriptures, are not the revelation but are the authoritative witness to the original revelation. The Christian confession is, "We believe *in*

---

[10] For an analysis here, see David Tracy, *The Analogical Imagination: Christian Theology and the Culture of Pluralism* (New York: Crossroad, 1981), pp. 233-339; Robert M. Grant with David Tracy, *A Short History of the Interpretation of the Bible* (London: SCM, 1984), pp. 174-87.

Jesus Christ *with* the apostles." The texts of the New Testament are the texts of apostolic witness to the revelation of God in the event and person of Jesus Christ. That original revelation continues, in the Christian community, by being re-presented through the primary "signs" of word (proclamation) and sacrament (which is the sign which renders present what it signified—recall Augustine on the Donatists).

To translate this theological hermeneutic into the terms of Books II and III: Augustine's principle concern is to discover the relationship of the authoritative signs of witness (the scriptures) to the supreme sign (incarnation) of the supreme *res* (God). Book I has articulated the needed principle of discovery or *inventio* (*caritas*). For Augustine, this principle is what Christian interpreters should use to interpret the authoritative texts of the Scriptures, i.e., these word-signs of witness to that supreme sign-event of the self-disclosure of the supreme *res*. To read the scripture as scripture is to read it theologically through the christomorphic and theocentric Augustinian principle of *caritas*. The signs of the New Testament should be read, for Augustine, typologically. Both Testaments, for Augustine, should be read both literally and spiritually, depending on the nature of the written "signs" involved and the interpreter's knowledge of "true things" through the principle of love of God and love of neighbor.

Even if we grant all these Augustinian terminological and hermeneutical-theological presuppositions, however, any reader of the scriptures realizes, with Augustine, that the interpreter still finds a host of difficulties in interpreting the word-signs of scripture. Some of those difficulties can be treated, as they are by Augustine, with relative ease. For example, we can distinguish, with Augustine, between "natural" and "conventional" signs. We can also take common-sense methods in dealing with many of the problems of "unknown signs." As an obvious example, we can learn the original languages: Augustine, in fact, knew Greek poorly and probably had no Hebrew at all: hence his great concern in *DDC* with the best Latin translation. Other Augustinian methods of textual discernment (e.g., his Pythagorean-like love of numbers and music) strike most contemporary interpreters of scripture as a part of the "common sense" of Augustine's late classical culture but not of ours. Still other Augustinian methods—viz., rhetorical analyses of the "tropes" in the scriptures—live on in new forms in contemporary historical-critical and literary-critical interpretations of the scriptures. Still other Augustinian suggestions (e.g., the importance of "context" and the relationship of parts to the scriptural "whole") were standard *topoi* of scriptural interpretation before Augustine, and have remained so, in modified forms, ever since (e.g., form-critical analysis of context, or redactional analysis of the whole of an individual gospel in order to understand the parts). Augustine's own candidate for a theocentric principle of understanding the *res* (viz., the principle of love of God and love of neighbor) and, thereby, the signs of scripture, survives, at best, as one candidate among several for that much disputed theological role.

These Augustinian analyses are important but familiar. However, three characteristically Augustinian positions in Books II and III came to bear practically a life of their own. They demand, by their novelty, further reflection.

1) The first question is how to value and understand "ambiguous" signs of the scriptures, especially how to discern "figurative" from "literal" senses of particular texts. To treat the latter problem first: Augustine is both clear and consistent in his use of the *caritas* principle as the principal way to distinguish the literal senses and the figurative senses of particular passages (e.g., Book III, X: "Therefore a method of determining whether a location is literal or figurative must be established. And generally this method consists in this: that whatever appears in the divine Word that does not literally pertain to virtuous behavior or to the truth of faith you must take to be figurative. Virtuous behavior pertains to the love of God and one's neighbor; the truth of faith pertains to a knowledge of God and one's neighbor").

So we do possess principle ("generally") that can help us discover the true meaning of difficult passages. But we also have a hermeneutical principle which defends not only "figurative" meanings but also the ambiguity and obscurity often present in the scriptures, that obscurity which gives rise to this difficult issue of what is "literal" and what is "figurative." Throughout Books II and III (and, under a new form in Books IV's defense of the "true eloquence" of the scriptures) we find Augustine providing one of his most original, debatable, and influential hermeneutical moves: a defense of obscurity and ambiguity. Among several examples, consider the discussion of Book II, VI. We are informed there (in the midst of Augustine's fascinating interpretation of the "teeth" and "shorn sheep" metaphors in the *Song of Songs*) that there are both good negative reasons for scriptural obscurity and good positive reasons. Negatively, these obscure passages help to conquer our pride by hard work. They discipline our natural disdain for what seems too obvious. Indeed, Augustine does not doubt that God has provided these obscurities for such discipline.

Positively, those obscure words and passages are wise (and, later, "eloquent") because "no one doubts that things are perceived more readily through similitudes and that what is sought with difficulty is discovered with more pleasure." This is an interesting (and debatable) hermeneutical principle—and one which will free Augustine from his earlier pre-conversion disdain for the "vulgarity" and "obscurity" of the scriptures. In sum, for Augustine, the principle of the theological value of obscurity and ambiguity allows him to argue for the scriptures as the new classic signs—wiser and even more eloquent (Book IV) than his own beloved pagan classics. Just as *caritas* can transform human *eros*, so, it seems, scriptural "obscurity" paradoxically can transform Augustine's earlier pre-conversion assessment of the status of these scriptural signs in relationship to the "clearer" signs of the pagan classics. This same principle of obscurity as a value, as noted above, will live a strange after-life in the Augustinian humanists of the Renaissance (Petrarch, Erasmus, Boccaccio). In yet another sea-change, the Augustinian principle will find another life among Romantics and Modernists under the rubric of the "priority of the symbolic" (obscure-ambiguous) over the conceptual, prepositional, literal—an ironic twist, surely, to Augustine's defense of scriptural obscurity.

2) This "defense of obscurity" can also illuminate another aspect of the Augustinian program—viz., the famous analogy (borrowed from Irenaeus) of Book II, XL on stealing "Egyptian gold." This Old Testament analogy is used by Augustine to insist that, even in the new rhetorical situation where the new classics of scripture are not the primary classics, the Christian rhetor can still use the classics of the pagan "liberal arts." Indeed, those disciplines, like the gold and silver of the Egyptians stolen by the departing Israelites, really belong to the new Israelites because these disciplines were not invented by the pagans at all. Rather, they were discovered as already existing by the grace of God who created them. Christians need not reject these treasures (*pace* Tertullian and Jerome's nightmare) since as the new Israelites they already own them.

The classics of scripture are for Augustine both wiser and more eloquent than the pagan classics, for the scriptures alone are the signs or witness to the direct self-disclosures of the divine. Still, the Christian rhetor, informed by the scriptures themselves through this new interpretation of the figurative meaning of the Israelite theft of Egyptian gold and silver, can now freely use all these treasures as their own. The original biblical image and the Christian analogical argument from it may be more than a little strained. However, if one considers the Tertullian option and the positive history of effects of this surprising theft-imagery, latter-day rhetoricians and theologians cannot but agree that Augustine's figurative reading of scriptural obscurity allowed the "gold and silver" of the "liberal disciplines" to find a continued life in medieval Christianity and, through the medievals, in Western modernity. The great modern discipline of theology and culture, to which Nathan A. Scott, Jr., has made such exemplary contributions, finds its original Western Christian impetus from the surprising imagery of theft.

3) A final note on how to interpret the signs of the scriptures is also worth noting: Augustine's defense of a plurality of readings of the scriptures (Book III, XXVII). What is hermeneutically interesting here is that Augustine does not allow the author's meaning in the scriptures to determine the meaning of the text. God, as the supreme author, can use the human author to state a meaning which even the author did not understand but which some later reader (e.g., Augustine) could then discern ("And certainly the Spirit of God, who worked through that author, undoubtedly foresaw that this meaning would occur to the reader or listener").

This theological principle provides for a remarkable flexibility of meaning to the scriptural texts and for a genuine plurality of readings. That plurality, moreover, was bound to increase once Augustine's own principle of *caritas* was also questioned. In sum, the more one moves into Books II and III, the more flexible do Augustine's hermeneutical principles of Book I actually become in practice: the ambiguity and obscurity of the scriptural signs are defended; the figurative begins to play almost as great a role as the literal sense (in contrast to Aquinas and Luther); the pagan classics of the liberal disciplines will continue to play a role for Christian interpreters and thereby provide more readings still; and, finally, since God is the ultimate author of these texts, any hermeneutical primacy accorded the "author's intention" becomes relatively unimportant. The "signs" of Books II and III will be dependent, of course, on the *res* of Book I. But as the Augustinian theological principle of *inventio* became more and more questionable both within later Christian readings of the scriptures as well as in secular interpretations on the scriptural texts, some modern hermeneutes turned rhetoricians have been tempted to find the hermeneutical principles of Books II and III as the true wisdom for rhetorical discovery in the "signs" of Augustine's own text. This would leave Books I, II, and III a theological truncated text but still a hermeneutically interesting one. That new text would bear strong family resemblance to Gadamer's hermeneutics and even to his suggestion that modern rhetorical theory needs hermeneutics for its own process of *inventio*. At the same time, modern hermeneutics may be construed as ancient rhetoric modernized (i.e., historicized). But that is, to be sure, another story—and one perhaps best entitled, "The Revenge of the Egyptians."

IV. Book IV: Eloquence and Clarity

If the claim that Books I-III present Augustine's discussion of rhetorical and theological *inventio* for discovering true wisdom by means of correct principles of interpretation of the new classics (the scriptures), then the familiar suggestion that the strictly rhetorical interests of *DDC* may be found in Book IV on style becomes highly unlikely. Rather, on my reading, Book IV's analysis of the need for the preacher to instruct, delight, and move (i.e, persuade to action) suggests that rhetorical structure, as first, always needs principles of discovery or interpretation (*inventio*) of Books I-III. Augustine is, to be sure, greatly concerned with style (or styles subdued, temperate, and grand) and does stretch Cicero a good deal in Chapter XVII to link the Augustinian styles directly to the "teach, delight, persuade" motifs of Cicero. I admit that the opening sentence of Book IV, II is somewhat disconcerting for my reading of *DDC* as providing a full rhetorical theory of *inventio* insofar as it seems to suggest a somewhat sophistic understanding of rhetoric—indeed, one which Augustine's own earlier anti-sophistic remarks seemed firmly to exclude. Yet even in that section, the rhetorical thrust of the whole chapter (as well as Augustine's reluctance to explicate his full rhetorical theory either here or elsewhere) suggest that Augustine's concern with a rhetoric of instruction (and thereby *inventio*) remains his central rhetorical concern. More exactly, by now familiar Augustinian motifs return, on this reading, in new guises: e.g., the true wisdom of the new classics, the scriptures, has also become true eloquence (especially in Paul and Amos). Still, the preacher of biblical wisdom and eloquence must not try to imitate the obscurity-profundity of the Bible. But why not—especially given Augustine's own plea for preachers to "imitate" classical models of eloquence as, in effect, a partial replacement for lack of formal rhetorical training?

The reason seems clear enough: the preacher is not the inspired author of scripture who can be used by God to speak obscure truths which even the author need not understand. Rather, the preacher is the interpreter of this true wisdom and eloquence. As interpreter, the preacher should not presume to imitate scriptural obscurity; the preacher should instead render biblical obscurity clear for the instruction, delight, and persuasion of the congregation. The preacher needs rhetorical and theological principles of interpretation of the scriptures if he is to instruct clearly (Books I-III). The preacher also needs some knowledge of "styles" (e.g., through imitation of classical styles or through rhetorical education in style) if he or she is to delight and thereby hold the congregation's attention and to move them, i.e., persuade them to action. But above all, the preacher, as interpreter of often obscure scriptural passages, must strive for clarity. Clarity alone can instruct the kind of mixed audience every preacher finds in the true wisdom and eloquence of scripture. And only such clear instruction can properly use whatever rhetoric is both available and necessary (e.g., to delight and to move). So Augustine is not sophistic after all: at least insofar as "delighting" and a "moving" are controlled by the demands of instruction and *inventio*—and that specified by the demands of the discovery of the rules for true interpretation of Books I-III.

Perhaps Augustine, the former professor of rhetoric, might even be able to agree that my interpretation of the rhetorical and theological theory sometimes obscure in the signs of *his* text is not forced. What the bishop of Hippo might think of his latter-day theological descendants is a more unsettling question which had best be left to another day. And yet, whatever the answer to that latter question, some of Augustine's rhetorical principles seem to live in new forms in our own rhetorical context: theological "charity" become, for example, Wayne Booth's hermeneutical model of the text as "friend"; scriptural "obscurity" become the "priority of the poetic" in modern hermeneutics and literary criticism; the divine impetus to a plurality of readings not determined by the author's meaning become the "loss of the author" of modern deconstructionists; the demand for clarity in communication become arguments over the relationships of a rhetoric of instruction to a rhetoric of delight and a rhetoric of *ethos*—and all three to a fuller rhetoric of persuasion in many contemporary rhetorical debates on the relationships of the topics and the tropes. What Augustine might add to those arguments rises or falls, I suggest, on whether we read *De Doctrina Christiana* as one text or two. If one wants Augustine's apologetic rhetoric, one should read his early dialogues. If one desires Augustine's rhetoric of conversion, one must turn to the *Confessions*. But if one wishes to find Augustine's rhetoric of *inventio* as a key moment in any Christian persuasion to action, then his deliberations on both *res et signa* for correct rhetorical-theological interpretation in *De Doctrina Christiana* makes that

great text the text to read and interpret. For all the new rhetorical theologies, therefore, *tolle, lege.*

II

Genres and
Types

Crossing a Shore:
A Glimpse into Contemporary Poetry in Welsh

A. M. ALLCHIN

One of the less expected characteristics of our century in Europe has been the resilience of a sense of national identity. In the Soviet Union, for instance, the three Baltic republics in the north, and Armenia and Georgia in the south, retain a stubborn sense of distinct and separate existence which expresses itself more and more insistently. So in the British Isles the small nations of the north and west, Ireland, Scotland, and Wales, refuse to be assimilated into a neutral Britishness. The English have to learn that England and Britain are not the same thing.

In Wales this phenomenon is particularly remarkable. The last independent Welsh princedom collapsed more than seven centuries ago. Since the reign of Henry VIII, Wales has been, for political purposes, simply a part of England. And yet the sense of a distinct, separate identity has never been lost. It has been sustained above all by the existence of the Welsh language and by the vitality of the literary tradition which that language sustains.

In this essay we take a brief look into that Welsh language tradition as exemplified in the work of two contemporary poets who are both academics, Bobi Jones and Gwyn Thomas, and in particular at a number of poems about specific places. The poetry of place has always had an important role in Welsh tradition. Celtic society in Wales, no less than in Ireland, remains in some ways ineradicably tribal. It is a society of intense local loyalties which feels threatened by the mobility and impersonality of much of our twentieth-century world. This sense of the particularity of place is not only a question of social attitudes and historical memories. It points to an awareness of the presence of the infinite and eternal within the limitations of time and space. A Welsh poet of the last generation, Waldo Williams, replies to the question, "What is living?" with the words, "Finding a large room between narrow walls." There is an implicit sacramental vision in the work of these writers, and since it is a vision with its roots in Christian faith and experience, it can confront the fact of death, as the ultimate form of our human finitude, with an unlikely courage. That courage has given a remarkable edge to the writing of these twentieth-century poets. I hope that these pages will give a glimpse of the quality of their work and encourage others to make an exploration of it for themselves.

It is a remarkable fact that the twentieth century should have seen a genuine renaissance of the Welsh literary tradition. In the last hundred years, the poetic tradition of Wales, which goes back unbroken to the work of Aneirin and Taliesin in the sixth century, has known a revival which has produced a number of poets whose work deserves to be known beyond the boundaries of Welsh-speaking Wales. A recent anthology of twentieth-century Welsh verse runs to over seven hundred pages. All this has happened at a time when the number of speakers of the Welsh language has been steadily diminishing. There are now only about half a million of them, less than twenty percent of the population of Wales. In a way that no statistician could have predicted, the decline in numbers has been accompanied by a cultural renaissance, whose leaders seem to have delighted in overturning the predictions of the pessimists. For a language to live under the constant threat of death can be a remarkable stimulus to poetic activity. There is something in the poetic act itself which bids defiance to death.

Equally surprising is the fact that since the 1930s, a very high proportion of these Welsh-language poets should have been explicitly Christian in their approach to their art. This does not mean that they all belong to the same school of thought or come out of the same denominational background. They are writers of considerable variety. But they have felt themselves to be the heirs of a literary tradition which has been impregnated with Christian ideas from the beginning until today. For them, their commitment to the struggle for the maintenance of their national language and their national identity has been linked with their commitment to a faith which speaks of the value of things which are small and vulnerable, and of the overcoming of death through death. They have been forced to meet the threats of annihilation and destruction which are part of the consciousness of us all in the late twentieth century in a very particular form. As a result, they have found themselves making their affirmations of life and meaning in a way which contrasts strongly with the predominant mood to be found across the border to their east. The notes of irony, self-questioning, and despair are not absent from the Welsh poetry of the last fifty years. But they are not the final or dominating qualities in it.

The very existence of the Welsh literary tradition remains in a curious way almost hidden from England and the whole English-speaking world. For fourteen hundred years the English have refrained from learning the language of their nearest neighbours. It would be an astonishing fact, were it not so familiar, that there is not a single university in England, as opposed to Wales, in which the post-reformation, post-renaissance language and literature of Wales can be studied. There are, it is true, one or two departments of Celtic studies in which Welsh and Irish are studied in their medieval forms, as if they were dead languages like Anglo-Saxon or Old Norse. But to get to know the modern literature of Wales, one has to go to Wales—to Bangor or Aberystwyth, for instance. There in the flourishing departments of Welsh it is possible to get a flavour of a tradition which is very much alive, still full of creativity. But in the English-speaking world, the study of the modern literature in Welsh is only just beginning, and until recently the lack of good translations has made it difficult to know even how to begin.

There has, however, been a change in the last twenty years or so as the number of translations into English from Welsh has multiplied. Among the translators, first place for fluency and industry must be given to the American scholar, Joseph Clancy, of Marymount College, Manhattan. Beginning in 1965 with his anthology, *Medieval Welsh Lyrics*, followed in 1970 by *The Earliest Welsh Poetry*, he has more recently produced four volumes of the plays of Saunders Lewis in translation, an anthology of twentieth-century Welsh verse in English, and a small selection of translations of the poems of Gwyn Thomas made in conjunction with the author. Most recently there has come a very much larger selection of the poems of Bobi Jones, who thus becomes the first contemporary Welsh-language poet to be presented in a representative way to the English-speaking world.[1]

[1] Joseph Clancy has published the following books: *Medieval Welsh Lyrics* (London: Macmillan, 1965; New York: St. Martin's Press, 1965); *The Earliest Welsh Poetry* (London: Macmillan, 1970; New York: St. Martin's Press, 1970); *Twentieth-Century Welsh Poems* (Llandyssul: Gomer Press, 1982); *The Plays of Saunders Lewis*, 4 vols. (Swansea: Christopher Davies, 1985). He has also produced Bobi Jones, *Selected Poems*, trans. by Joseph Clancy (Swansea: Christopher Davies, 1987); Gwyn Thomas,

The reader of English who wants to approach this whole body of unfamiliar verse is likely to begin by asking how far its contents are reflected in the work of the more notable Anglo-Welsh poets of our time and, in particular, the two most famous of them, Dylan Thomas and R. S. Thomas. Dylan Thomas was very insistent that he did not know Welsh. A careful study of some of his verse forms suggests that he was not quite so ignorant of the old language as he liked to pretend. But it is distinctly probable that the Welsh "feel" of some of his writing owes as much to Gerard Manley Hopkins, the one English poet whose work was manifestly and confessedly influenced by his knowledge of the classical Welsh metres, as it does to any direct acquaintance with the work of Welsh poets either of this or earlier centuries.

The case of R. S. Thomas is very different. R. S. grew up without a knowledge of Welsh and learned the language in adult life. He has mastered it so as to speak and write it with ease. He has published a considerable number of articles and reviews in Welsh, as well as his short autobiographical essay, *Neb* (1985). But he has never felt able, as a poet, to move from the language in which he grew up to the language of the country to which he so passionately belongs. There are, it is true, in his collections a very small number of translations from Welsh. It is tantalising that they are so few, for they are of outstanding quality. None of them comes from our own century, and the two most striking of them, "The Cry of Elisha after Elijah" and "Harvest End," come from relatively little known poets of the nineteenth century, not the best period in the Welsh literary traditions in the view of most Welsh scholars and critics.[2]

R. S. Thomas loves to surprise his readers, and it may be that he has hidden away a drawerful of translations from the Welsh with which to astonish us. There are few things which would do more to attract the attention of the world in general to the existence of the Welsh literary tradition than a volume of translations made by the greatest living Welsh poet who writes in English.

Of course, the whole question of the translation of poetry is full of problems. But as the twentieth century draws towards its end, it becomes

---

Living a Life: Selected Poems, intro. by Joseph Clancy (Amsterdam: Scott Rollins for Bridges Books), 1982). The other major translator from Welsh is Tony Conran. His *Welsh Verses* (Bridgend, Mid Glamorgan: Poetry Wales Press, 1982) has a particularly valuable and lengthy introduction.

[2] "The Cry of Elisha after Elijah" occurs in R. S. Thomas, *Song at the Year's Turning* (London: R. Hart-Davies, 1955), pp. 34-35, and "Harvest End" in R. S. Thomas, *Experimenting with an Amen* (London: Macmillan, 1986), p. 15.

clearer that in many ways the work of translation has been of the utmost significance in our time. The work of translation which has made the writers of Soviet Russia known to us—Pasternak, Mandelstam, Akhmatova, Tsvetayeva—has been of particular importance. It is significant that in *The Government of the Tongue*, the first of the four essays devoted to the poets of Russia and Eastern Europe is called, "The Impact of Translation," and that it follows directly on the review of *Poems of the Dispossessed*, in which Seamus Heaney stresses the vital importance for the poet writing in English in Ireland of being able through translation to re-possess the heritage of poetry written in the Irish language.[3] One of the things which has attracted me to the poetry of Wales has been a feeling that there is some deep affinity between the Celtic and the East European worlds. In Slavonic languages, no less than in Celtic, the public and even "sacred" role of the poet seems to be still strongly perceived. In the case of countries which have for a time maintained their nationhood primarily through their linguistic tradition, as with Poland in the nineteenth century, or as with Wales and Romania for the greater part of their history, the political and public significance of the language becomes particularly clear. The act of speaking, writing, or singing in a language whose very existence is considered by many an anachronism, a nuisance, or a political and financial handicap is inescapably an act of some social and political significance. Bobi Jones himself remarks on this in a letter addressed to Joseph Clancy: "I have a feeling that more of the poems are political than some readers consider—even most of the 'love poems'—and certainly the 'family poems.' . . . Living in Wales itself, it is rather difficult to deal with spring or water or people or places without being desperately political. To use a Welsh word is still a revolutionary action. Even to exist is just a little bit of a social attack."[4]

If we turn to Bobi Jones's poems about places, this resistance to oblivion emerges very clearly. In 1965, he published a poem called "Llanuwchllyn," the name of a village in North Wales at the end of Lake Bala. It is a village which for generations has been known as the centre of a Welsh-speaking district still particularly rich in the kind of popular cultural activity which is characteristic of Welsh-speaking Wales. The poem contains references to many places and to one of the most famous writers connected with the village, Owen M. Edwards, who in the early years of this century was an extremely influential figure in the field of

---

[3] Seamus Heaney, *The Government of the Tongue* (London and New York: Faber and Faber, 1988).

[4] Jones, *Selected Poems*, p. 13.

Welsh education. It is, as is often the case in Welsh, a poem of praise and celebration. It speaks of a culture which is still flourishing, though it looks back to it from a possible future when it will be scarcely a memory.

> If there's one left who'll understand me by means of a
>   dictionary,
> Let it be known that in the village of Llanuwchllyn
> In our day there were poets who would mount from their
>   farms
> Like thrushes, and singers who'd ripple in bright
>   crescendo
> Across the strings of river-banks, veined theologians
> Along the seats of Sunday Schools (museums of ancient
>   religion)
> Sprouting through the neighbourhood. And if there's any
>   comprehension
> By anyone of such a thing as living, let it be known
> That this was as natural as walking, that the foolery
> Of little children from a fifteen-hundred-year-old cradle
> Was an eating and a Welsh-speaking on street corners.
>
> If some, through great imagination, come to see
> How a country people deep in time could reap taste and
>   tradition
> Because their land was filled with them, it's fitting
>   I declare
> How the Lliw bewitched a character from the Arennig
> In the tales of its foam, and how there melted in the Dee
> Proverbs from the peat bogs of the Aran.
> And O. M. himself, a Twrch Trwyth along Cwm Cynllwyd,
> Broadcast classics and lullabies;
> And all this existed till the coming of our hurried
>   century's craving—
> That is, if there's one left who'll understand me by
>   means of a dictionary . . .
> And if there's no one—at least—saying it was a
>   blessing.[5]

It is difficult from outside to assess the value of much of the writing of verse which still goes on in Welsh-speaking Wales—some of it

[5] *Ibid.*, p. 95.

perhaps does not rise far beyond the ingenuity needed for the solution of a cross-word puzzle. But certainly it provides the soil out of which the amazing poetic achievement of the Welsh writers of our century has grown. In a poem written while he was spending a year teaching in Quebec, Bobi Jones salutes the Poetry Clubs of Wales, little societies in out-of-the-way places which bring together groups of people to work away at the techniques of poetry and to share their efforts with one another, continuing the practice of poetic rivalry or contention, competing with one another to find the right word for the right place.

> America doesn't know—no, nor any country of Europe—of
>   that contention
> Why they have it, those farmers, postmen, garage hands,
>   ministers.

This popular interest in poetry reaches its most public manifestation in the national Eisteddfod held at the beginning of every August, a great folk festival which has at its heart two classical poetry competitions. It is an occasion which mingles popular and academic, serious and comic, in a way which is rare in the English-speaking world, and which bears striking witness to the importance of the poetic word at the heart of the Welsh tradition. Each year, during the Eisteddfod itself, a volume is produced which contains the text of the two winning poems, together with the adjudications and comments of the judges on all the literary competitions, in prose as well as in verse, which have taken place during the festival. It is a volume with a surprisingly wide circulation, considering the nature of its contents.

The threat of extinction which hangs over small rural places like Llanuwchllyn is not only the threat of the gradual erosion of the language which gives it its name (the Church over the Lake) and articulates its story. Such places are vulnerable in more obvious ways. They are liable to physical obliteration. In the late 1950s, a campaign was waged in Wales which involved almost all the Welsh local authorities and a multitude of other organisations to prevent the flooding of Tryweryn Valley, a valley not very far from Llanuwchllyn. The valley needed to be flooded because the English city of Liverpool needed a new reservoir, and the political and financial interests of a large industrial city outweighed beyond question the views of those who were concerned with the preservation of the village community in the valley at Capel Celyn.

The thing they could not comprehend, that they have
   destroyed,
That ancient thing, so lofty and finely wrought.
How easily it was hidden, and now the sentence
That could not be repeated will not come back. Here they
   blotted it
In an inaccessible cwm that seemed so primitive.
The cynghanedd and the ballads, the close society and the
   prayer
They could never see at all: here is the full-stop.
And how it was drowned was by their own existence,
Not by water or earth, not by fire or air,
But their turds of sound and their stink of thought,
The thing they could not comprehend, the aristocratic
   spacious thing,
The treasure not hidden at all in any other place—
The warm priceless life, that they have destroyed
Unthinking: to be sure it was foreign, they did not hear of
   it
Nor feel its need on a beach trampled by sunbathers.
It could not be found in the file. And so, yes, it was
   shattered.
Today, it is quite attractive for an afternoon excursion,
And a haven for anglers, with their old desire to sleep;
And they, they all say, have paid their taxes.[6]

"They did not hear of it," naturally enough, because they had never learned Welsh, had never even learned of the existence of Welsh. For them, the village as a social, cultural entity was simply not there, and so it could be wiped out without guilt or anxiety. The "authorities" in London, the largely impersonal bureaucracy of the government administration, have remained and remain almost wholly unaware of the existence of Welsh and of its place in the history and tradition in the island of Britain. This lack of consciousness of who we are and who we have been in the course of our history on the part of so many people in Britain is part of a crisis of identity which afflicts the larger part of our predominantly English society. We need urgently to bring into consciousness elements of our own past and our own present which for too long we

[6] *Ibid.*, p. 207.

have ignored, if we are not to do irreparable damage to the fabric of our society. But if the tragedy of Capel Celyn seems in some ways a very local one, with a very specific application to late twentieth-century Britain, it is also universal. How many times has it been repeated over the last two hundred years, as the growth of industrial societies and the expansion of imperial languages has destroyed the places which preserved older and more fragile forms of human society? It is not surprising that when Welsh writers travel to North America or to Australia, they feel themselves instinctively drawn towards the plight of the indigenous peoples.

The poetry of Bobi Jones, who until 1989 was head of the Welsh department in the University College of Aberystwyth, is not always so overtly political. If we turn to the work of Gwyn Thomas, also a University professor, we find that the political commitment is there in his work, too, but usually expressed in ways that are implicit rather than explicit. The sense of the nearness of death is one of the primary characteristics of the Welsh language poets of the last fifty years. Their own linguistic situation has sharpened a perception which in one form or another is common enough in our North American/Western European world. A society which consistently puts financial interests before human ones can leave industrial areas to decay, no less than rural ones. So in a poem which dates from 1981, Gwyn Thomas meditates on "The Shut Down." It is common enough to contrast the industrial south of Wales, largely anglicized, with the rural north, where the Welsh language has held on more tenaciously. But the setting of this poem is most immediately one of the small quarrying towns of the industrial north, a place like Blaenau Ffestiniog, where the poet himself grew up. It is a place still predominantly Welsh in its speech but under constant pressure from outside. Here we see the situation through the eyes of someone who is inside it. There are television programmes in Welsh, but of course there are more of them in English. The graffiti on the Chapel walls, the symbol of the old non-conformist way of life, are in the original, written in English. Everything points to the end of an era, to the death of a society. The poem is, in this way, very precisely located. But it could refer to many places not only in Wales. The particular and the universal do not exclude one another.

> The factory's shutting down, and he's now fifty;
> A feeling of an ending comes, like soot falling,
> Dark about his heart.

And the future slams in his face.

A future on the dole in a poor place:
The son decides to join the army;
The daughter's looking for something in Birmingham,
Where his sister lives.
Houses for sale, shops closing down
And going to rack and ruin with those young men
Who take no pleasure in anything
But hanging about in pubs and breaking and destroying.
Even the chapel windows are full of holes,
And someone's been there painting, on the walls,
PUNKS RULE O.K. and profanities.

And on television every day—
Between chocolate dreams—
There are pictures of killing, hungry children dying,
And vicious people snarling.

And a nasty feeling grows on him,
Like a spider moving on the back of his neck,
That, soon, the whole show will be smashed.[7]

Not all Gwyn Thomas's poems have so strong an element of social comment as this. Many of them speak in a very personal and private way. But always what is personal is shown to have implications of a universal kind. One of his finest poems takes us into a day in autumn, when the reality of the passage of time and the inevitability of death suddenly confronts him in the midst of life's occupations. The poem ends with a Russian proverb, also used by Pasternak. In both poets there is a sense more implied than stated that the finitude and transitoriness of our life is held within an eternal reality which contains and redeems it. Life is not just a passage from past to future. It is also a passing over from time to eternity.

It was, that day,
September second.
And we're deciding, as a family,
To go to the seashore.

---

[7] Thomas, *Living a Life*, p. 87.

It was, that day,
Sunny but a trifle windy.
Across the big empty beach
The wind shook the shinings of sun,
Whistled its yellow across the sand,
And glittered the water as it ebbed in the distance.

And we began to do the things
That folks to at the shore—
Shovel sand;
Sit the baby down in its salty
Wonder; build a castle; kick a ball.
The boys even went, from a sense of obligation.
In bathing, cautiously.
But it was too cold, that day,
To stay long in the water.
And I stood watching.

They came out of the sea glistening, teeth chattering,
Laughing and splashing;
And then they're running in front of me
Across the wide strand
To their mother, to their sister,
To the shelter and the towels.
And I followed at a distance.
But crossing the shore, midway,
Here it struck me with a shock
That this happens only once;
This action won't ever, ever come back.

The moments just gone by are as firmly
Held as the Iron Age within eternity:
It's this sort of thing, our mortality.
And I felt a bit resentfully there and then—
This will never happen again.

But I kept on walking
And before long I came back
To the family,
To the fuss of drying off and changing,
To the noise of the present.
And between digging holes in the sand

And crunching a tomato sandwich
And trying to comfort the baby
That resentment passed away.

I had, as it happened,
My birthday that day:
Forty-one.

There's an old Russian proverb that says,
Life isn't crossing a field.
Right: it's crossing a shore.[8]

The Romanian Orthodox theologian, Dumitru Staniloae, loves to say that while it is inevitable that we die daily, there is a choice as to whether we die into death or die into life. In the perspective of the death and resurrection of Christ, the moment of death—and that is every moment—is always potentially open and not closed; it becomes a way through, it is no longer a dead end. The poet is far too discreet to spell all this out explicitly. But the contrast between "crossing a field" and "crossing a shore" is one which is full of latent possibilities of meaning. "Crossing a field" involves no more than a movement within our familiar world of space and time, of human action and consciousness. "Crossing a shore" suggests something more, for a shore is a place where one world meets another, quite specifically where the land meets the sea—the land, our native habitat, the place of human achievement and defeat; the sea, that symbol of immensity and the unknown, the place where we are no longer in control. To cross the shore as the poet does here is, as it were, to live in the presence of mortality, to recognise the reality of death. But it is also, at least implicitly, to see in that mortality the possibility of a greater reality, an eternal presence and an eternal life. The very fact that the poet does not state this in so many words is part of the source of the fineness and authority of his poem.

Gwyn Thomas is a writer acutely aware of "the flood of horror that is in our world," "the wretchedness and hatred and ugliness in it daily." In one of his most powerful poems, he comments very directly on the death of children in a terrorist incident in Belfast. But somehow he succeeds in not allowing this awareness of the darkness of our world to carry him into despair. He is a writer particularly sensitive to the lives of children. Some of the most delightful and humorous of his poems arise from the

[8] *Ibid.*, pp. 73-75.

amazed observation of the development of his own children. There are "songs of innocence" as well as "songs of experience" to be found in his work. In the last decade, his style has become more colloquial and relaxed. Many of the poems are written to be read aloud. Many would be particularly suitable for translation, since they speak so directly to our situation. The slim selection, published in 1982, certainly needs to be enlarged and diversified.

In *Negative Capability*, Nathan Scott speaks of the task of the poets as one of helping to reveal "the infinite depth and the radical mysteriousness of the human reality in the very disclosures that they bring to us of what is recalcitrantly finite in the world of the human creature. . . . It is, I believe, in some such way as this that the poetic experience is suffused, in its intensest modes, with an awareness of the world, in its concrete phenomenality, as a sacrament of the divine presence."[9]

It seems to me that it would be difficult to define more clearly what is the predominant quality of the Welsh poetic tradition from the beginning until today. This recognition through the limitations and finiteness of our human situation of its potential for an infinite depth, a radical mysteriousness, is present in an immense variety of ways. In our own century, poets as different as Saunders Lewis, Waldo Williams, Gwenallt and Euros Bowen have all written out of this underlying sense of the world as a sacrament of the divine presence. Perhaps because it has been denied a wide extension in terms of numbers and geography—because it has been, in some sense, constantly forced back on itself—the Welsh tradition has maintained an intense and astonishing sense of its own inner coherence, so that in its most contemporary utterance the remote past can sometimes draw very close to us. We are aware of the living presence of the past, of the experience of previous ages as a resource for human life now. But this is not only the presence of the past. It is also the presence of eternity: the sense that the whole world "in all its concrete phenomenality" is a sacrament of the divine presence which is never far away. Within what is finite, an infinite possibility is revealed.

Within a linguistic community of half a million people, an almost unbelievable wealth of poetic vision is articulated. Within a community which to all outward appearance is steadily dying, new possibilities of life are constantly emerging. From within the human spirit when it is

[9] Nathan Scott, *Negative Capability* (New Haven: Yale University Press, 1969), pp. 102-3.

touched by the Spirit of God, a new creation can come to birth. "The Wild Prayer of Longing" makes itself heard. Out of the moment of death there arises the sacrifice of praise and thanksgiving.

Nathan Scott, The Arts and Religious Journalism
LINDA-MARIE DELLOFF

From the late nineteenth century on, the number of Protestant religious general-interest magazines in the U.S. has increased dramatically. Virtually every denomination has published at least one, and a small number of nondenominational publications have also assumed important roles for Protestants—and for others who have been interested in learning more about American Protestantism by reading its publications. These magazines containing news, opinion, and, in some cases, spiritual guidance have existed quite apart from specialized and scholarly publications serving those with a professional or otherwise more analytical interest in various religious topics and questions. Presumably, the religious general-interest magazines have reflected the broadest spectrum of their readers' concerns and priorities.

One topic largely excluded from these publications, especially through the first third of the century, has been the arts and their relation to religious faith. The exceptions to this observation are notable because they are so few. One figure who did bring to a small number of these publications a vigorous message of the importance of art for religious belief was Nathan Scott—whose predominant, though not exclusive, focus was on the arts of the word. During the 1950s, Scott published numerous articles in these magazines, reaching outside the usual scholarly forums and thereby bringing his theories to a far larger audience than would otherwise have been the case. Indeed, some of his most imaginative and innovative criticism appeared in such magazines—in some cases to be revised as content for his major books. While he is more well known for those books, and for his other scholarly publications, one might suggest that he made an equally important contribution—and a unique one—by writing as much as he did for non-academic journals as well. This is an aspect of his career that has been heretofore unremarked. Nor, unfortunately, did his efforts in this regard stimulate any ongoing tradition of regular serious treatment of the arts by religious magazines.

Early in the twentieth century, even the most widely read and influential church magazines either ignored the arts completely or occasionally ran a brief book review if the subject seemed particularly "relevant." The more prominent denominational journals included the *Christian Advocate* (Methodist; many regional varieties existed at various times, the most important of which was published in New York; in 1940, this became the official denominational weekly); the *Congregationalist* (earlier and later called *Advance*); and the *Christian Observer* (Presbyterian). For the most part, these publications focused on church business, inspirational material, and, upon occasion, social issues such as prohibition.

Typically, when these publications did comment on the arts at all, it was in a brief notice of a popular novel in a review section dominated by books on churchly or social topics. For example, the *Christian Advocate* featured a section called "Our Book Table" (later "Methodists Ought to Read," then "Methodists and their Reading"). Most of the reviews therein were brief and unimaginative, and the editors made no general pronouncements of interest in the arts.

The case was similar with the other papers. In the *Congregationalist*'s book column, a 1921 notice in all seriousness designated *Moby Dick* as simply "a realistic story of whaling."[1] From time to time, this journal's editors seemed interested in the topic of religious drama, but they also issued statements like the following: "Will the stage degrade the spiritual . . . ? It is earnestly to be hoped that they will subordinate the art to its spiritual end, the properties to the proprieties, and the scenic effects to the religious results. But it is easy to cheapen by the misuse of the dramatic."[2]

Like other religious publications early in the century, the *Congregationalist* did run a "Favorite Poems" column, usually featuring explicitly religious or highly sentimental verse. The *Christian Observer* (published by Southern Presbyterians and taking a conservative stance on many issues) sometimes reviewed "Christian fiction," most often stories containing an obvious and simplistic "pious purpose." As with the other magazines, its editors were concerned that "its editorial pages

---

[1] The *Congregationalist*, September 29, 1921, p. 412.
[2] *Ibid.*, December 22, 1921, p. 812.

cover the more important activities of our Church and the religious world."[3] And this publication that claimed "more readers than any other Presbyterian Church paper in the World"[4] did not include art as an important element in that world.

In the first years of the nondenominational journal, *Christianity & Crisis*, which Reinhold Niebuhr founded in 1941, there was little emphasis on art. In one of its earliest issues, the journal's writers observed that they would "begin occasional brief surveys of literature. . . . The fields to be covered are international relations, theology, and domestic and social problems."[5] Later, *Christianity & Crisis* began to devote more space to the arts, but this interest was not a part of the magazine's early identity, nor has it ever assumed much prominence.

Alone among Protestant periodicals during almost the first half of the century, the nondenominational *Christian Century* displayed an interest in the arts—essentially from its "refounding" in 1908 by Disciples of Christ minister Charles Clayton Morrison (the paper became "undenominational" in 1916). Not only was the *Century's* consistent emphasis on art a radical departure from the practice of contemporary church journals, but, at the time, Morrison initiated his endeavor, there was as yet little academic interest in the relations between art and faith. Seminaries or divinity schools that included any study of art in their curricula were practically non-existent.

The *Century* writers expressed their views in major articles, editorials, series, and reviews; the journal also established a long (and continuing) tradition of publishing poetry. While they discussed music, sculpture, drama, and painting, the editors emphasized the literary arts more than any other. In this regard, the magazine in 1924 defined its chosen task: "For many years [the *Century*] has recognized its mission to be in considerable measure the interpretation of the best in books and the conveyance of the best books most advantageously to those who are set to lead the thought of our American communities."[6] The leaders invoked here were primarily understood to be pastors of local churches.

Among books favored by the *Century*, a special place was reserved for novels and poetry, especially the latter. For it was the editors' conclusion that "the things that are best worth saying can never be completely said in direct and categorical terms. Hence the need of poetry. . . . Great

---

[3] *Ibid.*, February 2, 1927, p. 23.
[4] *Ibid.*, p. 26.
[5] *Christianity & Crisis* (hereafter *C&C*), May 19, 1941, p. 2
[6] *Christian Century* (hereafter *CC*), October 23, 1924, p. 1359.

truths can be grasped and expressed only in imaginative form."[7] Because of their command of the imagination—the supreme human faculty, according to Morrison—poets and other artists are the public's "real leaders."[8]

In a 1924 editorial, "Religion as an Art," the editors summed up their artistic credo: "God as artist has been working through the age . . . filling the world with a beauty which is biologically superfluous, but spiritually necessary. . . . Man has no higher privilege than that of being, like Him, an artist both appreciative and creative."[9]

The early *Christian Century* editors deserve a great deal of credit for their insistence on the importance of art and its kinship with religious faith. However, there were serious limitations to their understanding of the arts. In general, their attitude was characterized by a profound ambivalence: on the one hand, high regard for art's salvific powers; on the other, sharp condemnation of much art being produced at the time. The editors, it seems, were hampered by a pervasive and stringent moralism that prevented them from appreciating many of the new artistic developments whose moral meaning was either unclear or, they decided, unacceptable (for example, sexual explicitness in the work of James Joyce). Furthermore, consistent with the social gospel and mainline Protestant thinking in general, they shied away from art that could be interpreted as too "sophisticated" for the common person, of which a prime example was the poetry of T. S. Eliot. Thus, the editors exhibited decided preferences for the classics: Bach, Beethoven, Shakespeare, the Romantic poets. When they favored a contemporary artist, it was apt to be a safely moralistic figure such as the poet Edwin Markham, or one whose artistic experiments they considered benign: Vachel Lindsay, for example.

It was not until the 1950s that the *Christian Century* began to display more openness to new artistic developments and to those whose work earlier editors had eschewed for its moral ambiguities: Faulkner, Joyce, even Sinclair Lewis (whose jibes at religion they could not tolerate). Also during the '50s, *Christianity & Crisis* began to include more pieces on the arts. Neither publication, however, ever revealed the conscious interest and dedication to the arts that informed the identity of *motive*, the publication of the Methodist Student Movement beginning in 1941. Interested

---

[7] *Ibid.*, September 14, 1924, p. 1134.
[8] *Ibid.*, April 29, 1920, p. 5.
[9] *Ibid.*, September 14, 1920, p. 1135.

primarily in the visual arts, *motive*'s editors included frequent features on the topic, as well as illustrating their pages with examples of original art by such talents as Margaret Rigg and Walter Hodgell.

Nathan Scott was a crucial figure for *Christianity & Crisis*, the *Christian Century*, and *motive*, especially during the 1950s, when some of his most original and pungent analyses of the relations between the arts and religion appeared in these three publications. Nor were Scott's contributions to these periodicals mere "outtakes" from his scholarly endeavors; rather, they were consciously targeted to the particular audiences addressed, in some cases later finding their way into his more academic treatises. He neither condescended to these magazine readers nor wrote "above" them. He took them seriously, respecting their intelligence but not making inappropriate assumptions concerning their knowledge or experience. These audiences included pastors, church workers, and a variety of other individuals interested in the relations between faith and culture.

Of the many contributions Scott made in his journalistic forays, three features stand out in their importance. First, he sought to articulate bold generalizations concerning recent developments in arts and letters, to discuss sweeping trends, and to draw broad summary strokes in order to give his readers a comprehensive outline of the current cultural and religious scene. Second, he went beyond analysis and description to prescription, prophecy, and exhortation. He spoke not only about the church and about artists; he also spoke to them. Like his implicit view that magazine journalism is of equal value with scholarly work, his exhortatory declamations evidenced a pastoral outlook as well as reflecting a rigorous theoretical base. Third, some of Scott's magazine articles broke new ground in original and innovative criticism, defying and challenging the conventional wisdom of contemporary religious thinking and occasionally that of the secular journalistic critics. In all of these efforts, Scott was vigilantly concerned to go beyond the work to the wider world, to assure that his readers understood the larger context of both art and religious faith.

A revealing example of Scott's efforts to scribe such a large panorama is "The Personal Principle in Recent Literature and its Religious Implication," appearing in *motive* in 1955. Wasting no time, he proclaims for the reader in the article's initial sentence that "we are moving into a new phase of development in the history of the modern imagination,"[10] a

---

[10] *motive*, May 1955, p. 19.

phase which, he later tells us, insists "ever more determinedly upon the primacy of the private life and the preciousness of personal relations."[11] Along with this new personal emphasis, writers were developing a radically new style as well, one

> which suggests that they no longer live under the dispensation of Hemingway but rather live now under the dispensation of the magisterial figure of Henry James. The new prose is very far indeed from the terse, tight-lipped telegraphy of Hemingway which was for so long the normative speech for the writer of our time, though it by no means represents a reaction toward a new baroque extravagance of diction. It springs rather from a renewed delight in the vivacious and brilliant processes through which the intellect asserts itself in imaginative literature, and it is characterized by the kind of richly personal complexity of style that is perhaps the common signature shared by such otherwise different writers as Peter Taylor and William Goyen, Flannery O'Connor and Jean Stafford, Truman Capote and Frederick Buechner.[12]

In sketching such large pictures, Scott always made pertinent comparisons, helping the reader to understand the importance of the new trend. In this article he contrasts the new "personal principle" with the type of writing normally expected during a post-war period. "We assume, of course, that . . . every postwar literature expresses the disenchantment, the defeatism, the despair, the sense of nullity, or whatever else it is that constitutes the predominant mood in the time that follows the time of anarchy and turbulence."[13]

In further delineating the context of the personal principle's significance, Scott draws parallels with recent Christian philosophy influenced by "the remarkably penetrating Jewish existentialist Martin Buber."[14] By the time the reader has completed the short (five-page) article, she understands not only what Scott sees to be the most original development in contemporary fiction, but also how it differs from the developments of other post-war periods, and how it parallels certain trends in philosophy, theology, and social analysis.

In another provocative article of the period, "Beneath the Hammer of Truth," appearing in *Christianity & Crisis* (later to become a chapter in his book, *Modern Literature and the Religious Frontier*), Scott outlines why it

---

[11] *Ibid.*, p. 20.
[12] *Ibid.*
[13] *Ibid.*, p. 19.
[14] *Ibid.*, p. 20.

was, above all, the literature of the time—and not the philosophy or the social science—that best captured "the deepest issues of our perplexity." He describes "the new congeniality"[15] of faith to literature and suggests several reasons for this new receptivity, especially as it contrasts with earlier stances: "This skepticism was never well-founded, being rooted not so much in theological principles as in a comfortable social-economic situation that closeted the Protestant consciousness from the bitter realities of the iron time which the modern artist was exploring. But the events of recent history have not only broken an earlier complacency about the human enterprise but have also compelled us to undertake deeper explorations of the meaning of the Christian faith itself—so that, the full implications of Gethsemane having been re-possessed, the austere and tragic vision of the great poets and novelists of our period is no longer the offense that it once was."[16]

In "The Meaning of the Incarnation for Modern Literature," also published in *Christianity & Crisis*, Scott proposes and analyzes another trait of Protestantism that had heretofore divorced it from its natural union with the arts. "Aside from the various socio-cultural factors that account for the historic divorce between Protestant Christianity and the arts, I suspect that the chief reason for our sense of being today without any radically Christian principles of aesthetic judgment in the Protestant community is to be found in what has for too long been our habit of withdrawing in alarm from the doctrine of the Incarnation."[17]

In virtually every instance of his journalistic prose, Scott goes beyond his description and analysis of current trends in art and faith to prescribe what the church ought to and ought not to do, and/or what artists ought to and ought not to do, to maximize the potential for their meaningful interaction. Thus, in "The Meaning of the Incarnation," he indicates the "deep need for a deep restoration of confidence in the stoutness and reliability and essential healthiness of the things of the earth—such a confidence, that is, as will permit the practitioner of a mimetic art really to look at the world instead of recoiling from it, and such a confidence as it is precisely the genius of an Incarnational faith to provide."[18]

In "Beneath the Hammer of Truth, " he also follows his initial mapmaking with some admonitions. First, what religious people must *not* do is to assume "a proprietary air about the Christian renascence in litera-

---

[15]   *C&C*, October 1, 1956, p. 124.
[16]   *Ibid.*
[17]   *C&C*, December 8, 1958, p. 173.
[18]   *Ibid.*, p. 174.

ture."[19] What that literature requires instead is "not any form of adulatory enshrinement—which would, in any event, hardly be a sufficiently active response to it—but rather the most rigorous questioning to which it can be submitted by the faith in which both we and its authors find the greatest illumination of the deep places of human life."[20] The goal is a prophetic one: "And if we succeed in bringing the Christian faith into a genuinely dialogical relationship with modern literature, so that art may speak to religion and religion to art, we may in due time get a renewal and a deepening of both."[21]

In "Faith and Art in a World Awry," appearing in *motive* (and in 1966 becoming an important part of his book *The Broken Center*), Scott says a good deal more about what the church should and should not do. The Christian thinker "had better not come prancing into the forums of our cultural life with a Christian system of aesthetics or with a Christian system of psychology or with a Christian system of anything else. For the world is one, the same for the Christian as for all other men of whatever persuasian: if Christ is truly the Logos, then He is witnessed to in all apprehensions of truth, whether they occur within a framework of Christian concern or not. And, this being the case, the Christian theologian will not be in a hurry to sponsor any particular system as the necessarily Christian way of ordering the data in a given field of inquiry."[22]

It is "the most outrageous kind of arrogance" for the Christian "even to attempt to produce some special *speculum mentis* for his brethren in the faith" because it indicates a profound misunderstanding of "the nature of the intellectual situation in which he must today do his work."[23] Instead, says Scott, again invoking Buber's "I-Thou" concept, the "fragmentation of modern intellectual life commits us irrevocably to an ethos of encounter and to the stance of attentiveness and listening."[24]

Scott is quite specific about how the Christian can undertake this encounter. "The task of those who are custodians of the Christian faith in our time is not, I think, to invent something called a Christian philosophy of art, and thus to add to the Babel of conflicting philosophies which so much oppresses us today. We shall want, I should think, a vigorous Christian criticism in the various fields of art. . . . For that which is, I be-

[19]   *C&C*, October 1, 1956, p. 126.
[20]   *Ibid.*
[21]   *Ibid.*
[22]   *motive*, November 1961, p. 23.
[23]   *Ibid.*, p. 22.
[24]   *Ibid.*, p. 23.

lieve, most needed is for theological interpreters to keep the Church alive to what it is in the nature of its own faith that requires it to be attentive to all the somber reports and prophecies and maledictions that the arts in our time are uttering."[25]

In another *motive* article, "Art and the Renewal of Human Sensibility in Mass Society," Scott analyzes and then calls into question the current social criticism of writers such as William Whyte in *The Organization Man* and David Riesman in *The Lonely Crowd*, works that assume "that we are all involved in the malaise of an enveloping totalitarianism from which no escape is possible; it does not focus upon a particular flaw in our societal structure, but, rather, it calls into question the whole fabric and design of contemporary society."[26]

He is careful to specify what bothers him about these works. "It is not, I think, the extremist character of contemporary criticism that is to be objected to—but, rather, it is the fatalism that it sometimes entails,"[27] a fatalism manifestly at odds with the religious promise. Against this fatalism, Christians must "exert a new pressure." In order to apply this pressure with any hope of success, theology must cooperate with the arts. For the first goal in combating hopelessness is to define a "theology of the imagination, the issue concerning how the imaginative style of a people may be renewed and reinvigorated at the concrete level of sensibility and lifestyle"—i.e., in order to combat the incipient nihilism of the social critics whom Scott has cited. And since "it is not within the competence of the theologian as theologian to deal directly with the order of sensibility," the church must enlist the help and cooperation of the artist. This is so because what the authentic artist is "concerned above all else to do is to make us see the fundamental order of the world"[28]—the same order that informs the substance of religious faith.

Thus Scott challenges the religious community "to enter a new and hitherto largely untried collaboration with the whole community of the modern arts" with the goal of deriving "a theology of the imagination that will be relevant to the spiritual crisis of the present time," a theology that ultimately may help to redeem the time by renewing and reinvigorating the human imagination now stultified by life in a mass society.[29]

[25] *Ibid.*, p. 28.
[26] *motive*, November 1960, p. 31.
[27] *Ibid.*
[28] *Ibid.*, p. 32.
[29] *Ibid.*, p. 34.

Nor does Scott neglect to speak directly to the artists concerning what might be their most helpful role in the redemptive project. In a *Christian Century* review article of Graham Greene's *The Quiet American*, he chides Greene for his shallow anti-Americanism but also, and more broadly and more significantly, for his misuse of both his talent and his religious sensibility. "Thus it is that the premises upon which Mr. Greene's imagination functions are such as to make him the rather curious figure he is: the leading Catholic novelist in the English-speaking world who today seems bent on using his art as a vehicle for the espousal of a romantic diabolism just as perverse and morally problematic as the dandyism of the late nineteenth-century decadents, of whom he puts us once again in mind." Scott concludes that "this is not, of course, in our time a very promising position, either religiously or aesthetically, and it is to be hoped that, in the future stages of his development, Mr. Greene will make his way beyond it."[30]

In "The Example of George Orwell," in *Christianity & Crisis*, Scott praises Orwell for his "radical humanitarianism" but locates the explanation for the novelist's ultimate gloom—as exemplified especially in *1984*—in the fact that he was "a Christian who had lost his Christianity." "May it not be that the attitude of utter horror with which he confronted the un-future of the modern world was in fact a result of his having been prepared to believe so little about what is ultimately possible for human existence?"[31]

Just as Scott saw help for the Christian endeavor in the work of artists, he also saw in the Christian faith succor for the nihilism infecting many artists. Articulating a condition, not a judgment, he concludes of Orwell that "having spoken of him as an exemplary figure for our period, it now becomes possible for me to specify just what he was an example *of*—and it is, I should say, the vulnerability of even the shrewdest and most knowledgeable secular liberalism before the rough and ungovernable weathers of modern history."[32]

The reader departs even such brief commentaries with the satisfaction of not simply having been informed regarding the artistic dilemmas of the day, but of learning, further, that this critic has specific suggestions for amelioration. It is a gratifying and fulfilling feeling—that the writer is consistently attempting to move beyond the text to the person of the

[30]   *CC*, August 1, 1956, p. 902.
[31]   *C&C*, July 20, 1959, p. 110.
[32]   *Ibid.*

artist and the person of the observer. And that finally he leaves the reader in the larger world in which the artwork is, certainly, but one discreet effort, yet one which may ultimately be seen as part of a larger project. This larger project, taken collectively, may actually offer some hope for the human condition.

It is no facile accomplishment to compress this much information within the scope of, and in the appropriate vocabulary of, a magazine article. Yet Scott was able to distill and summarize his agenda (while retaining his distinctive flowing style) such that the reader does not feel manipulated, i.e., the victim of a cryptic book summary. Presumably, one thinks, he elaborates upon these ideas in his books and longer articles, but he does not stint substance in the shorter, less theoretical offerings.

Indeed, some of Scott's brief review and commentary pieces make for downright exciting reading—the recognition that one has stumbled across truly ground-breaking criticism. A dramatic case in point was his 1957 *Christian Century* comment on the exceedingly controversial film, *Baby Doll*, directed by Elia Kazan from the Tennessee Williams play. Writing at a time when the sexually explicit and psychologically murky film "has thrown the country into a furor," Scott proceeds not to rip the work apart, as was the case with many other contemporary reviewers, and as was no doubt the expectation of his readers. Instead, he argues that critics had simply misunderstood the film, "as though what were central in Williams was a violent naturalism whose sole aim, in this instance was to dredge some dark cul-de-sac of southern life for the vilest scatological material it contains, and then serve it up for the titillation of the pornological mind."[33]

Williams, Scott protests, was not "serving up the realistic slice of life" but was using the material "for his wild and fantastic drollery and not for the sake of the prurient peep show." Indeed, ". . . the major point to be made, it seems to me, is that the ribaldry, unsalacious as it really is, is utilized for the sake of what it is often Williams' major purpose to do; namely to laugh at the very notion that human life might have a dimension of tragic significance." Accordingly, Scott reviews the movie "not as a pornographic exhibit . . . but as a comic grotesque."[34] His long and sensitive analysis, probing issues that had not occurred to other reviewers, is a masterpiece of provocative, creative criticism. (It is also an early instance of these publications' according to film an equally sustained and serious treatment as that accorded other artforms.)

[33]   CC, January 23, 1957, p. 310.
[34]   *Ibid.*

Also in the *Christian Century* that year, Scott published a review article of Faulkner's *The Town* which was notable for its departure from the
views of earlier *Century* critics, who had regarded the novelist as presenting a dour and perverse picture of reality. "Faulkner's role among us has
the very special exemplary quality," he argues, indicating that he
"continues to be in full possession of the most astonishing novelistic gift
of this century."[35] Read now, this evaluation seems unremarkable; but
considering the widespread distaste of that era's mainline Protestantism
for the perceived darkness and dankness of Faulkner's vision, its bold-
ness and confidence are to be noted.

It would, of course, be impossible to trace any direct influence from
Scott's innovative criticism—on his readers, his editors, or other writers.
In general, his articles did not seem to inspire any enduring increase in
these magazines' coverage of the arts. *motive* ceased publication in 1970
(for reasons having more to do with church politics than with its stance
toward the arts), though in any case, it had always tended to focus more
on visual forms than on those of the word. The *Christian Century* and
Christianity & Crisis both continue in publication, and both feature occasional pieces dealing with the arts, but that topic is not a major component of either journal's basic identity.

Simultaneous with the period of Scott's most frequent journalistic
pieces, the *Century* also offered regular drama reviews by Tom Driver,
who, while teaching at New York City's Union Theological Seminary,
wrote a weekly drama column conveying the highlights of new
Broadway plays to readers all across the country who would probably
never have the opportunity to see them. Driver was a perceptive and
careful critic who, like Scott, brought considerable theological insight to
his writing on the arts. Also like Scott, Driver reviewed works that
clashed with the longstanding preferences exhibited by the Morrison-
trained editors, who were strongly of the conviction that art must deliver
a positive moral message. Driver liked Shaw, he liked Brecht; he wrote
probing reviews of such new plays as John Osborne's *Look Back in Anger*,
the works of Dylan Thomas, Beckett's *Endgame*, Friedrich Durrenmatt's
The Visit ("a master-piece"),[36] Genet's *Deathwatch*, Williams's *Sweet Bird
of Youth* ("his best play");[37] did a humorous review attacking *The Sound of*

---

[35] *CC*, September 23, 1957, p. 1104.
[36] *Ibid.*, June 4, 1958, p. 688.
[37] *Ibid.*, April 15, 1959, p. 455.

Music as lightweight, and another calling *The Miracle Worker* "mock profundity."[38]

As the '60s opened, Driver reviewed Camus's *Caligula* and Genet's *The Balcony*, which he daringly called "the best play now running in New York."[39] He also wrote on Ionesco's *Rhinocerous*, Pinter's *The Caretaker*, and Williams's *Night of the Iguana*, which he found to be suffused with "a realism pregnant with spiritual yearning."[40] On trips abroad, he introduced the *Century* audience to a wide variety of European drama.

This period of regularly featured inventive criticism in the *Century* was short-lived—losing steam with the 1960 departure of the magazine's managing editor, Theodore Gill, who had provided strong encouragement for such efforts. In the early '60s, Driver's regular reviews ceased to appear; he withdrew of his own accord, but no replacement was sought for his frequent commentary.

After that time, Nathan Scott's journalistic contributions became less frequent as well, and he moved more fully into the publication of his numerous scholarly projects. In a general evaluation of Scott's complete corpus, it is certainly, first, his books and, then, his many scholarly articles for which he is most known. But any assessment of his seminal contribution to the examination of the relations between art and faith must also include his important work in the area of religious journalism.

---

[38] *Ibid.*, December 16, 1960, p. 1470.
[39] *Ibid.*, May 4, 1960, p. 546.
[40] *Ibid.*, February 17, 1962, p. 169.

The Grandeur of Humanity:
The Lure of Ideal Form in Classical Greece, The Renaissance, and Abstract Expressionism

JOHN DILLENBERGER

Throughout most of Western history, as Sir Kenneth Clark forcefully pointed out in *The Nude: A Study in Ideal Form*, human spirituality was conveyed either through the beauty of the human figure as an exercise that expressed human perfection, or through the corruptibility and pathos of the still inherently ideal human figure. But in the modern period, the conjunction, on the one hand, of beauty and perfection, and on the other, of corruptibility and form, dissolved. In the first instance, the belief in beauty, now devoid of ultimacy or perfection, and in the second instance, the belief in human corruptibility, now expressed without the dignity of form, resulted in an amalgam that turned human spirituality into sentimentality. Therefore the dignity of humanity, formerly associated with perfection or with corruptibility, was lost.

In the mid-twentieth century, the full dignity of humanity was reaffirmed in the conjunction of the first pair, beauty and perfection. But how ironic that the struggle to recover the spirituality and grandeur of humanity should occur, not through the depiction of the human figure, but through total abstraction as an exercise which connected grandeur, perfection, and beauty. In this sense, some of the Abstract Expressionist artists, particularly Barnett Newman (Plate 1), stand in the tradition of classical Greece (Plate 2) and the Renaissance (Plate 3) in the enterprise of connecting the perfection of beauty with the wholeness and grandeur of humanity.

Powerful and influential as these three moments have been, they represent special and short-lived moments in the history of art. Indeed,

Plate 1
"The Way No. 2" by Barnett Newman

Reproduced courtesy of Annalee Newman
insofar as her rights are concerned.

Plate 2
Polyclitus, "Doryphorus" (450-440 B.C.E.)
Roman copy, National Archeological Museum, Naples

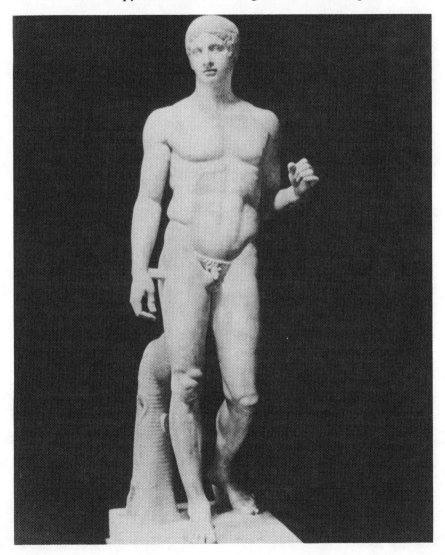

Reproduced courtesy of Alinari/Art Resource, New York.

Plate 3
Michelangelo Buonarroti,
"The Risen Christ" (1519–20) Rome; Santa Maria Sopra Minerva

Reproduced courtesy of Alinari/Art Resource, New York.

though the Western world prized classical Greece and the Renaissance, most of its history is either a derivative of that tradition or a following of what Clark has called "the alternative convention," that is, the Gothic impulse, in which the human form and its corruptibility are conjoined. By contrast, the zenith of Classical Greece, the Renaissance, and Abstract Expressionism lasted only a few decades. Preparations for these movements, and subsequent periods that lived off their accomplishments, comprised hundreds of years. We need not say that the brief periods were better; we need only to try to understand what was happening. It seems as if beauty, perfection, and a grand view of life coinhered only at brief moments in history, that such periods could not sustain themselves. That grand view of humanity was an echo and an imitation of creation or the creator, with the attendant dangers of such an identification; it was a conscious extension of nature, nothing less than an approximation of the God-like.

Not readily recognized by theologians is the fact that the preoccupation with the grandeur of humanity in classical Greece and the Renaissance held an awareness of something imaged beyond the self together with the recognition that humans only partially participated in that ideal. Even the theologian Paul Tillich was ambiguous on this point. While a chaplain at the Front in the throes of World War I, Tillich had an ecstatic experience when he saw Botticelli's *Madonna with Singing Angels*, finding it an anchor in the midst of the ugliness of war and psychic disorientation. But later he declared the religious significance of the Renaissance paintings to be meager. He was convinced that Renaissance painting stylistically suggested the secular rather than the God-like; so he focused instead on paintings that disclosed the disruption of the human condition; that is, he was more comfortable with "the alternative convention." Perhaps a similar instinct led him to prefer the archaic Greek works to the classical sculptures.

It has been suggested that classical Greece and facets of the Renaissance saw the human figure as the direct expression of human life in terms of an ideal beauty and perfection that placed humans between the realm of the gods and heaven, on the one hand, and the ordinary particular and finite form of the human body, on the other. In classical Greek sculpture, the body expressed harmony, for it was based on specific mathematical equations. Thus the female nude figure was depicted as having the same distance between the breasts, as from the breasts to the navel, and as from the navel to the pubic zone. In such a scheme, the square and the circle meet in the human figure, as illustrated in

Vitruvius. The Gothic nude, by contrast, has an ovoid form in which the distance between the breasts and the navel has almost doubled. It is surely not accidental that the Greek temple and the Greek gods, who exemplify the human ideal, have placed that harmony in our midst; it is surely not accidental that the Gothic body, with its elongated torso, typifies the architectural Gothic impulse that reaches upward, or represents another world in the midst of our earthly world.

Harmony and perfection as the expression of beauty demands that we abdicate canons of beauty that focus on parts of the anatomy, as in calendar art or in photographic poses. Instead, the beauty is an expression of the whole. Hence, the muscular armature is conveyed beneath the skin. Beauty is then not shapely but the shapes that fundamentally disclose the structure.

But two additional ingredients take us beyond the harmonies of the Greek body. First, the body expresses the harmony which it has, for example, in athletic pursuits or in affairs of the polis. Second, theories of harmony as well as the expression of harmony in the action of the human body are focused through the genius of the artist, a compounding into a whole which is more than the sum of the parts through a gift that borders on creation itself.

While recent Renaissance scholarship has deemphasized its classical dependence, the evidence is overwhelming that the rediscovery of classical sculpture did play a role in the Renaissance. Surely, this is evident in the early sculpture and in the painting of Michelangelo. While the cleaning of the Sistine ceiling makes it clear that Michelangelo no longer can be understood as a sculptor whose paintings are a translation from sculpture, the cleaning leaves intact the perceived volume of the figures. Ironically, the sculptural forms, now disclosed with incandescent color, appear analogous to Greek sculpture at a time when its painted colors were still visible.

Whether, with respect to the Sistine ceiling, one centers on the creation of the world, on the creation of Adam and Eve, or the expulsion from Paradise, the ingredients are the same as in classical Greece. First, there is a concentration in which form and perfection define beauty; second, a depicted drama that defines our existence; and third, the alchemy of the artist, whose liberties of genius disclose an imaginative Promethean psyche that skirts making the artist the creator. Surely it is Michelangelo's recognition of such Promethean facets that led him, as his faith changed, to change his art in his old age, though one should not say that the later works are consequently either better or worse.

Short-lived as the height of classical Greece and the Renaissance were, the power of their figural creations continue to haunt us, not only as periods that had their own life into which we could enter for our own enrichment, but also as an ethos in which the artistic process was to continue. While there were exceptions, by the time of the early twentieth century the heritage of Greece and the Renaissance had degenerated to sentimentality, or had generated a situation of revolt.

Abstract Expressionism, like classical Greece and the Renaissance, was a radical new creation in which grandeur and the sublime defined the human, but in Abstract Expressionism the sublime is without reference to the human figure or the gods or God. Moreover, its ingredients were the same as those of classical Greece and the Renaissance, as Barnett Newman himself indicated ("The Sublime is Now," *The Tiger's Eye*, #6 [December 1948]). In their perfection, Newman's canvasses hide the disciplined application of layers of paint. Their resonances of beauty reside in the studied modulations and adjacencies of color. Nor are they without the mathematical awareness of the circle and the square in their approximation of the human. But the canvasses also represent Newman's fiercely held conviction of the grandeur of humanity, a grandeur that is the basis even of tragedy. That conviction was anchored neither in a vision of the gods nor of a specific religion, but in the creative urge that defines humans on this planet, leading Newman to declare that the first human was an artist. That declaration places humans again on that border between transworldly and this-worldly dimensions, that is, dangerously and wonderfully near to what is represented by the gods. Moreover, in Newman as in classical Greece and the Renaissance, the artistic talent stretches and transforms both his artistic means and his convictions into an art form that stands on its own, a veritable creation.

Thus, in three relatively short-lived periods of history—two in terms of the human figure, one for the sake of the human—form as beauty succeeded in expressing the wholeness of humanity, a reality recognized as characteristic of ourselves even as none of us directly expresses or approximates it, either in our own lives or in artistic imitation. For most of Christian history, however, sorrow and pity, rather than wholeness, defined the iconographical agenda of art. Yet the ideals of Greece and the Renaissance persisted, a lure that could not be resisted, as in nineteenth-century Neo-Classicism. When the tradition of sorrow and pity had run its course in the late nineteenth century, it was as if only imitations of Greek and Renaissance, that enterprise which ended in sentimentality, was a possible avenue. It was for that reason that the revolt against late nineteenth- and early twentieth-century art was a conscious rejection of classical Greece and the Renaissance. In that period neither the perfection of form nor the alternative convention of sorrow and pity was possible. Different approaches were required; hence, art disclosed distortion without pity and forms that were consciously ugly. The concern with the past, which is also a part of the human scene, turned to primitive and less-Western cultures in the attempt to find a new vocabulary for art.

Barnett Newman, who had worked in the vocabulary of the primitive, Indian cultures, and ornithological explorations, abandoned all such attempts. Although they provided relief from the banality of nineteenth-century art, he felt they did not express the grandeur of humanity as developed in Western history. So, for him, a new creation, like creation itself, was required. That new creation took the form of total abstraction, at once free from the past and yet expressing every resonance of the human pilgrimage within it.

For those for whom art was the expression of the human figure, ranging from ideal form to transformations of the human figure, abstraction was anything but the reconstitution of the human figure or humanity. Yet elements of abstraction had always been a part of art, except for classical Greece and the Renaissance.

In the aftermath of the radical concern to express the grandeur of humanity in classical Greece, the Renaissance, and Abstract Expressionism, we need to retrain our eyes in ways that allow for abstraction that also echoes figuration and figuration that includes abstraction. Certainly, much of art in our time combines figuration and abstraction in ways not known to us before. In that venture, both the concern for figural form and for abstraction combine to give us both the grandeur of humanity and its fragility, its health and its sickness unto death.

Whatever Happened to the Catholic Novel?
A Study in Genre
MARY GERHART

Wherever religion has distinguished itself from aesthetics and in societies where literature has declared its autonomy from religion, scholars have been required to tell what the relationship of religion to literature is. One cogent response has been given by Nathan A. Scott, Jr. He has suggested several ways in which religion informs literature and through which literature, in turn, warrants an exposition of the sacred.

Nathan Scott's work both celebrates the presence of the sacred—whether this presence is muted or prominent—and takes notice of the absence of the sacred, in whatever mode that absence has been rendered. So extensive has been the evocation of the religious in literature of the modern period by scholars such as Scott, that many readers cannot read modern literature without hearing some religious thematization, some classical concept which at once illuminates the present by means of something known (however partially) in the past, and contemporizes the past by means of something known (however immediate) in the present. In his *Poetry as Civic Virtue*, having called into question any kind of transcendence that is outside the "dialogical world of human life," he argued, for example, that the polis can be understood as "time's covenant." By this apt phrase, Scott marked the turn from the "supernatural" to the "life of the human City" as the arena of the sacred and from a time- and race-bound notion of Covenant to one that is rooted in the "nature of our common humanity."[1] Such mediation between classical concept and

[1] Nathan A. Scott, Jr., *The Poetry of Civic Virtue: Eliot, Malraux, Auden* (Philadelphia: Fortress, 1976).

modern text creates an analogy sufficiently stable that readers are able to inhabit a world of common meaning and explore the interstices of that world, built on remnants of material retrieved from the past.

The advent of deconstruction, however, meant that this method of relating religion and literature would come under principled attack. Censure used to come from scholars, either religious or literary, who suspected that some kind of preconceived Christian perspective was being imposed on the text. If they allowed the question of religious meaning to arise, they preferred to explicate the religious significance of texts in terms of general religious concepts rather than historical themes. Today, however, the deconstructionists argue that the presence of meaning, its location either in the text or in the method of approach, is an illusion.

The contributions and limitations of the deconstructionist position have been well documented elsewhere, and we need not prolong or repeat that debate. Instead, we will turn to a process by which meanings become relatively stabilized without being reified, while at the same time, radically destabilized without becoming indeterminate. By means of genric analysis, we can trace the process by which a group of texts together constitute a literary monument,[2] a recognized element (including both classics and period pieces) in a literary canon. Frequently this process yields a literary history of texts whose genre has been completed: that is, as defined, the genre has ceased to produce new major texts that are candidates for becoming classics, even while the genre continues to produce meanings.

The genre Catholic novel[3] is a good candidate for investigating the process of the completion of a genre and its transformation into a literary

---

[2] The term "monument" harks back to Friedrich Nietzsche's use of the term in his essay, *On the Advantages and Disadvantages of History for Life* (trans. Peter Preuss [New York: Hackett Publishing Co., 1980]), and suggests the possibility of both a positive and a negative valuation. Monument is also distinct from and related to the notion of classic, as in David Tracy's and Frank Kermode's use of the term (see David Tracy, *The Analogical Imagination: Christian Theology and the Culture of Pluralism* [New York: Crossroad, 1981] and Frank Kermode, *The Classic: Literary Images of Permanence and Change* [New York: Viking Press, 1975]). Classic refers to texts; monument, to genres. I am indebted to A. M. Russell, Marianne Sawicki, and David Tracy for helpful comments on earlier drafts of this essay.

[3] In this essay I confine myself to the Catholic novels of the Roman tradition although the distinctions here may apply to novels of other Christian traditions as well. Novels of these other traditions—for example, the Anglican Catholic tradition,

monument. Novels like Graham Greene's *The Heart of the Matter* (1948) and *The End of the Affair* (1951), Sigrid Undset's *Kristin Lavrensdatter* (1920-22) and Francois Mauriac's *Viper's Triangle* (1932)—novels which referred to a Catholicism that is historically intact and assumed by definition to be superior to other religions—are no longer being produced. In a general sense, one can expect the Catholic novel to be a fictional interpretation of the religious experience of Catholics; but for most Catholics, current religious experience, informed by almost three decades of liturgical and theological reform—itself a reinterpretation of previous experience—has been subject to other interpretations than those given in the foregoing novels. As Mary Gordon commented in her essay, "Getting Here from There" on the art and craft of religious writing, "the enclosed garden of my childhood was enclosed by a system that said all acts found their meaning in the reiteration of the Truth. Capital T."[4] Gordon does acknowledge the positive aspects of her religious upbringing: "images of my religious life, its sounds, its odors, the kind of kinesthetic sense . . . of prayerfulness" and the sense of a "worldwide church that encompasses races and classes of all sorts."[5] Nonetheless, she also says that for this pre-Vatican II, fiction was superfluous: "the orthodox [had] no need of consolation, and a closed world [had] no need of descriptions of itself."[6] For most Catholics today, the church of the "Capital T" survives only as memory.

The crucial difference between Catholic novels and other novels is not the presence or absence of principles of belief (or doctrine)—whether with a capital or lower-case "T." All novels have such principles: what varies is the degree of ease with which these principles can be stated and

---

such as those of George Eliot, Lawrence Stern, and Dorothy Sayers—deserve a study of their own.

[4] Mary Gordon, "Getting There from Here," in *Spiritual Quests: The Art and Craft of Religious Writing: Mary Gordon, David Bradley, Jaroslav Pelikan, Frederick Buechner, Hugh Nissenson, Allen Ginsberg,* ed. William Zinsser (Boston: Houghton Mifflin Co., 1988), p. 47. Although the events in the Christian (here, Catholic Christian) religious tradition differ from those of the Jewish tradition, both traditions have undergone fundamental shifts in self-understanding in the middle of this century. On the possibility of developing a new religious understanding on the other side of an interruption in the tradition, see *The Jewish Way* (New York: Siummit Books, 1988), p. 322, where the author Irving Greenberg claimed, "There is no covenant so complete as a broken covenant." See also Alan Berger, *Job's Children: Post-Holocaust Jewish Identity in second Generation Literature* (unpublished), which treats of "second generation" Holocaust literature.

[5] Gordon, pp. 28, 47.

[6] *Ibid.*, p. 45.

the degree to which they in fact do or do not interfere with the action of the plot. Indeed, it can be argued that wherever such interference occurs—in black novels, feminist novels, Marxist novels, or Catholic novels—period pieces, as distinct from classics, are born. And period pieces, precisely because they are defined by their specific era and its ideologies, are more often apologues than they are action novels. With some notable exceptions, such as Muriel Spark's *The Mandelbaum Gate* (1965) and James Joyce's *A Portrait of the Artist as a Young Man* (1916), apologue characterized the ideal Catholic novel for both authors and readers. At the zenith of the Catholic novel, the understanding of doctrine as dogma—as Truth with a capital T—marvelously deepened and complicated the understanding of the human dilemma as it had previously been rendered in the wider tradition of the novel. At the same time, doctrine understood as dogma in those novels and their interpretation, all too frequently interfered with the action of the plot.

At the height of the genre, the action of Catholic novels represented the expectation that the Church, however it may be humanly flawed, was equivalent to its currently enunciated doctrine and that this doctrine was penultimate truth. Although it is also Catholic doctrine that an individual's conscience must be the final arbiter of choice and that one must follow one's conscience, even to the point of alienation from the church, this doctrine was little publicized: if this doctrine was acknowledged at all in Catholic novels previous to the '60s, it was never used to glorify the character who acted according to it when such action went contrary to other church doctrine. Mitigating circumstances, limits to what could be known about the disposition and deeds of the individual—these qualified the truth only by way of application. Little recognition of the time-bound character of truth can be found. Until the 1960s, the Catholic novel was characterized by the representation of the church as hierarchically structured in the necessary economy of salvation (see, for example, the conclusion of Graham Greene's *The Power and the Glory* [1961], in which the renegade priest dies and is unexpectedly succeeded by another) and by a trust and confidence in the teachings of the church as defined by the clergy (see the conclusion of Greene's *The Heart of the Matter*, in which the priest declares his conviction that Major Scobie loved God in spite of his suicide, although he probably loved no one else). In descriptive terms, these novels presented religious meaning unhesitatingly through the lens of a Catholicism untroubled by other religious expressions. But the pursuit of perfection coinhered with a grand view of human destiny in the early Catholic novel for a relatively short time.[7]

In contemporary theology, of course, doctrines are not immutable. It is difficult to state precisely for the genre when the relativization of doctrine occurred. It is fairly clear that previous to 1960, what was regarded as the quintessential Catholic novel too often tended in the direction of apologue. The question becomes how to refer to those novels being written today which, while they are informed by Catholic sensibility, are no longer referred to as Catholic novels. If we take them as a continuation of the genre, we must account for the strange "sea-change" that has occurred in the genre, namely, its current tendency away from apologue and toward the action novel.

When we move from descriptive terms to genric terms, however, two different and partially opposed arguments have been made. The first is that the genre Catholic novel ends with those written primarily before the decade of the '60s. In this view, Catholic novels are those in which doctrinal principles (presumed to be immutable) are explicit. To define the genre in this way is both to capture what has been monumental about it and to make apologue its essential mode. On this position, Catholic novel as a genre becomes a literary monument in the sense that although it is no longer productive of new texts, it continues to be productive of new meanings by continual interpretation. Genre as literary monument also allows for the possibility that some texts, such as Greene's *The Heart of the Matter*[8] in the current literary canon, can be read by different readers either as action novels or as apologues insofar as

---

[7] For a rhetorical analysis of the "drive to perfection"—in which Burke is especially interested as this search appears in speech as well as thought, see Kenneth Burke's *The Rhetoric of Religion: Studies in Logology* (Boston: Beacon Press, 1961).

[8] In his review of Norman Sherry's biography of Graham Greene, Robert Coles writes: "[Greene's] conversion to Catholicism enabled him to walk away from the cool, smug life he had inherited and that he sought in his twenties and thirties to advance. It was to be a conversion that haunted him, that gave him the strength to face down demons more scary, even, than those he describes in his essays of psychological examination and disclosure: self-centeredness and self-importance, the endless circus of self-promotion, the cynicism and callousness and pretentiousness that not rarely accompany the secular success he so ardently sought. Like the rest of us he had his fair share of 'nervous disorders,' but during an important part of his life he also was spiritually obsessed, and blessed with a genius to turn to good account such a state of mind. The man who might have been one more clever British satirist became, instead, the person who well merits Norman Sherry's long Boswellian venture." See Robert Coles, "The Gloom and the Glory," *New York Times Book Review*, 18 June 1989, sec. 1, pp. 30-31.

such texts continue to give rise to fruitful discussions about the human situation. Like other monumental genres, such as gospel or epic, the completion of a genre is no impediment but may assist it toward being a classic as well.

The second argument is that after 1960, the genre continues to produce texts as well as meanings. But the prevailing character of the genre shifts from apologue to action novel. At the same time (but not as a result), doctrine, which is implicit if it appears at all in the novel, shifts from being immutable to being relative.[9] On this position, certain texts, such as Mary Gordon's *Final Payments* (1978) and *Of Men and Angels* (1985) or Brian Moore's *The Lonely Passion of Judith Hearne* (1984), no longer treat exclusively of Catholics and their beliefs, even while the action of the novel may invoke some elements of Catholicism of a previous era. These novels are informed by Catholic sensibility or vision which is not easily restated in terms of doctrine.[10]

The problem with this second position is that it does not bear a name: "catholic novel" with a small "c" for universal is not accurate as a description and "religious novel" does not retain the distinctiveness of Catholic sensibility. A Catholic novel by no name or any other name is, for all practical purposes, no longer a Catholic novel.

The choice of either view of the Catholic novel genre rests on aesthetic preferences and religious dispositions, as well as on documentary evidence for the completion or the continuation of the genre. In the remainder of this essay, we will examine evidence for both views. But in order to identify this complex genre, it is first necessary to understand how one goes about formulating a genre.

I. What Are Genric Studies? General Issues

In Walker Percy's *The Moviegoer*, Binx Bolling elaborates on what he calls the "vertical search" to his cousin, Kate Cutrer:

[9] It is tempting to think that there is a causal relationship between the shift from apologue to action novel and from apodictic or immutable belief to relative or conditional belief. I agree with T. S. Eliot, who in "Shakespeare and the Stoicism of Seneca" (in *Selected Essays: 1917-32*, New Edition [New York: Harcourt, Brace and Co., 1950], pp. 117-18), explored a related question in his comparison of the beliefs and works of John Donne and William Shakespeare and concluded that a causal relationship does not obtain. See also Wayne Booth's comprehensive treatment of the issue in *The Company We Keep: An Ethics of Fiction* (Berkeley: University of California Press, 1988), especially pp. 421-23.

[10] The case for the "Catholic sensibility" and "vision" of each of the works cited in this essay would have to be argued, of course, in a further study.

"If you walk in the front door of the laboratory, you undertake the vertical search. You have a specimen, a cubic centimeter of water or a frog or a pinch of salt or a star."

"One learns general things?"

"And there is excitement to the search."

"Why?" she asks.

"Because as you get deeper into the search, you unify. You understand more and more specimens by fewer and fewer formulae. There is the excitement. Of course you are always after the big one, the new key, the secret leverage point, and that is the best of it."

"And it doesn't matter where you are or who you are."

"No."

"And the danger is of becoming no one nowhere."

"Never mind."[11]

It is tempting to understand this passage as a literary statement of what generic studies is all about. But is either the "vertical search" or genric studies anything more than formulating and categorizing?

This passage from *The Moviegoer* is a good starting-point for our study of the Catholic novel because it represents the popular view of genre, a view which we will attempt to surpass. Common sense expects that genre is a category—an after-the-literary-fact designation that would successfully distinguish the Catholic novel from other kinds of novels. Carrying this expectation further, common sense assumes that greater success in genric studies consists in understanding "more and more [literary works] by fewer and fewer [genres]." That is, once one achieves this greater success of putting them all together, one presumably is ready for the culminating point of the inquiry—"the big one, the new key, the secret leverage point" which would enable one to understand all of literature because one has the right formula, the one that includes all other formulae.

The passage from *The Moviegoer* tempts us furthermore to expect an isomorphic relationship between the disciplines of literary theory and chemistry: each, if practiced systematically and collaboratively, might be expected to have its period table in which specimens are known by

---

[11] Walker Percy, *The Moviegoer* (New York: Alfred A. Knopf, 1961), pp. 82-83.

means of definitive formulae and in relation to one another. But the iso-
morph fails for two reasons. The inorganic model only *seems* to work
nicely for chemistry (about which Kate observes, "it doesn't matter
where you are or who you are"); in our ecologically-minded world, even
this presumption has proved inadequate. Furthermore, only an organic
model is capable of disclosing the historicity of genric theory and the interpreter's horizon of understanding.

In place of a model of genre as categorical, I propose to employ a
model of genre as historical, as theoretical, and as praxis-oriented—a
model which I have elaborated elsewhere.[12] As historical, we shall expect
that both classics and minor writings will be included in the life of a
genre. Moreover, we will see intelligible relations among the Catholic
novel and other genres, especially those which attended its birth in the
early nineteenth century.

As theoretical, we shall define the genre in the form of a hypothetical
statement, foregrounding thereby the theoretical work that underlies every good definition and calling into question the expectation that every
novel called "Catholic" fits a single description. Instead, genre defined as
hypothesis maintains a testing attitude toward every new description
and encourages us to improve the hypothesis as needed.

As praxis-oriented, genres work to change the world and our understanding of it. Understanding a genre at the very least assists the reader
to move beyond a naive first reading. Ideally, genre provides a heuristic
method of ascertaining the effects of a text in relation to others and on its
readers.

II. What Have Genres to do with Belief?

No one seems particularly happy with the name "Catholic novel" for
this genre, but no one who admits dissatisfaction has suggested a better.
By appropriating T. S. Eliot's objections to the genre "religious poetry,"
we can state succinctly three analogous difficulties with the name
"Catholic novel," difficulties which are preliminary to the issue of belief.

In 1917, Eliot complained that the genre of religious literature—
specifically, for him, religious poetry—deals with a "confined part of the
whole subject matter of poetry." It is a genre, he went on to say, which
leaves out the "major passions" and is most likely ignorant of them.[13]

---

[12] I elaborate on these characteristics of genre in my forthcoming book, *Gender and Genre.*

[13] T. S. Eliot, "Religion and Literature," in *Selected Essays, 1917-32,* pp. 344.

Probably for this same reason thirty-three years later, he refused to speak of Dante as "the greatest religious poet"—even though Eliot thought that Dante surely was that—on the grounds that the title might detract from the poet's universality.[14] Eliot's criticism of the genre is also, of course, a criticism of the religious understanding of his time.

Eliot's position was that certain expectations are aroused whenever an investigation is made of literary texts designated as explicitly religious. These expectations can be described as three-fold: first, that the texts are minor and probably idiosyncratic; second, that as religious, the texts are devoid of human passion; third, that whatever the critical approach taken by a critic of religious texts, the religious aspect is likely to be at best a recapitulation of preformulated themes or beliefs waiting to be found in the text and at worst a summarily imposed meaning only remotely related to the particularities of the text.

The first two objections as applied to the Catholic novel are trivial and can be easily discounted by counter-examples. Against the charge that religious novels are minor and probably idiosyncratic, we can point out that two of the authors of Catholic novels treated in this paper were the recipients of the Nobel Prize for Literature. Sigrid Undset received the award in 1929 after the publication of *Kristin Lavransdatter*, and Heinrich Böll in 1972, after the publication of *Group Portrait with Lady*. Two other novels, James Joyce's *Ulysses* (1922) and *Finnegans Wake* (1939), have been lauded as revolutionizing the novel in this century. Against the charge that religious literature is devoid of passion, we notice that most of the texts we discuss treat explicitly of passion and suggest different relationships between sexual and other forms of passion. The narrator of Walker Percy's *Love in the Ruins*, for example, identifies himself as stereotypically male at the beginning of the novel, believing "in God and the whole business but I love women best, music and science next, whiskey next, God fourth, and my fellowman hardly at all."[15] His machine, More's Qualitative Quantitative Ontological Lapsometer, is an invention for "measuring and treating the deep perturbations of the soul."[16]

Eliot's third objection, namely, that the religious aspect to be found in the text is likely to be a recapitulation of preformulated belief or an imposition of extra-literary meaning from outside the text, forces us to re-

[14]   T. S. Eliot, "What Dante Means to Me," in *To Criticize the Critic* (New York: Farrar, Straus and Giroux, 1964), p. 134.
[15]   Percy, p. 6.
[16]   *Ibid.*, p. 29.

flect on the question of belief in relation to these texts. How valid, for example, is the assumption that the Catholicity of the author is essential to the definition of the Catholic novel? Early criticism of Catholic novels presumed a close link between the novel and the novelist's adherence to orthodox doctrine. In this sense, the early definitions, implicitly at least, require the Catholicity of the author. However, among major novelists treating of cultural, doctrinal, or moral matters pertinent to Catholicism are not only "first-born" Catholics and "converts" to Catholicism, such as Muriel Spark (some critics claim, somewhat gratuitously in my opinion, that the latter write the "best" Catholic novels). There are also "secessionists," such as James Joyce, perhaps the most prominent innovator in the Western novel tradition. At the other end of the spectrum are professed Catholics who write novels which are not considered to be "Catholic novels"—for example, Graham Greene's detective stories, or Ursula LaGuin's science fiction. Since these latter novels are *not* taken to be Catholic novels, we may conclude that the Catholicity of the author is not definitive for the genre.

Moreover, there is something of a naive circularity in defining a genre primarily by means of the author's beliefs. For surely there is a sense in which the "author" is created or constructed by the novel and its interpretation. We see this very clearly in the way Sigrid Undset's novels were received in this country. Undset won the Nobel Prize for Literature in 1929, a year after she published the first book of her trilogy *Kristen Lavransdatter*. Compared favorably with Jane Austen, her work was acclaimed as "the greatest Catholic fiction that has ever been produced."[17] The trilogy and her earlier books are all set in fourteenth- and fifteenth-century Norway. With pages of appended notes describing medieval architecture, political bonds, and social structures—similar to the material in J. R. Tolkien's *Simarillion* (1977)—the books received praise for their realism. "Her books are tales, wherein the narrative flows like a river, sometimes majestic, winding; sometimes rapid, breath-taking in its exuberance."[18]

But critics were surprised when the characters of her later novels, set in the twentieth century, embarrassingly held to the same moral and religious imperatives as had Undset's medieval characters. Whereas her first novels were praised for having presented "woman . . . to us in all

---

[17] Theodore Maynard, "Sigrid Undset: The Realist Who Reached Reality," *Catholic World* (April 1938): 22.
[18] *Ibid.*

her moral and physical beauty, . . . superhumanly strong, not dependent upon others, but only upon the unshakable faith which she preserves and which makes her almost unconquerable in the struggle for life, with all its ugliness, offensiveness, and evil,"[19] her later novels were criticized as being unrealistic in that the characters' views are unalterably medieval. At the appearance of one of her later novels, *Jennie* (1921), in which the main character, a "fallen woman," is made to perish under her sense of shame, sin, and regret, she was denounced by a group of militant feminists. Although Undset's Catholicism was never explicitly contested, its authenticity was repeatedly called into question—exemplifying the difficulty of defining novels exclusively by the professed beliefs of their authors. A better criticism of the novels could have been based on the implausibility of the action represented by the plots.

The relationship of belief to narrative is essentially an issue of genre. Only attention to genre can successfully mediate what is too often mistaken as a one-to-one equivalence between belief and action. In her historical-critical study of the Catholic novel, *The Vital Tradition: The Catholic Novel in a Period of Convergence*, Jean Kellogg wrote that "historic Roman Catholic theological and philosophical ideas furnished the mainsprings of dramatic action [for the Catholic novel]."[20] This descriptive statement lends itself to a new understanding of "mainspring": if you watch the action, she seems to mean, you will be able to deduce the mainspring. However, her statement would be misunderstood if it presumed that the action of the novel could be explained or accounted for without remainder by doctrine. Indeed, John Henry Newman may have been assuming one such easy transition from doctrine to narrative when he wrote in a preface to one of his two novels that he used "fiction when polemic or history do not suffice."[21] Whatever his assumption, his novels are clearly apologues and remain period pieces. If a distinction in genre is made, however, Kellogg's statement could appropriately describe action novels, as well as apologues.[22]

---

[19]   A. Lutz, "Great Norwegian Convert," *Catholic World* (February 1929): 607.

[20]   Gene Kellogg, *The Vital Tradition: The Catholic Novel in a Period of Convergence* (Chicago: Loyola University Press, 1970), pp. 1, 210. Jean Kellogg's pen-name was Gene Kellogg.

[21]   Joseph Ellis Baker, *The Novel and the Oxford Movement* (Princeton: Princeton University Press, 1932), p. 54.

[22]   On this issue, see Sheldon Sacks' three-fold typology of novels in *Fiction and the Shape of Belief* (Berkeley: University of California Press, 1967). Sacks differentiated among three kinds of fiction—the satire, the apologue, and the action novel—on the basis of their organizing principles. In his terms, the work of a satire is so organized

The case against the expectation that good novels require unwavering, all-encompassing beliefs on the part of the author is bluntly stated by Sartre in a devastating comment on Mauriac's work (a comment which ruined Mauriac's reputation among younger French critics). "In a true novel as in the world of Einstein there is no place for a privileged observer. . . . M. Mauriac preferred his own way. He chose divine omniscience and omnipotence. . . . God is not an artist; neither is M. Mauriac."[23] Although Sartre was wonderfully funny, he was also terribly

---

that it "ridicules objects external to the fictional world created in it"; that of an apologue exemplifies "the truth of a formulable statement or a series of such statements"; that of an action "introduces characters, about whose fates we are made to care, in unstable relationships . . . whose complication is finally resolved by the removal of the instability" (p. 26). Although Sacks hypothesized that a novel is, most properly the third kind of fiction, he recognized that a different set of problems is raised by each of these kinds of fiction in relation to belief. The ease, for example, with which the organizing principles of the apologue and satire enable us "to investigate their ethical content is almost matched by the obstructions [they offer] to any consideration of them as prose fictions" (p. 28). By the same token, the action novel gains the reader's involvement in the characters' convictions and dilemmas directly and readily, but it "offers no convenient access to consideration of ethical questions in novels" (p. 27). Sacks confined his discussion to ethical beliefs, but it is not difficult to see how it is relevant to religious beliefs as well. Sacks' point may be summarized as follows: not only do all three fictional forms have organizing principles which give rise to a discussion of beliefs, it is "foolhardy and critically irresponsible" not to inquire into the role of these beliefs in novels (*ibid.*). The further recognition that the beliefs that inform all fictional forms may *interfere* with the action enables us to distinguish within the genre of the Catholic novel, those which are apologues or satires, on the one hand, and those which are action novels on the other.

It is important not to minimize the problems associated with the action novel. In a footnote, Sacks anticipated the following problematic assumption: "There is the possibility that, while all works usefully classified as novels must contain characters introduced in unstable relationships which are later resolved, the development of these relationships may more accurately be described as subordinate to the change in a single character—i.e., the work is organized as a representation of character rather than an action. I am inclined to believe that we can best understand even such a work as Joyce's *Portrait of the Artist* as an action in which—as one of the variables possible in actions—the internal change of a major character is extremely prominent. *There are difficulties attendant on this view, but the consequences of its being wrong are not terribly significant . . . since, even if we were to include representations of character, action, or thought as novels, the general statements about the shape of belief in novels, as opposed to satires or apologues, would remain unchanged"* (emphasis mine, pp. 26-27n28).

[23] As quoted in Donat O'Donnell, *Maria Cross* (New York: Oxford University Press, 1952), p. 35. In *The Analogical Imagination*, David Tracy alluded to Sartre's classical conception of God in the following passage: "The surest sign of the artist is not a striking originality in the sense of novelty and is never a self unembodied in a finite

unfair and, according to Mauriac's biography, half apologized years later when the two had a reconciliation. Today we can see that Sartre took for granted the classical theological understanding of God, as well as deliberately identified Mauriac's literary point of view with his theological understanding.

To what extent must a reader "believe in" Catholicism in order to understand the Catholic novel? As with any fields of meanings embedded in literary texts, understanding the words is a requisite first level of reading. Nevertheless, at the more comprehensive level, a reader must have the ability to follow a story: that is, to differentiate between the time of the telling and the time of the originating action. Here is it useful to draw upon Paul Ricoeur's brilliant analysis of narrative,[24] an analysis in which narrative sentences refer to at least two time-separated events and aim explicitly to describe the earliest event to which they refer. The naive reader's view which needs to be overcome is the expectation that events in a narrative have a fixed meaning which can be determined line by line in a first reading of the novel. According to Ricoeur, a narration is not just a reenactment of what the actors originally thought, felt, or did, since their actions are described in the light of events that they did not and could not know.

Ricoeur's analysis brings into view the essential tension in any good novel—a space wherein the play of indeterminacy (in Roman Ingarden's sense) can take place. A story is the "distance" between two events: first, an original happening (narrated as the time of the action) and, second, the event of telling and accounting for (narrated as the time of the telling). The writer writes and the reader reads and reconstructs in an attempt to resolve the tension by making an entire set of events into a discernible unity or effect—whether in terms of an organic whole (as a hermeneutic approach would support) or in terms of an indeterminable series of fragmented meanings (as in a deconstructionist reading). As with any literary text, the conclusion of a Catholic novel need not be predictable but must be acceptable.[25] Looking backward from the conclusion

---

tradition—even if a despised tradition. The purely solitary self is not a human being. It is not even really the God of Jews and Christians who, *pace* Sartre, *is* an artist" (p. 125).

[24] See Paul Ricoeur, *Time and Narrative*, vol. 2, trans. Kathleen McLaughlin and David Pellauer (Chicago: University of Chicago Press, 1984), especially pp. 65-68.

[25] In a minimal sense, to be acceptable means to be conceivable or plausible. Once conceived, a specific sequence of events may appear acceptable or plausible to some readers but not to others. In Greene's *The End of the Affair* (New York: Viking, 1951), for example, some contemporary Catholic readers who have lived through Vatican II

to the episodes which led to it, we must be able to say that this chain of
events required this outcome. But this backward look is made possible
by the movement of our expectations when we followed the story, expectations which themselves have a life-orientation and which lead to
praxis.

With respect to belief and the Catholic novel, then, this minimal requisite remains: a reader must be able to understand the meaning and
significance of a religious interpretation of human existence. The reader
may expect a variety of expressions that have religious significance, significance best related to interpretations of the same text by other readers,
including both contemporary readers and those from the past. As Eliot
reminds us, each generation must reflect on its beliefs anew in relation to
the science, culture, and history of its time.

III. History of the Catholic Novel: Some Semantic Shifts in the Genre.

In his study, *The Catholic Literary Revival* (1935), Calvert Alexander
claimed that the first Catholic novel, written in 1824 and entitled *Father
Rowland*, was written to counteract a popular anti-Catholic novel, entitled *Father Clement*, and that the term "Catholic novel" seems to have
been used for the first time in 1858 by Barbey d'Aurevilly.[26] According to
Alexander, the development of this genre is best understood in relation
to the cultural history of Europe. In his view, the first stage (1845-1890)
evidenced the rise of the Catholic novel as an alternative to the great
English novel tradition, so rooted in the Anglican and Protestant culture
dating from the sixteenth century. The Catholic novels which are most
representative of this first period are the works of John Henry Newman,
Aubrey deVere, Robert Hawker, Nicholas Patrick, Stephen Wiseman,
and Henry Manning. Several of these names are also familiar as leading
figures of the Oxford Movement. None of them was a leading figure in
this first stage of the Catholic novel. According to Alexander, these novelists were persuaded that the novel must preserve truths which they
presumed were lost outside Catholicism.[27] The Catholic novel in France

---

and the changes it brought about may find Scobie's scruples about receiving communion in adultery—compared with his lack of concern for Asi's life and consequent
death—unacceptable. Pre-Vatican Catholics, on the other hand, may find the same
course of events compelling. Such divergence of opinion is fruitful in discussing the
novel and generally clarifies issues raised by the narrative as a whole.

[26] Calvert Alexander, *The Catholic Literary Revival* (Milwaukee: Bruce Publishing
Co., 1935), p. 4.

[27] *Ibid.*, p. 333.

of this period continued in the tradition of literature as an inquiry into spiritual development. The French novel grew out of general Romanticist aspirations in reaction against the "rigid mental and spiritual authoritarianism" of prevailing philosophies. Very quickly, however, the French Catholic novel went into schism from secular art altogether. Such art to Catholic novelists like Joris-Karl Huysmans could not account for the decadence bred by the passionate "fever of liberty."[28] In French Catholic novels, art and sanctity grew ever more adverse to each other, as can best we seen in novels by Chateaubriand, whose best novels *Atala* (1801) and *Rene* (1802), were published in the second stage. As far as I am aware, not one of the first-stage novels is other than a period piece.

The second stage of the Catholic novel (1890-1919) was dominated by the sense of apocalypticism—"that sense of world-crisis, of impending catastrophe"[29]—which Kellogg and others have argued is *the* distinctive thematic characteristic of the Catholic novel. In England, two women, Maisie Ward and Sheila Kaye-Smith, were well-known Catholic novelists; several others wrote under pen names. Gilbert Keith Chesterton and Hilaire Belloc transformed the Catholic novel from being an appreciation of the benefits of Catholic culture to being an aggressive, polemical defense of them. In France, Leon Bloy and Charles Peguy represented the world as a battleground for the forces of good and evil, where the misery of the poor staved off God's vengeance. In Germany, Gertrud von LeFort, Peter Dorfler, and Erich von Kuhnelt-Leddihn explored examples of victims as martyrs.

In the third stage (1929-1935) of the Catholic novel, Catholicism itself appeared as a major option in either-or worlds: for example, the choice between a militant Catholicism or a militant atheism, between Christ and anti-Christ, between Rome and Moscow. In the same period, however, the critical eye of the novels began to turn in toward the Catholic community itself. Francois Mauriac's castigation of corruption within bourgeoisie Catholicism as well as within secular society, George Bernanos' exaltation of chivalry, honor, and dedication over the hypocrisy and evil in Catholic decadence—the French novelists of this period spared neither peasant nor clergy in their exposure of hypocrisy and evil. With Graham Greene, Evelyn Waugh, and Robert Hugh Benson in England and Sigrid Undset, Johannes Jorgensen, and Jenryk Sienkiewicz on the Continent, the Catholic novel began to occupy a place of importance in the non-

---

[28] Kellogg, p. 15.
[29] *Ibid.*, p. 10.

Catholic world of literature as well as among Catholics. Alexander describes this third stage of the Catholic novel as the "war generation" that

> talks of returning to many strange things, to the Elizabethans, to the philosophy of Aquinas, to the classics, to monarchy, to baroque mysticism, to a healthy barbarism—but not to democratic liberation, nor to the promises of Science and Progress, nor to the parousia of Big Business and Industrialism, nor to reverent Rationalism, nor to charming bourgeois letters, nor to any of the other happy institutions and splendid ideologies of the society into which its members were born.[30]

In a very real sense, the Catholic novel came into its own during its third stage.

The fourth stage (1935-1970) is perhaps best characterized as a period of nostalgia—nostalgia not so much for an earlier age of faith (although such titles as J. F. Powers' *Morte d'Urban* [1956] suggest a focus on earlier times), as hope for the sudden swift injection of grace in the domestic situation. For the earlier age of faith was in the process of being demythologized: the thirteenth, "the greatest of centuries," was a faded dream along with Camelot. In this stage, Joyce's farewell to "old father fabricator" was just becoming known although his novels had been published earlier. Flannery O'Connor's novels qua short stories are recognized almost immediately as a unique contribution to American letters. For the first time, American Catholic novels are worthwhile taking into account.

The fifth stage (1970 to the present) is uncharted territory, or—if we accept Kellogg's stipulation "that [Catholic novels] must depend for their mainsprings of dramatic action upon Roman Catholic theology, or upon the thinking of one of the world's large Roman Catholic communities, or upon development of Roman Catholic ideas in Newman's sense"[31]— map without territory. That is to say, in the present pluralist theological situation it has become increasingly difficult to define the Catholic novel in the terms of its origin. Early in this period, the mood of one of the major American Catholic novelists, Walker Percy, was one of temporizing. Indeed, the titles of his novels, *The Moviegoer*, *The Last Gentleman* (1966), *Love Among the Ruins* (1971), and *Lancelot* (1977), have the taste of volcanic ash—as if the tradition once alive and vital were now no longer, as if the genius of its bloom, nipped by the frost of disillusionment, were

---

[30] *Ibid.*, pp. 4-5.
[31] Kellogg, p. 166.

already turning to inorganic dust. This is the view of those who argue that the genre has become a monument.

At this point it becomes important to put the Catholic novel in a larger context, that is, to compare it to other kinds of novels at a more general level. For the supposed demise of the Catholic novel may not be a singular event. In literary criticism, for example, in his book, *The Fabulators* (1967), Robert Scholes argued that the realistic novel, which had defined the novel tradition until then, had become obsolete and was being replaced by "fabulation." It is difficult, of course, to evaluate such predictions, especially in the face of significant evidence to the contrary that the tradition of the novel is alive and well and thriving in contemporary letters. Others, such as David Lodge, himself a novelist as well as a literary critic, refused to sing obsequies over the novel. Instead, he located it "at the crossroads." According to Lodge, "straight ahead" would be the continuation of the realistic novel, itself a compromise between fictional and empirical modes. But "the pressure of skepticism on the aesthetic and epistemological premises" of the realistic tradition is so intense, he thought, that novelists are likely to go in two other routes, opposed to each other. One route is toward the non-fiction novel, the other is toward "fabulation."[32] Since Lodge wrote *The Novelist at the Crossroads* (1971), other alternatives, for example, the "new" novel and the postmodern novel, have entered the field. We need not go further on any of these routes, however, to realize the sense of Lodge's theory: the traditional novel is not dead; its earlier forms are changing into new forms.

On the basis of this example it seems reasonable to understand the genre "Catholic novel" in two ways. The first way is illustrated by those who read the history of the genre as given above as essentially complete with the monumental novels (some of which are classics) of the third and fourth stages as described above. Indeed, there is some indication that the term, the "Catholic novel," is no longer widely used to describe works written today—although the term "Catholic novelist" continues to be used sparingly and seems to pertain to the novelist's identification as being or having been Catholic. In this reading, the genre is restricted to the third and fourth stages and no longer produces new texts. The evidence for this view is that Catholic novels are defined as raising questions from Catholic doctrine presumed to be immutable—which in turn is seen as providing the "mainspring" of the plot. This is not to say that

---

[32] David Lodge, *The Novelist at the Crossroads and Other Essays on Fiction and Criticism* (Ithaca: Cornell University Press, 1971), p. 19.

these novels—especially if they are also classics—need always be read as such: both as individual texts and as a group they may and do give rise to other readings—for example, feminist, Marxist, deconstructionist, Romanticist, etc. But it *is* to claim that this characterization of the early texts as a genre is likely to have a privileged position among the different interpretations of these texts that emerge as the novels continue to be read in the future.

The second way of understanding the genre "Catholic novel" is to distinguish its monumental form from those more recent action novels which are not related to an understanding of doctrine as immutable dogma, as were the novels in the prior stages. As is the case with the novel genre in general, the Catholic novel of the fifth stage exemplifies an alternative form to its tradition. As Catholic, let us suppose that these novels give rise to complex differentiations among naivete, belief, and religious meanings. Although they ordinarily refer to some aspects of Catholicism, their mainspring is to be located not in doctrine understood dogmatically, but rather in foundational principles, such as sacramental vision and a conception of human beings as themselves sacred before God. According to this second approach, the genre Catholic novel continues to produce new texts, as well as new meanings.

Examples of some of the alternative directions available at this crossroad of the genre are numerous. Heinrich Böll's *Group Portrait with Lady* illustrates one of the most promising directions: the "new" novel, or metafiction, a genre which foregrounds the act of writing. Böll, in whose novels a Catholic sensibility is unmistakable, set the novel in post-World War II Germany. The main character is ostensibly the "Lady" of the title, Leni, but the plot focuses on the effects of Leni on Au. (the Author), whose task it is to be a disinterested recorder of the facts of Leni's life. Au. is collating details about Leni, a "vulnerable and indestructible" 48-year-old woman who has survived both the War and its aftermath with remarkable insouciance. A third main character, Klementina, introduced as a source of information for Au., becomes increasingly involved in Au.'s work and life. At the end, Klementina helps to complete Au.'s manuscript, which is *Group Portrait with Lady*, the novel itself.

The ironic tone and the new novelistic techniques make it difficult to state the organizing principle of this work, even though the strong critical vision of the novel demands articulation. At the same time, the many explicitly Catholic elements of the novel, along with its "new novel" form and unconventional structure, stretch the genre Catholic novel and challenge the reader to find new ways to understand it.

Mary Gordon's first novel, *Final Payments* (1978), illustrates a second direction of promise for the Catholic novel: the realistic novel which examines the intrigue and precariousness of a secular/religious way of being in a world of meanings formerly informed by Catholicism. Thirty years old at the time of her invalid father's death, Isabel Moore finds herself having to invent a life. Her appetite for life is mixed with conflicting emotions and much residual guilt from the memory of her role in bringing on her father's stroke fifteen years before. The character of Isabel is structurally disclosed in the novel through her interaction with two childhood friends, an alcoholic priest-friend, people she visits as a social worker, and her lover. The plot is suspenseful, revolving around the tension between self-destruction and self-transformation. At the end of the novel, she understands for the first time what certain biblical passages, which she had known from childhood but not understood, might mean for her life. This novel confirms the continued viability of the action-novel form which may now come into its own in the Catholic novel tradition.

In different ways, perhaps both books also illustrate Muriel Spark's observation about her own writing experience: "The Catholic belief," she once said in an interview, "is a norm from which one can depart."[33]

---

[33] This quotation is in notes taken from a published interview which I am now unable to find.

The Humanities and "Other" Humans

CHARLES H. LONG

With us, it is an old conviction that Western philosophy is dangerously close to 'provincializing' itself (if the expression be permitted): first by jealously isolating itself in its own tradition and ignoring, for example, the problems and solutions of Oriental thought: second by its obstinate refusal to recognize any 'situations' except those of the man in historical civilizations, in defiance of the experience of 'primitive' man, of man as a member of traditional societies."[1]

The Humanities have traditionally been understood to form the basis for the college curriculum. This meaning of the college curricula is taken seriously in most distinguished universities as well as in the myriad of small liberal arts colleges that are spread across the landscape of this country. What is at stake in this concern for the humanities? It seems to me that this concern expresses the desire to form and inform students with a special and precise insight into the nature of the human mode of being. Stated in this way, it is the intention of the liberal arts or the humanities to provide a perspective from which one is able to understand human life as a total meaning—total in any one of its manifestations as well as total in the many configurations and manifestations that human existence might take. It is this sense of the totality of human life that allows for attention to and assessment of its essence as an intention and a possible realization. So it is through the humanities—in the main through the disciplines of art, history, music, re-

---

[1] Mircea Eliade, *The Myth of the Eternal Return* (Princeton: Princeton Univ. Press, 1954), p. x.

ligion, philosophy—that we are supposed to come to terms with the kind
of data from which these issues emerge. Through the natural sciences
our minds are able to contemplate the manner in which our species is
determined by and capable of the determining order of those human and
non-human forms of the world that contain us, form us, define the
possibilities for our enhancement as well as constrain us within the limits
of a common human community.

It is therefore the inter-relationship of *totality, essentiality,* and *value*
that forms the critical issue in the humanities. Notions of this sort
obviously give rise to contention regarding the value or worth of human
existence, whether as individual or cultural expression. But the
humanities must always be defined in terms of the actual or possible
worlds of those who undertake to be informed by this orientation. For
the most part in the Western world since the Enlightenment, the
humanities in this sense have formed, if not a "theology," at least an
ideology of the West. In most cases the humanities curriculum is
dedicated to those kinds of cultural data, those sorts of cultural meanings
that have emerged from the Hebraic, Greek, and Christian forms of our
culture. In other words, these data defined a normative meaning of our
actual and possible human worlds.

One of the crucial issues in the humanities today has to do with a
definition of the meaning of totality in terms of human worlds. In the
first instance, how are we to define the human species? Are all human
beings to be defined as constituting the human species? Are all human
cultures, both past and present, to be included in the study of the humanities? Are all human situations part of the possible constituting data of
the humanities? In other words, the question is raised, given the actual or
possible worlds we live in, is it adequate for the humanities to derive its
fundamental orientation, meaning, and data from simply the Hebraic,
Greek, Christian meanings of our culture?

Our late colleague, Mircea Eliade, often reminded us that the West
was in danger of provincializing itself by not taking account of other
human situations, those of past history—especially, he would say, those
of archaic cultures are other human situations in our contemporary
world represented by the cultures of India, China, and in other parts of
our globe.[2] In this sense, the meaning of the humanities as it relates to the
issue of totality must be rethought. One of the striking things about our
times is that all human beings in the world know about the existence of

---

[2] Eliade, *op.cit.,* x.

all other human beings. What has come to fruition is the notion that was enunciated some years ago by Wendell Wilkie, the Republican candidate for president of the United States in 1940; one of his slogans was "one world." Most of us at that time did not understand the full implications, theoretical and practical, of the meaning of one world. It is very clear today that this notion is no longer simply a slogan; we are conscious of just how we are inextricably bound to all other human cultures in all parts of the world. Any meaning of actual or possible worlds must perforce take account of all human beings.

Now to the issue of *essentiality*. The humanities in the American sense represent a translation of the German term, *Geisteswissenschaft*, which means the "science of the human spirit"; but the nuances of this term are lost in translation as we don't speak of "spirit" in this way. What is clear, however, is the notion that it is possible to undertake a serious and systematic investigation and understanding of that which is characteristically and irreducibly human, those expressions and qualities without which there would not be a proper way of even raising the issue of the specific mode of the human being.

There have been many ways by which this problem has been posed. More often than not, the posing of the issue itself has led to definitions, methods, and disciplines around the specific quality or meaning being essentialized; this is understandable. For example, there is the attempt to understand the human as a religious being, *homo religiosus*, and thus within this perspective any understanding of the human must take into account the predilection of human beings to live their lives in relationship to that which is sacred or holy; the implication is that this meaning is pervasive in all cultures and times. The totalizing and essentializing of a quality enables one to come to terms with that which is unique to each and common to all.

We also have definitions of this kind of essential quality of the human in art, music, literature, etc. Since the Enlightenment, other generalizing notions have been put forth: *homo socius*, human beings live in social groups; *homo geographicus*, human beings must orient themselves within their space. Rivaling religion, however, as one of the notions regarding the human is the meaning of history—human beings and human societies are what they are by virtue or their historicity. The notion of history is often confusing because it is weighted with a number of meanings and connotations. For the most part, within our Western tradition history has always carried theological baggage, even for the secular historian. The theological baggage has grown out of the normativity of the Hebrew and Christian orientations of our culture; that specific mode by which they call *history* is revalorized into a theological value. This meaning may be expressed in the following manner.

The historicity of the human community, the understanding that humans work in relationship to the deity and in the temporal arena can interact to create a new entity, gives a specific meaning to the notion of temporality. From this point of view, primacy is given to human events; those novelties in time that have come about because of the volition of human communities and individuals, which in turn forms the locus of value for an orientation in the societies of the Western world which is both theological and secular.

This orientation carries with it a critique—a critique of those cultures and societies who neither accept nor have acted upon this understanding of human temporality. For example, the long temporal period before the beginnings of urban communities in Mesopotamia is referred to as *pre-history*, an era before history! Now, in one sense, all human beings are historical beings insofar as we all live in a temporal-spatial continuum. When we say "pre-history," however, we are saying that there is something not quite normative, not quite authentic, about those persons and cultures who did not accept a certain valuational meaning of human time; therefore, most of our ancestors who lived before urban traditions came into being are said to have lived in pre-history.

Another valence of this same meaning is expressed in our regard for those cultures and societies of our modern world who have not been involved in history-making activities, that is, those societies and cultures in the world whose mode of being was not predicated upon bringing into being new historical constellations and meanings. These cultures have been variously referred to as "primitive," "uncivilized," "savage", etc. In other words, the very notion of history from the Western point of view creates other worlds, other peoples, and other cultures who by definition, given this categorization, are looked upon as being lesser in value than the history-makers.

Following closely upon this theological historical meaning of the human is the Marxist understanding. Marxists are nothing unless they are historical, and in this sense they keep alive that theological-historical tradition in the Western world, albeit from an anti-Western religious point of view. The meaning of history for Marxists must be looked for not simply in the volitional acts of human being and communities. For them, the fundamental meaning of the human act is not the amalgam or discernment of the action of a deity with the human community but through the modes of production and reproduction in societies; the modes of production and the meaning of the division of labor are for them the keys to the understanding of the nature of the human act and the mode of being.

Marxists hope that through history all human societies may be liberated; that is, attain the fullness of the human mode through discerning the right relationship between modes of material production and the creativity of human beings working together towards this end. On the level of material modes of production and distribution, this liberation would at the same time bring about a meaning of the human that is consistent with our understanding of the human through both the human and natural sciences. From this perspective, the Marxist understanding fulfills the ideal of the Enlightenment.

Presiding over or undergirding any notion of totality or essentiality is a more pervasive meaning of the human—a meaning so deeply imbedded in our tradition that we hardly ever bring it into consciousness: this is the notion of the human as a rational being. We posit this meaning at the beginnings of the West in the Greek classical tradition and see it as the enduring structure of the Western cultural tradition. It is the simultaneous extension and critique of this meaning of the rational in Enlightenment and post-Enlightenment traditions of the West that evoke the problematical nature of the humanities and the ensuing debates about the meaning of such an orientation.

One could argue that the critique of the Enlightenment orientation was brought about by the Enlightenment itself. Prior to the Enlightenment orientation, the meaning of the epistemological issue of meaning held together two necessary structures: the capacity and limitations of human reason and the givenness of the creation by God. Thus the proper understanding of any form of creation was predicated on an inherent order of its meaning as given in creation and upon the wisdom and grace of God as the provider of human reason for the purpose of understanding the created order. Knowledge as accumulated wisdom, as well as the processes of knowing, were predicated upon a transcendental meaning of the otherness given through creation by God and the inherent otherness of the forms of the world.

The epistemological issue of the Enlightenment centered around the proper way of knowing the forms of the world apart from an inherent structure of transcendence within these forms or within the knowing subject. Alexander Pope's aphorism that "the proper study of mankind is man" may seem commonplace to us today, but it represents a great divide on the epistemological level, for we have moved away from an understanding that presupposed that the proper locus for an understanding of the *human* was in and through God. Instead, we find emphasized the human understanding of humanity now acknowledged as the most certain, creative, and beneficial meaning of human understanding. The meaning of reason and rationality kept apace with this epistemological shift. All human beings are rational beings and this is the key to human understanding. Human understanding is possible because the person or community who wants to know is represented by a commensurate rationality in the beings or things to be known. All systematic acts of knowing must of necessity stylize what is to be known in the modality of an object. This stylization is the essential problematic of knowledge itself; it is also the basis for the possible resolution of the problem of knowing.

When the meaning and notion of God created the stylization of alterity and otherness in the manner of the "Wholly Other," as in the language of Rudolf Otto or Karl Barth—when God was that which was "wholly other," or when this "wholly other" represented the transcendent context of the problem of knowledge—the object to be known could never be exhausted by any mode of human understanding. Any object or being of creation could be known completely only in God and by God.

In the Enlightenment world-view, there was a denouement, an eclipse, a reversal, a distancing of the meaning of deity as a structure of the epistemological problem. Western culture, through its philosophical orientation, brought about the creation of other cultures and peoples as "empirical others"; that is, their alterity is not from this point of view rooted in their inherent givenness as a structure of the created order, but as a creation of the human order and orientation of simply another human culture, "with the right methods."

One is able to discern that these "empirical others" possessed in a debased form some of the characteristics of the archetypal meanings of a deity of former times. They were distantiated, not by an infinity of time and space, but in geographical space and empirical time. They were different from normative human beings but in terms of a qualitative superiority but as inferiors. One's relationship to them was ambiguous; they at once repelled and attracted. The discourse of the relationship to them expressed intimacy to the extent that they were members of the human family, but not an intimacy that defined the Hebraic tradition of justice and love but the more "objective intimacy" of objects of human knowledge.

The ambiguous, debased, and sentimental relationships to these "objects of human knowledge," created through the sciences and categories of Enlightenment reason, brought about what every Enlightenment epistemology had to face sooner or later: the antinomies of reason, those conundrums of reason that appear in its practical and instrumental expressions, that radical difference in reason that seems to lie at the heart of reason itself. We see this in the great work of Immanuel Kant, but it is equally present in Hume's *Dialogues* . . . and in the English empiricists' discussions of the philosophical origins of the human community. It appears in a quite different manner in Hegel's *Phenomenology*.

Hegel posed the problem of the antinomy of reason in the form of a dialectic and used the historical metaphor of the master-slave to illustrate this dialectic in a concrete form. Hegel's posing of the antinomy of reason in terms of this metaphor represents the concrete rendering of a meaning of reason, for it mirrors the historical times of the Enlightenment. The basic issue raised here is, how, within Enlightenment categories of reason and humanism, does one make sense of the practical and instrumental usages made of reason, given the mercantile imperialism of the nations of modern Europe? If otherness is to have no substantive transcendental structure, but is only a moment in the epistemological process, then there seems to be an internal necessity of reason to create "empirical others" for philosophical and economic reasons. These "empirical others" are the others of the New World, of Africa, of India, of China—of the entire extra-European world.

Now, Hegel's *Phenomenology* makes it clear that there is a relationship between the understanding of others and the political power over the objects to be understood. This is a different kind of meaning of the others in relationship to what we call civilization. I put it this way because the very notion of civilization—a notion and word that appears in Western languages only at the end of the eighteenth century—is directly related to the problematical issues of the "empirical others" and alterity. While the word "civilization" does not appear until this late date, all cultures have always had some discourse that enabled them to specify the difference between themselves and other cultures. This sort of difference, though often imputing superiority to one's own culture, was at heart made only on a descriptive level. The new meaning of "civilization" as it emerges from the Enlightenment world-view is not simply descriptive of the cultures of the West; it appears as a necessary philosophical construction within the problem of knowledge. The problem of knowledge is now formed and structured in relationship to a creation that in its very formation constitutes an epistemological problem.

The West is defined in terms of its geographical position in relationship to other parts of the world; more importantly, however, the West is what it is as that culture that has undertaken the economic, military, and *philosophical* creation and simultaneous conquest of a world. The "primitive" and/or the "Orient" constitute necessary meanings of the Western world: the empirical designations of "others" is both an issue of practical and theoretical reason. Antinomies of reason in this form life behind the problematical meaning of the Humanities in a post-Enlightenment world.

The cultural languages of the modern Western world, in both their popular and sophisticated discourses, all possess a special meaning for the "empirical others"; there is a place in every Western "sentence" for those necessary alterities. Sometimes this placement is explicit; as with a word at times it is the necessary and silent pause between the words; at other times it provides the basis for a negative definition (we are not like x). This placement of word or space is thus not so much a description as it is the embodiment of a conceptual and categorical orientation.

Wole Soyinka, Nobel laureate, Nigerian man of letters, once told of his invitation to deliver a series of lectures at Cambridge University. Upon his arrival at Cambridge, he discovered that the faculty of the Department of English Literature were very surprised that he had chosen to lecture on African literature. For them, there was no such category as African literature; this, despite the fact that he was at the time a professor of literature in Nigeria. His colleagues at Cambridge, however, determined that there was to be no category of African literature. Though his lectures dealt with African literatures, Soyinka ended up giving his lectures under the auspices of the Department of Anthropology.

The reason for this is very clear, and one should not fault the faculty of English Literature at Cambridge too severely, as they were being faithful to a received tradition of the academy. In Western cultural languages, to say anything about Africa means that you are dealing with "primitives," and the university discourse about primitives is found in the Anthropology department. It makes no difference whether one is talking about politics, music, economics, or whatever; all aspects and dimensions of the primitives belong in the same place. They belong there categorically and conceptually because this is the place we have made for them within the economy of our Western categorical languages.

This problem has led to various responces in American universities. In an attempt to redress the issue, new intellectual orientations have been added to our curricular structure; we now have African-American Studies, Women's Studies, Native American Studies, etc. All of these additions to our curricular structures are attempts to make up for a lack in our former understanding of the nature of the human and the Humanities. We are adding on; we are making a redress; we are reforming. It is precisely at this point that a peculiar problem arises—an antinomy. The Humanities as traditionally structured in our universities were based substantively, conceptually, and methodologically upon the exclusion of those whom we are now attempting to include. The "humanistic sentence" remains intact in the midst of the so-called reforms; the structure still holds.

We can see this clearly in the debates that have gone on over the last two decades in Anthropology when many scholars realized that the term "primitive" carried a negative valence. A name-change was called for: instead of "primitive," we'll use the terms "non-literate," "small-scale societies," "cold" societies" as over and against the West's "hot" societies—or whatever. What has occurred is simply the creation of tactful synonyms, an exercise in good manners. The sentence remains because as long as the only possible world for the meaning of *humanitas* is a world that is in continuity and consistent with the meaning, rise, and deployment of the Western world—i.e., the Western interpretation of these meanings—we will never raise the pressing problem of the Humanities in our time.

One discourse about the West creates it continuity and coherence through founding its *arche* in the Hebraic cultures of the Ancient Near East and the city-state polities of Hellenism. The modern West is understood as simply an extension of this continuity. The meaning of the modern Western world as a reciprocal relationship between the cultures of the world through the navigation of the Atlantic and Pacific Oceans and the founding of a stability for Northern Europe, and its ability to break from Mediterranean ideologies and powers, is overlooked in most meanings of the modern Western world.

The ideological foci of most interpretations of the West were choices to look backwards instead of forward. These ideologies created a glorious history precisely in the orientations that they were rejecting. The paradigmatic case is the Protestant Reformation's rejection of the

Mediterranean Christian Church; the most intense and ambiguous form is the American rejection of Europe without claiming the authenticity and related meanings of being in the world across the Atlantic. In these rejections, the meaning of the Humanities was allied with the historical thrusts of imperialism and colonialism. This alliance does not imply that all scholars and scholarly work were fueled by the ideological meaning of imperialism and colonialism; it does mean, however, that a corpus of scholarship about human beings and their worlds was fashioned within the context of this ideological construct. Any notion of the Humanities in our time must come to terms with the relationship of the continuity of the Western discourse with the correlative history of Western imperialism from the fifteenth century to the present.

It is for reasons such as these that many of us interested in the Humanities today might sound a bit nihilistic to many humanists and humanistic scholars. An attack is being waged upon every form of the Enlightenment meaning of the human. This attack grates the ears of many humanistic scholars because within the constellation of meanings and values, coming from both the Greco-Roman-Christian and the Enlightenment traditions, humanism—the highest values and valuation of the human mode—expressed as the norm and the epitome of religious and cultural possibility. But these attacks upon the various humanisms, whether they be Greek, Christian, or even Marxist, are really attacks upon the categorical and conceptual language that must of necessity create "empirical others" in worlds that must be conquered and dominated.

An example of this is found in Claude Levi-Strauss' account of a famous argument between Levi-Strauss and Jean-Paul Sartre reported in *The Savage Mind*.[3] Sartre had remarked that one of the great things that should and might occur after the Second World War was the decolonization of all areas of the globe: all of these peoples and cultures in the various parts of the world could join humanity by becoming a part of history. Levi-Strauss' rejoinder was that Sartre, because of his humanism, did not understand that all of these peoples and cultures in the several parts of the world had always been fully human—before colonialism, during colonialism, and, presumably, after colonialism. All peoples in all parts of the world were already, and had previously been, totally human!

[3] Claude Levi-Strauss, *The Savage Mind* (Chicago: University of Chicago Press, 1970), p. 245–69.

What meaning can the Humanities have if we take seriously the import of Levi-Strauss' rejoinder? While the discussion began in the terms of a political meaning, the rejoinder has implications for the order of knowledge. Given the world in which we live as both actual and possible, what directions are possible in the definition of a new form and structure of the Humanities? I, for one, am not of the opinion that we can solve this issue by simply making a smorgasbord, creating the Humanities out of a little bit of this culture and a bit of several other cultures. Any definition of the Humanities as an academic orientation should possess some systematic meaning. We might begin by trying to define the kind of world that is being experienced, understood, and participated in by most human beings.

The world we live in operates in a very different rhythm since the end of the Second World War. It contains different and varied modalities of the human and many of those previously categorized as "empirical others" in the past are now giving expression to a meaning of the Western world in terms of reciprocity rather than objectivity. The empirical and symbolic locus for a meaning of this kind may be seen in that phenomenon that anthropologists and historians of religion have called the "cargo cult."[4] Cargo cults resulted from the impact of modern Western culture on non-Western peoples in various parts of the world since the sixteenth century. The cargo cultists have taken account of the materialism and mercantilism involved in the contact; they have experienced this through technological and military power. They have also seen the destruction of their cultural meanings. By and large, they have been forced to live in two worlds at the same time. They have been forced to come to terms with a world that is not insured to them through tradition. They have assessed the impact and meaning of the relationship among humans as defined by a money economy; they have worried about work, its value and its structure. And through all this, they have attempted through their thought and behavior to create new human beings—new in the sense that these persons will be neither mimics of the West nor persons who wish to go back to their old traditions.

Such newness should be the case for Westerners also. The cargo cult presents us with the possibility that the study of the Humanities will reinstitute a structure of intimacy and reciprocity into its methodological

---

[4] There is an extensive literature on Cargo Cults. See first of all Peter Lawrence's entry on the topic in *The Encyclopedia of Religion*, edited by Mircea Eliade. The bibliography accompanying this article is excellent. See especially K. O. L. Burridge's *Mambu* (London: Methuen, 1961).

orientations. The goal of the cargo cultist might very well specify an ideal for the new structure of the humanistic venture.[5]

Before such an ideal can be attained, the reality of the humanity of the "empirical others" will continue to force a critique of the present order and the meaning of this orientation. The meaning of essentiality, wholeness, and value might well form the continuity in this debate and discourse, but these meanings will now have a new locus. The new placement of these meanings in the several cultures of the world will compel us to undergo what Ashis Nandy has called a debate among "intimate enemies"[6] before we are able to embrace a new and fuller meaning of a Humanities that, in fact, humanizes. Cargo cults are, on the one hand, an expression of the contact, but they are equally expressive of a response to this contact. In this response, the cargo cultist hopes to create a world that will afford both the Westerner and the extra-Western culture the opportunity to participate creatively in an-other world of human beings..

[5] I have explored the broader parameters of this possibility in a forthcoming article in *Beyond the Classic? Essays in Religious Studies and Liberal Education*, eds., Frank Reynolds and Sheryl Borkhalter (Atlanta: Scholars Press, 1990), pp. 19-40.

[6] See Ashis Nandy, *The Intimate Enemy* (New Delhi: Oxford University Press, 1983), *passim*.

III
Studies of Individual Authors and Texts

Integrity and Alterity: Death and the King's Horseman *In the Theater of Understanding*

LARRY D. BOUCHARD

> *Drama aims to make profitable terms with*
> *the alien powers surrounding man.*
>
> —G. Wilson Knight[1]

I.

Against Wole Soyinka's famous play is heard a paradoxical objection, that despite being among the great poetic dramas written in English or to come out of Africa, *Death and the King's Horseman*—or at least the mythopoesis informing it—lacks integrity. It lacks integrity in the way it interprets the history it represents, or the Yoruba myths it reveres, or because in reverencing them it romanticizes a past Nigeria should reject. What Biodun Jeyifo, one of Soyinka's most perceptive Marxist critics, finds intolerable is precisely the celebration of "Elesin Oba's honour—and the honour of the 'race'—[which] in the play hangs on a ritual suicide. However . . . the notion of honour (and integrity and dignity) for which Soyinka in the play provides a metaphysical realisation rests on the patriarchal, feudalist code of the ancient Oyo Kingdom, a code built on class entrenchment and class consolidation."[2] Another, otherwise insightful, commentator pleads, *au contraire*, that "Soyinka is surely questioning this kind of heavy communal demand which requires a man to

---

[1] G. Wilson Knight, *The Golden Labyrinth: A Study of British Drama* (London: Phoenix House, 1962), p. 3.

[2] Biodun Jeyifo, *The Truthful Lie: Essays in a Sociology of African Drama* (London: New Beacon, 1985), p. 34.

sacrifice his life for the sake of some unspecified benefit to the community."[3]

Others challenge not Soyinka's poetic achievements but the self-consistency and appropriateness of his critical thought: Even as he claims to exorcise the "alien gods" or Western ideologies and religions, his own dramatic theory is indebted to certain categories of European poetics. And his retrieval of the Yoruba *orisa* of war and metalcraft, Ogun, as the essence of creativity and revolutionary change is idiosyncratic, warranted less by Yoruba tradition than by his own disillusioning experiences as a political prisoner. As Isidore Okepewho writes in his fine, structuralism-informed study of myth in African literature, "The tragic element Soyinka sees in the African character has been projected largely through his own experience, and that in the end the tormented figure of the Yoruba god Ogun which Soyinka has constantly presented to us cannot be separated from the trouble-torn personality of our poet-dramatist."[4] Okepewho sees myth as a medium both of aesthetic play and speculative rationality that can be aligned with the transformative powers of fiction and philosophy. Writers are more mythical when, like Soyinka, they are "refining" or "revising" tradition than when they are "preserving" or "observing" it. Philosophers are properly mythical when using the local conditions of mythical play to explore questions of universal significance. Thus, myths are less the collective endeavors of communities lacking individual self-consciousness than the innovations of particular people whose works shape tradition. And this is as true of the modern writer as of the traditional oral story teller or poet.

Soyinka, then, would be a more effective story teller than philosopher. Where he is acclaimed, in Okepewho's view, is in refusing the rhapsodies both of "Negritude" (whose hope of world-redemptive African culture Soyinka thought morally and politically naive and dependent upon racist premises lauding African "intuition" while denigrating African rationality) and of doctrinaire Marxism. Where Soyinka is deluded is in desiring to articulate an exclusively African metaphysics; in employing Dionysus, Apollo, and Nietzsche on behalf of this desire; and in not seeing that the Ogun of his own innovation is not much related to

---

[3] Ketu H. Ketrak, *Wole Soyinka and Modern Tragedy: A Study of Dramatic Theory and Practice* (New York: Greenwood, 1986), pp. 89-90.

[4] Isadore Okepewho, *Myth in Africa: A Study of its Aesthetic and Cultural Relevance* (Cambridge: Cambridge University Press, 1983), p. 257.

the Ogun of Yoruba traditions.[5] The "eternal verities" and "irreducible truths" of Soyinka's African worldview seem meaningless beside the diversity and openness of Yoruba myth-making to foreign angles of vision.

Soyinka, of course, would resist these analyses. It is not obvious that he is exploiting European categories in behalf of an "exclusively" African truth, nor that the import of his critical theory obscures the concretely real—unless it is assumed that proper attention to reality must never raise questions that transcend the mundane. It rather seems that he finds in some African and some European traditions distinctive but shareable resources for seeking truth—a purpose at odds with a reticence among his Marxist and aesthetic critics to see that myth, even when transformed by a secular poet, may yet function in art religiously as an authoritative resource in community and tradition. Myth may function, as Okepewho himself shows, as a resource for envisioning and inquiring about reality, but a resource that also transcends the highly particular transformative play of the poet and to which the poet—in making poetry—may find him- or herself fundamentally accountable.

In this respect, *Death and the King's Horseman*[6] well represents Soyinka's poetry and poetics. Like his *Bacchae* and his criticism, it does invite comparison with Nietzsche and also with a noticeably existentialist and phenomenological approach to culture. But it also explores experiences, interpretive actions, and beliefs that resist, finally, such comprehension. *DKH* dramatizes a kind of hermeneutical negativity or "alterity" that resists comprehension in either worldview, African or Western. Its design incorporates traditional and ethical material in ways that are, in effect, intrinsically self-critical. The very word, "understanding" occurs frequently, and each scene creates dramas of understanding and misunderstanding: the allegory of the "Not-I-Bird," in which Elesin jauntily denies he has any fear of death; the misprision between Africans and Africans and Africans and colonists; and Elesin's despairing confession, "even I need to understand" (p. 69).

---

[5] *Ibid.*, pp. 187-203, 244-61. On Negritude, see Wole Soyinka, *Myth, Literature and the African World* (Cambridge: Cambridge University Press, 1976), pp. 126-39, and "The Fourth Stage: Through the Mysteries of Ogun to the Origin of Yoruba Tragedy," in D. W. Jefferson, ed., *The Morality of Art: Essays Presented to G. Wilson Knight by His Colleagues and Friends* (London: Routledge and Kegan Paul, 1969), pp. 126-27. On Marxist criticism of *Death and the King's Horseman*, see Soyinka's "Who's Afraid of Elesin Oba," in *Art, Dialogue and Outrage: Essays on Literature and Culture* (Ibadan: New Horn Press, 1988).

[6] Wole Soyinka, *Death and the King's Horseman* (1975; New York: Hill & Wang, 1987), hereafter cited parenthetically and referred to as *DKH*.

There is also the issue of integrity, which in this play does ask to be comprehended across cultural boundaries. But the way in which *DKH* is a drama of integrity transcends the paradigms of honor and shame particular to ancient Oyo. Rather, the play raises the question of what integrity means in relation to alterity, and exemplifies the way in which theater is an art form distinctly able to manifest integrity as a dimension of life and to inquire into what it manifests. Soyinka's tragedy, then, teaches us about understanding, integrity, and the powers of theater. Read thematically and as a work to be performed, it warrants a certain practical claim (i.e., while it may be proposed in the abstract, it is fully warranted only by the particular theatrical-literary *praxis* in which we discover it). We may infer the claim this way: personal and moral integrity may indeed founder in the encounter with the alien; nevertheless, the achievement of integrity is illusory apart from this encounter. Integrity is not integrity unless it is complicated by alterity.

II.

"Alterity" is a word that has achieved a certain currency of late, along with "otherness." While I do not wish to delimit all the connotations of the term, I do have in mind two senses of alterity. One we might call "dialogical" alterity, for it is the kind of negativity at the heart of the encounter of understanding envisioned by Hans-Georg Gadamer. Classic texts and works of art, and indeed persons, open for us horizons of experience other than our own by bringing forth subject matters and putting them into question. We project our own horizons of experience, assumptions, and traditions only to have them revised or negated, "called up short" before the claim of the other. Without the particularity of historical being and the negativity of having one's projections revised or refuted by the other, there is no understanding (*Verstehen*). Dialogical alterity, then, does affirm the otherness of the other, insofar as the other entails different histories, traditions, languages, and ranges of experience. Gadamer's "fusion of horizons" is not the merger of alien perspectives, which would negate the particularity of both self and other, but precisely a meeting about a question or subject matter, which can occur only if each participant in the dialogue speaks and listens from his or her own locus in time, culture, and tradition. But Gadamer does affirm that hermeneutical understanding is possible because all horizons "constitute the one great horizon," a kind of ultimate horizon of temporality and linguisticity that "embraces everything contained in historical consciousness."⁷ Were this horizon of horizons negated, so too would be broken the interplay of dialogue and understanding. The negation would entail—for lack of easier adjectives—a more "radical" sense of alterity.

This other sense of alterity is hard to specify. One might look for it in Jürgen Habermas's warning that dialogue is not immune from the "systematic distortions" arising from outside the hermeneutical encounter. The blindness caused by neurosis or ideologically rationalized interests must be located and clarified by the application of critical methods that distance us from the dialogical impasse; only when the distortion is resolved can conversation recommence. However, the alterity of distortion is radical only in that it defeats "dialogue"; the causes of the distortion are, in principle, open to explanation only by a self-critical science whose avowed interest is to liberate conversation. Paul Ricoeur's distinction between *explanation* (which can look "behind" the dialogical encounter to causes of distortion) and *understanding* (which can correct and be corrected by explanation) may show that neurotic and ideological pathologies are comprehensible within the context of nature and history, which constitute the "great horizon" of human communication.⁸

One might find another more radical sense of alterity in an aspect of the tragic vision that Ricoeur explores in *The Symbolism of Evil.*⁹ In his view, both the Hebraic notion of sin, which is "already there" in the primal scene of disobedience, and the Greek notion of *até*, which strikes at the tragic hero-victim's cognitive capacities, both resist reductive comprehension. Sin and *até*, however different, are both distortions that resist coherent placement in the horizon of horizons; we experience them as intractably perplexing. Thus in certain Christian theologies (i.e., Augustine, Kierkegaard, Karl Barth) we find conceptions of evil and sin that state the character of this perplexity without claiming to "understand" it. When Christianity locates sin in the turning of our will from God, there remains in the otherness of sin a "turning" that is already turning us. To turn away from sin, we must be liberated or turned

⁷ Hans-Georg Gadamer, *Truth and Method*, translation edited by Garrett Barden and John Cumming (New York: Seabury, 1975).

⁸ Jürgen Habermas, "On Hermeneutics' Claim to Universality," in Kurt Mueller-Vollmer, ed., *The Hermeneutics Reader* (New York: Continuum, 1988); Paul Ricoeur, "Hermeneutics and the Critique of Ideology," in *Hermeneutics and the Human Sciences: Essays on Language, Action and Interpretation*, ed. and trans. by John B. Thompson (Cambridge: Cambridge University Press, 1981).

⁹ Paul Ricoeur, *The Symbolism of Evil*, trans. by Emerson Buchanan (Boston: Beacon, 1967).

by grace—itself a mode of alterity that resists coherent comprehension and thus may seem a threatening as well as liberating prospect.

One may seek other liberating prospects of alterity in deconstructive criticism, as it unravels the diacritical texture of language. The critique of logocentrism in Derrida is readily grasped in terms of the centrality and yet arbitrary nature of the sign in Western thought. We want to trust signs, we want to be at home with them. In claiming to refer in our uses of language—including the language of dialogical encounter—we assume that we can trust the unity of signifier and signified (the two components in Ferdinand de Saussure's model of the sign).[10] When this trust proves unwarranted, when we find ourselves homeless before the inherent arbitrariness of this signifier/signified relationship, then an "Ariadne's thread"[11] has been exposed. And when pulled, it threatens (or promises) to unravel the coherence of signification, both within linguistic systems and in reference to the world.

All language is complicated by diacritical difference, but, again, distinctions must be made. The neologism *differance*—which indicates that all signifieds are signifiers *differing from* and always *deferring to* other signifiers—suggests a kind of alterity that is indeed common to the linguisticity of the human situation. Without acknowledging the *arbitrary*, hence alien aspect to our signs there can be no linguistic play, no encounter with others as others. Yet in saying this we again assume another "great horizon" of linguistic play which, while not guaranteeing the coherence of discourse, is a characterization of our *common* humanity in history and nature. And to those of us who find moral impetus in notions of solidarity with others as others, it is here that Deconstruction may have much to contribute.

But in the arbitrariness of signification one finds the alterity of embodiment, which may be a more radical problem for being less amenable to universalization. We might ask, whence these ghosts of presence and self-presence that haunt every naive act of speaking? If signs are but arbitrary linkings of signifier with signified (or even only with other signifiers), then may we not ask how the linkage is enacted? Any transcendental answer would announce no comprehensible divinity or ideality but a God whose otherness is always experienced as problem if also as

---

[10]   Jacques Derrida, *Of Grammatology*, trans. by Gayatri Chakravorty Spivak (Baltimore: Johns Hopkins University Press, 1976), pp. 27-73.

[11]   Mark C. Taylor uses this metaphor in *Erring: A PostModern A/Theology* (Chicago: University of Chicago Press, 1984); he distinguishes "altarity" from "differance" in *Altarity* (Chicago: University of Chicago Press, 1987), xxi-xxxiv.

promise, no more "present" than we are present to ourselves. Any practical answer—that it is our moving bodies that leave traces, that perform the linkages, that enact the play of signifiers—admits an alterity of embodiment that also betrays coherent explanation. Our bodies, as ephemeral as signs, enact the strange play of signifiers. Radical alterity, then, is what we experience when our embodied play is interrupted and we can give no coherent account of the interruption. Hermeneutics and Deconstruction both may give us languages that help speak of the alterity that differentiates us one from another and limits the power of our languages to reveal ourselves and the world. But the more radical alterity that embodies and disembodies us will be known by its resistance to both kinds of language. The resistance itself, however, may be dramatized.

III.

In the Yoruba city of Oyo the ancient tradition was that when the King (*Oba* or, more specifically, the *Alafin*) died, then the chief who was the King's Horseman (*Elesin Oba*), itself an inherited role of great status, must also die to insure the king's safe passage to the realm of the ancestors. So Elesin awaits in joyous equanimity the right moment in the moon's journey to begin a trance-like dance that will culminate in death, induced by ritual and the power of his own will. The people of Oyo, whose cosmic security and creative power depend upon Elesin's successful completion of this dance, encourage and warn him against complacency—especially Iyaloja, leader of the powerful women of the market where the opening scene transpires, and the Praise-Singer, whose chants will guide Elesin into his journey. But these preparations are discovered by the District Officer, Simon Pilkings, who is resolved not to permit a ritual suicide while the British prince is visiting the district. For it is World War II, and H.R.H. has been sailing abroad to bolster colonial morale.

Not only has Soyinka's play baffled many audiences, but so also has the Author's Note prefacing the script, which warns that the conflict in *Death and the King's Horseman* is "metaphysical" and not comprehended by the "facile tag of 'clash of cultures.'" Culture clash "presupposes a potential equality *in every given situation* of the alien culture and the indigenous, on the actual soil of the latter." But, the uninitiated may protest, if *DKH* is not a clash of cultures, what is? Okepewho observes[12] that this

---

[12] Okepewho, p. 244.

warning effectively contrasts the play with another work Soyinka mentions appreciatively in the Note. Duro Ladipo's opera, *Oba Waja* (The
King is Dead), is based on the same historical incident as *DKH* and treats
the District Officer far more sympathetically than does Soyinka: indeed,
Ladipo's D.O. in a sense is, as Soyinka says, "the victim of a cruel
dilemma." Against his better judgment, he is goaded by his wife into arresting Elesin and stopping the suicide, much to the horror of Oyo's
Elders and to the shame of Elesin. The latter's son, a trader in Ghana,
learns of the Alafin's death and returns to Oyo expecting his father's fu-
neral. Horrified to find Elesin alive, he fatally stabs himself, whereupon
Elesin takes his own life as well. The D.O. then states his view of the
tragic crux:

> O God!
> Can I be blamed for doing justice?
> Is kindness my crime?
> I was trying to save a life—
> And I have caused a double death.
> Man only understands the good he does unto himself,
> When he acts for others,
> Good is turned into evil; evil is turned into good![13]

There is much commendable about Ladipo's version of Elesin's
tragedy, not least of which the dilemma Soyinka refers to: Elesin fails because he meets an alien force he cannot understand and does not resist,
and the D.O. suffers the kind of catastrophe that can come from a blind
act of virtue. As is said, these things happen. Soyinka's objection has to
do with interpretations that would reduce such a conflict to a kind of anthropological equation in which the symbol system of each side simply
cancels out the other, leaving us at best with an abstract insight into cultural relativity and genuinely informed by neither side of the conflict.
Soyinka wants to interpret the drama in a way that shows the meanings
and indeterminacies of Elesin's side illuminating reality more adequately
than the colonial side, which for the most part is satirized. His Author's
Note concludes:

The Colonial Factor is an incident, a catalytic incident merely. The confrontation in the play is largely metaphysical, contained in the human vehi-

[13] Duro Ladipo, *Oba Waja*, in *Three Plays*, trans. by Ulli Beier (Ibadan: Mbari
Publications, 1964), p. 72.

cle which is Elesin and the universe of the Yoruba mind— the world of the
living, the dead and the unborn, and the numinous passage which links all:
transition. *Death and the King's Horseman* can be fully realised only through
an evocation of music from the abyss of transition. (p.6)

Thus, Soyinka asks us to interpret his play for the knowledge of reality it
may give us. But this does not mean that the distinction between alien
cultures is not a crucial possibility in this drama. It is perhaps more than
"catalytic," not only because of the scenes depicting the colonial factor,
but also because the play is written in the language of the colonists as
well as in the cadences and metaphors of Yoruba poetry, and it is offered
to audiences who include former colonists as well as Africans who may
be alienated from the traditions Soyinka evokes. The *juxtaposition*—not
"clash," and only rarely "encounter"—of cultures is built into both the
dramatic and the theatrical forms of *DKH*. Whatever is meant by the
metaphysics of transition, Soyinka wants it to spill out into the audience;
and I want to approach the play mainly as an unwitting participant in
the audience Soyinka addresses.[14] My claim is, in part, that *DKH* seeks to
disclose the effective reality of "transition" and to expose the inability of
thought to "understand" the alterity of transition except in terms of an
act of self-critical negation.

Soyinka's departures both from Ladipo's scenario and the historical
incident (which occurred in 1946, not during the war, and in which the
Elesin did not die) all serve a complex hermeneutical enterprise. By
changing Elesin's son from a trader in Ghana to Olunde, a medical student in England, an angle of vision is created that offers some minimal
possibilities for understanding across horizons and specifies more precisely the nature of nonunderstanding—especially, as we shall see, in
Olunde's encounter with Jane Pilkings. In Ladipo's version it was the
unnamed wife of the D.O. who was the most ignorant, while the D.O.
articulated a tragic awareness that somewhat balanced that of Elesin and
his community. Soyinka reverses this, making Simon Pilkings boorishly
uncaring not only of Yoruba traditions but also those of his Catholic
houseboy, Joseph, and him Muslim policeman, Sgt. Amusa—both of
whom take seriously enough what is happening in Oyo either to fear

[14] Westerners are not the only unwitting ones in Soyinka's audience; see Tundonu
Amosu, "The Nigerian Dramatist and His Audience: The Question of Language and
Culture," *Odu* 28 (1985): 35-45; and Chuck Mike, *Soyinka as Director: Interview* (Ife:
University of Ife, 1986). On theater performed between colonists and subjects, see
Max R. Harris, *The Dialogical Theatre: Dramatizations of the Conquest of Mexico and the
Question of The Other* (forthcoming).

what they ostensibly disbelieve (Amusa) or to explain it soberly (Joseph). The Pilkings themselves usually speak gratingly as if in a mannered British melodrama, while Elesin and the Oyo chorus speak in a high poetic style. By setting the action during the war, Soyinka juxtaposes the ritual systems of the cultures at a moment when both are in crisis, not to equate them but to contrast a fragile world of ethical meaning with an unassailable society that is morally vacuous.

We become aware of this juxtaposition in the second of the five scenes, in which we move from the market to the Pilkings' veranda, where they are preparing to attend a fancy dress ball in honor of the Prince. Sgt. Amusa, who has come to warn of the ritual suicide, is horrified by the sight of their costumes—the Yoruba ancestral masquerade, or *egungun*. The ironies here are both within the world of the play and between the stage and the audience. There is, in the first place, the belief that the ancestral realm coexists with the realm of the living; the Yoruba *egungun* is a kind of ritual drama that brings to bear, or instantiates, the reality of the ancestors.[15] The Pilkings' desecration of this ritual is not merely disrespectful but, for Amusa (a servile victim of halfway assimilation, who only at this moment demonstrates any capacity for integrity), seems to be an actual interference in the reality of the other: "Sir, it is a matter of death. How can man talk against death to person in uniform of death? Is like talking against government to person in uniform of police" (p. 29).

And there is, in the second place, a metatheatrical irony. After all, the play itself would seem to occasion a clash between audience and worldview: Western vs. African and contemporary political Africa vs. Soyinka's vision of an African worldview. If the desecration of the ancestral masks is efficacious interference, and if our perspective in the audience at this moment coincides with either that of the Pilkings or Amusa, then we ourselves are effectively desecrating the *egungun*. But the play creates this possibility of metatheatrical culture clash only to negate it.

This last point may be understood, in part, by way of the "ethical" and "performative" nature of theatrical art. In Aristotle, an argument from *ethos* (hence, "ethical" argument) is one that persuades us by eliciting our trust in the speaker's character, but the trust is created not by an antecedent impression we may have of the speaker, but "by the speech

---

[15] See Oludare Olajubu, "Iwi Egungun Chants—An Introduction," in Bernth Lindsfors, ed., *Critical Perspectives on Nigerian Literature* (Washington, D.C.: Three Continents Press, 1976).

itself." In an important sense, the ethos of the speaker is created in the speaking. Projected through the speech are shared resources of culture and language that the speaker now embodies; he or she invites us, then, to join in this rhetorical space created about the matter at issue. "It is not true," Aristotle says, "that the probity of the speaker contributes nothings to his persuasiveness; on the contrary, we might almost affirm that his character [*ethos*] is the most potent of all means to persuasion."[16] "Performance utterances" (including ritual) function similarly: a statement such as "I promise" brings into being a new situation, instantiates what it refers to—in this case the reality of a promise that effects a new relationship between speaker and audience.[17]

If our many uses of discourse entail ethical and performative speaking, so much more so does theater, where through language and gesture an ephemeral world is effected in real space and time before the eyes of a living audience. And if theater is ethical and performative, so much more is "metatheater," or theater conscious of itself as theater and of the audience (as in Brecht and Wilder). For in exposing, yet maintaining, the "fictional" world, the audience is invited into a theatrical space that includes real persons in the act of creating character through the negation of "characters."[18]

Soyinka's is theater that invites metatheater back into its fiction. His characters know that to live is to perform either paradigms that give life and shape to reality or roles that deny any relation to reality. (That Simon acts as if the world is but shifting social illusions is signaled by his cynicism about religion—including Joseph's Catholicism—and about culture—to him the Prince is little more than a "coat of arms." That Amusa

[16] *The Rhetoric of Aristotle* (I.2), trans. by Lane Cooper (New York: Appleton, 1932), pp. 8-9. On rhetorical *ethos*, see Jim W. Corder, *Uses of Rhetoric* (New York: Lippincott, 1971), pp. 72-95, and S. M. Halloran, "On the End of Rhetoric, Classical and Modern," *College English* 36 (1975): 621-30.

[17] J. L. Austin, *Philosophical Papers* (London: Oxford University Press, 1961), pp. 220-39. See Paul Ricoeur, *Interpretation Theory* (Ft. Worth: Texas Christian University Press, 1976), pp. 12-19. On "instantiation," see Robert P. Scharlemann, "The Forgotten Self and the Forgotten Divine," in Julian N. Hartt, ed., *The Critique of Modernity: Theological Reflections on Contemporary Culture* (Charlottesville: University of Virginia Press, 1986). On *mimesis* as performance, see William Schweiker, "Beyond Imitation: Mimetic Praxis in Gadamer, Ricoeur, and Derrida," *Journal of Religion* 68 (1988): 21-38.

[18] See Lionel Abel, *Metatheatre: A New View of Dramatic Form* (New York: Hill & Wang, 1963), and June Schueter, *Metafictional Characters in Modern Drama* (New York: Columbia University Press, 1979). On "efficiency" in theater, see Richard Schechner, "From Ritual to Theatre and Back," in R. Schechner and Mady Schuman, eds., *Ritual, Play, and Performance* (New York: Seabury, 1976).

is lost in social transition—he has no paradigm, only a humiliating role—
is obvious when the women of the market gleefully parody and shame
him in scene three.) The characters also know implicitly that paradigms
resist complete understanding, for they are "real" not as abstractions but
in their performance. We in the audience are invited to see that we also
live metatheatrically, performing either meaningful paradigms or
alienating roles. "Clash of cultures" is thereby negated, for we are no
longer merely translators of cultural signs but performers in the drama of
misunderstanding and discovery being performed in the play. We are
invited into a world defined not by the Pilkings, but by the egungun
masks they wear unwittingly. We may recognize that the masks effect
other realities more pertinent than those of the colonists. And this
recognition may challenge us to know the other, even if our knowledge is
largely that of ignorance. *DKH* invites a reading from its unwitting audience, but only if the reading is based upon a recognition of witlessness.
At some point each character fails to understand, before one kind of alterity or another. Pathos of understanding is thereby offered as a norm
for interpretation.

To us in the unwitting audience, this pathos is the norm not only because understanding is displaced by the arbitrary play of cultural differences but more crucially because we are confronting the embodied enactment of an alien cosmological vision that proffers a claim unto us. Our
recognition of the cultural other is subsumed into our discovery of the
cosmological other—Soyinka's "abyss of transition"—which by its own
"nature" would resist understanding in any culture. Our recognition of
Elesin's and Olunde's crises as being crises of integrity owes to our
recognition that the grounds of integrity—certain cultural or moral
paradigms—are at risk, that the grounds are "real" only insofar as they
are performed, and that the people of Oyo are ultimately no more able
than we to comprehend the shifting of the ground.

In *DKH*, the subsuming of cultural difference into ontological indeterminacy is integral to the fiction as well as to the dynamics of performance. The converging lines of action are, first, Elesin's fateful impulse
to marry a girl betrothed to Iyaloja's son and to conceive a child by her
immediately before his death—at the very boundaries of the living, the
ancestors, and the unborn—and, second, Pilkings' measures to prevent
him. The actions converge but do not meet, in that the causes of Elesin's
failure are given incommensurate meanings. Again, there is superficially
a conflict of cultural interpretation. Form one side, the failure is "caused"
by the intervention of the colonial police, the cultural other; Pilkings'

view is simply that his officers have at the last moment prevented a barbaric ritual that might have spoiled the royal visit. From Elesin's side, the failure came with a sudden fading of his will, his longing for his beautiful bride and, consequently, his loss of integration with his supreme vocational task.[19] In the last scene, Elesin stands in a cage enchained, a prisoner of shame and bewilderment, and makes several confessions—this one to the silent bride who remains near him:

> First I blamed the white man, then I blamed the gods for deserting me. Now I feel I want to blame you for the mystery of the sapping of my will. But blame is a strange peace for a man to bring a world he has deeply wronged, and to its innocent dwellers. . . . I needed you as the abyss across which my body must be drawn, I filled it with earth and dropped my seed in it at the moment of preparedness for my crossing. . . . My weakness came not merely from the abomination of the white man who came violently into my fading presence, there was also a weight of longing on my earth-held limbs. I would have shaken it off, already my foot had begun to lift but then, the white ghost entered and all was defiled. (p. 65)

Elesin also confesses to Iyaloja, who agreed to his usurpation of her son's marriage only if it would further empower Elesin's ultimate journey. In her is now concentrated the contempt and resignation of the people of Oyo:

> IYALOJA: Who are you to open a new life when you dared not open the door to a new existence? . . .
>
> ELESIN: My powers deserted me. My charms, my spells, even my voice lacked strength when I made to summon the powers that would lead me over the last measure of earth into the land of the fleshless. You saw it, Iyaloja. You saw me struggle to retrieve my will from the power of the stranger whose shadow fell across the doorway and left me foundering and blundering in a maze I had never before encountered. (pp. 67-68)

Again the colonial factor is subsumed into the ontological: both Pilkings' intervention and Elesin's tragic failure are moments across the indeterminate "doorway," moments in transition.

---

[19]   See D. S. Izevbaye, "Mediation in Soyinka: The Case of the King's Horseman," in James Gibbs, ed., *Critical Perspectives on Wole Soyinka* (Washington, D.C.: Three Continents Press, 1980).

IV.

As "transition" is the most crucial alterity theme in Soyinka's dramatic theory and practice, we need to leave for a time the unwitting audience and step behind the stage to fathom certain of his mythopoetic intentions. These involve the transformative and hermeneutical functions of theater.

Both theater and ritual integrate their onlookers and performers into a shared experience, which then leaves each participant a changed and perhaps transformed individual. The transformation itself has to do with one's apprehension of being in community and in nature, an effect of theater that has political as well as religious implications.[20] In an essay in which Soyinka articulates yet distances himself from a Marxist vision of social *praxis*, theater is nominated "perhaps the most revolutionary art form."[21] It is revolutionary not because it subsumes the individual into a process of social change, but because it shows the individual to be inseparable not only from various human communities but from the "chthonic" forces of creativity and destruction that impinge upon it from without and within. This potency of theater is evident in African, Greek, and Shakespearean drama and even, Soyinka observes, in such explorations of bourgeois neurosis as Edward Albee's *Who's Afraid of Virginia Woolf?*. The fulsome realization of ritual in theater can serve a critical function in modern culture, namely, to displace compartmentalized versions of reality that alienate persons from those inchoate depths of community and nature that are the real sources of human understanding and transformation.

This view of theater as transformation owes something to Brecht, something to Soyinka's mentor at the University of Leeds, G. Wilson Knight, something to Nietzsche, and much to Yoruba ritual and mythic traditions retrieved in behalf of a constructive interpretation of the "African worldview." While this worldview as such is relative and particular—"exclusive" as Okepewho says—its ontology is offered as a claim that claims all. In the seminal essay, "The Fourth Stage"—a single draft of which he managed to submit to a festschrift for Knight before be-

---

[20] For Soyinka on theater as transformation, see "The Fourth Stage," and also "Morality and Aesthetics in the Ritual Archetype," and "Drama and the African World-View" in *Myth, Literature*. For an excellent discussion of these and other sources, see Ann B. Davis, "Dramatic Theory of Wole Soyinka," in Gibbs.

[21] Wole Soyinka, "Drama and the Idioms of Liberation: Proletarian Illusions," in *Art, Dialogue and Outrage*, p. 45.

ing incarcerated in 1967—Soyinka proposes a fourth region of "transition" underlying the three separate but contemporaneous "aspects of time" to which the Yoruba are accountable: the unborn, the living, and the ancestral dead. The fourth region is one of chaos and nondifferentiation, a "numinous" abyss that is both radically alien yet near at hand. "Transition" is a hermeneutical category for Soyinka. He finds it implicit throughout Yoruba tradition, and he uses it to interpret these traditions as living possibilities.

Two Yoruba *orisa*, Obatala and Ogun, define the most important implications of transition, for Soyinka, and serve as dramatic paradigms in much of his imaginative work.[22] Obatala is the traditional creator god, whom Soyinka regards as the serene god of "plastic healing" and "patient suffering," whose primary function is to create the forms, not the living breath, of human beings. Ogun is the traditional god of war, of hunting, of iron and toolcraft, maker of roads.[23] But Soyinka collects various *oriki*, or praise-chants, suggesting that Ogun should be more profoundly understood as the god of creativity, of creative essence, of the unity of creative and destructive impulses. We can see, then, the parallel of Obatala and Ogun with Apollo and Dionysus; but the differences are evidently more profound that the parallels, for Soyinka is at pains to emphasize the essential realism of both Yoruba principles:

> Obatala the sculptural god is not the artist of Apollonian illusion but of inner essence. . . . [not] Nietzsche's Apollonian "mirror of enchantment" but a statement of world resolution. The mutual tempering of illusion and will, necessary to an understanding of the Hellenic spirit, would mislead us, confronted in Yoruba art by a similarity in the aesthetic serenity of the plastic arts to the Hellenic. But [Yoruba] art is not ideational but "essential." As for Ogun, he is best understood in Hellenic values as a totality of the Dionysian, Apollonian and Promethean virtues. . . . Ogun stands in fact for a transcendental, humane but rigidly restorative justice. The first artist and technician of the forge, he, like Nietzsche's Apollonian spirit, creates a "massive impact

---

[22] See Stephan Larsen, *A Writer and His Gods: A Study of the Importance of Yoruba Myths and Religious Ideas to the Writing of Wole Soyinka* (Stockholm: University of Stockholm, 1983).

[23] On Yoruba *orisa*, see Ulli Beier, *Yoruba Myths* (Cambridge: Cambridge University Press, 1980); Benjamin C. Ray, *African Religions: Symbol, Ritual, and Community* (Englewood Cliffs, N.J.: Prentice Hall, 1976), pp. 68-72; J. Pimberton III, "A Cluster of Sacred Symbols: Orisa Worship Among the Igbomina Yoruba of Ila-Orangun," *History of Religions* 17 (1977): 1-28; and Judith Gleason, *Oya: In Praise of the Goddess* (Boston: Shambhala, 1980).

of image, concept, ethical doctrine and sympathy." Obatala is the placid
essence of creation, Ogun the creative urge and instinct.[24]

The insistence that Ogun and Obatala are both irreducibly real means
that Soyinka's hermeneutics, in contrast to that of structuralists and
Marxists, is ontological or, as he says, metaphysical. In the parlance of
contemporary literary-philosophical debate, Soyinka asserts a
"foundational" semantics rather than a rhetoric of signs, and thus is liable to the critique that what he is really offering us is African logocentrism. But in his theoretical writings—and even more so in imaginative
works such as the novel *Season of Anomy* (patterned on the Orpheus
myth) and *Death and the King's Horseman*—the chthonic abyss of transition, of both possibility and annihilation, is chaotic and indeterminate,
functioning as much as ultimate question as ultimate referent. It marks
an intrinsically self-critical moment in Soyinka's thought. For transition
can be referred to only in performative *praxis*, which in ritual, on stage,
or in political process inherently entails disintegration; any subsequent
reintegration, while liberating, is always provisional. If, as Soyinka often
says, the goal of Yoruba morality is the harmonious resolution of relations among the cosmos, in his thinking such resolutions are ever encompassed by a profound awareness of conflict and fear of the dissolution of
the communal self.

That the *orisa* can serve as paradigms for both divine and human action is true because many of them also crossed the gulf from the realm of
the living to the realm of the ancestors: Ogun was a great warrior,
Obatala an artist, Sango a legendary Oyo king, and many of the traditional myths and ritual dramas recount events associated with their
apotheoses. Soyinka considers Ogun to be the "first actor": in
Promethean-like *hubris* he defiantly challenged the void, was torn asun-
der, survived the winds of dissolution by the sheer assertion of his will,
and emerged for the benefit of the human community. His passage recapitulates the primal cosmogonic act, when the first, unnamed *Orisa*
was fragmented by his slave Atunda (an "other" whose origin the myth
gives no account), who rolled a great rock upon him; other *orisa* then appeared to pick up the scattered pieces and reorder the world, often imperfectly. Ogun is also a model for the actor in ritual drama, one "who
prepares mentally and physically for his disintegration and reassembly
within the universal womb of origin, experiences the transitional yet in-

---

[24] "The Fourth Stage," p. 120.

choate matrix of death and being."[25] In many of Soyinka's works, characters who embody the spirit of Ogun challenge socio-political stagnation or oppression on the basis of a tradition that exalts, rather than resists, such revolutionary challenges.[26]

But *DKH* is preeminently about the ambiguities of embodying the paradigm of Ogun, and of Obatala as well. As we shall see, Elesin's son Olunde—the medical student in England—is a figure of Obatala who must become one of Ogun. For Obatala is a paradigm of healing and the reconciliation of opposites. He is the patient saint, ransomed prisoner, god of the suffering—of cripples and the misformed, of albinos—in part because in unwitting error he caused their suffering; once, drunk on palm wine, he slipped while molding the bodies of people (and so forbade palm wine to his devotees thereafter). There is the sense in which Elesin, when he desires to conceive a child on the boundaries of space and time as if to reconcile the three realms, forgets the paradigm of Ogun and embodies that of Obatala, including Obatala's intoxication. (This confusion of paradigms is more, not less, suggestive when we know that Ogun too was a seeker of women and abuser of palm wine.)

Transition itself is symbolized by no paradigm, embodied by no *orisa*, and so remains indeterminate. As Elesin ventured toward the abyss, not only did he risk the disintegration of his being, but also of his understanding. Thus his confession to Iyaloja: "I need neither your pity nor the pity of the world. I need understanding. Even I need to understand." He offers then a final interpretation: at the edge of transition, he was defeated by an intruding, impossible notion, that in the white man's intervention there might be a divine reprieve from transition.

> It is when the alien hand pollutes the source of will, when a stranger force of violence shatters the mind's calm resolution, this is when a man is made to commit the awful treachery of relief, commit in his thought the unspeakable blasphemy of seeing the hand of the gods in this alien rupture of the world. I know it was this thought that killed me, that sapped my powers. . . . My will was squelched in the spittle of an alien race, and all because I had committed this blasphemy of thought—that there might be the hand of the gods in a stranger's intervention. (p. 69)

[25] *Myth, Literature,* p. 30.
[26] Along with Okepewho and Larsen, see also Eldred Druosimi Jones, *The Writing of Wole Soyinka* (London: Heinemann, 1973).

V.

We have encountered alterity in both its aspects. We have met the stranger who performs other signs or paradigms, with whom we might create a shared space of understanding only if we put at risk our claims to understand; such dialogical alterity is what Soyinka fears may devolve into "clash of cultures." We shall see one more instance of it, but in *DKH* it is subordinate to a more radical alterity: the other that resists placement on even the most indeterminate horizon of horizons, not *differance* but "transition." What ultimately dislocates Elesin is not merely the speaker of other signs (hermeneutical difference), nor even the indeterminacy of his own signs (diacritical *differance*), but an active abyss that threatens the performance of signification, even while providing the theater of such performance. In the abyss Elesin must cross, Simon is one ephemeral danger; another is the confusion of Ogun and Obatala.

Does alterity in both its aspects make understanding not only elusive but impossible? That is one question, and in this play there is another. *DKH* ostensibly dramatizes the failure of Elesin—one upon whose integrity depends the integrity of a world—to act with integrity. Does alterity make integrity an impossible or meaningless virtue, an illusion masking the fact that every soul is but a muddle of scripts and performances with no beginnings, no centers, no ends and is, for all that, further threatened by the mischievous tricks of the Yoruba god Esu or the malevolent clouding of mentality that the Greeks call *atê*? And does not alterity in both aspects make it impossible to understand or reliably recognize integrity across the gulfs of difference and transition? Elesin represents one side of the problem: integrity entails performance and the other's recognition that the performance is appropriate and efficacious. Jane Pilkings and Olunde represent another side: to recognize another's integrity always entails an act of interpretation.

It is common to distinguish between personal and moral integrity. The former suggests the virtue of being a self-consistent, relatively autonomous, and eminently reliable person. "Honesty," "sincerity," and "authenticity" are often associated with personal integrity;[27] the idea ranges from allegiance to one's community and friends to reliance upon one's own creative resources. Polonius in *Hamlet* disingenuously defines

---

[27] See Henri Peyre, *Literature and Sincerity* (New Haven: Yale University Press, 1963), and Lionel Trilling, *Sincerity and Authenticity* (New York: Harcourt Brace Jovanovich, 1971).

its maxim, "To thine own self be true." Moral integrity connotes uncompromising commitment to certain fundamental and serious moral principles.[28] In both uses, integrity bears on the constitution of the self and the value of self to oneself, and thus usually—though certainly not always—suggests interiority. It is the interior, self-consistent self that typically is said to have integrity, not one who "only goes through the motions" or whose promises are clouded by "mental reservations."[29] To say someone has integrity is tantamount to making a judgment upon one's "soul." While the judgment may be based on outwardly observed actions and statements, it is often assumed that only a glimpse into the recesses of the other would authoritatively confirm or disconfirm such a judgment.

It is here that we take from theater two insights. First, because theater, unlike some forms of narrative, normally grants us no glimpse behind the mask directly into another's consciousness but demands that we learn everything from the embodied action and speech of live actors, character in theater recapitulates our normal relations with others. In the theater, as in life, character is effected in performance and in the presence and absence of the performances of others. Character is neither sheer self-creation, nor sheer role-determination, but arises in the interplay of inheritance and expression. What is "behind" each mask is what is created between and among the masks. Second, since the idea of the sheer interiority of the self is problematic to begin with—involving an infinite regress of enactments, so that even as we perform ourselves to ourselves we are never finally sure what is "behind" our own performance—the theatrical situation also implies that a character's integrity is established in performance. Integrity is enacted, effected, and interpreted in a public that includes our interior life. Even as we perform ourselves privately to ourselves, we are among an ensemble of other performers present or absent, living or dead, remembered or anticipated, virtual or possible. If integrity is, therefore, exceedingly public, then a better way to think about integrity and identity is in terms of the *integration* of present and absent

---

[28] See Bernard Williams, "A Critique of Utilitarianism," in J. J. C. Smart and B. Williams, *Utilitarianism: For and Against* (Cambridge: Cambridge University Press, 1973); Lynn McFall, "Integrity," *Ethics* 98 (1987): 5-20; Mark S. Halfon, *Integrity: A Philosophical Inquiry* (Philadelphia: Temple University Press, 1989).

[29] See especially Gabriele Taylor, "Integrity," *The Aristotelian Society*, supp. vol. 55 (1981): 143-59, with critique by Raymond Gaita, pp. 161-76.

relationships—with others, with tradition and history, with nature—
rather than in terms of a dichotomy between inside and outside.[30]

In the case of Elesin, to act with integrity entails the give and take of
performance. The "give," obviously, is that his personal task is also a
public task. Being true to himself coincides with being true to the vocation of King's Horseman; had he successfully performed the dance of
transition he would have been, in that dance, most successfully himself.
His community would have been complete as well, for its integrity and
that of Elesin are mutually implicated in vocation and performance.
Thus, Elesin's parody of those who flee death ends with a self-affirma-
tion to which the people willingly assent:

> ELESIN: I, when that Not-I bird perched
> Upon my roof, bade him seek his nest again,
> Safe, without care or fear. I unrolled
> My welcome mat for him to see. Not-I
> Flew happily away, you'll hear his voice
> No more in this lifetime—You all know
> What I am.
>
> PRAISE- [answering] That rock which turns open lodes
> SINGER: Into the path of lightning. A gay
> Thoroughbred whose stride disdains
> To falter though an adder reared
> Suddenly in its path.
>
> ELESIN: My rein is loosened.
> I am master of my Fate. When the hour comes
> Watch me dance along the narrow path
> Glazed by the soles of my precursors.
> My soul is eager. I shall not turn aside. (p. 14)

And so the "take": Elesin's integrity depends upon the performance of
others, especially the elaborate praise chants that serve not only to encourage him but to further establish his character. In reference to
Ladipo's *Oba Waja*, Robert Plant Armstrong has described praise names
as being a "syndetic," or "additive" means of constituting character.
"They represent an effective way . . . to bring a dramatic or a fictive char-

---

[30] Erving Goffman distracts more than helps this account of integrity, for in ostensibly offering us a socially constructed, performing self, he tacitly requires a radically
interior, inaccessible self. See *The Presentation of Self in Everyday Life* (1959; Woodstock,
N. Y.: Overlook, 1973), pp. 248-51.

acter into existence."[31] DKH records a similar phenomenon: throughout
the first and third scenes Iyaloja, the Praise-Singer, and the women of
Oyo contribute, through their praise, power to Elesin:

ELESIN: You who are breath and giver of my being
            How shall I dare refuse you forgiveness
            Even if the offense were real.

            . . . .

WOMEN: For a while we truly feared
            Our hands had wrenched the world adrift
            In emptiness.

IYALOJA: Richly, richly, robe him richly
            The cloth of honour is *alari*
            Sanyan is the band of friendship
            Boa-skin makes slippers of esteem

WOMEN: For a while we truly feared
            Our hands had wrenched the world adrift
            In emptiness.

PRAISE-   He who must, must voyage forth
SINGER   The world will not roll backwards
            It is he who must, with one
            Great gesture overtake the world. (p. 17)

Likewise, when at last Iyaloja and the Praise-Singer confront Elesin
and place the covered body of Olunde before him, their words both
enunciate Elesin's shame—the severing of all relationships—and yet
encourage him to complete his task, to send a message to Alafin, even if
only in the least desirable way.

PRAISE-SINGER: What now is left? If there is a dearth of bats, the pigeon
must serve us for the offering. Speak the words over your shadow which
must serve in your place.

ELESIN: I cannot approach. Take off the cloth. I shall speak my message
from heart to heart of silence.

[31] Robert Plant Armstrong, "Tragedy—Greek and Yoruba: A Cross-Cultural
Perspective," in Bernth Lindfors, ed., *Forms of Folklore in Africa: Narrative, Gnomic,
Dramatic* (Austin: University of Texas Press, 1977), p. 249.

IYALOJA (. . . removing the covering): . . . The son has proved the father, Elesin, and there is nothing left in your mouth to gnash but infant gums.

PRAISE-SINGER: Elesin, we placed the reins of the world in your hands yet you watched it plunge over the edge of the bitter precipice. You sat with folded arms while evil strangers tilted the world from its course and crashed it beyond the edge of emptiness . . . you left us floundering in a blind future. Your heir has taken the burden on himself. What the end will be, we are not gods to tell. But this young shoot has poured its sap into the parent stalk, and we know this is not the way of life. Our world is tumbling in the void of strangers, Elesin. (p. 75)

Whereupon Elesin stares at his son and stands rock still, then garrotes himself quickly with his looped iron chain.

Have we been prepared to accept these deaths as acts of integrity? Are we dizzied by the tumbling of the world? Or is the scene so inexplicable that we leave every bit as much the unwitting strangers as when we arrived? The play teaches us nothing explicitly of Ogun or Obatala. And if we find that we can translate its climax in terms of honor and shame then we are probably trading in the anthropology of "culture clash." To be sure, scene four might possibly invite this trade, and like the earlier scene with the Pilkings it recapitulates the play's relation to its alien audience. At the masked ball, as the Pilkings (in *egungun* costume) help entertain the Prince, Jane is left alone when Simon goes to investigate Sgt. Amusa's reports of a "riot." And immediately there appears in Western dress Olunde, expecting to receive from the District Officer his father's body. Jane has admired Olunde for studying Western medicine against Elesin's severe opposition; while Olunde says the English "have no respect for what [they] do not understand," he has found Jane "somewhat more understanding" than Simon (pp. 50, 52). But he offends Jane by speaking of her "desecration" of an ancestral mask, and she is unsettled to learn he is determined to participate fully in the traditions of his people. What Jane finds intolerable are his contradictory intentions, both to continue with medical training, at which he excels, and with the tradition that requires his succession as the King's horseman. All the while Olunde never doubts his father has successfully resisted the efforts of Simon Pilkings and has died.

The debate reaches a hysterical impasse—"You're just a savage like all the rest," Jane screams—and is interrupted by an officer who nearly arrests Olunde. When they resume, Jane is able to admit to a certain comprehension. There remains condescension in her manner, but she now understands that she does not understand Olunde, she can say that she knows she does not know. "Your calm acceptance for instance, can you explain that? It was so unnatural. I don't understand that at all. I feel a need to understand all I can" (p. 56). Hers is no more than an ephemeral haze of understanding, but it is that, and so an ephemeral achievement of integrity: she is beginning to relinquish self-possession. For his part, Olunde confesses his inability to fathom the self-defeating qualities of Western civilization; he has been surprised by its resilient capacities for self-sacrifice and survival. So Olunde also begins to engage the hermeneutical function of negation:

> By all logical and natural laws this war should end with all the white races wiping out one another, wiping out their so-called civilisation for all time and reverting to a state of primitivism the like of which has so far only existed in your imagination when you thought of us. I thought all that at the beginning. Then slowly I realised that your greatest art is the art of survival. But at least have the humility to let others survive in their own way. (p. 53)

Both Jane and Olunde have, in this encounter, revised their perspectives, but have done so finally only on the basis of an acknowledged lack of comprehension. This acknowledgement is the basis, then, of whatever integrity they achieve in relation to one another—which is fleeting, for Simon Pilkings soon arrives with Elesin in chains. Olunde is silent and stares blindly before his father, who must be considered lost in the shadows of transition. Olunde now confronts his own crisis of character and vocation.

If Elesin loses his integrity in a confusion of paradigms—being enamored of the reconciling peace of Obatala when what was required was the daring *hubris* of Ogun—Olunde enacts integrity precisely by giving up the medical vocation of Obatala for the venture of Ogun. When Elesin strangles himself with iron, he too is seeking reintegration with Ogun's task[32]—but it is very late, Iyaloja says, and little mitigates the impression that we have witnessed the ruin of a kingdom and a world. Little, unless

---

[32] That iron is specified signals that Elesin would integrate himself with Ogun's paradigm. But two other *orisa* are "present" here. Sango, god of thunder and kingship, ostensibly hung himself before becoming an *orisa* (see Duro Ladipo's play *Oba Ko So* [The King Did Not Hang]). For Soyinka, Sango is more a socio-political, less a cosmic paradigm; he is god of electricity, hence technology, "the tragic actor for the future age" ("Fourth Stage," p. 127). Once, Sango jailed the long-suffering Obatala for seven years (see Obotunde Ijimere's play *The Imprisonment of Obatala*) before, in the end, they were reconciled. Until he kills himself, Elesin enchained resembles Obatala imprisoned.

we find it in what is spoken to the young Bride, as she ritually places earth upon the eyes of Elesin, whose child she may carry. "Now forget the dead," Iyaloja commands, "forget even the living. Turn your mind only to the unborn" (p. 76).

VI.

We began by asking whether the awareness of alterity leads us inevitably to conclude that integrity is an illusion. In terms of dialogical alterity, integrity is threatened by the alienation that qualifies all understanding, of ourselves and others. In terms of the critique of logocentrism, personal integrity would be illusory because our moral paradigms are signs that unravel with Ariadne's diffuse web of signifiers. The radical alterity of the tragic vision might suggest, further, that integrity will be lost either in primordial sin or in the fall into some malevolent abyss (Mr. Kurtz in *Heart of Darkness*) or in the retreat from its edge (Marlow's lie at the end of a novel as blind to Africans as others as it is witting of the infernal colonists). Being what Murray Krieger calls "tragic visionaries,"[33] we might hope only to express another's expression of disintegrating "Horror," which, were we truly to understand it, would forbid our return to tell the tale.

But this skepticism about integrity is warranted only if we accept premises about the self that are unwarranted by the way we perform ourselves in life. Soyinka's tragic heroes are not isolated beings but people who find themselves not only in community but in relations that are ultimately always in transition. And the very developments in *Death and the King's Horseman* that show how integrity is always hedged by disintegration also show in what sense integrity is possible. Integrity is possible only when entangled in alterity and only when established in performance: when both the individual and the community submit themselves to the risk of creation and disillusion, which is the integrity of Ogun and Dionysus and Apollo and Prometheus, and in the self-criticism and relinquishment of self-possession, which is the integrity of Obatala and of the saint. What saves these paradigms of integrity from romantic delusion is that in both, the individual is inseparable from the encouragement, criticism, and possible rejection of character-sustaining communities and traditions (even plural communities, for the Pilkings are finally subsumed into these relations), and in both instances the loss

[33] Murray Krieger, *The Tragic Vision: The Confrontation of Extremity* (1960; Baltimore: Johns Hopkins University Press, 1973), pp. 154-65.

of the whole world is every bit as possible as its salvation. In Soyinka's vision there are revolutionary grounds for hope, but no apocalyptic guarantees.

An act of integrity, in this account, is an act of discovery. It is to discover one's accountability to an ever-changing nexus of relations: with various histories and symbolic traditions; with religious or moral paradigms; with many communities, political-economic realities, and vocations; with the complex truth claims of other persons, of nature, of reason, of circumstance; and with one's own anticipations of the future and the anticipations of others. The body with its physical-psychical processes mark a "center" to these relations, to be sure; the body marks our being here or being there; it is a proximate center of mind and matter— but a center subject to disintegration and change, pain and healing. Even our bodies are strangers unto ourselves.

Achieving integrity entails our finding ourselves and losing ourselves in the midst of these intersecting relations, trying to "integrate" them, however much they may be fragmented and fraught with uncertainty, and however much we know that when we act we always know too little and often know too late. These fragmented relations and our fragmented knowledge of them contribute, nonetheless, to the very constitution of the self, but do so in a way that makes claims to sheer self-possession an illusion (or, in Western religious terms, idolatrous or sinful).[34] Character, in this context, describes a self "spread about" its worlds; a self for whom "integration," "coherence," "wholeness" are both aims and problems; a self whose integrity is achieved but partially, and often recognized only in the aspect of the future, in the realm of the "unborn."

As we watch and think in the unwitting audience, we may recognize, in the first place, that the symbolic paradigms of the colonial social world have interfered with those of Elesin's social world, with disastrous results. We may or may not recognize the paradigms at work in either world, and in fact we may misidentify them. We may leave the theater impressed that we have seen something astounding, that our astonishment may be in response to an evocation of the tragic, but we may also be impressed that we do not know what we have seen. However, if *DKH* is performed effectively, our response may be more complicated than we at once know. If it transcends culture clash, for instance, it will resist any

---

[34] I owe such notions to Nathan A. Scott, Jr., "Hermeneutics and the Question of the Self," unpublished manuscript (1989).

fixation in cultural relativism: we will refrain from saying that "the British do not comprehend the Africans, nor the Africans the British, and from mutual incomprehension disaster comes." For one thing, the language of the British is too parodied and that of the Oyo market too noble. We may also find it insufficient to say that "because I have cultural paradigms, I can recognize that others have paradigms that are effective for them but which I do not understand." Our deeper response maybe twofold:

I may realize, first, that whatever paradigms are entangled in the lives of Elesin, Olunde, the Praise-Singer, Iyaloja, and the people of Oyo—paradigms I can barely intuit, much less understand—are "realized," "effected," or "instantiated" in the performance of those relationships one to another. To the extent I find myself implicated either in the interfering other (the British) or in the actions of those coopted by the bureaucratic regime, then I may find myself accountable to the paradigms being performed by Elesin and his people, which I glimpse but do not comprehend. And to the extent that the *mimesis* of this play— or of any art—is empowered by performative language and by the residue of ritual, then as those paradigms are performed in the play's fiction they are likewise performed in this theatrical space where our lives now happen to be. If we recognize this performative relationship to entail Elesin's, Olunde's, the Praise-Singer's, or Iyaloja's crises of integrity, then we recognize it because the reality of integrity as a complex and dynamic nexus of human relations has been created right before our eyes. What happens on stage and between the stage and the audience recapitulates what happens in life: integrity is achieved and recognized in the performance of relationships that radiate in and from the past, present, and future.

But there is another aspect to our deeper response, in addition to our being drawn into and implicated in the world created by performative language and movement. Our response to the performance of paradigms are interpretive responses. We in the unwitting audience may find ourselves implicated in Jane's hermeneutical response to Olunde: she confesses she doesn't understand and makes this confession the basis for further dialogue with Olunde, albeit possibilities for which are quickly destroyed. Likewise, there is the basis of negation in Elesin's hermeneutical response to being lost in transition: "I need understanding. Even I need to understand." And likewise Olunde: before the presence of his "former" father, now virtually a shadow, he relinquishes the vocation of Obatala for that of Ogun. These are extreme cases of one of the verities of comprehension. Integrity of understanding happens only in our projection of possibilities, in our recognition of resistance, and in our confessions of ignorance as well as understanding in the meeting of another—the moment when we may say "yes, here and there," or "no, not at all," or "neither this nor that."[35] Again, the theater—whose medium is that of embodied interpretation, living women and men—by its nature recapitulates and makes inquiry into the performances of life.

---

[35] Here I am indebted to an unpublished study of Mark C. Taylor by David Felty.

The Writer as Seeker: The Example of
Peter Matthiessen*

IHAB HASSAN

I.

In Peter Matthiessen, the ideal of quest finds its fullness. Motion, peril, hope, a self at risk, encounters with otherness, urgent spiritual pursuits, meet at the heart of his work. In that work, also, the several personae of Matthiessen—artist, naturalist, explorer, conservationist, social activist, mystic of the real—often blend into a prose writer of unchallengeable distinction.

We first enter Matthiessen's world through that luminous prose, luminous but also thick with shadows. It is a subtle, sinewy prose, resplendent and sometimes surreal, yet also bare and spare when the naturalist speaks, naming the land, the people, the fauna and the flora of the earth. It is the prose of a "closet poet," as Matthiessen modestly allows, perhaps a *haiku* poet who can see with the eyes of both the Zen adept and the Western scientist. It is a prose, however particular in description, that never loses sight of the whole, a sacramental order of existence. Indeed, at its best, the prose aspires to become a human whalesong, about which Matthiessen wrote: "No word conveys the eeriness of the whale song, tuned by the ages to a purity beyond refining, a sound that man should near each morning to remind him of the morning of creation" (B, 11).[1]

---

[1] Abbreviations and page numbers refer to the following editions of Peter Matthiessen cited in this chapter: *Blue Meridian: The Search for the Great White Shark* (New York: Random House, 1971), abb. as B; *Nine-Headed Dragon River: Zen Journals 1969-1982* (Boston: Shambhala Press, 1987), abb. as N; *Indian Country* (New York:

Though Matthiessen does not wear his spirituality on his sleeve, the qualities of his explorations, very much like those of his style, refer us back to the domain of nature and spirit conjoined. William Styron once wondered about his friend of nearly forty years: "From whence sprang this amazing obsession to plant one's feet upon the most exotic quarters of the earth, to traverse festering swamps and to scale the aching heights of implausible mountains?"; the motive, Styron supposed, a motive beyond wanderlust or adventure, is that of "a man in ecstatic contemplation of our beautiful and inexplicable planet."[2] Call it a visionary ecology, to which the self seeks lyric and elemental reconciliation.

Is there too much primitivism, romanticism, sentimentalism in all this? Of the first, there is very little in Matthiessen, neither in his prose nor in his stance, unless everything primitive or romantic be considered sentimental from the start. Indubitably, though, Matthiessen reveals much sympathy for the primitive, everything wild, simple, intact; indubitably, he manifests a romantic temper, which he avows and, in his best work, complicates or qualifies.[3] There is no shame, moral or intellectual, in a sensibility so sensuous and answerable to all things live. Nor can civilization banish from itself the spirit of quest, which is the spirit of romance.

II.

Questers and shamans also have a biography, a scattering of facts along their life's path. Peter Matthiessen is born in New York in 1927 to affluent parents; his father, a successful architect, has a strong interest in

---

Viking Press, 1984), abb. as *I*; *Under the Mountain Wall: A Chronicle of Two Seasons in Stone Age New Guinea* (New York: Penguin Books, 1987), abb. as *U*; *The Tree Where Man Was Born*, with Eliot Porter, *The African Experience* (New York: E. P. Dutton, 1972), abb. as *T*; *The Cloud Forest: A Chronicle of the South American Wilderness* (New York: Penguin Books, 1987), abb. as *C*; *The Snow Leopard* (New York: Bantam Books, 1979), abb. as *S*; *Far Tortuga* (New York: Vintage Books, 1984), abb. as *F*; *At Play in the Fields of the Lord* (New York: Bantam Books, 1976), abb. as *A*.

[2] William Styron, *This Quiet House and Other Writings* (New York: Random House, 1982), pp. 251f.

[3] Critics of the left as of the right tend to decry Matthiessen's alleged romantic primitivism, construing it as a powerful Oedipal antagonism to Western civilization. Their disapprobation even extends to Matthiessen's interest in Zen. Thus, for instance, Bruce Bawer: "More than anything else he has written, the Zen journals reflect the profundity and perverseness of Matthiessen's antagonism toward America, toward Western civilization, and toward the Christian idea of God; to read them is a tiresome and dismaying experience." In "Nature Boy: The Novels of Peter Matthiessen," *The New Criterion* 6, 10 (June 1988): 37.

wildlife and serves as trustee to the National Audubon Society. Matthiessen attends the Hotchkiss School, then Yale, with a stint in the U.S. Navy (1945-1947), and a junior year at the Sorbonne (1948-1949). In 1951, he marries Patricia Southgate, the beautiful daughter of a socially prominent diplomat; they take an airy apartment in Montparnasse. That same year, Matthiessen founds, together with Harold L. Hume, the celebrated and indestructible *Paris Review*, acting as its fiction editor. Paris is becoming a moveable feast again, after the war, and the "Paris Review crowd"—Matthiessen, Hume, James Baldwin, William Styron, Richard Wright, George Plimpton, Terry Southern, Irwin Shaw—is a bright and talented crowd, not lost like an earlier and perhaps more talented generation.

But the break, the turning point, comes for Matthiessen in 1958: divorce, the journey home. The glittering life, à la Fitzgerald, is not for him. Earlier, in 1956, he had visited every wildlife preserve in the United States; he had also worked on Long Island with commercial fishermen, and in the summer he had skippered charter boats. Now he commences to wander the world, cozier with death than most writers of his time. He travels to the Arctic, Alaska, Amazonia, Africa, Nepal, New Guinea, and on a converted whaler sails through several oceans in search of the Great White Shark. These are scientific expeditions, sponsored by the Sierra Club or the Harvard-Peabody Museum, not reckless adventures or flamboyant larks. These are also the journeys that give Matthiessen the firsthand experiences, the uncanny details, which thicken his work.

The books, more than twenty of them to date, achieve popularity and recognition—prizes, medals, National and American Book Awards, membership in the American Academy and Institute of Arts and Letters—but they fail, somehow, to enter the academic canon. This is predictable. Though many of the books espouse current social and ecological causes—the titles are revealing: *Wildlife in America* (1959), *"Sal si puedes": Cesar Chavez and the New American Revolution* (1970), *In the Spirit of Crazy Horse* (1983), *Indian Country* (1984), *Men's Lives: The Surfmen and Baymen of the South Fork* (1986)—none conforms to current, academic ideologies, "materialist" or otherwise.

Matter and spirit have never been separable in the practical ethos of Zen. As I have noted, Matthiessen is most reluctant to "brandish" his Zen: "It's just a quiet little practice, not a religion . . . just a way of seeing the world that is closely tied in with the way American Indian people see the world."[4] For him, Zen practice is simply life practice; self-conscious spirituality is what masters call the "stink of Zen." This "life practice" informs his most intimate, most autobiographical work, *Nine-Headed Dragon River* (1987), a journal of his encounters with *roshis* and himself.

III.

Matthiessen, however, did not spend his life in meditation halls. Some of his nonfictional works chronicle adventures; some, like *The Snow Leopard* (1978), turn adventures into quests; nearly all reveal a radical ruthlessness, an unappeased primal need. The need, however intimate, finally claims Nature as ally and claims all those who live in her harsh embrace: game wardens, migrant workers, commercial fishermen, conservationists, primitives.[5] Thus most of Matthiessen's expeditions meld personal, social, scientific, philosophic, and, above all, *literary* interests— the *New Yorker* did sponsor his earliest peregrinations.

But where is quest in all this? It remains virtual, implicit, in most of his earlier nonfictions. Full of engrossing actions and versatile knowledge, these works strike us finally as allegories of reconciled or failed existence: that is, allegories of man and beast in their natural element, of a wildness receding continually before civilization and nations wavering in the glare of history, of life itself, evolving or devolving in the invisible corridors of time—allegories of the human race, in all its unimagined variety, seeking to make sense of its destiny. Predictably, the allegories take on the hues of myth, prophecy, elegy, and monition all at the same time, as in this unattributed passage from *Indian Country*:

> One thing we know which the white man
> may one day discover. Our God is the same
> God. You may think now that you own Him
> as you wish to own our land. But you can-
> not.... The whites too shall pass—
> perhaps sooner than other tribes. Continue
> to contaminate your bed, and you will one
> night suffocate in your own waste. When
> the buffalo are all slaughtered, the wild
> horses all tamed, the secret corners of

---

[4] Quoted by Wendy Smith, "Peter Matthiessen," *Publisher's Weekly* 229, no. 19, 9 May 1986, p. 241.

[5] Matthiessen forthrightly says: "I like the values of traditional people who are closer to the earth. It's an attitude which I think is very precious and is in very serious danger of being lost, stamped out entirely" (*Ibid.*, p. 241).

the forest heavy with the scent of many
men, and the view of the ripe hills blotted
by talking wires, where is the thicket?
Gone. Where is the eagle? Gone. And
what is it to say good-by to the swift
and the hunt, the end of living and the
beginning of survival? (*I*, 8)

We cannot take this to be Matthiessen's own view, which in a Westerner today may seem a little tender. But we can take it as a view the West has proven unable to replace or even to mediate. "My hope is that these Indian voices," Matthiessen says in his introduction, "eloquent and bitter, humorous and sad, will provide what history and statistics cannot, a sense of that profound 'life way' which could illuminate our own dispirited consumer culture" (*I*, xii). This, at least, is a beginning, if only a beginning, of mediation.

The sentiment, in any case, expresses the intent of Matthiessen whose work always reaches for meaning, value, belief, even in the most descriptive, the most impersonal of narratives. *Under the Mountain Wall* (1962), for instance, set in the highlands of New Guinea, reads like an anthropological novel about Papuan chieftains, their warriors, families, enemies. Presumably, as Matthiessen says, the expedition offers a "unique chance, perhaps the last, to describe a lost culture in the terrible beauty of its pure estate" (*U*, xiv). But the third person narrative, blending local myths, ethnographic detail, and dramatic actions (nearly always violent) also raises overwhelming questions. The questions center, first, on the disturbing alterity of "Stone Age" Papuans and on their equally disturbing sameness to any reader; they center also on the history of Dutch-Indonesian colonization and the future of all "natives." Above all, the book powerfully evokes cosmic rhythms, the "wax and wane of ice-age seas."

The same cosmic rhythms beat through *The Tree Where Man Was Born* (1972). Vibrant with Eliot Porter's photographs, the work takes us on a spiritual safari through East Africa. As usual, Matthiessen has a pretext for starting out: in this case, an invitation from Jack Owen, Director of Tanzania's National Parks, to observe wildlife at the Serengeti Research Institute. There, true geophile, Matthiessen acts as witness to the earth, noting with wondrous concreteness its vital evidence, noting more sadly the ruin of vast ecosystems. There, too, as in all his journeys, he meets humanity on its own terms, meets the maimed, the indigent, the dispos-

250   *Ihab Hassan*

sessed, meets them as they submit—even the indomitable Masai!—to the trials of civilization.

Matthiessen observes accurately, without rote. He can be hard on unprivileged nations, he can be hard on himself; he has taught himself to regard death with clarity. Watching a dying lioness, he unexpectedly declares his sympathies "with the predator, not with the hunted," then goes on to note:

> Still grunting, she licked passionately
> at the grass, and her haunches shuddered
> in long spasms, and this last abandon
> shattered the detachment I had felt until
> that moment. I was swept by a wave of
> feeling, then a pang so sharp that, for
> a moment, I felt sick, as if all the waste
> and loss in life, the harm one brings to
> oneself and others, had been drawn to a
> point in this lonely passage between light
> and darkness. (*T*, 138)

There is nothing false here, nothing scanted. Nor is there anything false in this passage, at once radiant and poised, with which the book—*The Tree of Man*—starts:

> The tree where man was born, according
> to the Nuer, still stood within man's
> memory in the west part of the south
> Sudan, and I imagine a great baobab thrust
> up like an old root of life in those wild
> grasses that blow forever to the horizons,
> and wild man in naked silhouette against
> the first blue sky. That bodeful man of
> silence and the past is everywhere in
> Africa. One hears the silence, hears
> one's step, and stops . . . and he is there,
> in the near distance. I see him still:
> a spear point glitters in the sun. (*T*, 22)

The foregoing works suggest the ambience but not the particular character of quest in Matthiessen. Hints of that character, though, appear in two narratives, both told with the imminence of first person experience.

In *The Cloud Forest* (1961), Matthiessen undertakes one of his earliest voyages into the wilderness, prodigious Amazonia. Subtitled a "chronicle" again, the journey seeks, like future journeys, to penetrate time even more than space. Certainly he attends minutely to his spatial environment: a freighter is "warped swiftly from her berth," a stevedore lets "the last hawser slap into the water" (C, 1). But the sense of disjunction, time jarred out of its course, affects him even more deeply: "Now the tug is gone, and there comes a sense of uncertainty, of loss. This is not entirely homesickness; a continuity has been broken with the desertion of that tug, as if life must now start up all over again" (C, 1). This could have been the commencement of quest, its beginnings in a metaphysical twinge.

But the narrative, though rich in factual and poetic interest—Marston Bates has compared it with H. M. Tomlinson's *The Sea and the Jungle* and Peter Fleming's *Brazilian Adventure*, paragons of Amazonian travel literature—the narrative proceeds without any awareness of itself as a personal quest.[6] It proceeds, rather, as an adventure upon which the hero is almost too modest to intrude. Matthiessen perceives; unlike Theroux, he does not rush to judge. Thus, though repelled by the cluttered vulgarity of church interiors in South America, he typically admits his inability to comment fairly on colonial Spanish architecture (C, 64). Thus also, while braving genuine dangers—jaguars, anacondas, alligators, piranhas, murderous rapids, aroused Indians—dangers in the Urubamba and Ucayali basins, he describes himself neither as explorer nor seeker but simply a man on an "outing."

Hints of quest nonetheless flicker throughout the story. These do not refer to secret pre-Colombian ruins or giant prehistoric fossils (the *mandibula* of some extinct monster) that Matthiessen "discovers," or at least photographs. The hints pertain rather—since he is no Indiana Jones—to the mystery of human existence, his own. Matthiessen learns something about his moodiness, stubbornness, fits of garrulous jollity, about his fear as well as need for risk. He learns much about nature, and about his attitude to nature; at one point, "drunk with power," he cuts down crocodiles with a rifle, knowing in advance that he will keenly regret the impulse. Above all, he learns a unique kind of happiness, an intuition of a world seemingly complete, delivered from time, from death. The passage deserves to be given whole:

[6] Marston Bates, "Fortune Smiled on the Traveler in an Unmapped Part of the Earth," *The New York Times Book Review*, 15 October 1961, p. 3.

I haven't said that I've had
a magnificent morning. I have. And curiously, the magnificence did not consist
of finding what we were after—more poor
old bones, and thus a certain scientific
confirmation of the site—but lay instead
in the purity of this jungle stream. Only
a few woodcutters like Juan Pablo, seeking
the isolated *cedro* and *caoba* trees, may
ever have ascended this *quebrada*, and
there is no mark of the white man's heavy
hand upon it. Its still banks are laced
with the tracks of tapir, capybara, and
other creatures, and its clear water, running quietly on sandy shoals, sparkles
with the flash of the pretty *sabalo*. In
the bends the water runs beneath stone
banks and is a pure, limpid green, and the
trees which lend their leaf color to the water soar
away in great white columns. The queer
and clumsy boats in huffs everywhere in
the lower branches, and hidden birds of
unknown shape and color whistle and answer
down the cool silences, in counterpoint
and incredible clear harmonies. The tree
frogs loose their prodigious croaks, and
from a mile away resounds one of the mightiest
sounds in nature, like nothing so
much as an ominous moan of wind, the community
howl of the *mono colorado*—the red howler
monkey. In the stream itself lie the
striking shells of a variety of mollusks,
including a gastropod so large—the size
of a very large pear—that it is difficult
to believe it is not a marine creature.
(Louis Agassiz, a century ago, pointed
out the marine character of the dolphins,
fishes, and other aquatic fauna of the
Amazon basin.) We paused to breakfast
on a kind of nut, the Indian name for which
has now escaped me, and I wondered why
the stream itself was so much more exciting
than the bones we had found in it—more
exciting than the first sight of the great

jaw itself the night before. And it occurred
to me that, aside from its beauty—for
it is precisely this inner, mysterious
quality of the jungle, represented so well
by this lost stream, that I have been
searching for and feel I have found at last—
there was an adventure here, an exploration,
however timid. (*C*, 239f.)

Deliverance, we see, is momentary; it only serves to renew the promise of adventure, the whisper of a perilous quest almost fulfilled. Certainly *The Cloud Forest* simulates the form of classic journeys in "the heart of darkness," simulates the form without its density of allusions, its duskier self-apprehensions. For Matthiessen, the full achievement of quest was yet to come.

It does not come in *Blue Meridian: The Search for the Great White Shark* (1971), which nonetheless gestures at quest. Here Peter Gimbel, organizer of the expedition, holds the center. Another scion of affluence, Gimbel is a banker turned adventurer, and shares with Matthiessen, another Peter, many impulses—they both skydive, for instance, during the fifties, when skydiving was hardly a sport, and they both roam, independently, the Amazon. Gimbel longs for a confrontation with the formidable shark, "the white death," as challenge and exorcism; Matthiessen admits only to the challenge. Both are eager, indeed anxious, to test their limits, swimming with sharks—*not* the Great White—even in their feeding frenzy. Gimbel puts it simply: "We came, really, when you get right down to it, to see what the limits are, just how wildly—that's the wrong word—just how openly a man can expose himself in the water with excited sharks and still maintain control" (*B*, 160f.). And Matthiessen concurs: " . . . I am sympathetic with Peter [Gimbel]'s need to find out what the limits are; the original motivations may be ambiguous but attacks upon this [dangerous] life style are often ambiguous as well, as if the need to attack betrayed a fear in the attacker that his own life seeps away from him unlived" (*B*, 162). (Matthiessen has particularly in mind a woman who vehemently calls risk-takers "silly and childish.")

Blue Meridian ends with terrific and terrifying scenes of encounter with the "white death," filmed underwater from flimsy aluminum cages, and so proves itself, despite shades of psychic failure and fleeting introspection, a rousing adventure tale, not a focused human quest. Still, at the close of the book, Gimbel—*not* Matthiessen—reflects: "I was filled with a terrible sadness that we had indeed determined precisely the limits we sought, that the mystery was at least partly gone because we knew that we could get away with anything, that the story—and such a story!—has an end" (B, 204). This is indeed the sadness of quest, a quest hinted more than realized.

IV.

The preceding texts, I have already noted, delimit the interior landscape of Peter Matthiessen, the terrain of his imagination. Against their background, his best quest, one of the most compelling in this study, takes shape.

The journey in *The Snow Leopard* is both real, painstakingly real, and also mythic, both personal and universal. The work itself is rooted at every level in autobiography. Dedicated to three Zen *roshis* whom Matthiessen portrays reverently in *Nine-Headed Dragon River*, permeated by memories of Deborah Love whose agonizing death we have witnessed there, written in the first person as a series of diary entries, the book testifies to its author's felt self, his full life. Its incentive is also practical: Matthiessen accompanies the wildlife biologist George Schaller—they had met at the Serengeti Research Institute in Africa—who wants to observe the November rutting of Himalayan blue sheep, and perhaps glimpse that "shyest, rarest, and most beautiful of cats," the snow leopard. At the same time, the space of the journey teems with mountain gods and legendary beasts, monks, mystics, lunatics, and bandits roaming at altitudes of more than 17,000 feet, prophets riding the icy winds, astride snow leopards sometimes, and *bodhisattvas* who look like lowly porters. Then again, the destination of Matthiessen, the Crystal Monastery at Shey Gompa in Nepal's Inner Dolpo, appears on any good map of the region.

The journey does not begin auspiciously. Matthiessen himself starts in a troubled state. Deborah has just died, leaving him with two children. The widower nonetheless resolves to undertake his pilgrimage, as if to cleanse himself, come to terms with his wound. The snow leopard becomes for him a symbol of spiritual knowledge or attainment, though he never manages to see it—Scheller, a "stern pragmatist," does. Matthiessen's Zen teacher had warned him back in New York: "Do not expect too much"; that is, "You may not be ready to see the leopard."[7]

---

[7] In *Nine-Headed Dragon River*, which reprints Chapters 7 and 8 long sections on Buddhism and Hinduism from *The Snow Leopard*, Matthiessen also mentions that his teacher, Eido-shi, gives him a particular koan for the trip: "All the peaks are covered

But in Zen, the admonition could also mean: "To see or not to see the leopard is the same; *satori* simply comes." In any case, the journey begins ominously with thirty hours of continuous rain in Kathmandu. Later, a group of shrouded figures bearing a corpse crosses the path of his Land Rover, arousing in him feelings of "dim, restless foreboding." And a little later on the road, he sees an ancient Hindu, propped up on a basket, entirely "ravened from within": "I nod to Death in passing," Matthiessen soberly notes, "aware of the sound of my own feet upon my path" (*S*, 13).

Death attends this journey, attends it as awareness not simply quietus, though Matthiessen keeps his foot steady at the edge of dizzying mountain chasms. The journey itself proceeds in several dimensions: horizontal (from Kathmandu to the Crystal Mountain), vertical (from valleys, through mountain passes, close to unassailable peaks), temporal (present to past, modern to medieval), cultural (West to East and back again), generic (alternating between the forms of autobiography, didactic essay, theological tract, ecological disquisition, naturalist catalogue, poetic and philosophical meditation), and spiritual (a "journey of the heart," toward enlightenment). Taken as a whole, the diary appears as a continuous dialogue of heterocosms, straining for peace between the One and the Many in all their manifestations.

Matthiessen, however, does not write abstractly, and this is the triumph of his book. Though he hears "whispers of a paradisal age" in the mountains, his boots are full of blood from walking. Altogether *there*, he does not look away from children with broken legs or swollen bellies; nor will he allow himself, and us, to forget the face of the loveliest child he has ever seen, sitting with others in a circle, drinking buffalo blood. One day's trek may take him a century back; but he also recalls the turmoils of America in the sixties. And though he may read the universe as scripture like any good Zen or Christian adept, he can record each and every finite detail in its unalterable quiddity. A haunting immediacy characterizes his depictions of actions as well as objects. Here is Matthiessen, after crawling along a foot-wide ledge, waiting for the porters to catch up:

> For some time now, the chattering, laughing
> voices of the B'on-pos have been coming up
> behind. At that dangerous point of the cliff,

---

with snow—why is this one bare?" (47). Matthiessen confesses to great disappointment after he fails to attain illumination.

an extraordinary thing happens. Not yet in
view, the nine fall silent. . . . Then one by one,
the nine figures round the point of rock in
silhouette, unreal beneath big bulky loads
that threaten each second to bump the cliff
and nudge them over the precipice. On they
come, staring straight ahead, as steadily and
certainly as ants, yet seeming to glide with
an easy, ethereal lightness, as if some sort of
inner concentration was lifting them just off
the surface of the ground. Bent far forward
against the tump lines around their fore-
heads, fingers spread wide by way of balance, they touch the cliff face lightly to the
left side, stroke the north wind to the right.
Light fingertips touch my upper leg . . . but
their intensity is such that they seem not to
distinguish between cold rock face and
warm blue jeans. Mute, unknowing, dull
eyes glazed, the figures brush past . . . leaving
behind in the clear air the smell of grease
and fires. When the bad stretch is past, the
hooting instantly resumes, perhaps at the
point that they left off, as if all had
awakened from a trance. (*S*, 155f.)

Personal and social insights also root the book into the world. Thus,
for example, Matthiessen comments on his companion, George Schaller,
in a moment of strain:

Hunched in a cold and soggy sleeping bag
amongst the puddles, I have envied the
owner of the crisp blue tent next door, and
perhaps these base feelings fired our first
argument, this dark morning, when GS tossed
used cans and papers into the schoolyard.
He asserted that he did so because the local
people are always avid for containers,
which is true. But why not set the cans
upon the wall instead of littering the
place, and making the people pick them up
out of the mud? (*S*, 36).

The comment yields quickly, magnanimously, to others on Schaller's
dedication, intelligence, and great stamina.

Matthiessen also portrays with deft sympathy the Nepalese. Predictably, he most admires the Sherpas for their courage, dignity, altruism, their "merry defencelessness." His journey puts him in constant interaction with various natives, including porters, tribesmen, villagers, monks, lamas, who form a tacit hierarchy—lamas and Sherpas at the top precisely because they are the most selfless. He favors one particularly, Tukten by name, a rogue Sherpa who demeans himself by serving as porter. Part trickster and part *bodhisattva*, Tukten radiates an inner repose, the aura of a "crazy wisdom," a shade disreputable. In him, nonetheless, Matthiessen finds a kindred spirit, speaking an alien tongue.

But the worldliness of the book comes also from its roots in America, Matthiessen's own "psychedelic years." His eerie mountain environment, inhabited by the simplest human needs, acts on him as a mute critique of his own society, its "corrosive money rot," its "retreat from wonder," its "proliferations without joy" (*S*, 42). Thus, indirectly, Matthiessen remarks on race, sex, drugs, power, violence in America during the sixties, perceived now from the austere, wholly essential perspective of the Himalayas. Not that Asians appear altogether feckless, true innocents like the *sennin* or solitary mountain idiots. Repeatedly, Matthiessen shows that if Western colonialism seems inexpungable, even in the remotest Himalayan ranges, so is Asian caste prejudice, so is human venality, greed.

The world, in fact, may be too much with Matthiessen: continually, he recalls his wife, his children, his friends. The pangs of Deborah's love persist, an unfinished passion, though five months before her death, the couple had decided to divorce. Matthiessen also recalls Alex, their youngest son, who once stood rapt in his sandbox, "as doves and redwings came and went on the warm wind, the leaves dancing, the clouds flying, birdsong and sweet smell of privet and rose. The child was not observing; he was at rest in the very center of the universe. . . " (*S*, 41). But then, at eight, Alex has already begun to shut away "the wildness of the world," begun to fall into a more common day—precisely that dull, quotidian day from which his father, in the faraway Dolpo, is trying to awake.

Hence, despite all its worldliness, *The Snow Leopard* remains the quest of one man for another reality, another "day," or at least for a way to mediate between worlds. Matthiessen concedes at the start that he carries with him several "I"'s: one who observes, another who recalls, a third, exhausted, lies down to sleep . . . but always, somewhere, the one who pursues. He suspects that he may have contracted the Kierkegaardian "sickness of infinitudes," the wanderer's curse: "I only know that at the bottom of each breath there was a hollow place that needed to be filled" (S, 43). And so, in a ritual of dispossession—we have seen this gesture in other writers before—he removes his watch, shedding time; for the true *yeti*, "homegoing" is always Now.

Not that the journey lacks movement, difficulties to overcome. The dangers of snow blindness, frozen toes, rolling boulders, lost supplies, and sheer, transfixing heights are omnipresent. Nor are the dangers physical only. True to its moment, the quest swarms with ambiguities. Matthiessen recalls earlier *kenshos*, instants of provisional insight, only to relapse into black moods. When he reaches the remote Crystal Monastery, from which nothing is visible but snow and sky, he finds it deserted. He never glimpses the leopard, never answers the pertinent *koan*. He even begins to suspect that the willed act of searching may preclude the finding. And he worries that entrusting his experiences to the written work may falsify them irrevocably. Finally, in Patan, after journey's end, he awaits Tukten at a Buddhist monastery, waits at the rendezvous in vain. Thinking that he may have been spared the "desolation of success," Matthiessen looks, on the last day of his three-month journey, at his face in the mirror: "In the gaunt, brown face in the mirror—unseen since last September—the blue eyes in a monkish skull seem eerily clear, but this is the face of a man I do not know" (S, 328).

That stranger's face may be the face behind every human face, a face in and out of time. For even in the high, sublunary landscape of the Dolpo, where lungs gasp with each breath and life itself seems but a thin stain on eternity, history and politics continually obtrude. The wounded, whimsical Western seeker finds himself, recurrently, *between* worlds. All around him, the evidence of poverty is excruciating, and dogs eat human excrement. As Matthiessen puts it: "Confronted with the pain of Asia, one cannot look and cannot turn away" (S, 12). This may be the penultimate word on the interface between certain cultures, less interface than hideous scar which only a *bodhisattva* could steadily contemplate. As for the rest of us—perhaps even for Matthiessen—the ultimate word may be inconclusive quest, intermittent pain.

To say that *The Snow Leopard* may be inconclusive, however, is not to say that it fails either as spiritual quest or literary work. Indeed, the stunning achievement of the book is that it convinces a sympathetic reader that he has attained a measure of enlightenment himself; that he, too, could wake up some morning from a dream of white, supernal light. It all seems so near at hand, as in this epiphany of a wafted feather:

A white down feather, sun-filled, dances
before me on the wind: alighting nowhere,
it balances on a shining thorn, goes spin-
ning on. Between this white feather, sheep
dung, light, and the fleeting aggregate of
atoms that is "I," there is no particle of
difference. There is a mountain opposite,
but this "I" is opposite nothing, opposed
to nothing.
I grow into these mountains
like a moss. I am bewitched. The blinding snow peaks
and the clarion air, the sound of earth and
heaven in the silence, the requiem birds,
the mythic beasts, the flags, great horns,
and old carved stones, the rough-hewn Tartars
in their braids and homespun boots,
the silver ice in the black river, the Kang,
the Crystal Mountain. Also, I love the
common miracles—the murmur of my friends
at evening, the clay fires of smudgy juniper,
the course dull food, the hardship and simplicity, the contentment of doing one thing
at a time: when I take my blue tin cup into
my hand, that is all I do. (*S*, 238)

As a literary work, though, *The Snow Leopard* falls short of the perfection it seeks. The failure is largely due to its massive interpolations of
Oriental religion and personal history, homily and flashback, crammed
in. This forced quality stems from the ambition of the work itself. Written
as a journal, beginning September 28, 1973, and every day thereafter into
December, the book unfolds, Paul Zweig saw, "not as a story but as a
filled space of perception."[8] Matthiessen wants to jam his whole existence into three months. And he nearly succeeds, rendering his story in
the present tense, that eternal present of Zen. Yet with a little more reticence toward his illuminations—these, in all but the greatest masters,
skirt always narcissicism—Matthiessen may have consecrated his high
moments in a finer, tauter form. Still, *The Snow Leopard* must perdure as a
landmark in the literature of quest; for, in addition to all its spiritual values, it gives immaculate attention to the phenomenal world, to the

---

[8] Paul Zweig, "Eastern Mountain Time," *The Saturday Review* 15 (August 1978), p.
44.

abrupt glory of things as they are. Paradoxically, the seeker, a self at risk, comes closest to his end when he loses all self-concern, attending to attention and to the created world. With death the book began, with another kind of death it hopes to transfigure the quest.

V.

The scope of this essay does not permit me to discuss all Matthiessen's fiction, though as a young man in Paris, he had commenced his literary career by writing short stories, one of which won the prestigious *Atlantic* Prize in 1951. Since then, he has written five novels, *Race Rock* (1954), *Partisans* (1955), *Raditzer* (1961), *At Play in the Fields of the Lord* (1965), and *Far Tortuga* (1975), and has never ceased to cherish that genre. As he says about a forthcoming novel: "I'm extremely happy that I'm back to fiction—it's been a *very* long time—and I hope to stay there. I prefer writing fiction; I find it exhilarating. . . . I'm worn out by nonfiction."[9] Certainly, Matthiessen's earlier fiction is accomplished if sometimes ornate, written with the autobiographical intensity of youth, touching on themes—marital discord, the psychology of misfits, utopian or existential politics—rife in the fifties and early sixties. Only two of these novels bear on quest; they are his last two and by far his best.[10]

Far Tortuga is the more original of the two, the more astonishing achievement, but the less pertinent to the idea of quest. I turn, therefore, to *At Play in the Fields of the Lord*. Set in deep Amazonia, the work revels in contrasts: Nature and Civilization, South and North America, Animist and Christian religions, Catholic and Protestant missionaries, the Indian and the White Man. The novel, though, like its lush, jungle-green setting, finally overcomes its own antinomies. Thus, for instance, though Protestant missionaries—Leslie Huben, Martin and Hazel Quarrier— seem far more bigoted than the Dominican priest, Father Xantes, it is Martin Quarrier who achieves knowledge, a kind of bungling martyrdom in the rain forest. And though Indians seem guileless compared to the fanatic, genocidal White Man, they too, the Niarunas and kindred Yurimahas, can prove stupid, greedy, and murderous: at an earlier time, they enslaved the "filthy Tiro" tribe. There is no paradise in this novel, no edenic world that does not contain its Serpent, contain already its Cains and Abels.

---

[9] Smith, p. 241.
[10] See Styron, p. 251, who also prefers, like many critics, the last two novels.

The real focus of ambiguity in the novel, however, the real focus of its energy, is Lewis Meriwether Moon, a halfbreed Cheyenne-Canuck turned outlaw. Together with another soldier of fortune, Wolfie, a squat, knife-wielding, bearded Jew, he flies into Madre de Dios—Matthiessen does not identify the nation—in an old, pocked, stolen Mustang marked "Wolfie and Moon, Inc. Small Wars and Demolitions." Moon belongs to no world; his icy rage has closed his heart and snapped his teeth shut. Thus he appears the metaphysical drifter *par excellence*, owning nothing except bitter memories of humiliation and injustice, traveling always and traveling light. Even his sidekick, Wolfie, fears him, yet intuits an implacable contradiction in his character, a "beautiful" side and another "meaner than catshit" (*AP*, 69).

Still, something stirs in Moon's spirit. Even in the jungle, where no personal past or future counts, he thinks of himself, ironically, as the "great halfbreed of the world," precursor of a miscegenated earth. In a village latrine, recalling all the latrines he has visited, he broods that none has yielded him an answer; or "rather that it always came up with the same answer, a suck and gurgle of unspeakable vileness, a sort of self-satisfied low chuckling: Go to it, man, you're pissing your life away. / Standing there, swaying pleasantly, he grinned. I do not care, he thought, I no longer care" (*AP*, 58). Yet Moon cares, continues to care. He grins and yippies with fierce delight when a naked Niaruna warrior shoots an arrow at his plane, flying high above the tree-line. And unlike Wolfie, he refuses to bomb the Indian village at the behest of Comandante Guzman who wants to "clear" the forest. In this refusal, Moon tries to define himself, a Northern halfbreed among Amazonian Indians, an outcast of Western civilization, neither in nor out of its history.

The novel's action, however, remains always in context, a context rendered in various dramatic ways. Through Moon, for instance, Matthiessen can dramatize the plight of the Cheyennes as well as the Niarunas, the situation of each reflecting on the other. Through the missionaries, he can reveal how cultures, even in their idealistic moment, violate one another; as Leslie Huben puts it: "Before we are through, we hope to have an airplane survey, so that we may hunt out the last lost soul in this great wilderness. Not one will escape the great net of our Lord" (*AP*, 18). Through Comandante Guzman, Matthiessen can show how power still brutalizes human beings in the name of progress. Through Wolfie, half nice Jewish boy and half hippie turned thug, he can probe American society, its vices and antics. And through the women in the novel—Andy Huben, pretty and compassionate; Hazel Quarrier, ugly and devious; Pindi, the young Niaruna who becomes for a time Moon's "wife"—he can follow the transformation of eros, its blockage and flow in human life.

The central dramatic fact of the novel, though, is individual awakening, degrees of "conversion." Wolfie realizes his dependency on Moon, realizes his spiritual fatigue and solitude. Andy recognizes, without adultery in the flesh, her desire for Moon, and his desire for her. Young Billy Quarrier, a child beautiful in face and soul, sees through his mother's deceits, thorough the strange injustices of an adult world. And Martin Quarrier, mediocre in so many obvious ways, yet dogged, even strenuous in probity, rises to painful perceptions of himself, his wife, his lust for Andy, even his Christian mission and faith. After his contact with Catholics ("the Enemy," as Protestant missionaries say) and Indians, after his son's death of blackwater fever, he finds no solace in inert Christian pieties. Courageously, he assumes the full burden of his doubts as of his duties, till a venal twice-converted (Catholic to Protestant) Indian cuts him down with a machete.

The Wandering Jew, the Wandering Christian, the Wandering Halfbreed—none of them can affirm any value except in violent gestures of dispossession. Moon, who provides the dark, central energy of the novel, begins his dispossession in a three-day hunger vigil as a boy in the Dakotas, and continues it through his college career, his drunken rages and assaults, his psychedelic madness.[11] "He had flung himself away from life, from the very last realities, had strayed to the cold windy reaches of insanity. This perception was so clear and final that he moaned; he would not find his way back" (*AP*, 110). Under the influence of an Indian herb, *ayahuasca*, Moon steals Wolfie's plane and Quarrier's Niaruna dictionary, throws away his watch, and flies at dawn straight into the sun, then parachutes into impassable Niaruna country. The signs in his life, which once said Nowhere, suddenly point Now Here. Before leaving, he had said to Andy: "That's the only way to do it—*go*. When there's a jungle waiting, you go through it and come out clean on the far side. Because if you struggle to back out, you get all snarled, and afterwards the jungle is still there, still waiting" (*AP*, 130). That is how he plays in the fields of the Lord, not at all the missionary's way.

---

[11] Leslie Fiedler sees psychedelic derangement as the opposite of nostalgic primitivism, and sees Moon, in this regard, as a presage of the New Western hero. See *The Return of the Vanishing American* (New York: Stein and Day, 1968), pp. 172-75.

Among the Niarunas, Moon is considered a descendent of Kisu, the Great Rain Spirit, whom they ironically confuse with Jesu. Only Aeore, that same truculent warrior who had earlier shot an arrow at the sky, remains hostile to Moon. The latter, nonetheless, spends three idyllic months in the rain forest: "Days opened out, and furled again at night like jungle flowers" (*AP*, 200). Obscurely, though, he senses that he is at a "beginning and an end," a crux in his dread existence. Among the Indians, their myths and rituals, Moon recovers some atavistic knowledge of the blood, and begins to perceive the wilderness as host to multitudinous powers, neither benevolent nor malevolent only, but interdependent, and in this interdependence complete. The unabashed sensuality of the Niarunas, especially Pindi's, frees his instinctual energies. And, oddly enough, Aeore—jungle mentor, spiritual rival and brother, mortal enemy—imparts to Moon a sense of the great mystery which the former, also a "jaguar shaman," strains to realize.

But the idyll ends at gun and spear point; the world closes in. Lewis Meriwether Moon cannot finally identify with the Niaruna whom he perceives as irrational and primitive, more primitive than his own Plains Indians. Still alien in his adopted tribe, he carries from Andy, in a naked, sexually unconsummated scene, the flu virus that decimates the tribe; in the end, he must also shoot the relentless Aeore dead. Nor can Moon relate to Quarrier, though they share a certain doom:

> "I'm not really afraid of anything that
> may happen." Quarrier raised his eyebrows, as if
> surprised by this realization. "I've made such a
> disaster of my life that I'm not afraid of anything—
> that is, any change is welcome. Maybe you've never
> reached that point."
>
> "I've been there, all right. My trouble is,
> I never left it. I even *like* it." He turned the manioc
> tubers in the embers. (*AP*, 358)

Quarrier dies, stubborn to the last in his effort to make sense of a crumbling existence. Is Moon reborn? "Lewis Meriwether Moon: die soon" (*AP*, 396). In a long, hallucinating scene, drifting downriver prone in a funerary canoe, feverish with malaria, his legs intertwined with the corpse of Aeore, the smell of putrefying Indians wafted with every breath of wind, he expresses a pride equal to Ahab's: "He stared straight upward. Kill me or spare me as you like, but either way expect no thanks for it" (*AP*, 395). Yet the next moment, looking at the decomposing face of Aeore, he feels an immense compassion, "and a well of sadness for things irredeemable and gone flowed over him. . . . He wept and wept, and though toward the end he began to smile, he kept on weeping until as last he breathed a tremendous sigh and laughed quietly, without tears" (*AP*, 397). Reborn in his tears, at last, denying no part of himself, he drinks from the glittering river and bathes his heart; he rolls in the shallows like an otter and scrubs his skin with sand. Thus the book ends:

> The wind was bright. Laid naked to the sun
> and sky, he felt himself open like a flower. Soon
> he slept. At dark he built an enormous fire, in
> celebration of the only man beneath the eye of Heaven.
> (*AP*, 399)

Is this lasting rebirth, or simply a lambent pause, like legendary moths drawn to the moon, in an endless search? Matthiessen, of course, does not say; he only tells us, through every inflection of his novel, that Moon incarnates a radical human drive even as he radically threatens us all: "He don't care about nothing nobody else cares about" (*AP*, 377), Wolfie says, and he ought to know.

Sexual, political, ecological, religious themes crowd the novel; but its form is finally mythic, the shape of death and rebirth. Hence the recurrent Biblical *leitmotif*: "He that loseth his life for my sake shall find it" (*Matthew*, 10:39). The narrative form, though omniscient, also focuses on the mythic figure of Lewis Meriwether Moon who commands, even as an anonymous "he," the first and last sections of the novel, and much that is in between. His ironic words to Leslie Huben over the radio, just before he bails out into the jungle, give the novel its title. And Moon's tribulations, a self desperately at risk, give the novel its haunting interest.

This is not to say that the novel is flawless. Some of its unfavorable portraits—Comandante Guzman, Leslie Huben, Hazel Quarrier—seem caricatures. The action sometimes chokes on "colorful" anthropological details, and sometimes crawls—it takes us two pages to see Father Xante consume an egg. The novel, in places, also flaunts its verbal power, full of "fine writing" as Matthiessen himself admits, especially in the long hallucinatory sections when characters succumb to drugs or delirium—one wonders then if style does not substantiate for narrative structure and dramatic insight. Yet repeatedly, when the novel finds again its true passion and pace, such insights strike through the foliage to take our breath away. Then the words become one with their green, dangerous setting, one also with the more dangerous human heart. And Indian and

Christian myth blend into an utterance, stuttering the name of the unnameable.[12]

VI.

In this study's perspective—notably in *The Snow Leopard* and *At Play in the Fields of the Lord*—Peter Matthiessen comes close to realizing the form of quest, the ideal of selves at richest risk. This attainment reflects on both man and artist.

As a man, Matthiessen reveals extraordinary courage, moral stamina, a true longing of the soul. Modest too, lacking in the spiritual vulgarity of many adventurers, devoid of the grating egoism—though not of the egoism itself!—of many writers, he possesses a certain genial charm of self-preservation. The whim of the seeker is evident in him, the wound too. But the discipline of style, a style at home in alien cultures, attentive to the natural world, makes both whim and wound occasions for dramatic empathy. Man and artist also invite us to enduring mysteries. For as I have noted, Matthiessen seeks to penetrate time as he travels in space, and his allegories of reconciled existence put squarely before us the enigma of human, indeed of cosmic, evolution.

The question of belief thus becomes crucial to his work: what, in the decaying ecology of our values, remains still vital, worthy of our commitment and faith? Matthiessen's answer begins with nature, the history and future of the given world, its presence in us all. The answer reaches finally for an ecological vision, at worst intrusively didactic, at its best the vision of an artist and mystic of the real, casting the wide net of language on a universe he can never capture or own.

But there are really no answers, only ways. Matthiessen's way through Nepal or Amazonia, through ecology or Zen, may not be our way. It is nonetheless an emblematic way through our perplexities in the West.

---

*This essay is taken from the author's *Selves at Risk: Patterns of Quest in Contemporary American Letters*. Wisconsin Project on American Writers Series (Madison: University of Wisconsin Press, 1990). Permission to reprint has kindly been granted by the publishers.

---

[12] Quite rightly, Frederick R. Karl remarks about this work: "The only comparable novel to deal with such crucial issues is Bellow's *Henderson the Rain King*, also a marvel of language and insight. See *American Fictions 1940-1980* (New York: Harper and Row, 1983), p. 59.

Beckett and the Helping Hand
DAVID H. HESLA

We are well acquainted with the Samuel Beckett who portrays the decrepitude of the body, the aberrations of the mind, and a range of emotions running from the humorously cynical through the merely contemptuous to the casually vicious. We know, too, that as early as his twenty-fifth year, when he published his essay on Proust, he was convinced that there is no such thing as a self or ego that endures unchanged through time, and that consequently it is impossible for me to tell you who I am, impossible as well for two persons to know one another, much less love one another. And we are familiar with his vision of human existence as a mistake, a hoax, a bad joke too long in the telling, whose ending his tramps, bums, and seniles await out of habit, inertia, or even downright eagerness.

An assessment of the human condition as grim as Beckett's solicits an explanation, if not a justification. Critics who try to account for Beckett's pessimism, cynicism, and despair sometimes seek its etiology in "the Prudent affair."

In January, 1938, as he was returning home with friends after a late night out, Beckett was accosted by a man whom he recognized as a pimp named Prudent. The pimp demanded money, and Beckett refused. Prudent persisted, and Beckett—apparently unintentionally—knocked him down. Prudent jumped up and stuck a clasp knife in Beckett's chest. Beckett was seriously wounded, but was well enough five weeks later to confront Prudent in the courtroom. Deirdre Bair, from whose biography of Beckett I am taking this information, describes what happened next:

> After some insignificant chitchat, Beckett asked Prudent what he [Beckett]
> had done to inspire such drastic behavior. Prudent drew his shoulders up
> and with a Gallic shrug replied indifferently, "I don't know."[1]

Here indeed, in this act of motiveless, irrational cruelty, we may see
the model of Pozzo's treatment of Lucky, of Hamm's treatment of Clov,
Nagg, Nell, and Mother Pegg, of the trilogy's careless murders. We see
also the aleatory nature of human existence, for it was by chance that
Beckett encountered Prudent, by chance that he knocked him down, by
chance—and not out of some expressible motive—that Prudent stabbed
Beckett, and by most happy chance that Beckett was wearing an overcoat
so heavy that it absorbed much of the blow. So too, the world of Beckett's
art is governed not by love, justice, or reason, as theology, philosophy,
and science would have it, but by chance. We are conceived by chance,
we encounter others by chance and by chance fall in love with them; by
chance those we love are taken from us, by chance our work is neglected,
by chance we suffer disabling accidents and premature terminal ill-
nesses, and by chance we die.

If this is all we see in the Prudent affair, however, we are not seeing it
entire. For as Deirdre Bair also reports, as the fallen Beckett lay bleeding
to death on the ice-cold sidewalk of the avenue d'Orleans, a young
woman happened by. She took in the scene, then "quickly she helped to
wrap Beckett in Alan Duncan's overcoat and arranged a makeshift pil-
low before she called an ambulance" (*SB*, p. 254).

Let us suppose that, when he had recovered from his wound, Beckett
asked the young woman the question he asked Prudent. He would have
had opportunity to do so, of course, since the woman was Suzanne
Deschevaux-Dumesnil, she who was to become his life-long companion.
Let us suppose, then, that after some insignificant chitchat he asked
Suzanne what he had done to inspire such drastic behavior on her part.
What would she have replied? Perhaps what Prudent himself replied: "I
don't know." More likely: "Nothing."

---

[1] Deirdre Bair, *Samuel Beckett: A Biography* (New York: Harcourt Brace Jovanovich,
1978), p. 259; hereafter abbreviated *SB*. The information Deirdre Bair supplies must
always be used with discretion, nowhere more so than in this parable of the "Prudent
affair." I shall let the story stand, however, partly because any discrepancy of detail
(Suzanne apparently knew Beckett before the stabbing) does not affect my argument;
and partly as a modern instance of the way legends accrete to a saintly figure.

II.

In response to my inquiry, written in August 1983, Beckett proposed that we meet on November 4, at 11 a.m. in the lobby of the Hotel PLM. "No need to confirm." I was thirty seconds late. He was standing at the foot of the stairs leading to the lobby, hatless, black turtleneck, long gray overcoat, straight as a new pencil. He led me to the small restaurant, and ordered coffee in a French unblemished by any effort to disguise the fact that he was not a native.

By way of commencing the conversation, calming my nerves, and saying thank you, and because I knew he would not himself read it, I read to him the concluding paragraph of an essay I had written about him. He received it without emotion, and passed on to deplore the many automobile accidents that had happened over the recent All Saints holiday, the sad depletion of the plane trees that ornamented the boulevards of Paris; spoke of his mother, of Ireland, of the incongruity of showing on television films intended to be shown on giant movie screens.

The hour was drawing to a close. With his left forefinger he tapped quietly on the case of the small cigars he smoked. His eyes were less hawk-like, his countenance less intimidating than they appeared on an old photograph I had of him. He denigrated BBC television for its hurried and careless way of producing his work, and praised the Germans for their patience and attention to detail. He had just returned from Germany, where he had been working on a new piece for television. He seemed to be rather proud of it, even eager for approval. He explained that it begins with Schuber's "Nacht und Traüme." Could he sing it? He waited for noises in the kitchen, in the street, to subside (Pozzo: "Is everybody looking at me? Is everybody listening?") He la-la-la-ed his way through the melody, then described the scene: A dreamer dreams of a person's head, bent over, resting on the arms, the arms on a table. Ten seconds. A hand appears, rests gently on the person's head. Ten seconds. Hand is withdrawn. Hand reappears with a handkerchief, wipes the brow, withdraws. Hand reappears with a glass of water, gives the other to drink, withdraws. Hand and person's head are joined. Long pause, then "Da capo, in slow motion." And then he pushed himself back from the table, looked at me, and—almost—exclaimed, "The helping hand!"

I felt as if he had told me a joke, then punched me in the ribs with his elbow, and said, "Get it?" I wanted to say, "Yes, Sam, I get it. The helping hand."

I had to lengthen my stride to keep up with him. He stopped at a to-bacconist's, I continued on to the Metro station.

III.

The helping hand. It was there from the beginning, but disguised, obscured, disfigured. There is something of it in Celia's tender ministration to Mr. Kelly: "She took the assembled kite gently from his hands, backed along the path . . . and waited for the glove to fall."[2] It appears explicitly as a desperate plea addressed to the woman who, according to tradition, used her handkerchief to wipe the sweat from Jesus' face as he bore his cross to Golgotha:

> veronica mundi
> veronica munda
> give us a wipe for the love of Jesus
> ["Enueg II," *PE*, p. 26]

In its guise as pity, it is the substratum of "Dante and the Lobster," of which the superstratum is Belacqua Shuah's agenda for the day: prepare lunch, pick up the lobster for that evening's dinner with his aunt, and take a lesson in Italian from his tutor, Signorina Ottolenghi. Busy about the first item, he notices a newspaper photograph of McCabe the assassin, and he frets over the passage in Dante's *Paradiso* where Beatrice explains the reason for the spots on the moon. Beatrice's explanation is too much for him, and he settles for his mother's: "The spots were Cain with his truss of thorns, dispossessed, cursed from the earth, fugitive and vagabond. The moon was that [Cain's] countenance fallen and branded, seared with the first stigma of God's pity, that an outcast might not die quickly" (*MPTK*, p. 12). Later in the day Belacqua will learn that McCabe's petition for mercy has been rejected, and the man will be hanged at dawn the next day. "Belacqua, tearing at the sandwich . . . pondered on McCabe in his cell" (*MTPK*, p. 17).

In the course of the Italian lesson Signorina Ottolenghi suggests that Belacqua might study those episodes in Hell where Dante is moved to compassion. In reply he quotes what he calls Dante's "superb pun": *qui*

---

[2] *Murphy* (New York: Grove Press, 1957), p. 278; hereafter abbreviated *M*. Other works by Beckett are abbreviated as follows: *Collected Shorter Plays* (New York: Grove Press, 1984), *CSP*; *Endgame* (New York: Grove Press, 1958), *E*; *More Pricks Than Kicks* (New York: Grove Press, 1972), *MPTK*; *Poems in English* (New York: Grove Press, 1963), *PE*; *Waiting For Godot* (New York: Grove Press, 1954), *WFG*.

vive la pietà quando è ben morta. The pun results from the fact that *pieta* means both "pity" and "piety." The sense is that in Hell, piety lives when pity is dead. That is, pity for the sufferings of the damned must be replaced by a pious acknowledgement of the righteousness of God's justice. The Italian lesson is interrupted; and afterwards Belacqua asks the Signorina, "Where were we?" She replies acidly, "Where are we ever? . . . Where we were, as we were" (*MPTK*, p. 20).

At his aunt's house, Belacqua learns that the "lepping fresh" lobster is not dead, as he had supposed, and that his aunt proposes to boil the beast alive. "They feel nothing," she assures him. He ponders on the lobster's fate:

> In the depths of the sea it had crept into the cruel pot. For hours, in the midst of its enemies, it had breathed secretly. Now it was going alive into scalding water. It had to. Take into the air my quiet breath.

And the story briefly ends:

> Well, thought Belacqua, it's a quick death, God help us all.
> It is not. [*MPTK*, p. 22]

It may be that those last three words, unembraced by quotation marks, are spoken by the disincarnate voice that later will narrate the trilogy, as Hugh Kenner suggested. Or it may be the voice of the narrator of the story. But it is first of all the voice of the lobster—that, or the voice of the narrator speaking the words the lobster would utter if he could.

For "Dante and the Lobster" is a meditation, disguised and obscured by irony and blasphemy, on suffering, death, and pity. God exhibits his "pity" for Cain by condemning him to a life of vagabondage, thereby denying him the mercy of a quick death. True Christian piety must refuse to pity the suffering of the damned in Hell, for God's justice decrees that they deserve their agony. Folk wisdom and cliché combine to anesthetize Belacqua and his aunt to the torture which the lobster must undergo. And these three incidents triangulate the undescribed and undescribable misery of the assassin McCabe in his cell, waiting to be hanged. Everywhere the story looks—to the heavens, to Hell, to this earth—it is reminded of the truth that to live is to suffer. That is where we were, that is where we are.

The theme of the helping hand becomes slightly more discernible in *Waiting For Godot*. Shortly after the beginning of the second act, Didi removes his coat and places it over the shoulders of the sleeping Gogo.

Later in the same act, the fallen Pozzo cries out for help, and after much debate Vladimir says to Didi, "He wants us to help him to get up." Didi replies, "Then why don't we?" They help him up, they let him go, he falls, they get him up again and hold him up. "Pozzo sags between them, his arms round their necks" (*WFG*, p. 54a). That image is the culmination of the play, and it looks—should look—something like the late "Pietà" by Michelangelo.

In *Endgame* the theme is announced early on, in Nagg's solicitous concern for Nell. He has conserved a biscuit, and offers it to her. "I've kept you half. . . . Three quarters. For you. Here" (*E*, p. 18). It is given early so that, having seen what it is, we will recognize what it is not, as in the intercourse of Hamm and Clov. "Kiss me," Hamm pleads, but Clov refuses. Hamm holds out his hand and pleads again, "Give me your hand at least. . . . Will you not give me your hand?" Again Clov refuses (*E*, p. 67). The final tableau is that of two persons frozen in the immobility of near-maximum entropy, dying, like Mother Pegg, of darkness, of the absence of human kindness.

But it is the obese, bawdy, blasphemous, vital Maddy Rooney who finally enunciates the motif, fortissimo. She is trying to heave her huge bulk up stairs leading to the train station, and asks the dark Miss Fitt for assistance. Miss Fitt replies, "Is it my arm you want, Mrs. Rooney, or what is it?" And Maddy explodes, "Your arm! Any arm! A helping hand! For five seconds! Christ, what a planet!" Subsiding slightly, she adds, "Pismires do it for one another. . . . I have seen slugs do it" (*CSP*, p. 23).

Traces of the theme continue to appear in the shorter pieces for stage, radio, and television. The eleven pages of the radio play "Embers" (1959) are punctuated nine times by the word "Please," uttered in varying tones of desperate need. In "The Old Tune" (1963) the theme is present as absent, a request that is ignored. Two ancients, Cream and Gorman, are trying to get a light for a cigarette:

CREAM: . . . Perhaps we might ask this gentleman. [*Footsteps approach.*] Beg your pardon Sir trouble you for a light. [*Footsteps recede.*]

GORMAN: Ah the young nowadays Mr Cream very wrapped up they are the young nowadays, no thought for the old. . . .
[*CSP*, p. 181]

In "Rough for Radio II" it is present as a suggestion scorned. A (Animator), with the help of S (Stenographer), is interrogating F (Fox), with the use of a bull's pizzle swung enthusiastically by Dick. The results are unsatisfactory, and the sentimental S, interrupting, says, "I was going to suggest a touch of kindness, sir, perhaps just a hint of kindness." A caustically replies, "So soon? And then? . . ." [*CSP*, p. 118].

In "Rough for Theatre I," however, a favor is asked, and to the astonishment and consternation of the asker is actually granted. A (Billy) is blind, B wheelchaired. B strikes at A with the pole he uses to propel his wheelchair, repents his violence, and asks A to tuck in the rug around his remaining foot:

> B: Straighten my rug, I feel the cold air on my foot. . . . Do that for me, Billy. Then I may go back, settle in the old nook again and say, I have seen man for the last time, I struck him and he succoured me. [*Pause.*] Find a few rags of love in my heart and die reconciled, with my species. . . .

Making the effort, A stretches out his hand to B, and B exclaims in unbelief, "Wait, you're not going to do me a service for nothing? [*Pause.*] Good God! . . . " [*CSP*, p. 71].

Finally, almost finally, a quarter of a century after *All That Fall*, in the seventy-sixth year of his life, Beckett set out the theme again, but this time unobscured by vaudeville or irony or blasphemy. He did it in those four images of benediction, nurture, comfort, and communion—images as simple, sentimental, and utterly heart-breaking as the Schubert song after which the piece is named:

> 7. From dark beyond and above B's head L[eft hand] appears and rests gently on it.
>
> . . . .
>
> 9. From same dark R[ight hand] appears with a cup, conveys it gently to B's lips. B drinks, R disappears.
>
> 10. R reappears with a cloth, wipes gently B's brow, disappears with cloth
>
> . . . .
>
> 16. Together hands sink to table and on them B's head.
> 17. L[eft hand] reappears and rests gently on B's head.
> [*CSP*, pp. 305, 306]

It is only a dream, of course, a possibility for the human, but a possibility nonetheless.

And the image of the hand wiping B's brow takes us back fifty years, to the desperate plea of "Eneug II": "Give us a wipe for the love of Jesus."

<h2 style="text-align:center">IV.</h2>

Why should one person lend another person a helping hand? What is the motive for mercy?

Miss Fitt knows why she should help Maddy Rooney: "Well, I suppose it is the Protestant thing to do" (*CSP*, p. 23). Those first three words are heavy with the burden of duty imposed by religion on spinsters who live surrounded by the aged, the infirm, and the obese. If Miss Fitt had her way, she would be without company, alone with her Maker, oblivious to her co-religionists. But she knows that the Protestant thing to do, when asked, is to lend a helping hand.

In addition to religious motives there are ethical motives, founded for preference on the bedrock of pure reason. In the *Grounding for the Metaphysics of Morals*, Kant distinguished hypothetical imperatives from categorical imperative. There are many kinds of hypothetical imperatives, but they are all of the form, "If . . . , then . . . ," and are determined by interest—that is, by fear of punishment or anticipation of reward. There is only one categorical imperative, however, and in one of its formulations reads, "Act only according to that maxim whereby you can at the same time will that it should become a universal law."[3] In their discussion as to whether to help the fallen Pozzo, Didi and Gogo begin at the level of the hypothetical, and Didi suggests that they volunteer to help Pozzo in anticipation of some tangible return, to wit, a chicken bone. But immediately, in a flash of Kantian inspiration, Didi vaults to the plane of the categorical. At this place, he declares, and at this time, "All mankind is us." He summons the two of them to their duty: "Let us represent worthily for once the foul brood to which a cruel fate consigned us." This resolution is dissolved, however, by the consideration that the classic way to represent mankind is to be rational, so it follows that, "When with folded arms we weigh the pros and cons we are no less a credit to our species." After all, the lower mammals, a tiger for example, "bounds to the help of his congenors without the least reflection" (*WFG*, pp. 51, 51a). Kant is of no help to the two tramps, and it

<hr>

[3] Immanuel Kant, *Grounding for the Metaphysics of Morals*, trans. by James W. Ellington (Indianapolis: The Bobbs-Merrill Company, 1981), p. 30 (Ak. 421).

is not until six more pages of weighing the pros and cons that they actually help Pozzo get up.

There is also what could be called the motive of anticipated reciprocity. Its form is that of a hypothetical imperative, for it reads, if you want someone to have pity on you, then you must have—or have had—pity on someone else. It is on the basis of this formula that Hamm predicts Clov's fate: "Yes, one day you'll know what it is, you'll be like me, except that you won't have anyone with you, because you won't have had pity on anyone and because there won't be anyone left to have pity on" (*E*, p. 36). In the course of the play the truth of this principle is borne in on Hamm, and he is driven to declaim violently, "Get out of here and love one another." His cynicism objects to the verb, however, and he immediately vitiates it: "Lick your neighbor as yourself!" [*E*, p. 68]. Coming from a pitiless tyrant such as Hamm, this parody of one of Western culture's most reverend sayings is unspeakably hypocritical. But then, a hypocrite is one who can speak the truth even though he cannot do the truth; and Hamm's prediction concerning Clov turns upon its maker, as first Nell, then Nagg, and finally Clov leave Hamm in regal and total solitude.

What must now be immediately said, however, is that these three reasons for lending one's neighbor a helping hand—the religious, the ethical, and the pragmatic—are specious and ineffectual. Whatever obligation to kindness is imposed by "the Protestant thing" is called into questions when Miss Fitt's anxiety over her mother's fate is pretty well matched by her anxiety over the fate of the fresh fish Mother is delivering for lunch. Didi's rehearsal of Kant's argument leads not to the two tramps' enacting the categorical imperative but to behavior that is frivolous and cruel. When they finally do get around to helping Pozzo, it amounts to nothing more than taking advantage of what Didi calls a diversion (*WFG*, p. 52). In *Endgame*, Nagg's offering Nell a morsel of biscuit is the sole act of kindness exhibited or even described. The inference that Nagg is a kind person is invalidated, however, by his inhumanly vengeful speech to Hamm (*E*, p. 56).

I return to the event of Didi's removing his overcoat and placing it on the sleeping Gogo's shoulders. His act is motivated by none of the three reasons I have just listed. It is, rather, a deed inspired by compassion. In Beckett's ruined and desolate world, compassion is the only remaining viable virtue, and is as well the sole motive for lending one's neighbor a helping hand. As I have been trying to indicate, however, compassion, or pity, or kindness are present mainly as suggestion, request, prayer, or command—present, that is, as absent, unavailable.

We have it on Didi's word that the tiger springs without reflection to the aid of his congeners. Maddy Rooney declares that she has seen ants help one another, has seen slugs cooperate. And Hamm commands the audience—or someone—to behave like dogs, and lick one's neighbor as one licks oneself. There is in animals an instinct to lend a helping hand to others of the same species. In the human race, however, that instinct has all but atrophied, its place apparently taken by an instinct for cruelty, oppression, and revenge.

To be sure, if the human species lives according to its instincts for anger and revenge, it will eventually destroy itself, until perhaps there is one only left to tell himself stories, belatedly perhaps to repent, and then himself expire. Taking the long view, this might not be such a bad outcome, for the human is only one of thousands of species of the animal kingdom, amongst which one also names tigers, ants, and slugs. . . .[4]

V.

In Beckett's world, as in our own, there is no Foundation on which to ground the human enterprise, no Ultimate in terms of which to validate or judge it. What then does it profit the human to be kind rather than cruel, to be merciful rather than vengeful? What good does it do to lend a helping hand?

The grim reply must be that it profits nothing, and it does no good. Kindness goes unrewarded, cruelty goes unpunished. Gogo attempts to console the weeping Lucky, and gets kicked for his pains. Wheelchaired A strikes at blind Billy, and Billy tucks in A's rug around his foot. A character capable of kindness, such as Nagg, is capable also of hatred and vengefulness. A character incapable of pity, such as Hamm, is not without a certain stoic dignity. If at the end of *Endgame* Hamm sits in utter isolation, that is not a punishment for his cruelty (*pace* his curse on

---

[4] Compassion is also the pre-eminent virtue for the thinker who has influenced Beckett as much as anyone has, namely Arthur Schopenhauer. In deliberate and scornful disagreement with Kant, Schopenhauer declares that the only virtue that has genuine moral worth is compassion, the immediate participation in the suffering of another (*On the Basis of Morality*, trans. E. F. J. Payne [Indianapolis, 1965], 144). He puts his moral code in Latin: *Neminem laede; imo omnes, quantum potes, juva* ("Injure no one; on the contrary, help everyone as much as you can") (*Basis*, 147). Compassion is a mystery, for it asks me to feel the suffering of another. "We remain clearly conscious that *he* is the sufferer, not *we;* and it is precisely in *his* person, not in ours, that we feel the suffering, to our grief and sorrow" (*Basis*, 147).

Clov), but a simple statement of the human condition, for to be a human being is to be alone.

We are, as Heidegger says, thrown into existence. And what is worse, existence throws us by chance together with one another. The contusions that finite existence inflicts upon the human—loneliness, aimlessness, and, later on, it may be, the dastardly desertion of one's toes in the midst of the fray—these contusions are by themselves bad enough. But taken together with the abrasions that being thrown together add—as envy, guilt, shame, recrimination, anger, to name just a few—the contusions and abrasions may finally mount up, until one day the human says, "I can't go on." And having said it out loud at last, the human can then, perhaps, work up the courage to say, "I'll go on."

Now, if the human in fact decides to go on, it can be assured of two mishaps: first, it will fall down; second, it will get cold. Having opted for going on, the only other question to be resolved is this: In what company do I want to go on? Is it in the company of a person who for no good reason will attempt to knock me down and leave me to die of the cold? Or is it in the company of one who will, just as arbitrarily, help me to get up, or cover me with an overcoat or rug? In the company, that is to say, of a pimp named Prudent, or that of a young woman named Suzanne?

If the alternatives were that easy, of course, all would be clear. We would choose the person who is willing to lend a helping hand. The choice is complicated by the fact that in every Suzanne there is a Prudent.

Is it possible that in every Prudent there is a Suzanne?

The human being-with-one-another which existence by chance throws us into, then, is a gamble. To be human is to be alone. Is it better to be alone by oneself or to be alone in the company of another alone? That the other alone will hurt the one, the one the other, is taken for granted. But there is always the hope, the possibility, that if the one falls, the other will help him get up, that if the other gets cold, the one will help to warm him.

For the depth of understanding of the terror and emptiness of the being of the human, for the courage with which he has looked at the terror and not turned away, and for the power with which he has set it all before us, Samuel Beckett has few predecessors in the Western tradition. One thinks, perhaps, of the Sophocles of *Oedipus Rex*, the Shakespeare of *King Lear*, the Mahler of the Sixth symphony, the Grünewald of the Isenheim Crucifixion.

One thinks also of Koheleth, the Preacher, the author of the book of Ecclesiastes. No one has known better than he the vanity of human existence, the oppression of the poor by the wealthy, the injustice with which the powerful rule the weak, and even the helplessness of language:

> Whatever has already existed has been given a name, its nature is known. . . . The more words one uses the greater is the emptiness of it all; and where is the advantage to a man? (6:10, 11)

But when confronted with the choice between being alone and being alone together with another alone, Koheleth decides in favor of the latter; and he does so in two images, the first of which, it seems to me, Beckett appropriated for *Godot*, the second for *Endgame*. "Two are better than one," says the Preacher:

> Two are better than one; because they have a good reward for their labour. For if they fall, the one will lift up his fellow; but woe to him that is alone when he falleth; for he hath not another to help him up.
>
> Again, if two lie together, then they have heat: but how can one be warm alone? [Eccl. 4:9-11][5]

[5] An earlier version of this paper was originally read at the conference entitled, "Beckett at Eighty," held at Stirling University, Stirling, Scotland, in August, 1986. A slightly revised version was read at Agnes Scott College in April, 1987, as a part of "Beckett/Atlanta."

Walter Pater's Remoter and the Ever Remoter Possibilities

DAVID JASPER

> *It taught us to walk upon a rope, tightly stretched*
> *through serene air, and we were left to keep our*
> *feet upon a swaying rope in a storm*
>> William Butler Yeats on
>> *Marius the Epicurean*

It was through Nathan Scott's essay on Pater in *The Poetics of Belief* that I came to re-read *The Renaissance* (1873) and *Marius the Epicurean* (1885). Since Professor Scott's book was published, we have also had the benefit of a number of new studies of Pater by William Buckler, Paul Barolsky, and R. M. Seiler, but perhaps most important is the English translation of Wolfgang Iser's 1960 essay, *Walter Pater: Die Autonomie des Äesthetischen*.[1] As Iser recalls in his new 1985 Foreword, his book was written under the influence of the New Criticism of the 1950s, its focus upon the aesthetic dimension of the work as an autonomous object and to the exclusion of "extraneous factors" of history, environment, and sources.[2] Times have changed, of course, since 1960, and Pater's uneasy relationship with New Critical criteria has become an even more uneasy one with contemporary

---

[1] William E. Buckler, *Walter Pater: The Critic as Artist of Ideas* (New York: New York University Press, 1987); Paul Barolsky, *Walter Pater's Renaissance* (University Park, Penn.: Penn State University Press, 1987); R. M. Seiler, *Walter Pater: A Life Remembered* (New York: Routledge, Chapman and Hall, 1980); Wolfgang Iser, *Walter Pater: The Aesthetic Moment*, trans. by David Henry Wilson (New York: Cambridge University Press, 1987).

[2] Iser, *Walter Pater*, vii.

critical preoccupations. Nevertheless, with all his devotion to Art as an ultimate value, Pater does anticipate modernity and post-modernity in a number of crucial ways—the key term in Iser is "legitimation." In this search for a legitimation to bear out "the diversified intellectual commitments, social requirements, and multiple ideologies,"[3] I am brought back to Scott's emphasis that *Marius* inspires us to "'retrieve' the religious *possibility*," together with writers like G. M. Hopkins, Martin Buber, Simone Weil, and the later T. S. Eliot.[4]

How are we to understand Pater's "possibility"? Initially we need to join Scott in laying to rest T. S. Eliot's immensely influential essay of 1930, "Arnold and Pater." Eliot's contempt still rests heavily upon our reading. According to him, Pater was

> 'naturally Christian'—but within very narrow limitations: the rest of him was just the cultivated Oxford don and disciple of Arnold, for whom religion was a matter of feeling, metaphysics and not much more. Being incapable of sustained reasoning, he could not take philosophy or theology seriously; just as, being primarily a moralist, he was incapable of seeing any work of art simply as it is.[5]

It is difficult to imagine how a critic could be more wrong at every single point. I take systematic exception to Eliot's claims, but not, as Scott does, in order to reinstate Pater within a tradition of religious apologists. Pater's work certainly does have profound religious and theological implications, but of a very different and more radical nature, and the link with Eliot is not so much with the *Quartets* (although there is a link there) as with *The Waste Land*, anticipated most eloquently, perhaps, in Pater's description of the Mona Lisa in *The Renaissance*, "the embodiment of the old fancy, the symbol of the modern idea."[6]

Iser's work on Pater has taught us to consider neither Eliot's mindless aesthete nor Scott's prospective apologist. Scott himself, indeed, does not "foreclose the possibility of its (*Marius*) being regarded in its 'doctrine' as something more religiously ambiguous than I have been

[3] *Ibid.*, ix.
[4] Nathan A. Scott, Jr., *The Poetics of Belief* (Chapel Hill: University of North Carolina Press, 1985), p. 89.
[5] T. S. Eliot, *Selected Essays*. New Edition. (New York: Harcourt, Brace and World, 1964), pp. 390-91.
[6] Walter Pater, *The Renaissance: Studies in Art and Poetry* (London: New English Library, 1959), p. 90.

inclined to suggest."[7] But we need to go further, as Iser presents him as a figure often hauntingly anticipatory of our own post-modernist condition—deconstructive, defamiliarizing, perishing in relativities. Thus sceptically absorbed Pater attributes Coleridge's increasing dejection to his resistance to the necessity of the relative and his self-destructive grasping for the absolute. For, Pater asserts,

> The relative spirit, by its constant dwelling on the more fugitive conditions or circumstances of things, breaking through a thousand rough and brutal classifications, and giving elasticity to inflexible principles, begets an intellectual *finesse* of which the ethical result is a delicate and tender justice in the criticism of human life.[8]

Pater proposes a scepticism which counters the absolutism of such as Coleridge as systematic repression, and opens up the mind to experience, without theory and in recognition of "the basic condition of reality."[9]

Iser contrasts Pater with Ruskin, the last great proponent of the classic norm of mimesis, whose "exclusively theological concept of art"[10] seeks to portray God's presence in Nature. Pater's defamiliarizing art, on the other hand, instead of imitating what is given, achieves the triumph of the imagination over the compulsion exercised by reality. Abandoning any metaphysical interpretation of the world, art inhabits a region of undecidedness which does not even accept the responsibility of actually dismissing such an interpretation.[11] Determined by mood, art for Pater simply flashes the *illusion* of totalities before the mind's eye, set free from reality. Wolfgang Iser draws a detailed comparison between Pater's concept of art and history, and that of Hegel in the *Äesthetik*, upon which Pater drew heavily. In a typical spirit of revolution, Pater rejects Hegel's normative approach, abandoning any metahistorical idea which may lurk behind the philosopher's eschatology and ideology of progress.

Through Iser's criticism, Pater grows in stature as a thinker and as a brave proponent of a bleak, uncompromising vision which allows no resolution, no idealisation in religion and no comfortable limitation. In the end, *Marius* is to be read as an ultimate exercise in human experience in which the isolated aesthetic sphere is never abandoned for the ethical sphere of continuity. No final decision is reached by Marius in his per-

---

[7] Scott, *Poetics*, p. 89.
[8] Walter Pater, *Appreciations* (London: Macmillan, 1889), pp. 104-05.
[9] Iser, *Walter Pater*, p. 17.
[10] *Ibid.*, p. 33.
[11] *Ibid.*, p. 40.

petual dissatisfaction with the absolute as he dies, not a Christian, but aware only of a vague hope and "a pledge of something further to come."[12] Marius, like most of Pater's fictional characters, inevitably dies. To live aesthetically is to live without commitment and therefore without fulfillment, and to act is to abandon the aesthetic for the moral and the dubiously progressive. As Iser puts it, "action restricts and orientates life, thus destroying the liberty and unlimited receptiveness of the aesthetic way of life."[13]

And yet Pater is supposed to have said that the purpose of *Marius* was to "show the necessity of religion."[14] If that is so, its manner and preoccupation is peculiarly contemporary. For throughout his work, Pater's attempt to define art was made in order to release it from reality, making of it a kind of "negative theology," to use Walter Benjamin's term,[15] inasmuch as "art is rooted in temporal existence but has the task of transcending its basis."[16] Insofar as reality is conditional, art is a response to the one certitude of change, a moment which is momentarily experienced—the perpetual experience of dying—apart from the abstract and theoretical teleologies of evolution and ultimacy. It reveals the necessity of religion in a historical flux which denies the conclusive possibilities of theology.

In his essay on Winckelmann in *The Renaissance*, Pater indicates both his dependence upon Hegel's view of history and his abandonment of Hegel's normative approach. Recognizing that "a taste for metaphysics may be one of those things which we must renounce, if we mean to mould our lives to artistic perfection,"[17] Pater dismantles the ideological conditions which embrace and give direction to the Hegelian sense of change. Without determinate ideal or metahistorical idea, Pater is careful to preserve that "sense of freedom"[18] which art alone upholds in precious moments which dominate past and present and their necessities. The sole reality becomes that of the overwhelming moment, as Pater expressed it in the familiar, notorious Conclusion to *The Renaissance*: "for

---

[12]   Walter Pater, *Marius the Epicurean* (London: New English Library, 1970), p. 283.

[13]   Iser, *Walter Pater*, p. 166.

[14]   Quoted by Thomas Wright in *The Life of Pater*. 2 vols. (New York: G. P. Putnam's Sons, 1907), 2, 87. See also A. C. Benson, *Walter Pater* (London: Macmillan, 1906), p. 90.

[15]   Walter Benjamin, *Schriften*. 2 vols. (Frankfurt: Suhrkamp Verlag, 1955), 1, 374.

[16]   Iser, *Walter Pater*, p. 61.

[17]   Pater, *The Renaissance*, p. 154.

[18]   *Ibid.*, p. 155.

our one chance lies in expanding that interval, in getting as many pulsations as possible into the given time."[19]

Perhaps not surprisingly it is in his essay on Wordsworth, the celebrant of epiphanal "spots of time," that Pater explains most fully his vision in which means are the end apparently devoid of realisation. The moment is all.

> Wordsworth, and other poets who have been like him in ancient or more recent times, are the masters, the experts, in [the] art of impassioned contemplation. Their work is, not to teach lessons, or enforce rules, or even to stimulate us to noble ends; but to withdraw the thoughts for a while from the mere machinery of life, to fix them, with appropriate emotions, on the spectacle of those great facts in man's existence which no machinery affects. . . .[20]

Art, it may be said, absorbs the totality of history, discarding teleology and purpose. Its process is endless, its environment ceaseless flux. Its mode is never mimetic, but a constant aspiration to transcend those conditions which would define us within the purposes of history or theological resolution. Such transcendence amounts, perhaps, to no more than Marius' ambition, amidst the "perpetual flux," to live a little while "but in a fragment of perfect expression." Though to live thus is, perhaps inevitably, also to die.

In their recent book, *Joachim of Fiore and the Myth of the Eternal Evangel in the Nineteenth Century* (1987), Marjorie Reeves and Warwick Gould describe Pater's *Renaissance* as "a lonely document. It accepts without flinching an aesthetic relativism as the one constant index of experience. Life itself, objectively or subjectively considered, is reduced to that famous stream of impressions, every one of which records 'the individual in his isolation.'"[21]

Internalized, individuated, Pater's art is antinomian and subversive. Its logic is most ruthlessly pursued by Oscar Wilde in his philosophical dialogue, "The Critic as Artist":

> The artistic critic, like the mystic, is an antinomian always. To be good according to the vulgar standard of goodness, is obviously quite easy. It merely requires a certain amount of sordid terror, a certain lack of imaginative thought, and a certain low passion for middle-class respectability.

[19] *Ibid.*, p. 159.
[20] Pater, *Appreciations*, p. 62.
[21] Marjorie Reeves and Warwick Gould, *Joachim of Fiore and the Myth of the Eternal Evangel in the Nineteenth Century* (Oxford: Clarendon Press, 1987), p. 168.

Aesthetics are higher than ethics. They belong to a more spiritual sphere, To discern the beauty of a thing is the finest point to which we can arrive.[22]

From the artistic point of view, life is a failure, as, in Frank Kermode's words, "transition itself becomes an age . . . and we are left with eternal transition, perpetual crisis."[23] The transition is not progression, but utter subjectivity, individuation, abandoning all moral categories for the "pure" spirituality of aesthetic discernment which is without narrative or a sense of temporality. Such high disinterestedness in retreat from overt moral function characterizes the Conclusion to *The Renaissance*, and, more subtly in that work, Pater's celebrated evocation of the Mona Lisa.

> She is older than the rocks among which she sits; like the vampire, she has been dead many times, and learned the secrets of the grave; and has been a diver in deep seas, and keeps their fallen day about her; and trafficked for strange webs with Eastern merchants; and, as Leda, was the mother of Helen of Troy, and, as Saint Anne, the mother of Mary; and all this has been to her but as the sound of lyres and flutes, and lives only in the delicacy with which it has moulded the changing lineaments, and tinged the eyelids and the hands. The fancy of a perpetual life, sweeping together ten thousand experiences is an old one; and modern philosophy has conceived the idea of humanity as wrought upon by, and summing up in itself, all modes of thought and life. Certainly Lady Lisa might stand as the embodiment of the old fancy, the symbol of the modern idea.[24]

Mona Lisa embodies the synchronic, timeless abandonment of historical categories in every moment, which characterizes "modernity," perhaps even post-modernity. Beyond definition or abstraction, Lady Lisa embraces the supreme, destabilizing moment, when art is purely art, unresponsive to the "comfortable fictions of transparency, the single sense, the truth," and the only hard truth which is apparent is that: "I am no longer a child."[25]

[22] Oscar Wilde, "The Critic as Artist, Part II," in *Oscar Wilde*, ed. by Isobel Murray. The Oxford Authors (Oxford & New York: Oxford University Press, 1989), p. 295.

[23] Frank Kermode, *The Sense of an Ending: Studies in the Theory of Fiction* (Oxford and New York: Oxford University Press, 1966), p. 101.

[24] *The Renaissance*, p. 90.

[25] Frank Kermode, *The Genesis of Secrecy* (Cambridge, Mass: Harvard University Press, 1979), p. 123; Roland Barthes, *Roland Barthes*, in *Barthes: Selected Writings*, ed. by Susan Sontag, (New York: Hill & Wang, 1982), p. 419.

Although in his review of Mrs. Humphry Ward's *Robert Elsmere*, Pater is prepared to recognize Christianity as a perpetual "possibility,"[26] he radically opposes any sense, as claimed for example by John Ruskin, that art may propose any systematic or theological presentation of God in Nature. While for Ruskin art is an imitation and a celebration of an eternal divine order, for Pater its function is not imitative but experimental and expressionistic. The devices of art conspire to a "making strange" (*ostranenie*, in Shklovsky's term), a contradiction of habitual perceptions, a defamiliarizing. Thus art has a healing effect, unlike Ruskinian mimesis which merely reproduces the senselessness of the finite under the forms of our contrived fictions. For the essence of Pater's art is otherness, breaking through given reality and its claimed significances to the radically new with an "unconscious literary tact"[27] in a moment of transfiguration. It projects, in Pater's words,

> a world in which the forms of things are transfigured. Of that transfigured world this new poetry [the "aesthetic"] takes possession, and sublimates beyond it another still fainter and more spectral, which is literally an artificial or "earthly paradise."[28]

The language here is very precise, and within the context of the biblical experience of transfiguration. The world "sublimated" by poetry is "literally" an artifice which is not subject to the claims of temporality or the narrative flow of teleology. In Iser's words, "the beholder is released from activity and may bask in aesthetic quietism."[29]

In art the perpetual possibility of Christianity is infinitely deferred, a release from the burdens and moral demands of finitude. So that the religious image is perceived only as the spectral and artificial image reflected in a looking-glass, recognizably that of the original and yet its opposite in its reversal of form. In poetry we experience, therefore,

> a rival religion with a new rival *cultus*. . . . Coloured through and through with Christian sentiment, they are rebels against it. The rejection of one worship for another is never lost sight of. The jealously of that other lover, for whom these words and images and refined ways of sentiment were first devised, is the secret here of a borrowed, perhaps factitious colour and heat.

---

[26] *The Guardian*, 28 March 1888, n.p.
[27] *Appreciations*, p. 23.
[28] *Ibid.*, p. 213.
[29] Iser, *Walter Pater*, p. 36.

It is the mood of the cloister taking a new direction, and winning so a later space of life it never anticipated.[30]

The frame of Pater's aestheticism is familiar enough, but without metaphysical claim or moral structure. Means and ends are not divided, and purposefulness is fully absorbed in a pure *ascesis* of experience in which the end of life is life itself,[31] a phrase which may be understood in two ways; "end" as purpose, or "end" in terms of temporality. In his essay on Wordsworth, Pater wrote:

> That the end of life is not action but contemplation—*being* as distinct from *doing*—a certain disposition of the mind: is, in some shape or other, the principle of all higher morality. In poetry, in art, if you enter into their true spirit at all, you touch this principle, in a measure: these, by their very sterility, are a type of beholding for the mere joy of beholding. To treat life in the spirit of art, is to make life a thing in which means and ends are identified: to encourage such treatment, the true moral significance of art and poetry.[32]

Art, paradoxically, recognizes "morality" in presenting the vacuity of the ethical claims of a visible world organized upon the narrative demands of temporal structures. Its exploration in *Marius the Epicurean* emerges in an antinomian expression of perfectibility which is the moral and religious abandonment, finally, of the terms of morality and religion.

Marius is set in a historical moment of change, in the transition between the decayed culture of imperial Rome and the emergent, newly confident Christianity, the Church of "an earlier and unimpeachable *Renaissance.*" There is a clear connection to be seen between the spirit of Marius and, via Mona Lisa and the Renaissance, the contemporary inconstancy of the "modern idea." The vision is recognized only in the pure, unrealisable *écriture* or art, in the *aporia* which releases life rather than repressing it in concept or absolute. In the chapter entitled, "New Cyrenaicism," Pater proposes that:

> Such manner of life might come even to seem a kind of religion—an inward, visionary, mystic piety or religion, by virtue of its effort to live days "lovely and pleasant" in themselves, here and now, and with an all-sufficiency of well-being in the immediate sense of the object contemplated, independently of any faith or hope that might be entertained as to their ulterior tendency. In this way, the true aesthetic culture would be realisable as a new

[30] *Appreciations*, pp 61-62.
[31] See U. C. Knoepflmacher, *Religious Humanism and the Victorian Novel* (Princeton: Princeton University Press, 1965), p. 206.

form of the contemplative life, founding its claim on the intrinsic "blessedness" of "vision"—the vision of perfect men and things.[33]

Faith and hope abandoned, Christianity here gazes upon its mirror-image, it fulfillment and its extinction. And so in the novel's last chapter, entitled, *"Anima Naturaliter Christiana"*, matching the Conclusion to *The Renaissance*, the climax is both reached, and properly deferred. Marius' conversion to Christianity is achieved only in a moribund condition, the Host "like a snow-flake from the sky" administered in the "doubtful moment between life and death." His martyrdom, "a kind of sacrament with plenary grace,"[34] but only according to the "generous nature" of the Christians who tend him. All both is, and is not, accommodated where it is suitable to certain beliefs, but supremely for Marius a perpetual possibility, for him as for Leonardo da Vinci, the experience of "the last curiosity."[35]

> Surely, the aim of a true philosophy must lie, not in futile efforts towards the complete accommodation of man to the circumstances in which he chances to find himself, but in the maintenance of a kind of *candid discontent*, in the face of the very highest achievement; the unclouded and receptive soul quitting the world finally, with the same fresh wonder with which is had entered the world still unimpaired, and going on its blind way at last with the consciousness of some profound enigma in things, as but a pledge of something further to come. Marius seemed to understand how one might look back upon life here, and its excellent visions, as but the portion of a race-course left behind him by a runner still swift of foot: for a moment, he experienced a singular *curiosity*, almost an ardent desire to enter upon a future, the possibilities of which seemed to large.[36] (italics mine)

There is more to this than a kind of scriptural "sacred discontent,"[37] an ambivalence caught between the natural and the supernatural, a negative knowledge between culture and the denial of culture.[38] *Marius* is not Scott's "beautifully organized structure"[39] which leads to the thresh-

---

[32] *Appreciations*, pp. 61-62.

[33] *Marius*, p. 105.

[34] *Ibid.*, pp. 285-86.

[35] *The Renaissance*, p. 92.

[36] *Marius*, p. 283.

[37] See Herbert N. Schneidau, *Sacred Discontent: The Bible and Western Tradition* (Berkeley: University of California Press, 1976).

[38] See Amos N. Wilder, *Theology and Modern Literature* (Cambridge, Mass.: Harvard University Press, 1958), pp. 70-71.

[39] Scott, *Poetics*, p. 86.

old of Christian conversion and confession, except in the natures of those who wish to perceive it so. The true paradox lies in the Christian death of a pagan, in the resistance to system through the experience which is liberated by art and its replacement of the metaphysical with a mood, a blending of opposites, a transitional reality. Marius' greatest experience of life is the end of life, to live most fully is to die, an illusory totality flashed up momentarily by art, the supreme *possibility*.

Is art, then, simply a refusal to make a commitment, an abandonment of moral principles, a pure relativism? As an autonomous function does it become simply the prisoner of its own discourse, in Terry Eagleton's words, allowing you "to drive a coach and horses through everybody else's beliefs while not saddling you with the inconvenience of having to adopt any yourself"?[40] Does Pater's refusal to be caught in the trap of system and definition necessarily entail endless disappointment with simply occasionally glimpses of a *religious* possibility?

It does if our sense of that possibility is in the old metaphysical and ethical terms even though dusted free of the violence which they have exercised upon our minds, hearts, and imaginations.[41] But the alternative to them in Pater is not merely a shiftless and irresponsible relativism.

Walter Pater, I should wish to claim, is more important to us now than ever before, as his own *fin de siecle* awareness is matched by the uncertainties and disillusionments of our late twentieth century in the West. His voice may contribute to the debate now being heard in theology concerning its place and responsibilities in the "post-modern" world which, from Nietzsche, recognizes the long shadow of Heidegger and, more recently, of Derrida and Foucault. Just as in scholars like Carl Raschke we can now begin to re-engage in an imaginative rediscovery of theological discourse in an age in which relativity and quantum physics have begun to suggest to us new models of thinking, so we should also realize the serious and profound implications of Pater's work. For the end of theology and its conventional undertakings may be the blessed

[40] Terry Eagleton, *Literary Theory: An Introduction* (Oxford: Oxford University Press, 1983), p. 144.

[41] Cf. Scott, *Poetics*, p. 89: "it is only to say that—like the poems of Hopkins, like Martin Buber's *I and Thou*, like the books of Simone Weil, like Eliot's *Quartets*—it causes us to question the authenticity of our present mode of being in the world in such a way as, in effect, to make us 'retrieve' the religious *possibility*; and, thus, it makes 'a nonviolent appeal to our minds, hearts and imaginations, and through them to our wills.'" These last words are a quotation from David Tracy, *The Analogical Imagination* (New York: Crossroad, 1981).

rediscovery of "theological thinking," that is, "a return to the unthought origins of the discipline itself."[42] Such an adventure in thought, as Raschke has envisaged it, must be purely formal, cleansed of the distractions of Christian morality and ecclesiology. Thinking may then become an adventure in the depths of thought, a properly deconstructed exercise which escapes the referential byways of "theology" as such.

Raschke, like Pater in his own day, takes seriously the demands made upon presuppositions which direct our thinking processes and methods by the revolution in science which celebrates a "healthy suspicion toward everyday sensibility."[43] The movement away from reification and the drive to a metaphysic is safeguarded by self-conscious critical thought, a formal hermeneutical thinking whose sense of discipline matches in Pater "the idea of legitimation," that is, "the need for aesthetic existence to grapple with its own necessity."[44] It is this search for legitimation at the very heart of Pater's concerns which confirms him as a serious religious thinker, and as one who realized that theology and all its works must be abandoned as an attempt to *enclose the infinite*, forgetful of its origins or ultimate possibilities.[45] The realized/unrealized, affirmative, wry ending of *Marius* finds its proper theological commentary in the final paragraph of Carl Raschke's *Theological Thinking*. As is there suggested, thinking must now be into time and *through time*. The "text" of God must be deconstructed, so that, in Luther's words, we must "let God be God." The art must become autonomous, itself truly itself yet never the final word. Nothing has any proof, and we live by faith alone according, perhaps, to our own generous view of the matter.[46]

W. H. Mallock, in his novel, *The New Republic* (1877), parodied Walter Pater in his character of Mr. Rose, of whom Lady Ambrose shrieked: "He always seems to talk of everybody as if they had no clothes on." Any challenge to our fundamental notions about language and religious thought, which allows us no resting place upon which to cement our ideas or theories, will have that deconstructive, disrobing effect upon us. To feel ourselves naked may indeed be alarming—but Lady Ambrose's

---

[42] Carl A. Raschke, *Theological Thinking: An Inquiry* (Atlanta: Scholars Press, 1988), vii.

[43] *Ibid.*, p. 54.

[44] Iser, *Walter Pater, passim*. See also Ian Fletcher, "The In-Between Man." A Review of Recent Work on Pater. *TLS*, 5-11 August 1988, p. 858.

[45] See Raschke, *Theological Thinking*, viii.

[46] *Ibid.*, p. 153; Pater, *Marius*, p. 286.

point was well made and contained more truth than, no doubt, that civilised lady was aware of.

The Sadness of Sister Carrie

J. C. LEVENSON

According to Theodore Dreiser's account, he began *Sister Carrie* in September 1899 without a plan or a plot. He simply wrote the words "Sister Carrie" on the sheet of paper before him: "My mind was a blank except for the name."[1] Whether or not memory had reshaped the event, his story defines a special relation, a family closeness of the author to his imaginary subject. Along with intimacy, it expresses a willingness to draw on imaginative resources that he could not calculate or even define. Taking seriously the germ of the novel, I believe that the emotional cast of *Sister Carrie* is as important as the realistic detail. Such terms as incalculable feeling and devastating qualm, that usually describe spiritual aspects of a literary work, also serve a social and political analysis of *Sister Carrie*, which has lately been discussed in more narrowly economic terms. The moral economy of the novel, by which the literal economics is to be interpreted, in no way undoes the argument that the characters know scarcely any connection with one another except the cash nexus; rather, it underscores the problematic disproportion between feelings and commitments. Deep sentiments are evoked, but they do not link one person with another. Carrie the character is said to illustrate emotional greatness and yet in some ways she remains "a blank except for the name."

Dreiser, in his family experience, knew the paradox of powerful feelings and weak ties. Pressure of poverty had kept the family moving from house to house, from town to town, and then broke it up altogether.

---

[1] Dorothy Dudley, *Forgotten Frontiers: Dreiser and the Land of the Free* (New York Smith and Haas, 1932), p. 160.

When Theodore was eight, his father had to leave home to find work; although he presently returned, he never regained the parental authority that had begun to slip when he first started downhill economically. Although the mother remained a fixed center, as in so many poor families, the ten brothers and sisters gradually scattered. Two brothers landed in jail at various times. One sister eloped with an absconding bartender from Chicago, another came home to have a baby—and leave her for their mother to take care of. The dispersed and seemingly lost brothers and sisters sometimes managed remarkably to find one another when their help was most needed. Dreiser's brother Paul found him after his nervous breakdown. Dreiser himself helped the sister who had run off with the bartender. Yet each for the most part lived unconnected to the others, now in one city, now in another, it hardly mattered. For young Dreiser, Chicago, St. Louis, Toledo, and Pittsburgh were places in which to make good or go under, counting on no one for help. In such a world, family security was known by its absence, and the imagination of security was a form of loneliness.

Along with loneliness, the isolation and anonymity of city life brought out a more widely acknowledged American characteristic, self-reliance. But the self-reliance of the poor differs from that of the middle class—defeat comes early and often and at any time may look as if it has come to stay. The experience of defeat can breed either demoralization or tenacity of self-aggrandizement. Dreiser knew both. In the years immediately after the virtual suppression and financial failure of *Sister Carrie*, he suffered a collapse of ego that led him to the verge of suicide. Then, after rescue and recovery, he made his way almost to the top of Butterick Publications; he who had once so completely identified his life with his writing turned into a captain of the media industry. Either way, depending on himself alone, he demonstrated that the less smiling aspects of American life bear a grim resemblance to what goes on, apparently by choice, among the content and complacent. Self-reliance, the old-fashioned term but without the old-fashioned Emersonian tang, characterizes both the author of *Sister Carrie* and the protagonist of the novel.

Grim or smiling, self-reliance arrives at the stage of possessive individualism by a long route. "Individualism," the word Tocqueville invented to describe American experience as he had seen it in the 1830s, struck the French observer as something radically new, a loosening of bonds of intimacy that, among Europeans, supposedly reached far into the past. Among Americans, Tocqueville wrote:

the woof of time is every instant broken and the track of generations effaced. Those who went before are soon forgotten; of those who will come after, no one has any idea: the interest of man is confined to those in close propinquity to himself. . . . They owe nothing to any man, they expect nothing from any man; they acquire the habit of always considering themselves alone, and they are apt to imagine that their whole destiny is in their own hands. Thus not only does democracy make every man forget his ancestors, but it hides his descendants and separates his contemporaries from him; it throws him back forever upon himself alone and threatens in the end to confine him entirely within the solitude of his own heart.[2]

This American process, which Tocqueville saw as the process of modern society everywhere, describes the plot of *Sister Carrie* with remarkable accuracy. In the opening paragraph of Dreiser's novel, eighteen-year-old Caroline Meeber sets out by train with her pathetic little outfit of small trunk, satchel, wrapped lunch, and yellow leather purse. Ill-equipped save for the "illusions and ignorance of youth," she is to act out the historic theme that Balzac had set for the nineteenth-century novel: she is to be the young woman from the provinces who goes from the small-town Middle West to make her way in the great city of Chicago and then the still greater city of New York. As she departs Columbia City, Wisconsin, for Chicago, one thing she does not carry with her is the family feeling that Dreiser seemed to evoke in his title:

> A gush of tears at her mother's farewell kiss, a touch in her throat when the cars clacked by the flour mill where her father worked by the day, a pathetic sigh as the familiar green environs of the village passed in review, and the threads which bound her so lightly to girlhood and home were irretrievably broken.[3]

Tocqueville's ideal model helps us see much more than the irretrievable separateness of Carrie Meeber. When Dreiser wrote that "self-interest with her was high, but not strong," and yet it was "her guiding char-

---

[2] Alexis de Tocqueville, *Democracy in America*, 2, (1840), trans. by Henry Reeve as rev. by Francis Bowen (2 vols., ed. by Phillips Bradley. New York: Knopf, 1945), Second Book, Chapter II, "Of Individualism in Democratic Countries."

[3] Theodore Dreiser, *Sister Carrie*, (New York: Doubleday, 1900), p. 1. Further references are made in parenthesis, citing page numbers of this edition; the same pagination obtains in the 1907, 1911, and Modern Library editions. The Pennsylvania edition (1981), edited by James L. W. West III, prints Dreiser's manuscript draft, a version with more circumstantiality of detail and less interpretive coloration than the book which Dreiser published—and republished—as his final text.

acteristic" (p. 2), he was virtually restating the older writer's distinction between individualism and *égoisme*, or selfishness. In Tocqueville's view, selfishness arises from depraved instincts, whereas individualism "originates as much in deficiencies of mind as in perversity of heart." Carrie's intellectual limitations, about which Dreiser is explicit, make her at once a specimen for Tocqueville and, in an ironic sense, an ideal subject for literature, for she cannot conceive of abstract ideas or personal goals apart from what she experiences directly through the senses. Her "rudimentary" mind, too crude to be violated by ideas, fits her to act out in novelistic terms what Tocqueville tried to understand by shrewd analysis. In the analyst's logical scheme, "individualism, at first, only saps the virtues of public life; but in the long run it attacks and destroys all others and is at length absorbed in downright selfishness." When the analysis is put to the test of Dreiser's fiction, the etiology of individualism is roughly as Tocqueville described it, but the word "selfishness" does not seem adequate to the outcome of the process.

Tocqueville began on the right track, however. As Dreiser's would-be censors recognized almost at once, Carrie's public virtues are negligible. In her casual relation to family and, later, to marriage, she evinced an indifference to historic institutions which, in 1900, was less likely to be excused as naive or sublime than to be condemned as vicious or subhuman. But Dreiser did not portray her as vicious or make her out to be less than human. A more sophisticated naturalist like Frank Norris, who knew his Zola, might show that when socially-engendered conscience and institutional obligations cease to control, the veneer of civilizations is stripped off and animal appetites are released. The naturalist's beast-at-the-bottom-of-the-psyche hardly figures in Dreiser's conception of character. Rather, when abstract injunctions fade into ineffectuality, sensuous attractions become the stronger. And when specific obligations lose their hold, the mind responds to more general outside pressures. On page two of the novel, he declares:

> The city has its cunning wiles, no less than the infinitely smaller and more human tempter. There are large forces which allure with all the soulfulness of expression possible in the most cultured human. The gleam of a thousand lights is often as effective as the persuasive light in a wooing and fascinating eye. Half the undoing of the unsophisticated and natural mind is accomplished by forces wholly superhuman. A blare of sound, a roar of life, a vast array of human hives, appeal to the astonished senses in equivocal terms. (p. 2)

The sensuous appeal of the city is crucial to Carrie's experience. While she is staying in the Chicago working-class flat of her sister's family, she feels "the drag of a lean and narrow life" (p. 13). But from the beginning she is solicited by the glow and murmur of the vast metropolis, by "the lights of the grocery stores" and "the sound of the little bells upon the horse-cars, as they tinkled in and out of hearing" (p. 12). In that modern urban institution, the department store, which Dreiser carefully dates from the year 1884,[4] she feels object after object assert a personal claim on her: "The dainty slippers and stockings, the delicately frilled skirts and petticoats, the laces, ribbons, hair-combs, purses, all touched her with individual desire" (p. 24). What she see, feels, and desires so intensely takes on a life of its own; things seem to reach towards her as much as she towards them.

With her responsiveness to *things*, Carrie moves easily from the free-floating individualism of Tocqueville into the moral economy of Thorstein Veblen—with a difference. Her desires are quickened by those whom she meets, so that for most of the novel she climbs the endless ladder of acquisitive emulation. Yet her acquisitiveness is not disguised aggression in a universal war of competitive consumption. Although she enters barbarian society, she lacks the barbarian temperament. She is indeed self-centered, but with a simplicity that is the opposite of calculating. In her private world she learns the irksomeness of labor by day and contemplates her dreams of pleasure by night. Her changes of status, when they result from choice at all, are not prompted by invidious comparison on a pecuniary basis. At first she chooses between actual hardship and the illusion of pleasure. When hardship becomes a memory, when the murmur of crowds, the clanging of horse-cars, and the texture and look or goods on department-store counters no longer constitute the ever-receding objects of desire, she remains incapable of a more complex hedonic calculus. As June Howard observes, "at the end of the novel, when Carrie has succeeded in attaining all the desires to which she can put a name, she is as desirous as ever."[5] At the end she finds herself confined within the solitude of her limited consciousness, and bafflement at trying to breach those limits creates its own kind of suffering.

---

[4] The narrator established historical authenticity and objectivity with such details, duly noting that he is recording the first such stores in the United States. Rachel Bowlby, in *Just Looking: Consumer Culture in Dreiser, Gissing, and Zola* (New York and London: Methuen, 1985), dates the department store from the 1850s in Paris.

[5] *Form and History in American Literary Naturalism* (Chapel Hill: University of North Carolina Press, 1985), p. 43.

Carrie's consciousness, limited though it may be, is what principally defines the world of the novel. That world is made up not only of things in their particularity, but also of massed effects. On her first day in Chicago she walks among the tall buildings and imposing stores to the streets of drab workshops, where she suffers the discouragements and humiliations of seeking work. When she finally gets the promise of a job at a shoe-factory, she feels a revival of spirit and sees once again with the eyes of hope. Responding to the cityscape and the crowds, to the collectivity of Chicago, she comes as close as she ever does to formulating a controlling purpose for the action:

> She walked into the busy street and discovered a new atmosphere. Behold, the throng was moving with a lightsome step. She noticed that men and women were smiling. Scraps of conversation and notes of laughter floated to her. The air was light. People were already pouring out of their buildings, their labor ended for the day. She noticed that they were pleased, and thoughts of her sister's home and the meal that would be awaiting her quickened her steps. She hurried on, tired, perhaps, but no longer weary of foot. What would not Minnie say! Ah, the long winter in Chicago—the lights, the crowd, the amusement! This was a great, pleasing metropolis after all. Her new firm was a goodly institution. Its windows were of huge plate glass. She could probably do well there. . . . She boarded a car in the best of spirits, feeling her blood still flowing pleasantly. She would live in Chicago, her mind kept saying to itself. She would have a better time than she had ever had before—she would be happy. (pp. 30-31)

The pursuit of happiness, the goal that determines Carrie's action in general, provides the clue to particular choices. At first the choices are simple. When, a few months after coming to Chicago, Carrie is out of work, weary with job-hunting, and shivering for lack of a proper coat, she meets again the traveling salesman who had talked to her on the train-ride that brought her to the city. The genial Drouet takes her to lunch at a splendid restaurant. The gleam of the linen and silver, the shine of Drouet's rings, and the newness of his suit that *creaks* as he carves and serves, captivate the senses—and so captivate the girl. When he hears that she is almost ready to return to her home town in defeat, Drouet spontaneously offers help: "Come on . . . I'll see you through all right. Get yourself some clothes." And he presses into her hand "two soft, green, handsome ten-dollar bills" (p. 69). Carrie becomes Drouet's mistress, and in her fall begins her rise.

The sympathy for Carrie that is created at the beginning of the novel, which seems to me crucial, is a matter of critical dispute. Her story in its external outline hangs on a reversal of fall and rise that flouts conventional morality. In "realistic" terms, the country girl smartens up and turns into a ruthless gold-digger. When Carrie contemplates the twenty dollars that Drouet has given her, she thinks of money as "something that was power in itself" (p. 70), and it has been suggested that in that moment the story of desire turns into a story of power. If this were the case, she could be said to have joined Veblen's "universal pantomime of mastery . . . and subservience."[6] But Carrie lacks both aggressiveness and sensitivity to aggression. On the one hand, she can hardly conceive of power over people, even when she puts herself in the hands of others. On the other hand, Dreiser is at pains to illustrate that she has a limited grasp of abstractions: she cannot turn people or even things into objects of calculation, into abstract entities that can be accumulated, traded, and amassed. Although the narrator may claim to understand money and economics, she certainly does not. Dreiser, in deleting numerous moments of pecuniary consideration between his original draft and the final version of the novel, focused his narrative on the non-pecuniary aspect of the first and crucial transaction. For Carrie, the feel of those "two soft, green ten-dollar bills" (p. 70) (the phrase repeated like an incantation) conveys a talismanic power to make concrete wishes come true: "a nice new jacket . . . a nice pair of pretty button shoes . . . stockings, too, and a skirt, and, and— . . . " (p. 71). Her system of values cannot be computed; abstract numbers are nothing to her compared to tangible things.

The paradox of the novel is that Carrie, though she seems to turn outward, is an isolated individual turned in upon herself. True, she builds her world entirely out of the things and circumstances of the modern city. Impelled by limitless wants, she engages in the primary activity of an acquisitive society. Despite starts and stops and even going back a step or two, she rises on the ladder of conventional success. Her goal, however, is not simply acquisition; she is engaged, as Tocqueville would have recognized, in the pursuit of happiness. Material things are for her the only evidence of things unseen.

Carrie's happiness is in the longing, not in the attainment of any object. Specific objects of desire constantly change, and specific satisfactions dissolve. At the end of the novel, when Carrie has become a leading lady in Broadway musicals and gets a raise to one hundred fifty dollars a week, the money means nothing. She cannot think of jackets or shoes or

---

[6] Thorstein Veblen, *The Theory of the Leisure Class* (New York and London: Macmillan, 1899), p. 47.

coats enough to convert her getting to spending. Economically speaking, she cannot rise above the elementary functions of wage-earner or consumer. The idea of amassing pecuniary power is totally foreign to her. She lives in a simpler, and radically different, world, of which the premise is made clear in the question put by Nietzsche in *Beyond Good and Evil*:

> Supposing that nothing else is "given" as real but our world of desires and passions, that we cannot sink or rise to any other "reality" but just that of our impulses . . . are we not permitted to make the attempt and to ask the question whether this which is "given" does not *suffice* for the understanding even of the so-called mechanical (or "material") world?[7]

The radical departure is worth specifying. The novel of consciousness, when *Sister Carrie* was being written, was the Jamesian novel of fine intelligence, in which experience could be defined as "our apprehension and our measure of what happens to us as social creatures."[8] Dreiser revolutionizes the process by moving from what Nietszche defined as the Apollonian consciousness to the Dionysian. Carrie, in her immediacy of response to her world, is far from taking the measure of anything; she scarcely perceives relations; precision, particularity, and prudence are not part of her nature. Because moral judgment is as foreign to her as economic calculation, she can be said to live beyond good and evil. On the other hand, she is so alive to the look and sound and feel of things that she virtually loses herself in her immediate surroundings. Insofar as the novel is presented from her point of view, it establishes a world of desire that is boundless and, once entered, offers no way out. Although Carrie, if her measure be taken as a social creature, is to be judged deplorable, she becomes more and more the embodiment of pathos. She is not a Becky Sharp celebrating the career open to talents, but a latter-day Constance adrift, "a lone figure in a tossing, thoughtless sea" (p. 11).

Sister Carrie may be usefully thought of as a mock-romance, for just as mock-epic invokes the dimensions and categories of the epic, her story invokes those of romantic tragedy. The difficulty in having such a ro-

---

[7] Friedrich Nietzsche, *Beyond Good and Evil* (1885), ch. 2, section 36 , trans. by Helen Zimmern, in *The Philosophy of Nietzsche* (New York: Modern Library, 1927), pp. 421-22. The suggestion is not new: in 1917, H. L. Mencken, who had met Dreiser the media bigshot and perceived in him the novelist of genius, first linked Dreiser with *Beyond Good and Evil*.

[8] Preface (1907) to *The Princess Casamassima*, in *The Novels and Tales of Henry James*, 24 vols. (New York: Scribner's, 1907-09) V, x.

mantic figure as protagonist is that her world by definition escapes our ordinary schemes of judgment. So, as the novel progresses, the narrator less frequently interjects views of conventional morality and economic analysis. Not that such views are invalid: they help us see the genesis of Carrie's character, but as the novel progresses, they become less and less relevant to the controlling consciousness. The realistic historian gradually gives way to the choric figure. Dreiser the story-teller, commenting less from outside or above the action, speaks more and more with the voice of empathy with the characters. Immersed in their world of feeling, he seems to give up the authority to judge it. If as outside commentator he can be said to accept without question the political and social economy that engendered Carrie, as empathizing chorus he seems entirely to accept the phenomenology of desire. Dreiser the actual novelist reinforces the impression: when he revised his manuscript draft, he eliminated much economic detail, whether in the comment of the narrator or in the thought-process of the protagonist, and he added the final pages that now conclude with a lyrical apostrophe to Carrie. In cutting out overspecification and letting his emotional closeness to his subject have full expression, he did not, however, simply abandon realism for romance. For he had discovered a way to take the measure of Carrie's world from the inside.

Hurstwood's story, the second plot of the novel, defines the seemingly limitless world in which Carrie is adrift, for Hurstwood *enters* the Nietzschean world of nothing-but-desire by his own act and leaves it betimes by the only way out. His life and destiny are absorbed into hers, and yet it has a different underlying pattern if only because he starts out as a have rather than a have-not. In Dreiser's view, the saloon-manager is first seen as a member of "our great American upper class" (p. 50), and that historical estimate of Hurstwood's upper-classness is dramatically confirmed in Carrie's intuitive reaction to what she sees at first meeting—coat lapels that "stood out with that medium stiffness which excellent cloth possesses," a vest of "rich Scotch plaid, set with a double row of round mother-of-pearl buttons," a silk tie "not loud, not inconspicuous," and shoes "of soft, black calf, polished only to a dull shine" (p. 107) that are obviously superior to Drouet's patent leather.

Carrie's relation to Hurstwood begins in invidious comparison of clothes and manners. Dreiser makes it clear that the manager of a "truly swell saloon" (p. 48) like FitzGerald and Moy's is altogether a bigger man than a drummer like Drouet, and he gives him the appearance that goes with the role—"not loud, not inconspicuous." But Hurstwood's desire to win Carrie undermines his habitual presentation of self. She elicits in him a romantic discontent:

> "If you were to meet all day with people who care absolutely nothing about you, if you went day after day to a place where there was nothing but show and indifference, if there was not one person in all those you knew to whom you could appeal for sympathy or talk to with pleasure, perhaps you would be unhappy too." (p. 142)

Although he expresses himself in the cliches of the tired business-man, Hurstwood discloses that same hatred of appearance, manipulation, and aloneness that Nietszche describes in *The Birth of Tragedy*. He too would like to enter the Dionysian world in which "all the stubborn, hostile barriers, which necessity, caprice or 'shameless fashion' have erected between man and man, are broken down."[9] As Nietszche observes, the recoil from reason, prudence, and duty becomes an impulse towards desire, passion, and extinction of individuality. In Dreiser's version, such an abandonment of appearances and duty is irrevocable. The instant after the confused Hurstwood has stolen the money from the safe at FitzGerald and Moy's, the rational Hurstwood says, "I wish I hadn't done that. . . . That was a mistake" (p. 289).

In rationalist terms, Hurstwood's error of judgment leads to a fall from a relatively high estate; he falls by his own act. Hi story has a tragic dimension, that is to say, apart from the romantic pathos that proceeds from his yielding to passion and undergoing the long, slow descent to extinction. The ambiguity of generic suggestion, rationalist and romantic, is important to the novel: given that Carrie dwells instinctively in the world of desire and has experience of nothing else, the Hurstwood plot provides a measure of her rise in terms other than her own. The pity and fear that are aroused by the fall of Hurstwood help to account for the sadness of Sister Carrie.

Carrie's appeal, closer to sympathy or perhaps even empathy than to pity and fear, has an etiology of its own. Francis Fergusson, in his analysis of *Tristan and Isolde*, develops the hypothesis of Denis de Rougemont that the spirit of romance derives from the heretical cult of courtly love.[10] The ritual pattern that underlies the basic plot begins with the taking of the love potion; permits a single exchange of kisses and then by setting

---

[9] *The Birth of Tragedy* (1872), section 1, trans. by Clifton Fadiman, *The Philosophy of Nietzsche*, p. 956.

[10] Francis Fergusson, *The Idea of a Theater* (Princeton: Princeton University Press, 1949), ch. 3.

obstacles to the fulfillment of passion keeps desire at the flood; attains its climax when confronting death, the ultimate obstacle to fulfillment and thus the guarantor of perpetual longing; expresses the moment of entering this perpetual state in a paean to love and death. In Dreiser, the magic potion is the effect of the great city on the sensibility, of "the atmosphere of the high and mighty" on the small and lowly:

> Little use to argue that of such is not the kingdom of greatness, but so long as the world is attracted by this and the human heart views this as the one desirable realm which it must attain, so long, to that heart, will this remain the realm of greatness. So long, also, will the atmosphere of this realm work its desperate results in the soul of man. It is like a chemical reagent. One day of it, like one drop of the other, will so affect and discolour the views, the aims, the desire of the mind, that it will thereafter remain forever dyed. A day of it to the untried mind is like opium to the untried body. A craving is set up which, if gratified, shall eternally result in dreams and death. Aye! dreams unfulfilled—gnawing, luring, idle phantoms which beckon and lead, beckon and lead, until death and dissolution dissolve their power and restore us blind to nature's heart. (p. 322)

As mock-epic takes on the dimensions of epic, mock-romance may take on the dimensions of its ideal model. The distance between *Sister Carrie* and *Tristan and Isolde* is not bathetic because Dreiser so carefully keeps us aware of what is lost—and what is gained—in translation. In the magic potion passage, the narrator becomes in effect the chorus and prefigures the final lyric apostrophe to Carrie, at the book's end, while at the same time the "chemical reagent" simile asserts the milieu and the moment as surely as the author's dating of the first department store or the first pay-telephone booth. But what gives the romantic plot its realistic credibility runs deeper than that. Dreiser never lets us forget that whatever the magic potion is called, the passion that it generates is not the same as love. In the single "erotic" scene of the novel, Hurstwood's "You know . . . that I love you?" (p. 141) goes unanswered, and in reply to his "Tell me . . . that you love me," Carrie proffers only silent assent. When Hurstwood takes silence as "victory," the scene leads to their first kiss, which is, dramatically speaking, their only kiss. After which Hurstwood claims possession—"Now . . . you're my own girl aren't you?" (p. 144)—and Carrie glows with pleasure in "her affection for Hurstwood and his love" (p. 145). Neither of them is said to love; each basks in the thought of possessing the other's love. Moreover, as Dreiser puts it rather clinically, Hurstwood's forty-year-old kind of passion lacks the power that belongs to youth—lacks the power, that is, to impose itself on Carrie. And so, at most, "she might have been said to be imagining herself in love, when she was not" (p. 242).

Such unpassionate passion might not be strong enough to unseat reason and directly control the plot, but it helps shape other causes that converge in the climactic theft and flight. Mrs. Hurstwood's role as archetypal conspicuous consumer—she is a "pythoness" (p. 239) in her own right—moves to a new level of aggressiveness when she suspects her husband of philandering. Carrie has reasons enough to be dissatisfied with her position as appurtenance to Drouet, but it is her relation with Hurstwood that brings matters to a quarrel. The wife-harassed bar-manager plays the role of genial host just a bit more than usual and so is somewhat "roseate" (p. 283) with drink at the evening's end when he finds the office safe ajar. Wavering between the "entanglement" (p. 286) of the day and the simple solution of making off with the day's receipts, he repeatedly takes out the money to see and feel and count it. After the fourth time the safe clicks shut—a will too weak to enact the theft is assisted by chance. His decision thus made for him, Hurstwood virtually abducts Carrie—except that her own entanglements make her first gullible and then acquiescent—and they board the train for Montreal and then New York. Yet, with all the detailed logic of realistic plausibility, the mock-romance is not lost. Both the principal characters have entered the world where duty has yielded to passion, where drift is stronger than purpose, where strength of desire matters more than clarity of reason. In this world "beyond good and evil," ethical judgments of ordinary prudence are not invoked and do not apply. Instead of individuality and choice, there are only strong wills and weak wills, intensity of desire and dwindling of desire, the waxing and waning of life.

Carrie, whose nature brought her early to such a world, has both youth and temperament in her favor:

> To the untravelled, territory other than their own familiar heath is invariably fascinating. Next to love, it is the one thing which solaces and delights. . . . It was an interesting world to her. Her life had just begun. She did not feel herself defeated at all. . . . She was saved in that she was hopeful (p. 305).

In contrast, Hurstwood has no such advantage. As a fugitive hoping to start a new life, he tries out changes of name but he can barely stand the change of identity: "What hurt him most was the fact that he was being pursued as a thief" (pp. 314-15). For Carrie, not remembering is a function of living only in the present; for Hurstwood, not remembering is mere regression: "He forgot that he had severed himself from the past as by a sword" (p. 315). Carrie, from almost the first scene of the novel to the very last, rests from action by sitting and rocking and dreaming; the rocking chair becomes an emblem of her affinity for primordial rhythm and inchoate hope. Hurstwood, in his long, slow decline, tends to sit and rock, scrunched up close to the artificial heat of the steam radiator, absorbed in the artificial life of newspaper stories. For him, primordial rhythm substitutes for purposive activity; inchoateness, replacing what was once a directed will, takes the form of apathy. He begins not to care for neatness of dress, and he starts to shave less and less frequently.

Appearance, which for Hurstwood is only a half-remembered token in the play of competitive personalities, is for Carrie still the substance of immediate pleasure. The sensibility to things that had made skirts and jackets and ribbons on department-store counters come alive radiated energy in other ways. Back in Chicago, to please Drouet, she had ventured into amateur theatricals, and her "sympathetic, impressionable nature" proved to be a gift for the stage. As Dreiser saw it, "she was created with that passivity of soul which is always the mirror of the active world"; she instinctively tried "to re-create the perfect likeness of some phase of beauty which appealed to her" (p. 173). In New York, when Hurstwood's capital had run out and his job-seeking faltered, Carrie turned to the theater when it became necessary for her to find work. Her instincts and her looks were good enough for a job in the chorus of a musical comedy, and thereafter they were good enough for the improvised response that lifted her out of the chorus line. In time she got to see her name in lights. Her success hardly seems to come from a predetermined chain of events, but the circumstances suggest one reason why determinism so often comes up in the discussion of Dreiser. The term fills a vacuum: Carrie's rise, like Hurstwood's decline, entails no awareness of moral choice or rational judgment.

Memory and judgment hardly affect the flux of desire. At one moment Carrie feels the pathos of the ex-manager whom she has sent to the store for flour and meat and who has brought back the exact change of twenty-two cents: "There was something sad in realizing that, after all, all he wanted of her was something to eat" (p. 431). But "that very evening," as the next paragraph immediately reports, she sees a chorus girl in a pretty tweed suit and the need for clothes fills her mind. Before long, she comes to see that she can no longer support him, but she does not "want to make anyone who had been good to her feel badly" (p. 482). In her last days with Hurstwood, she takes a kindly tone with him, and with her farewell note she leaves twenty dollars in soft green paper money.

Carrie and Hurstwood are linked, even after they separate. As they live out the implications of having submitted to the flux of desire, their stories intertwine. With them, the prophesied effects of desire—"dreams and death"—appear to be so much alike as almost to be interchangeable, except that they elicit pity in radically different ways. Once Hurstwood has severed himself from the secure world of custom, prudence, and rational will, his downward course is made credible in realistic terms by Dreiser's gift for detailed specification. Fugitive, bartender, unemployed, strikebreaker, panhandler, flophouse client, he endures mortifications that make death almost a relief. Even worse than his first begging Carrie for help is the failed attempt to beg of her a second time. Thrown from the stage door steps into the snow, he cries and curses the doorman in a moment of shame and memory: "'God damned dog!' he said. 'Damned old cur,' wiping the slush from his worthless coat. 'I—I hired such people as you once'" (p. 547). Eventually, beyond shame with its illusion that he is still the person he once was, Hurstwood comes to the recognition of helplessness. There is a minimal but crucial reassertion of will in the neatness with which he folds his clothes and places them to stop the crack of air in his flophouse room, and there is minimal reassertion of judgment as he yields himself to the unlit gas with "What's the use?"(p. 554). In the end he resumes a modicum of individual dignity. Death—not blank nothingness, but a man's actual dying—is one way in which the world of "gnawing, luring, idle phantoms" can be given a boundary.

Carrie's world of desire, on the other hand, is indefinite and boundless. Self-absorbed as she is, she can scarcely conceive of something beyond self which she cannot reach; and yet, if her romantic longing is to be more than an infinite regression of immediate desires, she must have a glimpse at least of the unobtainable. Dreiser's solution to the problem is to introduce a minor character—Ames, a young engineer from the Midwest and a cousin of Carrie's friend Mrs. Vance, who joins the Vances and Carrie for dinner at Sherry's Restaurant. It doesn't matter that he is a flat; that only strengthens his otherness from Carrie and her controlling point of view. Looking at the smart crowd and the lavish setting, he makes the proper prudent comment on conspicuous consumption: "A man doesn't need this sort of thing to be happy." Carrie reacts with surprise and incomprehension: "'He probably could be happy,' she thought to herself, 'all alone. He's so strong'" (p. 358). At a later meeting he advises her that youth and beauty are perishable and that, if she wants her stage career to last, she should give up musical comedy for serious drama: "If I were you . . . I'd change" (p. 538). At his suggestion she begins to read seriously, and with her responsiveness she is said to catch "nearly the full sympathetic significance" (p. 548) of *Pere Goriot*. Yet she will never understand things as Ames does. Unlike the $150 a week that she does not know how to spend—a limit that can be extended in kind—mastering a new level of artistic awareness requires that she become someone other than who she is. Against that possibility, all the detail of the novel argues that her given character is unalterable. For her to become a different person would be nothing short of a miracle.

Carrie may wish to escape the fact-conditioned world in which she has lived, but she cannot think of changing the flux of consciousness which is a given of her being. Moved though she is by the story of Old Goriot, she soon tires of reading, yawns, and wanders to the window of her fancy apartment at the Waldorf and looks out at the snowy street. Her roommate Lola hopes there will be snow enough for a sleigh ride, to which Carrie, her sympathies still aroused, responds: "Aren't you sorry for the people who haven't anything tonight?" Lola's "Of course I am" sounds frivolous, especially when she almost immediately sees someone fall and exclaims, "How sheepish men look when they fall, don't they?" But Carrie's mind shifts just as quickly, and she answers "absently" that on an evening such as this they will have to take a coach to the theater (p. 549). In these constant shifts of attention, nothing seems to hold. But the reader is unlikely to forget that this Fifth Avenue scene immediately follows that of Hurstwood pushed into the snow from the stage door and, after a moment of anger, turning into Broadway again "begging, crying, losing track of his thoughts, one after another, as a mind decayed and disjointed is wont to do" (p. 549). In the world of flux where neither anger nor empathy can be sustained, any ties between one person and another are dissolved. Carrie can be sorry for suffering mankind, but she is incapable of "love in particular."[11]

The juxtaposition of the two denouements, Carrie's and Hurstwood's, is one way in which Dreiser makes the reader see the world differently from either of them. The irony, while it conveys the absoluteness of the gulf between then, also makes for a parallelism between Hurstwood's dying and Carrie's drift. Ironic juxtaposition implies rational critical judgment; it takes the reader into an Apollonian world in

[11] The phrase is from John Malcolm Brinnan's fine early poem of that title, in *No Arch, No Triumph* (New York: Knopf, 1945), p. 23.

which individuation and obligation exist. But the novel as mock-romance does not give up the complementary, Dionysian mood that invites sympathy, the breaking of the bounds of self: when the limits of one's own consciousness are transcended, shared community of experience is possible. The wholeness of experience that Nietzsche had in mind when he invoked the idea of Apollonian *and* Dionysian in *The Birth of Tragedy* is necessary if both individual identity and imaginative identification with another are to exist. Without such wholeness, Carrie is full of feeling and incapable of love.

It is not through any of the characters, but through the narrator that the novel affirms such wholeness. In the terms of nineteenth-century realism, it might be argued that an omniscient narrator who can break into the private consciousness of individual characters shows a reader the way to a widening of sympathies. But that is crude and arbitrary compared to the effect achieved by the narrator as choric commentator, detached from the characters and yet able to feel for them. On Hurstwood's last night, he stands in the street among the other derelicts waiting for the flophouse door to open:

> Still they waited and still the snow whirled and cut them with biting flakes. On the old hats and peaked shoulders it was piling. It gathered in little heaps and curves and no none brushed it off. In the center of the crowd the warmth and steam melted it, and water trickled off hat rims and down noses, which the owners could not reach to scratch (p. 553).

Among men reduced to poor bare forked animals, the narrator speaks both for the sympathizer who might like to brush away the snow and for the suffering men who cannot "reach to scratch."

And wide as the gulf between the worlds of Carrie and Hurstwood, the narrator can enter both. Although the original draft of the novel ended with the somber dignity of Hurstwood's suicide, Dreiser added a coda that returns the focus to Carrie. To define the "mind that feels," as against the "mind that reasons," the choric voice adopts the romantic figure "harps in the wind." If Carrie has in some sense gone beyond all the thing-conditioned desires she has ever adopted, she still thinks that "the world of fashion and the world of stage" stand for a realm of beauty that she may hope to reach, that beyond appearances she may hope to enter a "world of dreams become real" (pp. 555, 557). The language is awkward but not inaccurate, and it rises to a kind of choral ode in the final paragraph of the book:

Oh, Carrie, Carrie! Oh, blind strivings of the human heart! . . . Know, then, that for you is neither surfeit nor content. In your rocking-chair, by your window dreaming, shall you long, alone. In your rocking-chair, by your window, shall you dream such happiness as you may never feel (p. 557).

Except for the narrator, no one can break into the isolation of Carrie any more than of Hurstwood. But the Liebestod of the final paragraph makes a difference. From Hurstwood's extinction of self there is nowhere to go. From the extinction of self that makes Carrie a harp in the wind there is a sense of possible continuance beyond illusion, beyond unnameable desire, to a reconstituted order of reality. It is impossible to imagine, in natural terms, how Carrie herself could change. Only a radical break could release her from the absoluteness of being who and as she is. Yet, at the final paragraph, narrator, chorus, and reader share an intimacy with her that is based in sympathy, in a vague but nonetheless felt self-recognition. The upwelling of desire for change helps explain why the novel, in which the explicit economics is so thoroughly conformist, has impressed so many readers as somehow revolutionary. That such change can be conceived only as a total departure from what seems absolutely the given state of things helps explain why the novel turns our minds to questions of ultimate value.

Auden's Doubleness

EDWARD MENDELSON

In the summer of 1939 W. H. Auden began work on a book of prose titled *The Prolific and the Devourer*, which he abandoned before he finished it. About a year later, in the autumn of 1940, he sent his publishers a book of prose and of verse titled *The Double Man*. The first, whose title was taken from Blake's *The Marriage of Heaven and Hell*, contrasted two types of personality, the Prolific who nurtures and creates, and the Devourer who organizes and consumes. The purest examples of these types were the artist and the politician. The second book, whose title Auden took from Montaigne, evoked the divided state of every individual personality, artist and politician alike. Auden's turn from the first book's vision of two opposed personal types, one admirable, one contemptible, to the second book's recognition of a divided self corresponded to his return, in his early thirties, to the religious beliefs he had abandoned as an adolescent.

That return effectively began when Auden left England for America in January 1939. Early in his career he had made or found himself the most prominent young spokesman of the English literary left, invited to write analytic essays on Marxist thought, celebrated in newspapers when he went to Spain in 1937 in the hopes of driving an ambulance for the beleaguered forces of the Republic. Auden was ambitious enough to cultivate his reputation, but he was surprised by its intensity and unsettled by the stark political choices that he felt were demanded by the times. He hoped to find in Spain a clear distinction between the virtues of the Republic and the evils of Franco, between an admirable Us and a contemptible Them. He was disturbed to discover instead that the Republic had boarded up the churches and committed, partly under the direction of Stalin's agents, its own violent injustice. Auden wrote in vigorous partisan terms about the Civil War before he left for Spain. When he returned, after about half the three-month visit he had planned, he said little or nothing about his experiences there.

Auden's politics had always included a sane and lucid note of self-doubt. During the 1930s he reminded himself and his readers that those who opposed the undiluted evil of fascism did not, simply by the fact of their opposition, achieve unambiguous goodness. Auden journeyed to the East in 1938 to observe the war between the Chinese defenders and the Japanese invaders—a war in which the division between justice and injustice was far clearer than it was in Spain. Even there, in a sonnet sequence about the causes and details of the war, he remembered that even the apparently peaceful among us pursue unjust wars in the privacy of their imagination:

> Behind each sociable home-loving eye
> The private massacres are taking place:
> All Women, Jews, the Rich, the Human Race.
> ("In Time of War," XIV)

Auden's subject, the issue he could write about most usefully to others and most truthfully to himself, was in fact the private imaginary massacres committed by the good rather than the bloody public massacres committed by the evil. But the ethical imperatives of the moment seemed to him to demand that he write against the more immediately urgent public evils committed daily by Germany and Japan.

Auden left England early in 1939 partly in order to find a different set of imperatives. In England his political pronouncements were taken seriously by a large and influential public. (He later said that had he remained in England he would have inevitably become a member of the Establishment.) In America, where the literary and political worlds had always kept a greater distance from each other than they did in Europe, he could look forward to seeing his political opinions virtually ignored. Or so he hoped. In fact, soon after he arrived, he found that his politics were taken more seriously than he expected. Invited in March 1939 to deliver a speech on Spain to the Foreign Correspondents' Dinner Forum in New York, he found, as he later wrote to a friend in England, that "I could really do it, that I could make a fighting demagogic speech and have the audience roaring."[1] He added: "It is so exciting but so absolutely degrading; I felt just covered with dirt afterwards."

Within a few weeks Auden resolved never to speak again at a political meeting. His renunciation was part of a larger refusal to use poetry as magic, as a means of persuading others to a political position through the seductive force of his verbal powers. (As he later wrote, "Orpheus who moved stones is the archetype, not of the poet, but of Goebbels."[2]) Yet Auden was not yet ready to renounce partisan politics in 1939. Instead, he merely shifted the political dividing line from its normal position, between political parties, to a more subtle division, between those who were political and those who were not. In *The Prolific and the Devourer*, during the summer of 1939, he praised the type of the artist and denounced the type of the politician (while acknowledging the necessity of his existence), and he began to blame the political disasters of the 1930s less on those who belonged to a different party from his own and increasingly on those who belonged to *any* party.

A few weeks after Auden gave his rousing political speech in New York, he gave a very different speech in which the divisions essential to partisan politics were no longer the means to achieve justice but the barrier to justice. At the University of North Carolina, on April 4, 1939, he asked his audience "to forget that he had certain political sympathies so that he could talk to them simply as a human being."[3] As the student newspaper paraphrased his speech:

> There are, he said, only two philosophies of life, one being true and the other false. The false is called, philosophically, dualism. It says that man has a body and a soul and that the soul is good and the body, passion, is bad. Or it reverses this with Hitler and Rousseau and says that energy and feeling are good and the intellect is bad. The true philosophy is monism or "organized common sense." It recognizes no sharp division of body and soul, no body as distinct from soul. For Auden Jesus was an exponent of this monist philosophy in general human conduct, Blake, Voltaire, and Goethe were its exponents in culture and partly Marx was its exponent in the political realm. . . . "People" he added "accept dualism because they lack confidence in their ability to put this world right."

[1]   Letter to A. E. Dodds [July 1939], in the Bodleian Library, Oxford (MS Eng Lett c464).
[2]   "Squares and Oblongs," *Poets at Work*, introduction by Charles D. Abbott (1949), p. 180.
[3]   Auden's speech was reported in *The Daily Tar Heel*, 5 April 1939, p. 1.

The romantic dualism of Hitler, with its celebration of energy above reason, was one source of the world crisis; another source, Auden implied, was the rational dualism of the revolutionary. "The dualist often escapes by saying that good and decent living is only possible in another world"—as some communists were willing to postpone the moral life until after the revolution. The political expression of dualism was a partisan politics that claimed virtue and power for one party alone.

Auden's speech at North Carolina was the first occasion when he explicitly named Jesus as an ethical exemplar. Through the rest of 1939 he continued to write of Jesus as an ethical rather than as a religious figure, and as a model who was followed more closely by the artist than by the politician. During the summer, in *The Prolific and the Devourer*, Auden linked the scientist and artist as the types that value unique particulars and use those particulars as the means of comprehending the universal. Against the scientist and artist he placed the politician, who divides the world into categories and assigns particulars to one category or another. Jesus belonged to the camp of the scientist:

> The teaching of Jesus is the first application of the scientific approach to human behaviour—reasoning from the particular to the universal. The Church only too rapidly returned to the Greek method of starting with universals and making the particulars fit by force, but the seed once sown, grew in secret. What we call Science is the application of the Way to the non-human world.[4]

Auden was sane enough to disclaim any belief that the types of the artist and the type of the politician were mutually exclusive, but he argued as if in fact they were. Near the start of *The Prolific and the Devourer* he wrote of "Three kinds of people: three roads to salvation":

> Those who seek it
>   1) through the manipulation of non-human things:
>   the farmer, the engineer, the scientist
>   2) through the manipulation of other human beings:
>   the politician, the teacher, the doctor
>   3) through the manipulation of their own phantasies:
>   the artist, the saint.

> Everyone combines these three lives in varying proportions, e.g., when we are eating we are scientists, when we are in company we are politicians, when we are alone we are artists. Nevertheless, the proportions vary

---

[4] *The Prolific and the Devourer*, published in *Anteus* 42 (Summer 1981): 30-31.

enough to make individuals inhabit such different worlds that they have
great difficulty in understanding each other. (8-9)

But after this mild acknowledgement that even artists engage in political
life (in a passage that incidentally aligns the artist with the saint), the rest
of the book treats artists and politicians virtually as different species. The
book as a whole is a cornucopia of categories, in which the type of the
politician is set variously against the artist and the scientist, or against
the a-political. And the hindsight offered by the stark distinction between
artist and politician in *The Prolific and the Devourer* subtle alters the tone
of the lines Auden wrote a year earlier about the private massacres
"Behind each sociable home-loving eye." Those eyes were not, as they
must have appeared to Auden's readers at the time, merely the eyes of
those who do not make war in the public sense. They were the eyes of
those who live in company, the eyes of the politician.

The political argument of *The Prolific and the Devourer* is more or less
explicitly pacifist, although the book recognized that "to think that it is
enough to refuse to be a soldier and that one can behave as one chooses
as a private citizen, is to be quite willing to cause a war but only unwilling to suffer the consequences" (56-57). Progress, the book argues, is real,
and—as in the 1930s Marxist interpretations of historical change—can
only be hindered, never prevented. What hinders progress is the divisiveness of political action:

> Socialism is correct in saying that the world will inevitably become socialist,
> and that the actions of an individual can only either accelerate of retard that
> development, but in accepting the use of violence and hatred now, in
> believing that the laws which govern history today differ from those that
> will govern it tomorrow [like the dualists who believe that good and decent
> living is possible only in another world], they are doing the opposite of
> what they imagine: they are ranging themselves on the side of the retarders.
> (51)

In contrast to the divisive hatreds of politics were the unifying
teachings of Jesus:

> If Jesus was right, then
>   A) The general direction of history must have been and be towards
>   1) The unity of mankind and a recognition of the common
>   humanity of all men,
>   2) The equality of men, through a recognition that all men are
>   subject to the same divine law,

and B)

    1)   The Way of love and understanding [the Way practiced by the artist and the scientist], which must by its very nature intend this direction, must always have assisted events so to move,

    2)   The Way of hate and coercion, whether it intended Unity and Equality or their opposites, must have always hindered events from moving, but also must have always failed finally to prevent them.

This list is written in the conditional tense: "If Jesus was right." But elsewhere in the book Auden wrote: "Jesus convinces me that he was right because what he has taught has become consistently more and more the necessary and natural attitude for man as society has developed the way it has. . . . Neither the heathen philosophers, nor Buddha, nor Confucius, nor Mohammed showed his historical insight" (30). Yet the confidence voiced here and elsewhere in *The Prolific and the Devourer* because increasingly hard to maintain as the summer of 1939 drew to its violent close. In September, as Auden recalled in an essay a few months later, "whenever I listened to the radio, I started to cry."[5] (He added that the year before, during the Munich crisis, when he had still been thinking in more partisan political terms, "I listened to the radio with a happy excitement, secretly hoping there would be a war, a hope for which I found excellent political reasons.") By the end of September he told friends he probably would not publish *The Prolific and the Devourer*. But he had no alternative to its confidence in progress and in the saving power of the artist. In "September 1, 1939," he contrasted the dualistic lies of the politician and their public to the monist truth of the artist and the scientist:

> All I have is a voice
> To undo the folded lie,
> The romantic lie in the brain
> Of the sensual man-in-the-street
> And the lie of Authority
> Whose buildings grope the sky:
> There is no such as the State
> And no one exists alone . . .

And the poem ended by invoking those who spoke that truth to each other:

[5] "Poet and Politician," *Common Sense* 9 (January 1940): 24.

> Dotted everywhere,
> Ironic point of light
> Flash out wherever the Just
> Exchange their messages:
> May I, composed like them
> Of Eros and of dust,
> Beleaguered by the same
> Negation and despair,
> Show an affirming flame.

Yet even while writing this, Auden sensed that his confidence in an inevitable progress encouraged by the acts of the Just was itself a dualistic illusion. (The "ironic points" of light were a revision in the typescript from "little points" of more unambiguous light.) Evil was not something found only in other people; the Just, as a category, did not exist. But Auden evaded this knowledge for two more months, until he was forced to acknowledge it through an event that seemed like the result of chance but was one that he had evidently planned unconsciously.

In November 1939, he walked into a German-language cinema in the Yorkville district of New York, an area where he had lived briefly six months before. A newsreel sent from Berlin portrayed the Nazi conquest of Poland, and, as Poles appeared on the screen, some of the audience shouted, "Kill them!" Shocked by this experience, Auden wondered "why I reacted as I did against this denial of every humanistic value. The answer brought me back to the church."[6]

What Auden recognized at that moment was, among other things, the intransigence of and persistence of personal evil. And with that recognition, he could no longer believe that progress was inevitable, or that artists were innocent of the divisiveness of politicians. The Hitlerian denial of every humanistic value could be answered only by an affirmation of values that were superior to the humanistic ones taught by the secular Jesus of *The Prolific and the Devourer*. Since the start of Auden's career he had sought an all-embracing system of understanding, first in psychoanalysis, then in politics. Both systems permitted the illusion that through a process of rational investigation he could choose to be among the party of knowledge and the vanguard of the future. It was an illusion that encouraged him to adopt covertly another form of the dualism that he overtly condemned. Auden's pervasive sense of guilt, which he sup-

---

[6] Alan Levy, "In the Autumn of the Age of Anxiety" [interview with Auden], *New York Times Magazine*, 8 August 1971, p. 42.

pressed in *The Prolific and the Devourer* and in the allegiance to the Just that he declared in "September 1, 1939," did not allow him to be satisfied with that illusion long. In Christianity—as distinguished from the teachings of a secular version of Jesus—Auden found a vocabulary in which to rebuke and comprehend the evil of Hitler while acknowledging the reality of evil in himself.

In the final weeks of 1939, Auden began planning a long philosophical poem, and he began writing it on New Year's Day 1940. In its early stages "New Year Letter" retained some of the artist's pride he had expressed a few months earlier in *The Prolific and the Devourer*: the poem spoke of an artist as "one of those / The greatest vocations chose." But only a hundred lines later, the poem had already begun to shift from the artist's glory to the artist's weakness and temptation:

> still the weak offender must
> Beg still for leniency and trust
> His power to avoid the sin
> Peculiar to his discipline.

And the rest of the poem acknowledged that artists faced the moral choices and moral dilemmas that everyone else faced. Artists, as a group, may have understood the nature of the choices sooner, but now the obligation and the capacity to choose are universal:

> Each salesman is not the polite
> Adventurer, the landless knight
> *Gawaine-Quixote*, and his goal
> The *Frauendienst* of his weak soul;
> Each subway face the *Pequod* of
> Some *Ishmael* hunting his lost love . . .
> In labs the puzzled *Kafkas* meet
> The inexplicable defeat . . .
> And all the operatives know
> Their factory is the *champ-clos*
> And drawing-room of *Henry James*,
> Where the *debat* decides the claims
> Of liberty and justice . . .

The division of humanity into categories, classes, and types was a distracting error. The division that mattered was the division within each individual self.

Early in 1940, a few months after it was published in 1939, Auden read Charles Williams' "history of the Holy Spirit of the Church," *The*

Descent of the Dove. In it he found the title for the book of poems that he was then planning, a book that would include "New Year Letter," some other poems, and a few passages salvaged and rewritten from the wreckage of *The Prolific and the Devourer.* Williams quoted Montaigne's aphorism against any dualistic claim to authority: "The conviction of wisdom is the plague of man." Williams expanded on this aphorism with another quotation, from Montaigne's essay, "De la gloire": "We are, I know not how, double in ourselves, so that what we believe we disbelieve, and cannot rid ourselves of what we condemn." Auden used this quotation as the epigraph of his book, and took the book's title, *The Double Man,* from Williams' phrase in the sentence immediately following that referred to "The 'double man' of Montaigne" (192).

During the spring of 1940, Auden wrote a Prologue to *The Double Man* in which the voice of the sacred made itself heard above the circle of the seasons and the crises of the hour:

> neither a Spring nor a war can ever
> So condition his ears as to keep the song
> That is not a sorrow from the Double Man.

Seven years earlier, in the sestina, "Hearing of harvests rotting in the valleys," Auden had summed up all human failure and phantasy in the stark phrase, "It is sorrow." Now he could hear, beyond the realm of the human, the song that is not a sorrow. During the autumn, he attended church for the first time since childhood, and, in October 1940, joined the Episcopal Communion. A year before, in "September 1, 1939," he had hoped to unfold a lie and show the light of an affirming flame. Now, in a poem that he wrote as the Epilogue to *The Double Man* in October 1940, he looked for truth and light somewhere beyond the shadows of himself. He ended the poem with a prayer that

> the shabby structure of indolent flesh
> Give a resonant echo to the Word which was
> From the beginning, and the shining
> Light be comprehended by the darkness.

Doubleness had moved from the world of politics, where each side convinced itself that it was just, to the world of the divided self, which knew that its own division required it to look elsewhere for justice.

George Eliot's Final Experiment: Power and Responsibility in Daniel Deronda

ANNE E. PATRICK

"WAS she beautiful or not beautiful?" Thus begins George Eliot's *Daniel Deronda* (1876), a novel that has inspired a range of responses to the question of its own aesthetic merits. Daniel asks this question as he watches a woman lose her fortune at a roulette table, and wonders further, " . . . what was the secret of form or expression which gave the dynamic quality to her glance? Was the good or the evil genius dominant in those beams?"[1]

This opening scene supplies a metaphor for approaching the novel as well as its female protagonist, for the risks George Eliot took in designing this last of her "experiments in life" yielded a text that continues to raise questions for readers and critics: Is it Daniel's story or is it Gwendolen Harleth's? Is the "Jewish plot" a success or a failure? And is the novel itself "beautiful," in the sense of being aesthetically pleasing and, above all, unified, or is it an incoherent construct that deserves the harsh judgments made by influential critics over the years? In a contemporary review Henry James had objected to the "Jewish part" of the novel, and in 1948 F. R. Leavis went so far as to propose in *The Great Tradition* that this half of the text be cut away, leaving a substantial masterpiece to be called *Gwendolen Harleth*.[2]

---

[1] George Eliot, *Daniel Deronda* (1876), ed. and intro. by Barbara Hardy (Harmondsworth: Penguin, 1967), p. 35. Subsequent references to this edition are cited parenthetically by page numbers in the text.

[2] Henry James, "*Daniel Deronda*: A Conversation," *The Atlantic Monthly* 38 (December 1876): 684-94; this review was reprinted as an appendix to the Anchor

Although other critics have defended the text's artistic merits and unity, *Daniel Deronda* has generally been consigned to the status of a "problem text," which has been thought to suffer from the artist's having "overidealized" the main Jewish characters, for reasons varying from her "immaturity" and "feminine emotional indulgence," as Leavis alleged, to her admirable intent of combating anti-Semitism, as more sympathetic critics of *Daniel Deronda* such as Barbara Hardy and Irving Howe have emphasized.[3] But with certain developments in the theory of fiction and criticism, the last fifteen years have seen studies that place the novel in a new and more favorable light. Whether or not *Daniel Deronda* is thoroughly "beautiful," it has at least been found to be interesting, and particularly so in the Jewish sections dismissed as tedious by James and Leavis. Indeed, scrutiny of recent interpretations of this text suggest that the problems in its reception have been due less to artistic lapses or excessive ambition on George Eliot's part and more to blind spots in the backgrounds of critics and other readers, and particularly to ignorance of

---

edition of F. R. Leavis's *The Great Tradition* (Garden City, N.Y.: Doubleday & Co., 1954), pp. 300-19. See pp. 101-110 and 150-54 of this edition for Leavis's ideas about revising and renaming *Daniel Deronda*. Some years later Leavis withdrew this suggestion in the essay, "George Eliot's Zionist Novel," which appeared first in *Commentary* 30 (October 1960), pp. 317-25, and subsequently as an introduction to a 1961 edition of *Daniel Deronda* published by Harper Torchbooks. But this late acknowledgement that the "flawed" sections of the novel were too tightly bound up with its "greatness" to be removed did little to offset the influence of the original suggestion, which was much more widely circulated than the retraction.

[3] David R. Carroll makes a good argument against "amputation" of the Jewish sections in "The Unity of *Daniel Deronda*," *Essays in Criticism* 9 (1959): 369-80. Twenty years later Henry Alley, as if in testimony to the residual power of Leavis's long-retracted suggestions, concludes his article, "New Year's at the Abbey: Point of View in the Pivotal Chapters of *Daniel Deronda*," with the claim that chapters 35 and 36 form a "masterpiece of technical skill . . . which makes a total separation of the two stories and destines [sic] a critical impossibility." The essay appears in *The Journal of Narrative Technique* 9 (1979): 147-59. Barbara Hardy finds much to praise aesthetically in the novel, but she agrees with the judgment that it is flawed by excessive idealization of Daniel, Morah, and Mordecai. She compares George Eliot's "bias" to the "categorized sympathies" that affect James Baldwin's work ("Introduction" to Penguin edition of *Daniel Deronda*, p. 21). Irving Howe describes Daniel as "abundantly virtuous but only intermittently alive" in his "Introduction to *Daniel Deronda*" (New York: New American Library, 1979). Howe insists, however, citing the opinion of Lionel Trilling, that the idealization needs to be understood in light of the need to oppose the Fagin-stereotype of the Jewish villain with a "counter-myth," a necessary step toward allowing a "fully shaded humanity to characterization of the Jews" (xiii).

the literature—imaginative, philosophical, religious, and scientific—that informs the work. What interpretations by critics such as Sara M. Putzell, Judith Wilt, E. S. Shaffer, George Levine, and Mary Wilson Carpenter make clear is that there is much more to the design of *Daniel Deronda* than was previously believed. These critics have provided new reasons for appreciating the novel by tracing intertextual links with other important materials, including the Arthurian legend (Putzell), the Gothic literary tradition (Wilt), Ernest Renan's *Vie de Jesus* and Goethe's *Wilhelm Meister* (Shaffer), G. H. Lewes' *Problems of Life and Mind* (Levine), and the biblical Book of Daniel as well as nineteenth-century writings on its significance (Carpenter).[4]

My purpose here is to add to the mounting evidence for the excellence and importance of *Daniel Deronda* by returning to the text itself and the question of its internal coherence, considering this matter of unity in terms of its philosophical as well as its religious significance. My point of departure is the hypothesis that George Eliot succeeded quite well in her stated aim of making "everything in the book to be related to everything else there."[5] I shall argue that the work's unity is discernible not only at the level of ideas, but also at the more concrete levels of plot and imagery, if only one looks carefully at what is there, that is assumes the attitude of the questioner that Deronda himself exhibits at the beginning of the story. Is *Daniel Deronda* beautiful or not beautiful? Perhaps if we view it closely, our ideas of what makes a novel beautiful—or for that (not-unrelated) matter, a human being attractive—may be altered, and our selves along with them. For what is at stake in this question of the text's unity is much more than a matter of aesthetics alone. Something of great human significance was being reflected in *Daniel Deronda* by an author whose work exemplifies Nathan A. Scott's insight that "finally, there is no separating the poetic and the imaginative from the reflective and the

---

[4] See Sara M. Putzell, "The Importance of Being Gwendolen: Contexts for George Eliot's *Daniel Deronda*," *Studies in the Novel* 19 (1987): 31-45; Judith Wilt, *Ghosts of the Gothic: Austen, Eliot, and Lawrence* (Princeton: Princeton University Press, 1980); E. S. Shaffer, *"Kubla Khan" and The Fall of Jerusalem: 1770-1880* (Cambridge: Cambridge University Press, 1975); George Levine, "George Eliot's Hypothesis of Reality," *Nineteenth-Century Fiction* 35 (1980): 1-28; and, Mary Wilson Carpenter, *George Eliot and the Landscape of Time: Narrative Form and Protestant Apocalyptic History* (Chapel Hill: University of North Carolina Press, 1986).

[5] Letter to Madame Bodichon (October 2, 1876), in Gordon S. Haight, ed., *Selections from George Eliot's Letters* (New Haven: Yale University Press, 1985), p. 475.

metaphysical."[6] Somehow it seems fitting that the novel's own unity has been a recurring critical question, for a central thematic concern of the text is precisely how to recognize the fundamental unity of human beings in a world that no longer presupposes a Divine basis for human community. Rigorous scientist and philosopher that she was, George Eliot was testing in this imaginative work the hypothesis of human unity against the corrosive criticism of new scientific and historical discoveries.

What distinguishes my argument from a standard "New Critical" approach is the claim that in the case of *Daniel Deronda* the issue of textual unity is bound up with the philosophical question that engaged George Eliot, and that also occupied such great thinkers as Dostoevsky and Camus: What will support ethical respect for others, especially those who are "different" from one's self and one's kind, when there is no longer a widely shared belief in a Divine Creator of human life and ultimate judge of human action?

The present essay seeks to steer a middle course between two unproductive fetishes identified by Gerard Graff as, on the one hand, the "organic unity or bust" approach of New Criticism and, on the other, the deconstructionist "fetish of disunity, aporias, and texts that 'differ from themselves.'"[7] If *Daniel Deronda* was once likely to be read halfway or halfheartedly, thanks to James and Leavis, it is now in danger of being misread entirely by critics who find its chief contribution to be a statement of skepticism concerning human ideals and action. In contrast, I am persuaded that the key to understanding this novel is to see it as part of a complex cultural conversation of its time.[8] I am also convinced that its poetic wisdom, which is ethical as well as metaphysical, has a good deal to say to our cultural and political conversations today, which are the poorer because inadequate modernist and postmodernist views of fiction would keep such texts isolated from public discourse as wards of the lit-

[6] Nathan A. Scott, Jr., *The Poetics of Belief* (Chapel Hill: University of North Carolina Press, 1985), p. 12.

[7] Gerald Graff, *Professing Literature: An Institutional History* (Chicago: University of Chicago Press, 1987), pp. 232, 242.

[8] In this I am influenced by Graff, who praises the work of Robert Scholes, *Textual Power: Literary Theory and the Teaching of English* (New Haven: Yale University Press, 1985), for arguing that "to teach the literary text one must teach the 'cultural text' as well." Graff also cites the contributions of Mikhail Bakhtin on "dialogics" (as interpreted by Don Bialostosky) and concludes that "the pedagogical implication of dialogics seems to be that the unit of study should cease to be the isolated text (or author) and become the virtual space or cultural conversation that the text presupposes" (*Professing Literature*, p. 257).

erary elite. It is no accident that the reception of *Daniel Deronda* has had from Christian and secular readers differs markedly from that of most Jewish readers, and although for reasons of space I shall focus here on the text rather than on the history of its reception, the influence of ideology on interpretation is something that should not be forgotten.[9]

What the case of *Daniel Deronda* suggests is that preconceptions about fictional excellence can function in ways that are similar to the prejudices we have about people. The important thing in approaching a text is not to answer definitively the question, "Is it excellent or beautiful?" but simply to *ask* this with full attention. Because to answer it negatively too soon, to prejudge, is precisely to miss the truth and the possibilities that are there. Perhaps standards of fictional "beauty" have changed, as we are coming to find excellence in more and more novels that go beyond the conventions of realism. In any event, the presupposition of the textual analysis below is that the aesthetic question about unity remains crucial where *Daniel Deronda* is concerned, and that it is appropriately linked with the intellectual, moral, and religious concerns that inspired the artist's efforts. Indeed, although I cannot argue the point fully here, I am inclined to regard the novel's difficulty in "achieving" unity (or being perceived to have it) as a metaphor for the philosophical difficulty of finding or recognizing the fundamental unity of human beings, which is the ethical and religious concern of the scientific experiment that is *Daniel Deronda*.

Scientific Concerns and Artistic Rebuilding

Although the established critical wisdom regards *Middlemarch* as George Eliot's masterpiece and *Daniel Deronda* as the flawed capstone of her career, from the author's own perspective her last novel is an attempt to transcend the limitations of *Middlemarch*. In this work she probes for still better answers to her own questions, at the same time striving to convey the knowledge she believed to be empirically verified and valu-

[9] Although the James-Leavis objections to *Daniel Deronda* have to some extent been accepted by many Christian and secular interpreters, Jews have from the first tended to read the novel in a much more favorable light. In *George Eliot: The Jewish Connection* (Jerusalem: Massada, Ltd., 1975), Ruth Levitt traces the influence of this text on figures including the influential Zionist, Henrietta Szold; the first president of the Jewish Theological Seminary, Solomon Schechter; and, the American poet, Emma Lazarus. Levitt asks, "Did George Eliot . . . not influence Zionism in [Theodore] Herzl's time by preparing the very air which Herzl breathed in England, by planting the seeds of his acceptance with her idealistic hero and her unforgettable and prophetic words?" (p. 74).

able for life. She says as much in a January 26, 1876, letter to Dr. Joseph Payne, written while she was completing *Daniel Deronda*. There she describes her works as "experiments in life," efforts to discover "what gains from past revelations and discipline we must strive to keep hold of as something more sure than shifting theory."[10]

As in *Middlemarch*, George Eliot is concerned in *Daniel Deronda* with discerning the causes of a character's success or failure in leading a good and effective life. Just as the description of Lydgate at the microscope provides an image of the author's efforts to probe human nature in *Middlemarch*,[11] so also the reference to an astronomer tracing the planets

---

[10] Haight, ed., *Selections from George Eliot's Letters*, p. 466. Although for some purposes it is appropriate to distinguish the actual author from the implied author and the narrator of a story, in view of the well-documented identification of George Eliot with the values of her fictional narrators, I shall not stress such distinctions here. This decision is reflected in my use of feminine pronouns to refer to the narrator, the gender of whom as been the object of some critical discussion. In treating the designs of *Middlemarch* and *Daniel Deronda*, I assume that writing fiction is a human action whose intentionality is to some degree discernible from textual and extra-textual evidence, though I make no claim to provide absolute or final interpretations of the "meanings" of the works I discuss. The effects of texts are, like those of other human actions, "incalculably diffusive" to borrow a phrase from the narrator of *Middlemarch*, p. 896), and this entails that novels may at times undermine or "deconstruct" their basic intentionality in interesting ways. My concern here, however, is not with this undermining, but rather with the artistic design of *Daniel Deronda*, which has not begun to receive the sort of sustained critical attention given to *Middlemarch*. The present essay is part of a larger comparative study of these two texts, entitled *Faith, Ethics, and Fiction: The Case of George Eliot's Last Novels*.

[11] Toward the end of chapter 16, the narrator observes of Lydgate: "he was enamoured of that arduous invention which is the very eye of research, provisionally framing its object and correcting it to more and more exactness of relation; he wanted to pierce the obscurity of those minute processes which prepare human misery and joy. . . ." W. J. Harvey concludes his "Introduction" to the Penguin edition of *Middlemarch* (1871-72; Harmondsworth: Penguin Books, Ltd., 1965) by asserting that Lydgate's researches are an apt metaphor for those of George Eliot (p. 22). References to this edition are cited parenthetically by page numbers in the text. Important critical studies that analyze the relationship between George Eliot's scientific interests and her fiction include George Levine, *The Realistic Imagination: English Fiction from Frankenstein to Lady Chatterly* (Chicago: University of Chicago Press, 1981); Bernard J. Paris, *Experiments in Life: George Eliot's Quest for Values* (Detroit: Wayne State University Press, 1965); Diana Postlethwaite, *Making It Whole: A Victorian Circle and the Shape of Their World* (Columbus: Ohio State University Press, 1985); and Sally Shuttleworth, *George Eliot and Nineteenth-Century Science* (Cambridge: Cambridge University Press, 1984).

in chapter 16 of *Daniel Deronda* is associated with the "narrator of human actions":

> Men, like planets, have both a visible and an invisible history. The astronomer threads the darkness with strict deduction, accounting so for every visible arc in the wanderer's orbit ; and the narrator of human actions, if he did his work with the same completeness, would have to thread the hidden pathways of feeling and thought which lead up to every moment of action, and to those moments of intense suffering which take the quality of action.... (p. 202)

These two images differ in terms of the scope of the scientific inquiry involved. Whereas *Middlemarch* is designated "A Study of Provincial Life," *Daniel Deronda*'s interests go beyond the provincial to the intercultural. And since the alternate culture selected for study is Judaism, a religious tradition typically denigrated by Christians in Victorian England, George Eliot's appreciative interest in it represents a daring enlargement in subject matter. For all its scope and innovativeness, however, there is a sense in which *Daniel Deronda* involves a return to concerns governing *Middlemarch* and an attempt to transcend the limitations of the earlier novel.

One problem, which has generally escaped critical attention, is that of a basic harshness in the narrator's treatment of Rosamond Vincy, which seems to violate the author's canon of sympathy.[12] This limitation is amply compensated for in *Daniel Deronda*, where the Rosamond-like Gwendolen is handled fully, critically, and compassionately. A second problem involves moral transformation. In *Middlemarch*, the regenerated characters, Fred Vincy and Will Ladislaw, seem to depend on fulfilled romantic love for their redemption from irresponsibility (in Fred's case) and despair (in Will's). This association of romantic love with moral growth fits their situations, but leaves open the question whether romantic fulfillment is necessary for significant and lasting moral influence.[13] This question is addressed and answered in a well-nuanced

---

[12] For a fuller discussion of this problem, see Anne E. Patrick, "Rosamond Rescued: George Eliot's Critique of Sexism in *Middlemarch*," *Journal of Religion* 67 (1987): 220-38.

[13] Moreover, this association in *Middlemarch* fuels the reader's resentment toward Rosamond, insofar as it implies that Lydgate's failure is more his wife's fault than his own. If she had been more like Dorothea, the reader may tend to assume, then the doctor would undoubtedly have accomplished great things for society. This reading ignores the ways in which Lydgate thinks and behaves like Casaubon in relation to his wife.

negative manner in *Daniel Deronda*. Third, there is the matter of the origins of moral goodness itself. How is it that Caleb Garth, Mary Garth, and Camden Farebrother developed into such noble characters in the first place? Their formative struggles are not depicted in the novel, and this invites wonder about where influence for good originates. This is the question that particularly occupies *Daniel Deronda*: What empowers moral goodness, and makes it worthwhile despite personal loss and suffering? Here George Eliot pushes the exploration beyond provincial boundaries to ask what grounds the ethical universalism she believed essential for human fulfillment.

Thus *Daniel Deronda* represents a continuation of the author's scientific research, and a broadening of the scope of her experiment. But at the same time as it expands the scope of inquiry, *Daniel Deronda* can also be said to tighten its focus. This is evident especially in the Gwendolen plot, where the story involves a reworking of the moral situations of three characters from *Middlemarch*: Rosamond, Lydgate, and Bulstrode. All three fail in the earlier work, but in Gwendolen's transformation they are rescued.

The link between Gwendolen and Rosamond Vincy is most obvious. Gwendolen is the very type of feminine egoism, the pretty young woman misled by her elders to think herself the center of the world. George Eliot's use of neck imagery to symbolize arrogance and horseback riding to suggest recklessness in both women reinforces the association. Gwendolen also carries Lydgate's moral agenda. Like him she is fiercely proud and independent; like him she is angered and alienated by the setbacks of life. And finally, Gwendolen's moral situation resembles that of Bulstrode, in that she marries for financial benefit, accepting the injury done to others as unavoidable, and later hopes for deliverance from a painful situation through the death of her tormenter. One element shared by all three failed characters from *Middlemarch* is their moral isolation: each comes to decisions as an alienated agent, whose deepest problems are kept within the self. They all lack that which Gwendolen comes to have—a mentor who can assist in a moral rescue.

There are also elements of *Middlemarch* in Daniel's story, though these are less abundant and less pronounced. Like Dorothea, Daniel has a vague idealism that seeks some concrete outlet. And like her, he is wrought upon by a dying scholar to carry on a project the latter deems important. But whereas George Eliot is critical of Casaubon's project and saves Dorothea from having to complete it, she endorses Mordecai's dream and applauds Deronda's acceptance of his mission.[14]

Jewish Subject Matter

Although *Daniel Deronda* develops material from *Middlemarch*, this last of George Eliot's novels has an intentional structure of its own, in which the Jewish subject matter, the double plot, and the imagery of power combine to support an inquiry into the process of moral conversion and maturation. The Jewish material is essential to the experiment George Eliot is conducting, in that this religious tradition is being tested as a possible source of grounding for the ethical universalism she believed essential for human fulfillment. Her answer to the question of whether Judaism can offer a valid principle of transcendence to the individual is largely affirmative: constituting a form of inheritance much more valuable than money or property, the Jewish tradition can summon a man like Daniel to live meaningfully for the sake of a noble cause. However, the fact that Judaism provides a "solution" for him does not entail a blanket endorsement of the tradition nor a claim that all persons must affirm Judaism or another such religious tradition. In fact, Gwendolen's moral transformation is accompanied by neither a return to Christian piety nor a conversion to Judaism, and the criticisms Daniel's Jewish mother makes of the tradition are never answered within the novel, nor could they be.

Besides its connection with the fictional experiment, the Jewish subject matter reflects a second strand of intentionality, namely, disabusing Gentile readers of their prejudices against Jews. The author made this clear in an October 29, 1876, letter to Harriet Beecher Stowe:

> As to the Jewish element in *Deronda*, I expected from first to last in writing it, that it would create much stronger resistance, and even repulsion than it has actually met with. But precisely because I felt that the usual attitude of Christians towards Jews is—I hardly know whether to say more impious or more stupid, when viewed in the light of their professed principles, I therefore felt urged to treat Jews with such sympathy and understanding as my nature and knowledge could attain to. . . . There is nothing I should care more to do, if it were possible, than to rouse the imagination of men and

---

[14] George Levine draws out another connection in "George Eliot's Hypothesis of Reality," where, citing the earlier work of Jerome Beaty, he observes that Will Ladislaw is "a more trivial, or less solemn, anticipation of Deronda—the alien, abstracted dilettante" (p. 22).

women to a vision of human claims in those races of their fellow-men who most differ from them in customs and beliefs.[15]

Her fictional method for doing this is complex. At times she is subtle, as when in chapter 16 she sounds the theme of transcending provincialism by noting Daniel's wish to study abroad—"' . . . I want to get rid of a merely English attitude in studies'" (p. 224)—and when in chapter 17 she observes that Mirah's features "seemed to have given a fuller meaning for him to the human face" (p. 233). But she can also be quite direct. The question Mirah asks Daniel in chapter 17 is addressed to the reader also: "'Do you despise me for [being a Jewess]?'" And the dialogue that ensues is calculated to bring the reader along out of a spirit of fairness:

> "Why should I?" said Deronda. "I am not so foolish."
> "I know many Jews are bad." [replied Mirah]
> "So are many Christians. But I should not
> think it fair for you to despise me because of that." (p. 234)

Irony also serves George Eliot's didactic aim, as when she comments in chapter 33 on Daniel's dislike for the "unpoetic" shopkeeper, Ezra Cohen, "It is naturally a Christian feeling that a Jew ought not to be conceited" (p. 443), and when she has Lady Mallinger describe Mirah in chapter 36 as "a bigoted Jewess" (p. 492).[16]

This last instance also illustrates George Eliot's technique of having prejudicial remarks made by subordinate, often ridiculous characters, thereby undermining such remarks by their contexts. Mrs. Arrowsmith's description of the musician Klesmer as someone "'who is nobody knows what—a gypsy, a Jew, a mere bubble of the earth'" (p. 289) is another instance of indirect criticism. Klesmer's own words and behavior testify to his genius and nobility of character, and the reader easily shares Catherine Arrowpoint's esteem for him.

Finally, a particularly effective educational technique involves having the attractive, apparently Christian Daniel gradually come to appreciate the Jewish tradition and discover his own Jewish background. If the reader has identified in any measure with the book's hero, then he or she

---

[15] *Selections from George Eliot's Letters*, p. 476.

[16] A similarly ironic statement is voiced by Hans in chapter 47: "'Deronda is getting perfectly preposterous about those Jews,' said Hans with disgust, rising and setting his chair away with a bang. 'He wants to do everything he can to encourage Mirah in her prejudices'" (p. 640).

has shared in this educational process also. In the early stages of the story Daniel betrays some of the bigoted views typical of his society:

> Spite of his strong tendency to side with the objects of prejudice, and in general with those who get the worst of it, his interest had never been practically drawn towards existing Jews, and the facts he knew about them, whether they walked conspicuous in fine apparel or lurked in by-streets, were chiefly of the sort most repugnant to him. Of learned and accomplished Jews he took it for granted that they had dropped their religion, and wished to be merged with the people of their native lands. (p. 246)

Some chapters later, the narrator signals a development in the young man's views. Whereas Daniel, "like his neighbors, had regarded Judaism as a sort of eccentric fossilized form, which an accomplished man might dispense with studying, and leave to specialists" (p. 411), Mirah's appreciation of her heritage stimulates him to remedy his ignorance of something that is vital to her. Thus after visiting a synagogue in Frankfort, Daniel has reached the point where he is voicing George Eliot's own position: "Our religion is chiefly a Hebrew religion; and since Jews are men, their religious feelings must have much in common with those of other men—just as their poetry, though in one sense peculiar, has a great deal in common with the poetry of other nations" (p. 424). And by the end of the novel Daniel has embraced the heritage that enables him to enjoy "the very best of human possibilities," namely, "the blending of a complete personal love in one current with a larger duty" (p. 685).

The Double Plot

In contrast to *Middlemarch*, *Daniel Deronda* lacks the structural elements of Prelude and Finale, but its opening and closing chapters disclose the work's central action. Thus by asking "What has happened?" and "What has changed?" from chapter 1 to chapter 70, one can discover much about the design of the fictional experiment. Both Gwendolen and Daniel are prominent in these chapters, and a comparison of their situations at the end of the story indicates how balanced and unified the plot is designed to be. On the surface, Daniel appears to be easily the book's "winner." He enters a joyful union with Mirah, receives a supportive letter from a woman he has helped ("'Do not think of me sorrowfully on your wedding day. . . . It is better—it shall be better with me because I have known you'" [p. 882]), witnesses the final moments of the friend to whom his own life has meant fulfillment, and prepares to undertake his

Zionist mission in the East. Gwendolen, by contrast, is present in chapter 70 only through her brief letter, and on the surface she seems to have lost out: she has neither husband nor lover, she has been deprived of nearly all her fortune, and she faces an uncertain future. But Gwendolen's letter to Daniel—both the fact of her sending it and the nature of its message—testifies to the moral victory she has won, and makes the reader willing to apply to her situation the passage from Milton's *Samson Agonistes* that concludes the novel:

> "Nothing is here for tears, nothing to wail
> Or knock the breast; no weakness, no contempt.
> Dispraise, or blame; nothing but well and fair,
> And what may quiet us in a death so noble." (p. 883)

The narrator links these lines directly with Mordecai's death, but they also fit Gwendolen's situation, which involves a death to her old egoism: Gwendolen is only apparently a loser; in terms of essential values she has gained what she needed.[17]

In fact, what is accomplished by this double plot is that two characters, each of whom was initially incapable of sustained effective action, are transformed into responsible moral agents. This claim may seem too strong in Daniel's case, but scrutiny of the opening and closing situations of both protagonists suggests that the fictional experiment is designed to portray a double moral rescue, which involves a transformation from irresponsibility to responsibility, and which can be understood in terms of the agent's relationship to power.

Daniel's early moral situation is less problematic than Gwendolen's; he is generous, good-natured, and sympathetic. But there is a danger posed by a certain indecisiveness in his character, a tendency to doubt, wonder, and dream. The opening lines of the novel not only draw the reader into thinking about Gwendolen, but also reveal something about Daniel's customary uncertainty:

> Was she beautiful or not beautiful? and what was the secret of form or expression which gave the dynamic quality to her glance? Was the good or the evil genius dominant in those beams? . . .

---

[17] This has been foreshadowed in the first two chapters, in which Gwendolen loses her money at the gaming table and begins the relationship with Daniel (chapter 1) and pawns her necklace to obtain money for her trip home, only to have the necklace redeemed and returned by him (chapter 2).

> She who raised these questions in Daniel Deronda's mind was occupied
> in gambling . . . .(p. 35)

The fact that the novel opens with an "inner debate" (p. 38) would
not be significant in itself, were this theme of indecisiveness and its connections with lack of commitment not stressed subsequently in the text.
But the matter is singled out for attention later; in fact, the narrator goes
to some lengths in chapter 32 to suggest that Daniel is in danger of failing
to accomplish anything in his life:

> His early-wakened sensibility and reflectiveness had developed into a
> many-sided sympathy, which threatened to hinder any persistent course of
> action. . . . A too reflective and diffusive sympathy was in danger of
> paralysing in him that indignation against wrong and that selectness of
> fellowship which are the conditions of moral force . . . .(pp. 412-13)

Daniel, we are told, "did not attempt to hide from himself that he had
fallen into a meditative numbness" (p. 413), but the fact was that he had
yet to focus his energies in any particular direction, and seemed incapable of pulling himself out of his drift away from a productive life. At
this stage the reader does not see how the rescue can occur, but later it is
clear that his Jewish heritage supplies what is needed to transform
Daniel from the uncertain lounger we meet in the gaming room at
Leubronn into the dedicated agent who is able to commit himself in
marriage and political involvement.

Whereas Daniel's transformation is from a kind of impotence (the
imagery of such terms as "neutralise," "paralysing," and "numbness"
connotes lack of power), Gwendolen's conversion begins at precisely the
opposite point. She is portrayed initially as enjoying a feeling of omnipotence, a kind of reckless independence symbolized by her indulgence of
gambling and her desire to appear unflinching even while her stake is
disappearing. Gwendolen's rescue, like Daniel's, involves becoming capable of responsible action, and like his it requires an outside force to
succeed. In her case Daniel is the rescuing agent, whereas his rescue depends largely on the Jewish tradition, mediated by his friends and
mother. As with Daniel, the change in Gwendolen is evident in the differences between chapters 1 and 70. In the opening scene, Gwendolen is
acting out of her false sense of "omnipotence," relying on luck and personal power. When she begins to lose at the gaming table, her overriding
concern is to appear unaffected by circumstances and other people.

Though she has in fact felt the influence of Daniel's gaze, any acknowl-edgement of such influence is out of the question.

What a contrast between this affected young woman and the person who sends the letter at the end of the book! Gwendolen's brief message to Daniel on his wedding day is not only a unifying device in the novel, balancing as it does her reception of the news of financial loss in chapter 1 and of a guilt-exacerbating message from Grandcourt's mistress Lydia Glasher on her own wedding night (ch. 31), but it also reveals her moral transformation. Whereas the "spoiled child" of Book One would have thought only of her loss, and would likely have feigned indifference to Daniel's actions, Gwendolen is concerned here to insure that his happi-ness not be marred on her account. The letter reflects her growth in sym-pathy and signals a newly-won ability to acknowledge Daniel's influence as a positive factor in her life. This is precisely what she could not do when the story began; hence the significance of the letter as a sign of her conversion from a self-centered state of pseudo-omnipotence to a state wherein she is capable of genuine concern for others and of responsible action on their behalf.

Thus from choices the artist has made, especially in the first and last chapters, we may infer that the action of the double plot of *Daniel Deronda* is designed as a balanced analysis of moral rescue from two op-posite forms of irresponsibility.[18] "What happens" in these intertwined tales is that Daniel is cured of an incapacitating excess of sympathy, and Gwendolen is healed of a debilitating lack of the same virtue. Moreover, since the essence of this double plot involves a movement from "impotence" in Daniel's case and "pseudo-omnipotence" in Gwendolen's, toward in both instances the capacity for effective action, a major concern in the novel is that of power.

Imagery of Power

Power is a name for that which causes or can cause something to happen. It can be thought of as impersonal (luck, fate, circumstance, nat-ural or mechanical forces) or personal (human or divine). It can be expe-rienced as coming from outside the individual (through physical, histori-cal, or interpersonal events) as well as from within (through passions such as desire, anger, or fear). In every case it connotes energy and influ-

---

[18] The intention of moral rescue is also evident in another sense, namely, the artist's didactic interest in rescuing her audience from "moral stupidity," and particu-larly from the stupidity of anti-Jewish prejudices.

ence, and thus the imagery of power is an effective way of expressing the novelist-experimenter's basic interest in the causality associated with individual and social influence.

George Eliot's investigation of this sort of power is thoroughly sensitive to its ambiguities. Individual influence, the work demonstrates, can be harmful, as in Grandcourt's manipulative power over Gwendolen, or beneficial, as in Deronda's ability to inspire Gwendolen, and Mordecai's ability to inspire Daniel. Likewise social influence is shown to cut two ways. The same Jewish tradition that liberates Daniel from his paralysing uncertainty has been experienced only as bondage by his mother.

Two kinds of power images are dominant in *Daniel Deronda*, both of which express its negative as well as its positive aspects: images of organic life and images of action. A prominent example of the first is the title of Book Eight, "Fruit and Seed," the implications of which are multiple: Mordecai's life has ended, but has borne fruit in Deronda; Deronda's moral transformation has been completed, while Gwendolen's is only beginning; and, Daniel's dream of "'restoring a political existence to [his] people'" is at the seedling stage. George Eliot interprets this title in her motto for chapter 70:

> In the chequered area of human experience the seasons are all mingled as in the golden age: fruit and blossoms hang together; in the same moment the sickle is reaping and the seed is sprinkled; one tends the green cluster and another treads the wine-press. Nay, in each of our lives harvest and springtime are continually one, until Death himself gathers us and sows us anew in his invisible fields. (p. 879)

This motto is interesting for two reasons. In the first place it serves a unifying function, for by stressing the mingling of seasons in human experience the passage recalls the motto for chapter 1, which acknowledges the artificiality of fictional beginnings and the partial nature of fictional accounts. Both mottos, in other words, testify to the complexity of human experience and the limits of fiction. And second, the final motto recalls an organic image the narrator had employed to describe Gwendolen in chapter 7. Criticism of Gwendolen's selfishness had been virtually unremitting up to this point (Book One is entitled "The Spoiled Child"), but here the critique is softened with an observation on the heroine's potential for good:

> For some of the goodness which Rex believed in was there. Goodness is a large, often a prospective word; like harvest, which at one stage when we talk of it lies all underground, with an indeterminate future: is the germ

prospering in the darkness? at another, it has put forth delicate green blades, and by-and-by the trembling blossoms are ready to be dashed off by an hour of rough wind or rain. Each stage has its particular blight, and may have the healthy life choked out of it by a particular action of the foul land which rears or neighbors it, or by damage brought by foulness from afar. (pp. 99-100)

It is Gwendolen's salvation that she has "a root of conscience in her" (p. 733); and yet, as her own theory puts it, human potential is not always well served by its environment. Gwendolen's botany is faulty here, but the following lines from chapter 13 contain some accurate social criticism and psychology:

"We women can't go in search of adventure—to find out the North-West Passage or the source of the Nile, or to hunt tigers in the East. We must stay where we grow, or where the gardeners like to transplant us. We are brought up like the flowers, to look as pretty as we can, and be dull without complaining. That is my notion about the plants: they are often bored, and that is the reason why some of them have got poisonous." (p. 171)[19]

It is, of course, Grandcourt, to whom Gwendolen is "rather nervously" addressing these words, who has grown poisonous from boredom. Although the narrative never relents on its critique of social limitations on women, the fact that it is a male who thus develops complicates the analysis. Grandcourt has enjoyed the freedoms available to a wealthy man of his society, and yet he is consumed by boredom. Later in the story the image of the poisonous organism ("torpedo") is used of him, along with other animal images conveying mastery and cruelty:

Already, in seven short weeks, which seemed half her life, her husband had gained a mastery which she could no more resist than he could have resisted the benumbing effect from the touch of a torpedo . . . she had found a will like that of a crab or a boa-constrictor which goes on pinching or crushing without alarm at thunder. (p. 477)

By choosing to marry Grandcourt, Gwendolen has elected a way of life that makes the poisoning of her own nature all the more likely. The problem of the drama is thus centered on the question of whether or not the "root of conscience" that is in her can experience enough positive influences to transcend its poisoned destiny.

---

[19]   The image of the poisonous plant recalls Lydgate's perception of Rosamond as a "basil plant" in the Finale of *Middlemarch* (p. 893).

Even more prominent in this novel than organic images are images of action. These sometimes express positive uses of power, as in the case of such images as the "ray" (p. 494) and the "electric shock" (p. 507) describing Daniel's kindly intervention on behalf of others. But action imagery is more often negatively weighted, critical on the one hand of an agent's failure to act, and on the other, of one's acting heedlessly, without taking account of consequences. Imagery of drifting and gliding expresses the author's concern with the former problem, which represents an abdication of responsibility, an unwarranted reliance on powers beyond the self. For example, Gwendolen's acceptance of Grandcourt's proposal in chapter 27 is described as a "drifting" for which Gwendolen ought, but does not want, to claim responsibility: "She seemed to herself to be, after all, only drifted towards the tremendous decision:—but drifting depends on something besides the currents, when the sails have been set beforehand" (p. 348).[20] And in chapter 32, the narrator criticizes Daniel for "gliding farther and farther from that life of practically energetic sentiment which he would have proclaimed (if he had been inclined to proclaim anything) to be the best of all life, and for himself the only life worth living" (p. 414).

Still more pronounced is the action imagery that deals with the opposite problem, that of reckless activity. A notable example involves gambling, where an agent trusts blindly to luck or a sense of personal exemption from the ordinary laws of cause and effect. Occasionally a gamble pays off, but George Eliot is severely critical of this form of the corruption of power because the gambler's losses tend not only to be personal ones, but also losses for one's family or others who have a right to expect more responsible behavior. Gwendolen's conversion entails learning this lesson in causality and revising a deep-seated assumption that her superiority over others will guarantee success and fulfillment.

Closely allied with gambling imagery is that of the reckless rider.[21] The horse is traditionally associated with primitive energy, and George Eliot capitalizes on this association by portraying Gwendolen on horseback on occasions when she is enjoying a sense of personal power, with-

[20] The motto of this chapter underscores the author's critical point: "Desire has trimmed the sails, and Circumstance/Brings out the breeze to fill them" (p. 340).

[21] Both the gambling temptation and the imagery of reckless riding recall *Middlemarch*, and reinforce my claim that Gwendolen is working on the "ethical agendas" of Lydgate and Rosamond. Lydgate, it will be recalled, is rescued from a disastrous game of billiards by Fred in chapter 66, and Rosamond suffers a miscarriage because of an ill-advised ride with Captain Lydgate, reported in chapter 58.

out regard for the effects her actions may have on others. In chapter 7, for example, she gallops after the hounds, feeling "as secure as an immortal goddess, having, if she had thought of risk, a core of confidence that no ill luck would happen to her" (p. 103), and leaving her frustrated cousin Rex to follow on a nag that falls and breaks its knees. The riding image is reinvoked on the symbolic level in chapter 28 when Gwendolen deliberates about putting on the ring that will signify her betrothal to Grandcourt: "At last she raised herself with a determination to do as she would do if she had started on horseback, and go on with spirit, whatever ideas might be running in her head" (p. 357). As the marriage approaches, the image is modified to suggest Gwendolen's actual loss of control, which she herself is reluctant to admit. Thus in chapter 29 she begins to recognize the loss of autonomy involved in her indebtedness to her fiance, and hardens herself to stay with her chosen course:

> She was conscious of having received so much, that her sense of command was checked, and sank away in the perception that, look around her as she might, she could not turn back: it was as if she had consented to mount a chariot where another held the reins; and it was not in her nature to leap out in the eyes of the world. (p. 373)

The chariot image recurs when thoughts of Deronda's situation "tempt" Gwendolen to reconsider her marriage plans out of sympathy for Grandcourt's mistress Lydia Glasher and her children. However, she persuades herself that breaking the engagement would not do any good; besides, "turning round was out of the question. The horses in the chariot she had mounted were going at full speed" (p. 381). George Eliot returns to gambling imagery to describe Gwendolen's excitement on her wedding day:

> ... she had wrought herself up to much the same condition as that in which she stood at the gaming-table when Deronda was looking at her, and she began to lose. There was enjoyment in it: whatever uneasiness a growing conscience had created, was disregarded as an ailment might have been, amidst the gratification of that ambitious vanity and desire for luxury within her which it would take a great deal of slow poisoning to kill. (p. 401)

Marriage, the narrator implies, will mean a loss of power for Gwendolen—"the cord which united her with this lover and which she had hitherto held by the hand, was now being flung over her neck" (pp. 401-2)—but she refuses to allow apprehension to surface in her consciousness. Any "agitating experience" left over from ominous impressions gained during her brief courtship, Gwendolen

> ... surmounted and thrust down with a sort of exulting defiance as she felt herself standing at the game of life with many eyes upon her, daring everything to win much—or if to lose, still with *éclat* and a sense of importance. (p. 402)

Gwendolen is naive, and blind to her real situation. The narrator completes the description of the reckless gambler by adding a metaphor of intoxication, another image that connotes a false sense of power:

> But this morning a losing destiny for herself did not press upon her as a fear: she thought that she was entering on a fuller power of managing circumstance—with all the official strength of marriage, which some women made so poor a use of. That intoxication of youthful egoism out of which she had been shaken by trouble, humiliation, and a new sense of culpability, had returned upon her under the newly-fed strength of the old fumes. (p. 402)

Finally, after the marriage, the riding imagery has a significant new variation, as in the telling narrative comment in chapter 35, "Grandcourt inwardly observed that she answered to the rein" (p. 482). Indeed, the reversal of her expectations to enjoy unlimited power once she became Mrs. Grandcourt has brought Gwendolen to a point of decision. One course is to "carry her troubles with spirit," to distract herself from guilt and boredom without concern for the consequences of her actions. The riding and gambling images are combined for the first time as she considers this option:

> By-and-by she promised herself that she should get used to her heartsores, and find excitements that would carry her through life, as a hard gallop carried her through some of the morning hours. There was gambling: she had heard stories at Leubronn of some fashionable women who gambled in all sorts of ways. (p. 483)

However, Gwendolen has no appetite for such distractions; she is at the point of a moral conversion, at the dawn of a new realism about causality: "Her confidence in herself and her destiny had turned into remorse and dread; she trusted neither herself nor her future" (p. 484).

These two factors—herself and her destiny—are precisely the elements that had once fed her false understanding of causality. By assuming she was a superior being, whose every success "determined another"

(p. 137), Gwendolen had acted without consideration for the feelings of others. The distance between her selfish ignorance and the effective knowledge she needs for responsible action is considerable; the narrator suggests what a challenging educational task is involved by means of the motto for chapter 29, an unusually long motto that contrasts knowledge and ignorance in terms of power:

> It is a common sentence that Knowledge is power; but who hath duly considered or set forth the power of Ignorance? Knowledge slowly builds up what Ignorance in an hour pulls down. . . . Of a truth, Knowledge is power, but it is a power reined by scruple, having a conscience of what must be and what may be; whereas Ignorance is a blind giant who, let him but wax unbound, would make it a sport to seize the pillars that hold up the long-wrought fabric of human good, and turn all the places of joy dark as a buried Babylon. And looking at life parcel-wise, in the growth of a single lot, who having a practised vision may not see that ignorance of the true bond between events, and false conceit of means whereby sequences may be compelled . . . precipitates the mistaken soul on destruction? (p. 268)

Besides focusing attention on two sorts of power—the responsible power guided by accurate knowledge of causal operations and the reckless power of ignorance—and reinforcing the imagery of animal energy and motion, the motto also alludes to the story of Samson, the biblical "blind giant" who slew the Philistines.[22] In Judges 16 Samson's destructive act, to be sure, is the reverse of sporting irresponsibility: by a well-calculated use of his restored physical strength he atones for past transgressions and destroys the enemies of his people. George Eliot has taken liberties with this text, but by alluding to Samson she prepares the reader for subsequent associations with Milton's epic *Samson Agonistes*, and particularly for the concluding judgment that Gwendolen's suffering, like Samson's, is cause for celebration, not mourning: "'Nothing is here for tears . . .'" (p. 883).

The import of the motto for chapter 29 becomes evident well before the novel's conclusion, however, for knowledge of the laws of cause-and-effect is directly connected with Gwendolen's rescue. When, in chapter 36, she is able to admit to Deronda her own selfishness and ignorance, she has taken the first step toward conversion. She is prepared to begin applying the lessons he offers:

---

[22] George Eliot's use of this Jewish legend is particularly poignant in view of her aim of combatting English "Philistinism."

" . . . some real knowledge would give you an interest in the world beyond the small drama of personal desires. It is the curse of your life—forgive me—of so many lives, that all passion is spent in that narrow round, for want of ideas and sympathies to make a larger home for it." (p. 507)[23]

The knowledge Deronda has in mind involves recognizing the interconnectedness between persons and events: " . . . you know more of the way in which your life presses on others, and their life on yours" (p. 508).

Thus by chapter 36 Gwendolen is involved in a slow and painful process of learning about causality. Invoking the equine associations of her past recklessness she declares to Deronda, "'when my blood is fired I can do daring things—take any leap; but that makes me frightened of myself'" (p. 508). Deronda invites her to make the most of this emotion: "'Take your fear as a safeguard. It is like quickness of hearing. It may make consequences passionately present to you'" (p. 509). It is precisely this ability to anticipate consequences realistically that the gambler and the reckless rider lack. Deronda encourages Gwendolen toward knowledge and responsibility, and she both accepts the advice and acknowledges her indebtedness. Her words signify how much she has grown since the opening scene at Leubronn, and also anticipate her concluding message to Deronda: "'It may be—it shall be better with me because I have known you'" (p. 510).[24]

From the above discussion it is clear how important to the experimental inquiry of *Daniel Deronda* is the phenomenon of power, which is the dynamism of causality itself. Power in the form of personal and social influence is central to this text, and imagery expressing this sort of power—particularly organic images and images of action in ignorance or defiance of the laws of causality—reinforces the book's experimental agenda, which involves probing the causes of human moral success and failure, especially those causes that reverse a character's tendency toward failure and support his or her transformation from irresponsible action or immobility to effective activity. *Daniel Deronda* shares *Middlemarch*'s basic intentionality, but adds more dynamism to the experimental design. *Middlemarch* studies the connectedness of persons and events; it is domi-

---

[23] These lines recall not only Lydgate's self-pitying resignation to his "narrowed lot" (*Middlemarch*, p. 858), but also the final line of Milton's *Samson Agonistes*: "And calm of mind all passion spent." Quoted here from *The Poems of John Milton*, edited by James Holly Hanford, 2nd ed. (New York: The Ronald Press Company, 1953), p. 597.

[24] Her message on Daniel's wedding day is only slightly reworded: "'It is better—it shall be better with me because I have known you'" (p. 882).

nated by the image of the web; and, it yields an ontological claim about the essential unity of all living creatures. *Daniel Deronda* takes this imagery of connection and, as it were, sets it in motion. It replaces the web imagery with the imagery of interaction and power, and yields insight into the relationship between power and human good.[25] Thus the experiment supplies new data to support an hypothesis long held by George Eliot—namely, the claim that the laws of causality must be understood and respected.

From the perspective of ethics, *Middlemarch* asserts the necessity of having a correct ontological vision, and, particularly in Lydgate's failure, demonstrates the tragic effects of living defensively in relation to other beings. *Daniel Deronda* assumes the need for this correct vision of the unity of all beings, and concentrates on the question of how one is empowered to see life this way, and more importantly, to act in accord with the fact of human interdependence. What enables an agent to take up the ethic of sympathy in the first place? What enables an agent who subscribes to this ethic to channel his or her compassion into beneficial action? These are the questions governing the experiment that is *Daniel Deronda*.

We have already seen how the characters and plot of George Eliot's last novel involve reworking of some *Middlemarch* material, and from an aesthetic perspective it is worth noting how this rebuilding ties in with the theme of power. Gwendolen, the one time "empress of luck," has exercised three types of power associated with three failed characters from *Middlemarch*. Like Rosamond she has enjoyed the power of fortune, the sense of being "special" that comes with beauty and privilege; like Lydgate she has vaunted the power of independence, the sense that one can control the environment solely by one's talent and industry; and, like Bulstrode she has indulged in the power of manipulation, the sense that it is wise to arrange circumstances for one's own advantage regardless of the harm this may involve for others. In *Middlemarch* these characters discover that such power is illusory—it is eventually unseated by the balancing forces of life, by the inexorable laws of cause and effect. The problem with these false types of power is that they assume a division between the self and other beings; they are manifestations of what H.

---

[25] In distinguishing the emphases of these two novels, I do not intend to suggest that elements dominant in each are not present in the other. As J. Hillis Miller has demonstrated, the "web" of *Middlemarch* is far from static. See his article, "Optic and Semiotic in *Middlemarch*, in Jerome H. Buckley, ed., *The Worlds of Victorian Fiction* (Cambridge, Mass.: Harvard University Press, 1975), pp. 125-45.

Richard Niebuhr calls the "ethics of defense," which denies precisely the vision of unity that Dorothea comes to affirm in chapter 80 of *Middlemarch*.[26] The heroine of *Daniel Deronda* is at first misled by this false vision and places much confidence in these false types of power. Eventually, however, Gwendolen comes to recognize her unity and interdependence with others. How is it that she succeeds where Rosamond, Lydgate, and Bulstrode have failed? The chief factor in her transformation is the influence of her mentor Deronda, which she experiences as liberating rather than oppressive or manipulative.

Finally, the mentor himself requires liberation from the paralysis of unfocused sympathy. Like Dorothea Brooke, he needs some way of channeling his energies of compassion; his potential for devotion, sympathy, and dedication seems unlikely to be realized if he cannot find an appropriate social context for it. Dorothea lacked a social "medium" to give shape to her "ardent deeds," and thus her influence remained largely hidden—"incalculably diffusive," as the narrator puts it (p. 896). Although George Eliot affirms the value of this hidden influence in the Finale of *Middlemarch*, in *Daniel Deronda* she presses on to investigate the possibility that a generous idealist might influence history in a more visible way. The factor making this difference possible, the novel suggests, is the religious tradition of Judaism, which provides for Daniel the influence that "would urge him into a definite line of action, and compress his wandering energy." By acknowledging his Jewish heritage he can become "an organic part of social life, instead of roaming in it like a yearning disembodied spirit. . . ." And this integration and channeling of his energies gives him hope that his life can "make a little difference for the better" (p. 413).

In recounting the way Daniel's transformation is finally communicated to Gwendolen and gradually comprehended by her, George Eliot lays great stress on the theme of power. Gwendolen's recognition that Daniel has found a cause worthy of lifelong devotion is tied up with a sense of her own smallness in the world. The narrator observes that when history intrudes into the private lives of people through events such as invasions and civil wars,

> Then it is as if the Invisible Power that had been the object of lip-worship and lip-resignation became visible, according to the imagery of the Hebrew poet, making the flame of his chariot and riding on the wings of the wind,

[26] See H. Richard Niebuhr, *The Responsible Self* (New York: Harper & Row, 1963), pp. 98-99.

till the mountains smoke and the plains shudder under the rolling, fiery visitation. Often the good cause seems to lie prostrate under the thunder of unrelenting force, the martyrs live reviled, they die, and no angel is seen holding forth the crown and the palm branch. Then it is that the submission of the soul to the Highest is tested, and even in the eyes of frivolity life looks out from the scene of human struggle with the awful face of duty, and a religion shows itself which is something else than a private consolation. (pp. 875-76)

This is a complex and difficult passage. It should not be interpreted as a strong theistic claim on George Eliot's part, for the reference to "the Invisible Power" is, after all, hypothetical. But this notion obviously reinforces the thematic centrality of "power," and makes its ethical significance quite clear. Moreover, the narrator's reference to the "imagery of the Hebrew poet" and her selection of the imagery of chariot and riding both recall and transcend the earlier use of such imagery in connection with irresponsibility. And clearly the narrator recommends a sort of religion, which is defined negatively as "something else than a private consolation." Thus although the passage cannot be regarded as making a theistic claim, it does make a religious one. It communicates the narrator's judgment that, for Daniel, Judaism has served as an authentic means of self-transcendence and significant historical action. Further, it prepares for the following description of the effects of Daniel's religious dedication on the consciousness of Gwendolen, effects which include a new understanding of her position in the world:

. . . she was for the first time feeling the pressure of a vast mysterious movement, for the first time being dislodged from her supremacy in her own world, and getting a sense that her horizon was but a dipping onward of an existence with which her own was revolving. (p. 876)

This involves a "shock" for Gwendolen, one going "deeper than personal jealousy," one associated with "something spiritual and vaguely tremendous" (p. 876). In sum, this scene of the final conversation between Daniel and Gwendolen reports the findings of George Eliot's last "experiment in life." "What gains from past revelations and discipline" should be held to as "something more sure than shifting theory?" Those capable of summoning the individual beyond the narrow confines of self-preoccupation, whether in the form of desolation or consolation; those which carry the individual into responsible unity with others; those, in other words, which truly serve the human good.

Invocation as Interruption in *Augustine's* Confessions

LYNN POLAND

One of the oddities of the scholarship on Augustine's *Confessions* is the persistence with which Augustine's addresses to God are described as a "dialogue" or "conversation."[1] The description is odd not only because the reader of Augustine's text has only the words of human invocation inscribed on the page before her; it is also unfortunate because it overlooks the complexities of Augustine's notion of divine "speech." Augustine, to be sure, confesses that he "hears" God's voice, but he also makes plain that this is not a voice heard outwardly, by the ears of men, but "within" (*intus*): "It is there, Lord, that I hear (*audio*) your voice as you speak to me; for it is our teacher who speaks to us (*docet nos*). . . . And who is our teacher except the steadfast truth?"[2] It is essential that the Truth, the eternal *Verbum*, be both steadfast and apprehensible, "because if it did not remain there would be nowhere to which, after going astray we could return. But when we return from error, we return

---

[1] See, for example, A. Solignac's influential introduction to the French translation of the *Confessions* by E. Tréherel and G. Bouissou, based on the text of M. Skutella, in the "Bibliothèque Augustinienne," vol. 13 (Paris: Desclée de Brouwer, 1962).

[2] *Confessions* XI.8. Hereafter, citations from this work will appear in the main body of the text. English quotations are taken from the translations by R. S. Pine-Coffin (New York: Penguin Books, 1961), and Rex Warner (New York: New American Library, 1963), with occasional modifications of my own.

Augustine's understanding of interior illumination is much discussed. Helpful summaries of the debate can be found in Eugene Teselle, *Augustine the Theologian* (New York: Herder and Herder, 1970), pp. 103-04; and David Chidester, "The Symbolism of Learning in St. Augustine," *Harvard Theological Review* 76 (1983): 73-90.

by realizing the Truth, and it is by His teaching that we do realize the Truth, because he is the Beginning and speaketh unto us" (*ibid.*). While the interior master "speaks," however, it is not in a voice that others can overhear; it "is neither Hebrew nor Greek nor Latin nor Barbarian and which speaks without the aid of mouth or tongue, without any sound of syllables" (XI.3). This is an odd form of speech indeed.[3]

The analogy between human *vox* and divine *Verbum* is as imperfect and troublesome as it is familiar, and in many places in the *Confessions* Augustine calls attention to these difficulties by pointing to the limitations of human language and its utter difference and distance from the eternal Word.[4] Nonetheless, while the reader who describes the *Confessions* as a "conversation" may be rightly accused of supplying Augustine's text with words that are not there, it is also easy to see why such descriptions are so persistent: from beginning to end, the *Confessions* provides such a profound sense of the relationship between Augustine and his divine auditor that one's perception of the difference between human and divine "speech" is blurred, now slipping away, now

---

[3] God "speaks," according to Augustine, in many other ways as well: in the events leading up to his conversion, in the Scriptures, in the example of other Christians, and through the *magisterium* of the Church. Of his mother's pleas, for example, he writes, "Whose words were they except yours, which, by the means of my mother, your devoted servant, you kept crying in my ears?" (II.3). There is, of course, a vast literature on Augustine's use of the analogy of the Word. For helpful summaries and intelligent analyses of the classical scholarship, see: Mark D. Jordan, "Words and Word: Incarnation and Signification in Augustine's *De doctrina christiana*," *Augustinian Studies* 11 (1980): 177-96; Marcia L. Colish, *The Mirror of Language* (Lincoln and London: University of Nebraska, 1983), pp. 7-54; Ulrich Wienbruch, "'Signum,' 'Significatio,' und 'Illuminatio' bei Augustin," in *Der Begriff der repraesentation im Mittelalter*, ed. Albert Zimmerman. Miscellanea mediaevalia Bd.8 (Berlin: W. de Gruyter, 1971), pp. 76-93; Douglas W. Johnson, "*Verbum* in the early Augustine, *Recherches augustiniennes* 8 (1972): 25-53. For some contemporary perspectives, see Joseph A. Mazzeo, "St. Augustine's Rhetoric of Silence," *Journal of the History of Ideas* 23 (1962): 175-96, with Marcia Colish's reply, "St. Augustine's Rhetoric of Silence Revisited," *Augustinian Studies* 9 (1978): 15-24; Ralph Flores, "Reading and Speech in St. Augustine's Confessions," *Augustinian Studies* 6 (1975): 1-13; Eugene Vance, "Augustine's Confessions and the Grammar of Selfhood," *Genre* 6 (1973): 1-28; Margaret Ferguson, "Saint Augustine's Region of Unlikeness: The Crossing of Exile and Language," *Georgia Review* 29 (1975): 842-64.

[4] For example, Augustine stresses the transience of language and its likeness to time (4.10-4.11); its opacity on the human level, and its complete inadequacy before the ineffability of God: "What does any man succeed in saying when he attempts to speak of you? Yet woes to those who do not speak of you at all, when those who speak most say nothing" (I.4).

returning to view, now disappearing again. The reader who "hears" more than is written in the text participates in this relationship, supplying the principle by which human word and divine word are brought together: *caritas*. Indeed, the reader who supplements Augustine's text in this way is the kind of ideal reader Augustine imagined for his work. In his scattered addresses to his eventual readers, Augustine makes it clear that the human audience to which his work is directed is a faithful one, one that believes so that it may understand:

> It is a brotherly mind that I would wish for, not the minds of strangers . . .
> that brotherly mind which is glad for me when it sees good in me and sorry
> for me when it sees bad in me, because, whether it sees good or bad, it loves
> me. It is to people like this that I shall show myself (X.4).

Augustine hopes for readers bound to him by *caritas* because he knows that written texts, even his text, can be read, and misread, in multiple ways. While language, for Augustine, is defined from the outset as a vehicle for communication (persons use words for "conveying, in so far as they are able, the motion of their spirits or something which they have sensed or understood"), it is nonetheless the case that verbal signs and the spirit's "motion" are of two incommensurable orders.[5] While one seeks to discover an author's or speaker's intention through the words that convey it, the reader or auditor has no independent access to this intention against which to measure the accuracy of her understanding. This Augustine recognizes as the case even with scripture: "If Moses himself appeared to us and said 'This was what I was thinking,' we should believe what he said, but still would not actually see what was in his mind" (XII.25).

The situation becomes even more complex when the question is not only what an author intended, but whether what an author says is true. Moses wrote, and "went his way"; his intentions cannot be discovered by questioning him. But even if Moses were present, Augustine observes, "how should I know whether what he said was true? And if I did know

---

[5] *De doctrina christiana* II.ii.3. Several of the best discussions of Augustine's sign theory are: Colish, *Mirror*; B. Darrell Jackson, "The Theory of Signs in St. Augustine's *De Doctrina Christiana*," in *Augustine: A Collection of Critical Essays*, ed. by R. A. Markus (Garden City, N.Y.: Anchor Books, 1972), pp. 92-147; R. A. Markus, "St. Augustine on Signs," *Phronesis* 2 (1957): 60-83, reprinted in the above anthology, pp. 61-91; G-H. Allard, "L'articulation du sens et du signe dans le *De doctrina christiana* de S. Augustin," *Texte und Untersuchungen zur geschichte der Altchristlichen literatur* 117 (Part III, 1976) (=Studia Patristica 14): 377-88.

it, would it be from him that I know it?" (XI.3). The answer is no: Augustine would know the truth not from Moses' words, but from the Interior Teacher, the eternal Truth. Augustine wishes for readers, then, who will read his book as he reads the book of Moses—with *caritas*. "But charity believeth all things (that is, among those whom it binds together and makes one)," Augustine writes; "and so, Lord, I make my confession to you in such a way that men may hear it, though I cannot demonstrate to them that I am telling the truth; yet those whose ears are opened to me by charity believe what I say" (X.3). Charity "binds," we could say, by bridging the gap between verbal sign and speaker's intention, filling the space with loving belief—with what in *De doctrina christiana* Augustine speaks of as "the whole current of love" (I.xx.21). This current is effective when both speaker and listener, writer and reader, stand in relation to the same single and eternal Truth. *Caritas*, more than words, then, is the vehicle of communication, for it is the medium by which the incommensurable orders of verbal signs, speaker's intention, and Truth are joined. *Caritas* believes not the words themselves, but the intention of the speaker to speak truly.[6]

Not every reader of the *Confessions* is a brother, however. Another kind of reader—let us call her, following Kermode, the "outsider," or even "carnal" reader—finds in Augustine's invocations to God not conversation, but interruption. For this reader, what is most immediately striking about the *Confessions* is the way Augustine's addresses to God alternate with narration, as though he can move his text forward only by repeatedly halting to consult the divine author, God. The disparity between invocation and narration is perhaps most apparent to the reader who comes to Augustine's text with expectations shaped by modern narratives, and particularly by autobiographical narratives—the reader guided by the history of the *Confessions'* own influence. For such a reader Augustine's continual addresses to God can be puzzling and trying; they appear as deviations from the narrative norm, as interruptions or addenda to the narrative that retard its progress. Rather than supplying the principle of cohesion that binds spirit to letter, this reader instead

---

[6] The brotherly reader to whom Augustine appeals not only hears Augustine in conversation with God; his supplement of *caritas* also resolves the troubling question of the *Confessions'* unity, by finding beneath its apparent discontinuities an "interior" principle of cohesion. As one preeminent fraternal reader puts it: "On peut légitime-ment préférer voir dans les *Confessions* une unité plus *intérieure* que logique: unité d'esprit et d'intention plus que suite cohérente et progressive de developpements. . . ." Solignac, p. 20.

observes the spaces in the fabric of the narrative that mark the work's formal shape. While the fraternal reader may hear more than is written, the outsider, of course, can be charged with misreading as well. As the scholar will be quick to point out, to see Augustine's addresses to God as wholly separate from his act of narration is to misunderstand the intimate relation between invocation and telling that makes Augustine's work a confession rather than an autobiography. If one looks at the content of Augustine's invocations to God, for example, one finds a clear, if partial, indication of the polysemy of the work's title: Augustine sometimes avows his sinfulness and blindness, sometimes praises God for God's mercy and grandeur, sometimes petitions or thanks God for the capacity to read and understand the texts of scripture and of his life. If one examines the content of the story Augustine tells, one can add to this list the notion of confession as witness: his individual life displays a universal pattern, the economy of redemption in Christ, in which the reader is called to participate. As Solignac's masterful summary of the meaning of the work's title points out, these multiple aspects of *confessio* are intimately related: for Augustine to avow his fault in the humility of repentance is to proclaim simultaneously his creaturely nothingness and misery and the grandeur of the God who created and pardons him. The interdependence of invocation and narration follows from this relation: Augustine's dialectic of avowal and praise is made possible and authenticated by being enacted in the light of God's presence, and it is only in this divine light that Augustine can see his own history as the story of salvation.[7]

Nevertheless, to think of Augustine's invocations as interruptions, it seems to me, is to recognize something significant about their structure and function that the brotherly reader fails to see.[8] What is helpful about this perception is the way it invites us to imagine the formal structure of Augustine's work: the invocations, it suggests, insert a set of "spaces" or "gaps" into the narrative's temporal progress. It allows us to note that *caritas* not only binds the gaps between written word and author's intention, and between human *vox* and eternal *Verbum*; it is also the condition for narration. Narratives are structures that overcome gaps, forging intelligible connections between disparate events by assimilating them to a common plot. Yet as we shall see, stories also depend upon

[7] Solignac, pp. 9-18.

[8] To the carnal outsider, as Frank Kermode puts it in the *Genesis of Secrecy* (Cambridge, Mass.: Harvard University Press, 1979), is sometimes given understanding denied to the *exégètes de metier*.

certain kinds of gaps as the condition for their being told. Difference, as we shall see, is as central as similarity to storytelling. This binding of differences occurs in Augustine's invocations to God. The fraternal reader participates in this process; the outsider sees in the invocations the conditions for narration made visible.

I.

The story Augustine tells is the story of redemption; it is a story about interruption as well as a story that depends upon interruption to be told. The Christian narrative begins, after all, in the arresting middle, with the interruption of Christ, a "space" inserted into the history of Israel. For the Christian this gap becomes the turning point of history, the axis around which emerges a new before and after, another beginning and end, a different story. As Frank Kermode observes, the gospel is inserted into world-history at the crucial moment of transition—between the main body of history and its end, "between past and immediately future time, establishing a continuity which makes sense only in terms of that which interrupts it."[9] Augustine's conversion, like any other story of Christian conversion, repeats this habit of interruption and continuity. It turns on the spiritual division between old, fallen, unconverted self and the new self born with conversion, and on its temporal coordinate, the divide between before and after. To both correspond a familiar literary division: the author is divided into two, into a teller and the one whose tale is told, an I who speaks and an I who is described. We see the simultaneous origin of these crucial divisions in the moments of torment immediately preceding Augustine's conversion in the garden at Milan. These are the moments when the rhetorician is on the brink of appropriating the Christian plot—that is, of letting it provide the new, and "proper," meaning of life—and we see him both willing and resisting this rewriting. Both the desire and the resistance concern division.

---

[9] *Genesis of Secrecy*, pp. 133–34. Kermode is actually describing the gospel of Mark here, with its persistent use of intercalation. His point is both a theological and a literary one—interruption refers both to theological content and to the work's formal shape. Indeed, Kermode is willing to wonder if the theology is the result of habits of language, content a result of literary form, rather than the other way around: "Perhaps," he writes, "there is a secret at the heart of Mark which is not a theology and perhaps not even really a secret; but rather some habit of narrative paradox or conjunction that might, in the end, be best represented without the use of words, in a diagram or by algebra" (p. 127).

Throughout the *Confessions*, Augustine has described the condition of his fallen, pre-conversion self as one of enslavement, which he pictures as a chain:

> From a perverse will came lust, and slavery to lust became a habit, and the habit, being constantly yielded to, became a necessity. These were links, hanging each to each (which is why I called it a chain), and they held me fast in hard slavery. (VII.5)

The image of a chain suggests narrative, for it links, sequentially, fragment to fragment. This enslaving chain is an endless one, however, and without closure it lacks narrative potential; caught in a seamless chain, one cannot look back with the eye of difference to plot events. Augustine's chain, we could say, is like the condition of the neurotic, its bonds the "compulsion to repeat." In the Freudian account, one repeats what one cannot remember: ". . . a thing which has not been understood inevitably reappears; like an unlaid ghost, it cannot rest until the mystery has been solved and the spell broken."[10] The neurotic endlessly reproduces rather than remembers the past, and so she cannot tell her story. Narration requires repetition of another kind: to narrate is to repeat in the mode of difference; plots go over the ground of "what has already happened" again to interpret it and so to transform it into another order. To "represent" events in narrative form is not to redouble presence, as Ricoeur points out, but to break open a space where retelling is possible.[11]

In the moments of torment immediately preceding his conversion, Augustine clings to his chain of slavery, resisting its division. It is God who forcefully breaks the chain, and divides Augustine from himself, inserting into time, and into the sequence of habit, a "space" that introduces difference. Augustine writes:

> But you, Lord . . . were turning me around so that I could see myself; you took me from behind my own back, which was where I had put myself during the time I did not want to be observed by myself, and you set me in front of my own face so that I could see how foul a sight I was—crooked

---

[10] Sigmund Freud, "Analysis of a Phobia in a Five-Year Old Boy," (1909) *Standard Edition* X, 122.

[11] Paul Ricoeur, *Time and Narrative*, vol. 1, trans. by Kathleen McLaughlin and David Pellauer (Chicago: University of Chicago Press, 1984), p. 45. On narrative as repetition, see also Peter Brooks, *Reading for the Plot* (Oxford: Clarendon Press, 1984), and J. Hillis Miller, *Fiction and Repetition* (Cambridge, Mass.: Harvard University Press, 1982).

(*distortus*), filthy, spotted and ulcerous. I saw and I was horrified, and I had nowhere to go to escape from myself. If I tried to look away from myself, . . . again you were setting me in front of myself, forcing me to look into my own face, so that I might see my own sin and hate it. I did know it, but I pretended that I did not. I had been pushing the whole idea away from me and forgetting it (VIII.7).

Where there was only a continuous chain and a single Augustine, there is now, thanks to God's interruption, a series of doublings: before and after, remembered and forgotten, front and back, the self unseen and the self seen, the self who gazes and the image of the self it sees. Conversion will come later, when the foul, deformed image Augustine now sees will be exchanged for another less deformed, an image that more closely resembles the "image of God" he was created to be. But first Augustine must "see" his sinfulness, and this scene depicts the crucial divisions that make this possible. The mirror into which Augustine is forced to gaze creates a place from which to look, and therefore creates a past that did not "exist" before. Before Augustine was "turned around" to look at it, the self enslaved in the chain of habit was neither forgotten nor remembered, and neither enslaved nor free; it was simply the same. The moment that Augustine sees himself doubled in the mirror in effect creates the self that he can now say he "was" all along, "behind his back," unobserved and forgotten. Augustine depicts his resistance to conversion as an unwillingness to see himself and to remember. God forces him to do both, by prising open a space in the chain of reproduction; this space creates simultaneously the conditions for memory, for conversion, and for narration. Without the interruption and the doubling of the mirror, Augustine would be neither converted nor a narrator.

This scene of struggle is, of course, the turning point of the story that the converted narrator tells about his past. Yet we can also think of Augustine's transaction with the mirror here as the paradigm for his transactions with God. What happens in Augustine's confrontation with the mirror is repeated each time he interrupts his narrative to address God; just as the mirror scene is necessary for his conversion, so are the invocations the condition for that conversion story to be told. Augustine's account of his resistance in the mirror scene provides us with a vivid sense of contending forces: we imagine God forcing open a chain of habit that could at any moment close again. Augustine's invocations have a similar quality of tension and fragility, as though his words, in the speaking of them, create and hold open a space that threatens to close again. This is suggested not only by their content, but also by their sheer number; Augustine repeats the act of invocation so often because he must. Surely one of the urgent needs the invocations meet concerns the relation between his act of narration and his keen sense of the sorrows of temporality, a concern that comes to fruition in his speculations on the enigma of time in Book 11. We recall his lament that the present does not take up any space:

> If anything can be meant by a point in time so small that it cannot be divided into even the most minute particles of moments, that is the only time that can be called "present." And such a time must fly by so rapidly from future to past that it has no duration and no extension. (XI.15)

As long as Augustine is speaking to God, however, the present achieves a kind of measureless duration, like the recitation Augustine describes in the same meditation: "A voice that has never ceased to sound cannot be measured. . . . But when it has ceased to sound it will no longer exist" (XI.27). The invocations create the space of a present that continually threatens to vanish, and so must be continually recreated, by speaking again. This is missed by readers who stress the retrospective character of Books 1 through 9, for they suggest that the narrative is told from the perspective of its end. On this reading the converted Augustine who narrates stands in a fixed—and thus atemporal—place, re-reading his past with God's eternal eye.[12] This understanding of the *Confessions* is problematic, because for Augustine, the complexity of the work, like the complexity of Christian life, springs from the multiple ways in which reader and writer stand not at the end, but always in the middle. For Augustine the human condition is always "in between": the life span moves between birth and death, just as it stands between the beginning of creation and the promised revelation of the end. Even the converted Augustine therefore remains on a journey of perpetual conversion in which time never comes to a "stand" (XI.11). One of the functions of Augustine's invocations to God, then, is to create and sustain, *in media res*, a necessary present. As Ricoeur points out, the experience of temporality is qualitatively diverse; "there can be a hierarchy of levels of

[12] This perspective is developed at length, for example, by William C. Spengemann, in *The Forms of Autobiography* (New Haven: Yale University Press, 1980), pp. 1-33; so too Eugene Vance, in "The Grammar of Selfhood." For a recent attempt to counter this "metaphysical prejudice," see the interesting, if confusing, analysis by Geoffrey Galt Harpham, *The Ascetic Imperative in Culture and Criticism* (Chicago: University of Chicago Press, 1987), pp. 92-106.

temporalization, according to how close or how far a given experience approaches or moves away from the pole of eternity."[13] While for Augustine time never comes to a stand, in the space of the present established by his invocations to eternity, he achieves a kind of "steadiness" that permits him to retell his story. We see that this vantage always remains a fragile one, however; for Augustine evokes this steadiness only to contrast time and eternity once again: "But if only their minds could be seized and held steady (*ut paululum stet*), they would be still for a while and, for that short moment, they would glimpse the splendour of eternity which is forever still (*semper stantis*). They would contrast it with time, which is never still, and see that it is not comparable" (XI.11).

II.

The Augustine who gazes in the mirror and sees his "sin" is not so much seeing "himself" as "seeing-as": he sees himself as fallen, and to be fallen is already to participate in the Christian plot. What Augustine sees is himself as Prodigal Son, dwelling in a "far country," and himself as the humiliated Christ. Indeed, throughout the *Confessions* Augustine casts his narrative as a repetition of the pattern of the Prodigal Son, whose exile and homecoming, in turn, duplicate the model of Christ's death and rebirth. Every conversion story shares this plot—which is why Book VIII of the *Confessions*, the book that narrates Augustine's resistance to conversion and his moment of turning in the garden at Milan, consists of an intricate series of stories within stories, stories told and stories heard, each a story of conversion that serves as a kind of parable or mirror for Augustine's own conversion at the end of the book. Each conversion story in the *Confessions* is situated inside another, like a Chinese box. Another story of conversion is always already going on. Augustine's encounter with the mirror in chapter 7, for example, takes place "while [Ponticianus] was speaking": while Ponticianus, that is, recounts not only a conversion story, but a story about persons converted by reading yet another narrative, a life of St. Anthony. French literary critics call this kind of repetition a *mise en abyme*, a casting into the abyss. By duplicating in miniature the larger pattern, a scene like this creates the effect of uncontrolled repetition, of a potentially endless series of duplications,

---

[13] Ricoeur, p. 28.

which thus explodes the possibility of narrative closure.[14] What prevents the multiplication of conversion stories in the *Confessions* from extending to infinity, of course, is precisely Augustine's Christian belief that each of these repetitions is grounded in an originary model: in Christ, the Alpha and Omega—a model written into the very grammar of creation. Nevertheless, for the convert *in media res*, access to this originary model of not an affair of direct, immediate knowledge but instead a matter of faith in the plot made visible in Christ. The reader does not see, but repeats, the plot. It is the continual reduplication of the model in history—by enacting the pattern in one's own life, and by recognizing the pattern hidden within the often opaque signs of scripture, history, and creation—that confirms the presence of the origin.

The moment when Augustine sees his foul ulcerous self, then, not only breaks the enslaving links in the chain of habit, allowing Augustine to retell his life in narrative form. This moment of liberation, the gaining of a self to remember and narrate, is also a moment of obedience, and of substitution, the point at which Augustine exchanges one story for another. In the Christian economy, one must lose to gain; Augustine's appropriation of the Christian plot is thus simultaneously a moment of self-dispossession. There can be only one story: "Every good and true Christian should understand that wherever he may find the truth, it is his Lord's" (DDC II.xviii.28). To tell a single story, however—to tell this story rather than that one—one must check other narrative possibilities. Narratives, we could say, are at once agents of liberation and suppression: if to tell a story is to bring events into the arena of intelligibility, it is also to deny other stories their telling. The moment when Augustine gazes in the mirror is thus an act of self-crucifixion in a double sense; seeing his sin, Augustine both mimes Christ's humiliation and is dispossessed of all other possible narrative selves. This act of self-crucifixion is preserved and continually repeated throughout the *Confessions* in his invocations to God. As readers quickly observe, a rhetoric of humility, submission, and sacrifice dominates the text: the former orator repeatedly prays, "Let your mercy give ear to my desire. . . . I want to sacrifice to you the service of my thought and my tongue" (XI.2). In this act of submission Augustine repeatedly re-casts himself as reader rather than teller, as participant rather than author of a plot. The need for these acts of self-dispossession is continually renewed as

---

[14]   On the *mise en abyme*, see Neil Hertz, "Freud and the Sandman," *The End of the Line* (New York: Columbia University Press, 1985); and J. Hillis Miller's useful description of two forms of repetition in *Fiction and Repetition*, chapter 1.

Augustine writes, since in the act of narration the words he writes, the images he elaborates, and the patterns he discovers and forges, would seem to be his rather than God's. This converted rhetorician, the man who wept for Dido, knows the pleasures of word play and the power of profane eloquence to transport. Even as he writes, then, Augustine must dispossess himself of his words and of his power to signify. He must become the Christian orator he describes in the last book of *De doctrina christiana* who acts as "a petitioner before he is a speaker," one whose activity is a surrendering of agency, an emptying of himself so that "when the hour in which he is to speak approaches," he may "raise his thirsty soul to God in order that he may give forth what he shall drink, or pour out what shall fill him" (IV.xv.32). In the *Confessions* this occurs in Augustine's invocations to God. Here, divine and human discourse circulate and are exchanged, Augustine sometimes appropriating God's own scriptural speech by substituting biblical citation for his own words. At other times he divests himself of potency through petition: "From all rashness and all lying circumcise my lips both within and without" (XI.2).

Circumcision of the "lips within"—of one's *verbum interioris*, one's intention to say—is the most crucial, for as we have already seen, there is in the verbal sign already a divergence between language and thought, a disjunction between the perceptible sign and the thought it signifies.[15] Augustine therefore knows well that in a sense one is always already dispossessed of one's words: readers of one's own text may find in it other senses than what one intended, just as interpreters of scripture may each read it differently.[16] Meanings "increase and multiply," as Augustine explains in his allegorical reading of creation in Book XIII: "For I know that what is understood by the mind in a single way can be represented corporeally in a number of ways, and also that what is understood by the mind in a number of ways may have only one corporeal expression" (XIII.24). "There is no danger" in this proliferation

[15] Augustine describes the sign differently in different works. In *On Dialectics*, for example, he analyzes the speech situation in terms of four elements: "These four are to be kept distinct: the *verbum* (word), the *dicible* (expressible), the *diction* (expression), and the *res* (thing)" (v). See the essays by R. A. Markus and Darrell Jackson for hypotheses concerning the way Augustine's distinctions vary depending on whether he is concerned with speaking or listening, communication or designation.

[16] See, for example, *Conf.* X.3, XI.3, and II.25. G-H. Allard develops the theme of dispossession in relation to inspiration by the Holy Spirit. As Allard notes, Augustine's definition of *signa translata*, figurative signs, already includes the notion of violation or theft: "ad aliud aliquid significandum usurpantur" (DDC II.x.15).

for the circumcised speaker or reader, however, because the multiplicity now belongs to God. Augustine states this most boldly in his familiar pronouncement in *De doctrina christiana*:

> For he who examines the divine eloquence, desiring to discover the intention of the author through whom the Holy Spirit created the Scripture, whether or not he attains this end or finds another meaning in the words not contrary to right faith, is free from blame if he has evidence from some other place in the divine books. For the author himself may have seen the meaning in the words we seek to understand. And certainly the Spirit of God, who worked through that author, undoubtedly foresaw that this meaning would occur to the reader or listener. Rather, he provided that it might occur to him, since that meaning is dependent on truth. For what could God have more generously and abundantly provided in the divine writings than that the same words might be understood in various ways?. . . (III.xxvii.38)

The meanings of words may "fly," increasing and multiplying as they emerge from the corporeal body of the text, just as the birds (*volatilia*) in Augustine's allegory of creation are born in the "deep" but emerge from it to fly above the earth. These wheeling birds filling the sky with an excess of meaning are nevertheless contained, for they fly within the space marked out by the Christian story—they fly "beneath the firmament," under the unfolded scroll of scripture. Augustine's depiction of this release in semiotic flight is a wonderful image of the fruits of dispossession: a picture of both Christian freedom and of the inclusiveness of the Christian narrative, a single story which subsumes within it all of history and creation, even unto the beginning before there was no story to tell. Yet this picture of polysemy is also hierarchically arranged: all *res* of creation and history become *signa* whose referent is the "proper" sense inscribed in the divine eloquence of creation. The "danger" in reading and speaking is therefore not excess of meaning but absence of humility; indeed, the misreader and the man who lies, in Augustine's definitions, are those who insist on retaining their own meaning, those who refuse to surrender proprietorship of sense. That is why, when Augustine takes up the question of scriptural interpretation in Book XII, he is not troubled by readers who interpret the first verses of Genesis differently than he has. He saves his anger for those who insist that their reading is the only proper one.

> They are speaking out of pride; they do not know what Moses thought, but they love what they think themselves, and they love their own opinion not because it is true, but because it is their own. . . . In fact, it ceases to be theirs

just because it is true. . . . For whoever claims as his personal possession what you have given for the enjoyment of all, and wants to have as his own what belongs to everyone, is driven out from what is common to what is really his own, that is, from truth to a lie. For he that speaketh a lie, speaketh it of his own (XII.25).[17]

This is the economy of redemption applied to the economy of words: he who would save his meaning must lose it. In this economy one must lose to gain. Those who insist on keeping their senses are "driven out" from the great common space of verbal exchange under the firmament. Like the servant in the parable of the talents, they are divested of what they have kept: "Wicked servant . . . thou therefore oughtest to have committed my money to the bankers."[18] Augustine thus describes the words of the Manichees spoken in "private gatherings" as *inbecilla* (V.xi.21), just as he depicts the man who refuses to look at the truth as witless, as one who has "weakened the acuteness of his mind" (DDC I.ix.9). These hoarders of meaning are of course not really driven out; they lose their senses by being included in Augustine's narrative precisely *as* senseless. The *Confessions* is therefore filled with the errors Augustine has escaped or abandoned: they are not so much driven out as rewritten. They reappear as reflections in the mirror of the Christian narrative—the single plot that aims to include within it all of history from beginning to end—as the wrong turn, as the moment of sin, as the period of the fall, as the old dispensation, as the Jew.[19]

III.

Carnal and spiritual readers offer complementary rather than contradictory perspectives on the *Confessions*. This work, more than any of Augustine's other writings, provides a vivid sense of the aporias— between time and eternity, language and thought, sign and meaning— that the Christian believes are reconciled in the mystery of the eternal Word, Christ. These tensions persist in Augustine's thought as productive, for the space between them is the place where faith is acted out. Passage between these incommensurable orders is accomplished by

[17] See also DDC I.xxxvi.40-xxxvii.41.
[18] Matthew 25:26-27. Augustine cites this passage in a similar context in *De doctrina christiana*, Prologue 8.
[19] Part of the effectiveness of the *Confessions* as moral example may lie here. While the reader is presented these errors as wrong turns, their narrative potential is evident enough in the text that the reader can imagine other stories. In choosing Augustine's story, the reader cooperates in the suppression.

enacting it: by speaking and reading, the "whole current of love" is created and maintained. What I have reflected on here is the way these productive tensions are also present as the conditions of narration. Christ is the Way, and the way is preeminently a narrative one—the repetition of the Christian plot of redemption, the pattern of Christ's death and rebirth. We could say that in the Christian narrative the mystery of Christ is stretched out into time; the "metaphor" of Christ is extended into the metonymy of narrative, so that the antimonies that Christ reconciles can be made visible and played out in the particular life in time.[20] Augustine's invocations to God display the conditions of narration: they show us both the aporias and the enacting of the passage between them. The brotherly reader for whom Augustine hopes is a participant in this enactment. The outsider see just how much *caritas* is called upon to do.

---

[20] Cf. Peter Brooks's observation that "narrative is the acting out of the implications of metaphor. . . . We read the incidents of narration as 'promises and annunciations' of final coherence, that metaphor reached through the chain of metonymies" (pp. 24-36; 93-94).

The Alienated Self and the Absent Community
In the Work of Walker Percy

RALPH C. WOOD

As more and more one becomes spirit,
it causes no pain that one is unlike others.
Spirit precisely is this: not to be like others.
Soren Kierkegaard,
Attack upon "Christendom"

Walker Percy regards the modern self as a paltry and pusillanimous thing—an atrophied and attenuated affair of needs and drives that can be given mere anthropoid satisfaction. Percy blames the regnant scientific humanism of our age for this shrinkage of the modern self into virtual animality:

Man can be understood as an organism in an environment, a sociological unit, an encultured creature, a psychological dynamism endowed genetically like other organisms with needs and drives, who through evolution has developed strategies for learning and surviving by means of certain adaptive transactions with the environment.[1]

Percy's work offers a withering attack on this diminished idea of human nature, even as it seeks to restore the self to its native anguish and grandeur.

Against the grain of our sub-human humanism, Percy the converted Catholic humanist presses but a single question. It is the selfsame query

[1] Walker Percy, *The Message in the Bottle: How Queer Man Is, How Queer Language Is, and What One Has to Do with the Other* (New York: Farrar, Straus and Giroux, 1975), p. 20.

which Percy's own scientific education, far from enabling him to answer, failed even to make him ask: What does it mean to be a solitary self, an individual who lives and suffers and dies? It was this staggeringly simple question which Kierkegaard alleged that Hegel's massive system could not meet. Like the Dane to whom he is so deeply indebted, Percy answers it with admirable candor: "the only way to be yourself is to be yourself transparently before God."[2]

So long as Percy remains within this Kierkegaardian frame, he writes brilliant satire. He knows what he loathes: a humanism that has jettisoned its theological ballast. Yet insofar as he ignores the individualist and anti-communal limits of Kierkegaardian selfhood, Percy often fails to convince. His protagonists recover their lost selves apart from any sustaining community of faith that might nourish positive life. They know what they hate far better than what they love. Thus are they often thrust back into an alienation almost as deadly as the torpor from which they have escaped. The aim of this essay is to mark the alienated self-obsessiveness of Percy's main characters, while also suggesting communal and confessional sources for its remedy.

I.

Percy's understanding of the self is thoroughly Kierkegaardian. The outward social self, he learned from the Great Dane, can be described by the sociologist and psychologist as a creature of desires and urges to be satisfied from within the environing social and physical world. Like all other animate things, this external self has the capacity to "coincide with itself." Those who possess an untroubled public identity become the virtual sum of their constituent parts. Their social actuality is commensurate with their social possibility, i.e., with all the conditions and causes that have gone into their making. Binx Bolling, the narrator of *The Moviegoer*, describes his own ancestors as men who—with one notable exception—are thus "serene in their identities":

[2] Bradley R. Dewey, "Walker Percy Talks About Kierkegaard: An Annotated Interview," in *Conversations with Walker Percy*, ed. by Lewis A. Lawson and Victor A. Kramer (Jackson, Miss.: University of Mississippi Press, 1985), p. 110. Percy is true to Kierkegaard's own individualist idea of what constitutes Christian faith: "to venture wholly to be oneself, as an individual man, this definite individual man, alone before the face of God, alone in this tremendous exertion and tremendous responsibility" (*The Sickness Unto Death*, trans. by Walter Lowrie [Garden City, N.Y.: Doubleday Anchor, 1954], p. 143).

Each one coincides with himself, just as the larch trees in the photograph coincide with themselves: Judge Anse with his drooping mustache and thin cold cheeks, the hard-eyed one who is still remembered for having publicly described a Louisiana governor as a peckerwood son of a bitch; Dr Wills, the lion-headed one, the rumpled country genius who developed a gut anastomosis still in use; and Alex, serene in his dream of youth and of his hero's death to come. But my father is not one of them. His feet are planted wide apart, arms locked around an alpenstock behind him; the katy is pushed back releasing a forelock. His eyes are alight with an expression I can't identify; it is not far from what his elders might have called smart-alecky. . . . Again I search the eyes, each eye a stipple or two in a blurred oval. Beyond a doubt they are ironical.[3]

It is the inward individual self who has this capacity for irony, who lives at an enabling distance from his outer social self, and who cannot be described by the objectifying and classifying categories of science. The misery and bliss of this hidden spiritual self have far more mysterious motives than science can specify. Far from being the product of social and behavioral influences, one's personal identity is a delicately forged synthesis of life's fundamental contraries: transcendence and immanence, thinking and feeling, freedom and necessity, the infinite and the finite.

Yet a mere synthesis of these contraries does not constitute a self. As Johannes Climacus says, "the self cannot of itself attain and remain in equilibrium and rest by itself, but only by relating itself to that Power which constituted the whole relation."[4] The Dynamic that galvanizes these converse realms into unity—thus forming the basis for the uniquely human self—is the prevenient grace of God. One's repeated decisions to become and remain a self are exercised in the unaccountable freedom made available when one exists transparently before God. Such divinely endowed liberty of soul is what all scientific systems, whether Hegel's or Freud's, inevitably miss.

Percy seeks to give literary life to this Kierkegaardian claim that the self is born in reiterated acts of passionate inwardness. "Truth," Kierkegaard extravagantly insisted, "is subjectivity."[5] This celebrated

---

[3] Walker Percy, *The Moviegoer* (New York: Noonday, 1967), p. 25.

[4] Kierkegaard, *The Sickness Unto Death*, p. 147.

[5] Hence the celebrated analogy used by Kierkegaard's pseudonymous author in *Concluding Unscientific Postscript*: "If one who lives in the midst of Christendom goes up to the house of God, the house of the true God, with the true conception of God in his knowledge, and prays, but prays in a false spirit; and one who lives in an

dictum does not entail a moral relativism which declares anything good
so long as one sincerely wills it. Such is the stuff of a terribly romantic
fascism. Kierkegaard's equation of truth with subjectivity is, as Louis
Mackey observes, a Kantian means of universalizing the summons to
selfhood: "The Good is the same for all men, of every shade of better or
worse, and it is in fact efficacious precisely . . . in the consciousness of
guilt, where all men are equally condemned each by his own conscience."[6] It is exactly at this point—in crediting the universal sense of
shame—that Percy is most Kierkegaardian.

Percy's tour-de-force "scientific" description of the self's origins
should not obscure his existentialist outlook.[7] For fifteen billion years,
Percy argues, the entirety of cosmic life was an affair of dyadic causation:
"particles hitting particles, chemical reactions, energy exchanges, gravity
attractions between masses, field forces, and so on."[8] The world constituted by dyadic events provided the matrix for organic life to develop
some three-and-a-half billion years ago. Whether by genetic coding or by
trial-and-error learning, organisms began "responding" to significant

---

idolatrous community prays with the entire passion of the infinite, although his eyes
rest upon the image of an idol: where is there most truth? The one prays in truth to
God though he worships an idol; the other prays falsely to the true God, and hence
worships in fact an idol" (trans. by David F. Swenson and Walter Lowrie [Princeton:
Princeton University Press, 1968], pp. 179-80).

[6] Louis Mackey, *Points of View: Readings of Kierkegaard* (Tallahassee: Florida State
University Press, 1986), p. 30. Exactly because this universal moral sense is unerring
in its work, Percy can make his own heroes answer their inner call without any overt
Christian witness: transcendent Truth is already immanent within their own
subjectivity.

[7] Despite his conversion to Christian faith by way of Kierkegaard, Percy confesses
that he "was always put off by Kierkegaard's talk about inwardness, subjectivity, and
the absurd" (Dewey, p. 120). But the real point of contention is that, for Percy the
Catholic humanist, Kierkegaard makes too sharp a divide between the divine Gospel
and human self-understanding. Though Kierkegaard is right to insist on the distinction between transcendent and immanent truth, he is wrong to deny our deepest
spiritual urges. Humanity has an irrepressible longing, Percy insists, for the Good
News that does not originate immanently within our own human sphere. Even when
most at home in the world, we remain castaways who secretly desire another country, a city not made with hands. To be truly human, therefore, is to be more than a
citizen of the earth; it is to comb the beach daily in search of "the message in the bottle"—not for immanent island news, but for transcendent tidings from beyond the
seas: *"It is this news and this news alone that [the castaway] has been waiting for"* (*Message
in the Bottle*, p. 146).

[8] Walker Percy, *Lost in the Cosmos: The Last Self-Help Book* (New York: Farrar,
Straus and Giroux, 1983), pp. 85-86.

elements in their environment: "eating, fighting, avoiding some, approaching and mating with others"(*Lost in the Cosmos*, p. 90). Though often conducted by means of *signals* (grunts, whistles, scents, etc.), such organic behavior remained dyadic in character.

With the beginning of human life roughly 100,000 years ago, something genuinely new and unprecedented occurred: human consciousness made breath become articulate, giving birth to the *sign* and thus to the self. Unlike the signal operating dyadically within its environment, the sign creates a world of meaning wherein both sign-giver and sign-receiver have their life. Annie Sullivan spelling the word "water" in Helen Keller's hand is not sending her a signal to flee or approach, but giving the girl a sign that will enable her to understand (and to misunderstand) her world. From this triadic language event springs not only a distinctively human society of co-namers and co-discoverers; it also leads to the total construal of the world by signs:

> The Cosmos is accounted for willy-nilly, rightly or wrongly, mythically or scientifically, its past, present, and future. All men in all cultures know what is under the earth, what is above the earth, and where the Cosmos came from" (*Lost in the Cosmos*, p. 99).

That certain signs (e.g., hobbits and elves) have no identifiable counterparts in the universe hardly keeps them from being real.

This wondrous semiotic breakthrough entails an inevitable, even if not a necessary, calamity. While our sign-using consciousness is able to place everything else within a world of meaning, it cannot place itself:

> Semiotically, the self is literally unspeakable to itself. One cannot speak or hear a word which signifies oneself, as one can speak or hear a word signifying anything else. . . . The self of the sign-user can never be grasped, because, once the self locates itself at the dead center of its world, there is no signified to which a signifier can be joined to make a sign. . . . You are *Ralph* to me and I am *Walker* to you, but you are not *Ralph* to you and I am not *Walker* to me (*Lost in the Cosmos*, p. 107).

The moment we become conscious of our irreducible and unplaceable selfhood, we are banished from our own world of signs. We become exiles and wanderers; pilgrims and wayfarers; "a creature which is ashamed of itself and which seeks cover in myriad disguises" (*Lost in the Cosmos*, p. 108).

II.

It is this vision of human selfhood as an inherently catastrophic—born to trouble as the sparks fly upward, Percy often quotes from the Book of Job—that makes his work so incorrigibly existentialist. Percy's stated aim is to move the modern secular mind from the dyadic world of Sir Isaac Newton to the triadic world of Charles Sanders Peirce, employing Gabriel Marcel's notion of intersubjectivity and George Herbert Mead's social understanding of consciousness. Yet Percy's central commitments remain Kierkegaardian and individualist: "the self locates itself at the dead center of its world." However communal the self must eventually become, Percy's most notable characters remain essentially isolated and self-obsessed.

What few critics have noticed is that the Percy hero comes to his potentially saving self-knowledge always in solitude: Binx Bolling watching a dung beetle as he lies wounded in Korea, Will Barrett sitting miserably alone in his Princeton room unable to share the gaiety of his fellow students, Thomas More hitting upon his idea for the lapsometer while recovering from attempted suicide, and Lancelot Lamar discovering his wife's infidelity as he examines his daughter's blood type. In every case, the awakening revelation arrives by way of solitary self-awareness. Percy's protagonists come to *themselves*.[9]

Once stirred from their subjective slumbers, Percy's characters are embarked on the troubled quest for authentic selfhood. "The search is what anyone would undertake," says Binx Bolling in a memorable echo of Heidegger, "if he were not sunk in the everydayness of his own life.... To become aware of the possibility of the search is to be onto something. Not to be onto something is to be in despair" (*The Moviegoer*, p. 13).[10] Yet the Percyesque search has no discernible destiny within any specifiable

[9] For all his complaints about lonely Protestant anguish, Percy shares Kierkegaard's conviction that the self is born in negation. His protagonists require a revolutionary deliverance, first of all, from the deadly torpor of not being a self. Hence their need to experience a shattering encounter with that unrecognized despair which Kierkegaard calls "the sickness unto death."

[10] Elsewhere I have sought to show that, in *The Moviegoer*, Percy creates a veritable catalogue of the damned who lack such saving self-consciousness—a hierarchy of the spiritually dead ranging from those who (like Jules Cutrer) are inwardly so torpid as to be near animals, to those who (like his wife Emily) are ethically so energetic as to be almost angels. See *The Comedy of Redemption: Christian Faith and Comic Vision in Four American Novelists* (Notre Dame, Ind.: University of Notre Dame Press, 1988), pp. 163-66.

community. On the contrary, Percy is fond of citing Cervantes' dictum that the road is preferable to the inn. Any reachable goal would short-circuit the soul's itinerary before God. An attainable shrine, whether ethical or religious, would make outward and visible what must remain inward and invisible.

Not only do Percy's protagonists come to truth about themselves in solitude; they also maintain their new-won selfhood largely in isolation. The most singular—also, alas, the most unconvincing—exception to this rule is Will Barrett in *The Second Coming*. He recovers his own lost self-hood by undertaking communal life with a woman who is a third his age and who is possibly his own daughter. They are aided in this act of restoration by Father Weatherbee, a priest whose main interest is Lionel trains. Far more memorable are the Percy protagonists whose spiritual awakening leaves them in lonely isolation. Only at the very end, and usually in a brief Epilogue, do they undertake their *vita nuova* amidst the obligations of work and worship, of political and familial existence.

The typical Percy hero becomes an authentic self by means of that purity of heart which, according to Kierkegaard, wills but a solitary thing. Such integral volition derives always from one's individuality:

> Do you now live so that you are conscious of yourself as an individual; that in each of your relations in which you come into touch with the outside world, you are conscious of yourself, and that at the same time you are related to yourself as an individual? Even in these relations which we men so beautifully style the most intimate of all [i.e., sexual love], do you remember that you have a still more intimate relation, namely, that in which you are related to yourself before God?[11]

Kierkegaard's description of the "pure in heart" reveals why Binx Bolling can be on the road to true selfhood despite his seeming atheism. Bolling admits that a curtain lowers in his head whenever the word "God" is uttered, that conclusive proofs for God's existence would not matter, and that his own existential quest is not a proverbial "search for God." Ninety-eight percent of all Americans believe in God, Binx complains,

---

[11] Soren Kierkegaard, *Purity of Heart Is to Will One Thing*, ed. by Douglas V. Steere (New York: Harper & Brothers, 1956), p. 187. Kierkegaard adds: "In eternity there are chambers enough so that each may be placed alone in one. For wherever conscience is present, and it is and shall be present in each person, there exists in eternity [either] a lonely prison, or the blessed chamber of salvation. On that account this consciousness of being an individual is the primary consciousness in a man, which is his eternal consciousness" (p. 193).

but hardly anyone is "related to oneself as an individual." Hence his refusal to finish dead last in a race everyone else has won! That Bolling has
an ineradicable consciousness of his own self is, by contrast, a sign of his
incipient faith—his purity of heart.

The problem for Percy no less than Kierkegaard is that the individual
self, no matter how intensely and inwardly alive, cannot exist for itself
alone. Its "selfish" life needs social corroboration; it needs ethical expression; it needs, above all else, a sustaining community of worship and
service. In the absence of such communal sources of selfhood, Percy's
characters often maintain an appalling solitude of heart, an angry individuality of soul. Like the Kierkegaard of the *Attack upon "Christendom,"*
they will one thing alone: their own alienation from the spirit-slaying
world.[12]

Binx Bolling's rebirth into self-conscious life, far from relieving,
serves to sharpen his sense of alienation. Despite his marriage to Kate
Cutrer and his return to medical school, Bolling claims in the end to possess "no more . . . than a good nose for *merde*." In what is surely the most
crapulent diatribe in the whole of Percy's fiction, Bolling calls ours

> . . . the very century of *merde*, the great shithouse of scientific humanism
> where needs are satisfied, everyone becomes an anyone, a warm and cre-
> ative person, and prospers like a dung-beetle, and one hundred percent of
> people are humanists and ninety-eight percent believe in God, and men are
> dead, dead, dead (*The Moviegoer*, p. 228).

Thus is Percy's work filled with alienated selves who, having themselves
been jolted into spiritual life, are consumed with rage against those who
refuse the troublous career of being selves. Like the Psalmist hating those
who hate God, his progatonists find a strange kind of sustenance in de-
spising the despicable.[13]

---

[12] Kierkegaard describes the suffering required for being a true self and thus for
becoming "spirit" in unlikeness to others: ". . . never to live a single day without being reminded that one is not like the others, never to be able to run with the herd,
which is the delight and joy of youth, never to be able to give oneself out expansively,
always, so soon as one would make the venture, to be reminded of the fetters, the isolating peculiarity which, isolatingly to the border of despair, separates one from everything which is called human life and merriment and joy" (*Attack Upon
"Christendom" 1854-1855*, trans. by Walter Lowrie [Princeton: Princeton University
Press, 1944], pp. 285-86).
[13] A world populated with subhuman creatures drives the Percy protagonist not
only to drink and fornicate but also to hate. "No man is now believable," says Sutter
Vaught, "unless he is derisive" (*The Last Gentleman* [New York: Farrar, Straus and

III.

Percy's spleen receives its most convincing expression in the figure of Father Rinaldo Smith, the utterly convincing character who stands at the moral center of *The Thanatos Syndrome*. Here again Percy attempts to show the apocalyptic moral consequence of a behaviorist humanism that denies the necessary suffering of the self. Though he sets his novel in the imminent future, sometime before the turn of the century, Percy offers up the same minatory cry that he has shouted from the start. He fears not so much that we may soon incinerate ourselves physically, but that we have already annihilated ourselves spiritually. Yet now for the first time, and with an anger exceeding even the wrath of his earlier work, Percy likens the moral malaise of late twentieth-century America to the complacency of Weimar Germany.

Father Smith makes harrowing comparisons between our decently demonic behaviorists and the German scientists who practiced euthanasia during the day while reading Rilke and Schiller by night. It was these cultured doctors who proved that the venerable humanistic and theological terms no longer "signify." The brotherhood of humanity, the sacredness of life, the dignity of the individual, heaven and hell, sin and salvation—these words and phrases have ceased to register because they have been set adrift from their metaphysical moorings, subsumed under alien categories, and even put to satanic uses.

The grand guidewords of Greece and Rome and Christendom have been replaced by such slogans as "caring and sharing," "improving the quality of life," "fulfilling one's potential," "wellness training," and "the helping professions." In the name of this vacuous new humanism, a group of Louisiana behaviorists has drastically modified human conduct. By doping the local water supply with heavy sodium, these scientific humanists have put a virtual end to many crimes and evils: child abuse, wife battering, teenage pregnancy, venereal disease, etc. Though it leads to a flattening of speech and a vacancy of character, this chemical method

---

Giroux, 1972], p. 357). His sister, the nun Val, makes the same point by way of a rhetorical question: "Do you think it possible to come to Christ through ordinary dislike? Can dislike be a sign?" (*The Last Gentleman*, p. 211). "I believe in the whole business," Val later affirms, "God, the Jews, Christ, the Church, grace, and the forgiveness of sins—and . . . I'm meaner than ever. Christ is my lord and I love him but I'm a good hater and you know what he said about that. I still hope my enemies fry in hell" (*The Last Gentleman*, p. 301).

of soul control also enhances IQ scores and enables total recall of numbers and facts.[14]

Father Smith makes the drastic case that our theoretical and scientific tenderness, once it is severed from Christian faith, leads to the gas chambers.[15] A Whitmanesque lover of humanity in the abstract is probably harmless, the priest explains, just as a Skinnerian theorist of human behavior usually confines his researches to the laboratory. But once abstract theory and abstract love are combined, the result is totalitarian terror. Stalin, Hitler, Robespierre, and their successors at work in south Louisiana are all determined to save mankind from its own suffering, even if it means the slaughter of millions.

Father Smith's main contention is that the Nazi extermination camps were not the product of a peculiarly German wickedness, nor even of man's inveterate inhumanity to man. They were the result, on the contrary, of a distinctively modern mindset. Because this same abstract mentality has taken terrible root throughout the West, Jewish genocide could occur in America no less than in Germany. In a passage calculated to offend many of his readers, Percy has Father Smith link the Holocaust to abortion and euthanasia. There is a slippery precipice, he warns, whereon a society plummets from the killing of the unneeded and the unwanted to the gassing of Jews. Hence Smith's vitriolic denunciation of More's fellow physicians and the whole scientific-humanistic establishment:

> "You are a member of the first generation of doctors in the history of medicine to turn their backs on the oath of Hippocrates and [to] kill millions of old useless people, unborn children, born malformed children, [all] for the good of mankind—and to do so without a single murmur from one of you. Not a single letter of protest in the august *New England Journal of Medicine*. And do you know what you are going to end up doing? You, a graduate of Harvard and a reader of *The New York Times* and a member of

[14] What troubles Dr. More about the satanic Louisiana experiment in behavior modification is not that it makes people truly ill but that it makes them falsely well. This so-called mental "health" produces a simian tranquility in supra-simian creatures. It removes the uniquely human life-signs of spiritual suffering: "such peculiarly human symptoms as anxiety, depression, stress, insomnia, suicidal tendencies, chemical dependence. Think of it as a regression from a stressful human existence to a peaceable animal existence" (Walker Percy, *The Thanatos Syndrome* [New York: Farrar, Straus and Giroux, 1987], p. 180).

[15] His thesis is plagiarized directly from Flannery O'Connor's "Preface" to *A Memoir for Mary Ann*. It is reprinted in *Mystery and Manners*, ed. Sally Fitzgerald (New York: Noonday Press, 1970), p. 227.

the Ford Foundation's Program for the Third World? . . . You're going to end up killing Jews" (*The Thanatos Syndrome*, pp. 127-28).

Jews and targets for pogroms and holocausts, Smith contends, because they are the single people who refuse to be subsumed under the abstracting and generalizing categories so highly valued by modern culture. They retain their identity against all pressures to assimilate. This is not due altogether to their religious practice, the priest insists, since many non-observant Jews are secularists. He agrees with the Pauline dictum of Romans 11 that, even in its unbelief, Israel remains God's elect: "Since the Jews were the original people of God, a tribe of people who are still here, they are a sign of God's presence which cannot be evacuated" (*The Thanatos Syndrome*, p. 123).

It is crucial to notice that, for Percy, the Jews have scandalous significance because they are the consummate peregrine people, the unsettled vagabond race. They figure forth, in graphically historical terms, the perpetual pilgrimage of the self, the inward displacement of every human soul. They are unwelcome reminders of the anguish that is intrinsic to human existence and necessary to the achievement of true selfhood. That Jews remain the wandering people of God thus constitutes a dire offense against our secular at-homeness in the world. *Shoah* is its consequence.[16]

Given this existentialist understanding of Jews, it should come as no surprise that Rinaldo Smith is himself an *isolé*. Though a priest of the Roman Catholic church, he does not live and move and have his being within the community of faith. On the contrary, he is a confessedly solitary and "spiteful man" (*The Thanatos Syndrome*, p. 243). His bilious disgust for our subhuman world makes him dwell, like a latter-day Simeon Stylites, in scornful solitude atop a firetower. Though Smith has begun celebrating Mass again at the end, and while he assumes courageous responsibility for a newly opened hospice, he remains most memorable as a *furioso*. It is not enough that the vile behaviorist experiment in human manipulation has been stopped, for this Cassandra-like priest hurls im-

---

[16] Father Smith romanticizes the suffering and the dying for the same reason he is attracted to Jews—because they acknowledge our incurable condition as spiritual voyagers in search of a homeland:

"You can't fool children and you can't fool dying people. They knew I was a drunk, a failed priest. Dying people, suffering people, don't lie. They tell the truth. Death makes honest men of all of us. Everyone else lies. Everyone else is dying too and spends their entire lives lying to themselves" (*The Thanatos Syndrome*, p. 244).

precations to the very last: "Everyone here is creaming in his drawers from tenderness!" (*The Thanatos Syndrome*, p. 316).[17]

Even Smith's youthful conversion to Christian faith was prompted less by attraction to the Gospel than by revulsion at his own romantic admiration of the Hitler youth. Like Percy himself,[18] Smith elected Christianity because all of the alternatives were paltry: "In the end one must choose—given the chance." "Choose what?" asks Tom More. "Life or death. What else?" replies Smith (*The Thanatos Syndrome*, p. 257). This is a typically Percyesque passage, and it reveals his continuing adherence to Kierkegaardian decisionism. The human act of solitary will seems always to matter more than the divine gift of communal faith.

In *The Second Coming*, Will Barrett boasts about all the species of death that he will not allow to conquer him—neither the new Christianity nor the old Christendom, neither facile belief nor equally facile unbelief, neither marriage nor family nor children:

> Death in the form of isms and asms shall not prevail over me, orgasm, enthusiasm, liberalism, conservatism, Communism, Buddhism, Americanism, for an ism is only another way of despairing of the truth.

---

[17] Thomas More seems drawn to Father Smith less because he is a man of faith than because the priest shares More's scorn for those who deny the self's necessary perplexity. Yet More's loathing, like Smith's, runs the risk endemic to all moral fury: it threatens to create a perverse interest in the thing it denounces. This danger becomes especially vivid in More's description of the school behaviorists having kinky sex with happily drugged children. More also takes a depraved delight in forcing the "qualitarians" to drink their own medicine and thus to re-enter a pre-primate state: they pooch out their lips, make *hoo hoo hoo* sounds, groom and search each other for fleas, and mount their partners from the rear. The most cynical of More's ironies is to arrange for an ape trained in sign language to re-educate the satanic Van Dorn in the art of communication. Though sardonically funny, these scenes border on the misanthropic.

[18] "This life is too much trouble, far too strange, to arrive at the end of it and then to be asked what you made of it and have to answer 'Scientific humanism.' That won't do. A poor show. Life is a mystery, love is a delight. Therefore I take it as axiomatic that one should settle for nothing less than the infinite mystery and the infinite delight, i.e., God. In fact I demand it. I refuse to settle for anything less than Jacob, who actually grabbed aholt of God and wouldn't let go until God identified himself and blessed him. . . . I took it as an intolerable state of affairs to have found myself in this life and this age, which is a disaster by any calculation, without demanding a gift commensurate with the offense. So I demanded it" ("Questions They Never Asked Me," in Lawson and Kramer, eds., *Conversations with Walker Percy*, pp. 175-77).

.... *What is missing? Where did it go? I won't have it! I won't have it! Why this sadness here? Don't stand for it! Get up! Leave! Let the boat people sit down! Go live in a cave until you've found the thief who is robbing you. But at least protest. Stop, thief! What is missing? God? Find him!*

.... It is a matter of knowing and choosing. To know the many names of death is also to know there is life. I choose life.[19]

In the novel's final scene, Barrett asks whether it is madness to want both marriage to young Allison Huger and faith in the transcendent God. He answers his own question: "No, not want, must have. And will have" (*The Second Coming*, p. 411).

For the classic biblical and theological tradition common to Catholics and Protestants alike, faith is the single thing one *cannot* demand: "it is the gift of God" (Ephesians 2:8). There may be more of Nietzsche than St. Paul in these sovereign declarations of will. The "life" that Will Barrett and Rinaldo Smith elect seems, moreover, to be an intrinsic and timeless good akin to what Kierkegaard calls "spirit." Though he finds its temporal location in the Mass, Smith generalizes his life-advocacy into a moralistic proposition that makes abortion and euthanasia tantamount to Judaicide. The deadly tenderness of modernity derives not so much from

---

[19] Walker Percy, *The Second Coming* (New York: Washington Square Press, 1981), pp. 313-14. Percy's versions of Genesis 32 and Deuteronomy 30 may be wittier than they are true. Jacob is no solitary self who, coming to existential self-awareness, chooses transcendent faith over all the contemptible alternatives. He is the inheritor, instead, of the call that came to Abraham and Isaac, a summons sustained by the communal worship of Yahweh, and thus a vocation that the angelic night-wrestler passes on to Jacob himself. For while Jacob may "grab aholt" of the divine intruder and demand his blessing, it is not Jacob but the messenger of Yahweh who remains the real agent. Not only does the angel refuse to reveal his own name; he also renames Jacob and leaves him with a permanent limp. This thigh-wound is a reminder that the determinative activity belongs not to man but to God. Jacob the supplanter of Esau has thus been made Israel the father of God's people—not because of any willful existentialist bravado, but because "I have seen God face to face, and yet my life is preserved" (Gen 32:30).
Concerning the celebrated Two-Way Schema of Deuteronomy 30:19-20, Jon D. Levenson makes the salient point that Israel is not put into fearful existentialist straits about whether she is to obey or not to obey. In responding to the covenant Yahweh makes with his people, the one true freedom always lies in obedience: "Israel will live only if she freely makes the right choice. Covenant is an offer that the vassal cannot refuse, especially if the suzerain is omnipotent" (*The Persistence of Evil: The Jewish Drama of Divine Omnipotence* [San Francisco: Harper and Row, 1988], p. 142).

our rejection of the God of the Gospel, therefore, as from our scorn for the sacred life of selfhood.[20]

IV.

Like Walker Percy, the social philosopher Alasdair MacIntyre seeks to account for what has gone awry in this most murderous of all centuries, the Age of Thanatos. In *After Virtue*, his widely praised book of 1981, MacIntyre traces the death-dealing loss of community to the secularized Protestantism of the Enlightenment. It was Immanuel Kant who, in making the rational structure of the self determine the nature of reality, elevated the individual to primacy. The Kantian rational self is not understood as having been formed by any communal tradition. The reasoning individual is regarded, on the contrary, as the source rather than the product of common life. Kantian rational psychology finally failed, but its legacy remains very much alive, MacIntyre argues, in the modern existentialists. Soren Kierkegaard was the first important thinker driven to make the irrational choice that Kantian reason refused: the leap into the absurd, where truth is subjectivity.

MacIntyre maintains that Enlightenment individualism also marks the fall of human character as a social phenomenon, even as it means the rise of the abstract and ghostly self endemic to modern Western societies. In traditional cultures, the self is irreducibly social. It is formed through a union of communal roles and individual wills. The requirements of personal life are at once imposed from without and assumed from within. Character thus becomes a moral ideal legitimating certain modes of social existence. Wife, brother, cousin, household servant, village tribesman: these social roles are not *accidental* characteristics which must be sloughed off to disclose the "real self." They provide the very framework for one's *essential* social being:

> They are part of my substance, defining partially at least and sometimes wholly my obligations and my duties. Individuals inherit a particular space within an interlocking set of social relationships; lacking that space, they are nobody, or *at best a stranger or an outcast*. To know oneself as such a social person is however not to occupy a static and fixed position. It is to find one-

[20] "Please do this one favor for me, dear doctors. If you have a patient, young or old, suffering, dying, afflicted, useless, born or unborn, whom you for the best of reasons wish to put out of his misery—I beg only one thing of you dear doctors! Please send him to us. Don't kill them! We'll take them—all of them. . . . God will bless you

self placed at a certain point on a journey with set goals; to move through
life is to make progress—or to fail to make progress—toward a given end.
Thus a completed and fulfilled life is an achievement and death is the point
at which one can be judged happy or unhappy. Hence the ancient Greek
proverb: "Call no man happy until he is dead."[21]

This affirmation goes straight to the heart of Walker Percy's fiction.
Like MacIntyre, Percy laments the disappearance of the substantial self
into a vapor of indeterminate potentiality. "Lucky is the man," declares
the narrator of *The Last Gentleman*, "who does not secretly believe that
every possibility is open to him" (*The Last Gentleman*, p. 4). Percy would
also join MacIntyre in repudiating a Newtonian science which reduces
every effect, whether in the human or natural order, to necessary or sufficient causes that reside wholly within antecedent conditions. Percy affirms, above all, MacIntyre's conviction that the self has its true life in the
quest for happiness rightly conceived—a bliss both temporal and eternal.

Despite these agreements, there is a fundamental divide between
Percy and MacIntyre concerning the nature of human selfhood. What
Percy proposes as the *cure* to our modern malaise, MacIntyre understands as the heart of the *sickness* itself—the notion, namely, that the self
is a sovereign wayfarer and wanderer, the metaphysical stranger and
outcast who "comes to himself" in the solitude of his own spiritual
search. Whereas MacIntyre's idea of selfhood is social and historical
through and through, Percy's remains Kierkegaardian and existentialist.
Thus may Percy be tangled in the very same Enlightenment snares from
which he seeks to wrench us free.

Yet there is also danger in MacIntyre's yearning for a return to tradition and community. As the critics of communitarianism point out, Nazi
society comprised a democratic, cohesive, and legally constituted community. Richard Rubenstein makes the chilling observation, in fact, that
"the Nazis committed no crime at Auschwitz":

> Once defined as a Jew, by the German state bureaucracy, a person was pro-
> gressively deprived of all personal property and citizenship rights. The final
> step in the process came when he was eliminated altogether. The destruc-
> tion process required the cooperation of every sector of German society. The
> bureaucrats drew up the definitions and decrees; the churches gave evi-
> dence of Aryan descent; the postal authorities carried the messages of defi-

---

for it and you will offend no one except the Great Prince Satan, who rules the world"
(*The Thanatos Syndrome*, p. 361).

nition, expropriation, and deportation; business corporations dismissed their Jewish employees and took over 'Aryanized' properties; the railroads carried the victims to their place of execution, a place made available to the Gestapo and the SS by the *Wehrmacht*.[22]

For Percy no less than for MacIntyre, the real question is what might shape the life of a faithful community—and thus of the culture where it makes witness—in order to verify the inscription at Dachau: *Nie wieder*. Against Father Rinaldo Smith, I would argue that the answer to totalitarian will-to-power does not lie in an existentialist reverence for the sacredness of life itself. Israel in diaspora does not scandalize the world because it bodies forth human homelessness, but because it is the community called and constituted by the God of the covenant.

It is important to recall that Jews were not the only people who refused to be subsumed under the abstractions of race and nation. Gypsies and homosexuals who declined membership in the Nazi state—not to mention faithful Catholics and Protestants—were also executed by the thousands. What offends every epoch and culture, medieval Christendom no less than modern totalitarianism, is Jewish *faith*. The Jews are a scandal precisely insofar as they are a people animated by the faith that not the state, not humanity, not even life itself, but God alone rules human existence.[23]

For Christians, it is faith in Jesus Christ that forms the basis for such a claim. The Lutheran theologian Eberhard Jüngel denies that this faith is lived in solitary existence before God. He argues against the popular notion that the Christian life is essentially inward rather than outward. It is not because our outer nature is social that it must pass away (II Cor 4:16), but rather because it is constituted by its own externality—by its denial of God in allegiance to false claims and values. A strictly external self would never be capable of coming to itself exactly because it could never

---

[21]   *After Virtue*, 2nd ed. (Notre Dame, Ind.: University of Notre Dame Press, 1984), pp. 33-34. Emphasis mine.

[22]   *The Cunning of History: The Holocaust and the American Future* (New York: Harper Colophon Books, 1975), pp. 4-5, 87.

[23]   Stanley Hauerwas points out how such biblical faith scandalizes our Enlightenment assumption that a free and self-determining people must emancipate itself from all historical particularity and heteronomous authority. He also observes the awful irony inherent in the call for a universalist idea of humanity to prevent another Holocaust. It is always the Jews—Hauerwas cites disturbing passages from Kant—who are the first to be persecuted in the name of a universally valid ethic. See *Against the Nations: War and Survival in a Liberal Society* (Minneapolis: Winston, 1985), pp. 71-77.

exist outside itself. A worldly self is no real self at all. Our inner nature, by contrast, is meant to go out of itself and to be turned away from itself. Far from being buried within its own solitude, the inward self has its true life in engagement with others and knowledge of God.

Yet in sin the inner self has forfeited such out-going freedom. It has immured itself within the walls of its own solitude. Hence Martin Luther's insistence—despite the standard judgment of him to the contrary—that inwardness is not the realm of liberty but of slavery. Why else, asks Jüngel, would Luther agree with Paul in speaking of the fallen inner self as *flesh* (cf. Rom 8:3-8)? Having surrendered its liberty of movement, the sinful inner self now dwells in the same bondage as the outer—namely, in the captivity of a selfhood which remains within itself, unable to emerge from itself, acting inwardly as if it were an outer self.

Jüngel insists with Luther that the proclaimed and enacted Word alone can deliver the inner self from its miserable confinement. Like the Prodigal Son, we come to ourselves in order to leave ourselves behind. Only in the abandonment of false inwardness do we find what Luther regarded as true liberty rather than dread servitude of will: "If God is *in us*, then *we are outside ourselves.*" Freedom is thus a divine possibility before it can become a human reality. In putting off our old nature for a new (Eph. 4:22f., Col. 3:9f.), believers become something which they cannot possibly generate through self-awareness: a new creation, God's own people.[24]

It is this Christological formulation of freedom that Percy's fiction imperfectly mirrors. Percy rightly understands that the self is not created through its own autonomous activity.[25] With St. Augustine and the entire Western theological tradition, he stresses the utter prevenience of God's grace. Lancelot Lamar is damned precisely for believing that his valorous and murderous works constitute his real self. And Will Barrett

---

[24] Eberhard Jüngel, *The Freedom of a Christian: Luther's Significance for Contemporary Theology*, trans. by Roy Harrisville (Minneapolis: Augsburg, 1988), p. 76.

[25] Jüngel rightly insists that this notion of the will has having sovereign freedom is not biblical but pagan: "Christian understanding lives from the fact that God cannot be managed. If we were to forgo distinguishing the inner and outer man—in whatever terminology—then humanity would have to be conceived as acting subject and in is activity as realizing itself. Then I am my deed. . . . Then God, like the world, is treated as a means to the end of human self-realization—or since God cannot be an intelligible theme for the person whose self is realized through activity, is entirely ignored. . . . And this is in fact the goal of all self-realization through activity, that finally I may have or possess myself. The goal of all self-realization is self-possession, having myself without restriction" (p. 81).

is correct in calling subjectivity a vortex, "the great suck of self" (*The Second Coming*, p. 16).

So deep is Percy's understanding of "the grace that prevents us everywhere" that, at least in his first four novels, his unheroic heroes are all miraculously *delivered* from evil—despite and not because of their willful efforts. In *The Moviegoer* Binx Bolling backs inadvertently out of antic detachment and into marital love for Kate Cutrer. Tom More is spaced an apocalyptic fate at the end of *Love in the Ruins,* and not chiefly because he has fought it off. In *The Last Gentleman* Sutter Vaught wondrously waits for Will Barrett, thus offering the addled engineer a chance to learn from a failed suicide what it might mean to live.

That three of Percy's first four protagonists move beyond solitude into solidarity with at least one other person is a modest communal corrective to Kierkegaardian notions of selfhood. That the Catholic Mass figures as a sign of their restored solidarity indicates that the Christian reality is sacramentally received before it is ethically imitated. But that Percy's central characters retain much of their spleen and nearly all of their alienation marks their continuing need to be emancipated from a furious self-obsession.

Although they have come *to* themselves, they have not yet been delivered *from* themselves. What they have still to learn is, in Jüngel's phrase, that "the outer man is to be related to the inner man as the inner man to God." He explains:

> the same Jesus Christ, if he has been at work without our aid as *sacramentum,* now also intends to be recognized as our *exemplum* by calling those he has freed to discipleship. And for that purpose those who are freed must in turn become active. The hearer of God's Word must in turn become a doer of the Word, faith thus active in love. And this occurs when the outer man is made conformable to the inner man, since the free lord of all who is subject to none becomes the dutiful servant of all [who is] subject to all (p. 79).

The *vita christiana* is not lived, therefore, in angry solitude before God but in glad priesthood to each other. Thus would I suggest that the redemptive community of faith is the true alternative to alienated selfhood no less than to scientific humanism.

IV

Bibliography of
Nathan A. Scott Jr.

Bibliography of Nathan A. Scott, Jr.

Compiled By
KIMBERLY R. CONNOR & CAROLYN M. JONES

BOOKS

Rehearsals of Discomposure: Alienation and Reconciliation in Modern Literature (New York: King's Crown Press of Columbia University Press, 1952; London: John Lehmann Ltd., 1952).

Modern Literature and the Religious Frontier (New York: Harper and Bros., 1958).

Albert Camus (London: Bowes and Bowes Ltd., 1962; New York: Hillary House, 1962). [in the series Studies in Modern European Literature and Thought, Ed. Erich Heller].

Reinhold Niebuhr (Minneapolis: University of Minnesota Press, 1963). [University of Minnesota Pamphlets on American Writers, no. 31].

Samuel Beckett (London: Bowes and Bowes, Ltd., 1965; New York: Hillary House, 1965) [in the series Studies in Modern European Literature and Thought, Ed. Erich Heller].

The Broken Center: Studies in the Theological Horizon of Modern Literature (New Haven: Yale University Press, 1966).

Ernest Hemingway (Grand Rapids: William B. Eerdmans Publishing Co., 1966).

Craters of the Spirit: Studies in the Modern Novel (Washington, Cleveland: Corpus Books, 1968; London: Sheed and Ward, 1969).

Negative Capability: Studies in the New Literature and the Religious Situation (New Haven: Yale University Press, 1969).

The Unquiet Vision: Mirrors of Man in Existentialism (New York: World Publishing Co., 1969).

Nathanael West (Grand Rapids: William B. Eerdmans Publishing Co., 1971).

The Wild Prayer of Longing: Poetry and the Sacred (New Haven: Yale University Press, 1971).

Three American Moralists—Mailer, Bellow, Trilling (Notre Dame: University of Notre Dame Press, 1973).

The Poetry of Civic Virtue—Eliot, Malraux, Auden (Philadelphia: Fortress Press, 1976).

Mirrors of Man in Existentialism (New York, Cleveland: William Collins, 1978; Nashville: Abingdon Press, 1979).

The Poetics of Belief: Studies in Coleridge, Arnold, Pater, Santayana, Stevens, and Heidegger (Chapel Hill: University of North Carolina Press, 1985).

EDITED VOLUMES

The Tragic Vision and the Christian Faith (New York: Association Press, 1957).

The Climate of Faith in Modern Literature (New York: Seabury Press, 1964).

The New Orpheus: Essays Toward a Christian Poetic (New York: Sheed and Ward, Inc., 1964).

Forms of Extremity in the Modern Novel (Richmond: John Knox Press, 1965).

Four Ways of Modern Poetry (Richmond: John Knox Press, 1965).

Man in the Modern Theatre (Richmond: John Knox Press, 1965).

The Modern Vision of Death (Richmond: John Knox Press, 1967).

Adversity and Grace: Studies in Recent American Literature (Chicago: University of Chicago Press, 1968).

The Legacy of Reinhold Niebuhr (Chicago: University of Chicago Press, 1975).

ESSAYS IN BOOKS

"Religious Symbolism in Contemporary Literature," *Religious Symbolism.* Ed. F. Ernest Johnson (New York: Harper and Bros., 1955).

"Dostoevski: Tragedian of the Modern Excursion Into Unbelief," *The Tragic Vision and the Christian Faith.* Ed. Nathan A. Scott, Jr. (New York: Association Press, 1957).

"The Collaboration of Vision in the Poetic Act," *Literature and Belief.* Ed. M. H. Abrams (New York: Columbia University Press, 1958).

"The Broken Center: A Definition of the Crisis of Values in Modern Literature," *Symbolism in Religion and Literature.* Ed. Rollo May (New York: George Braziller, Inc., 1960).

"Art and the Renewal of Human Sensibility in Mass Society," *Christian Faith and the Contemporary Arts.* Ed. Finley Eversole (New York, Nashville: Abingdon Press, 1962).

"The Broken Center: A Definition of the Crisis of Values in Modern Literature," *Society and Self.* Ed. Bartlett H. Stoodley (Glencoe: The Free Press, 1962).

"Graham Greene: Christian Tragedian," *Graham Greene: Some Critical Considerations.* Ed. Robert O. Evans (Lexington: University of Kentucky Press, 1963).

"Faith and Art in a World Gone Awry," *The Climate of Faith in Modern Literature.* Ed. Nathan A. Scott, Jr. (New York: Seabury Press, 1964).

"Mimesis and Time in Modern Literature," *The Scope of Grace: Essays for Joseph Sittler.* Ed. Philip Hefner (Philadelphia: Fortress Press, 1964).

"The Modern Experiment in Criticism; A Theological Appraisal," *The New Orpheus: Essays Toward a Christian Poetic.* Ed. Nathan A. Scott, Jr. (New York: Sheed and Ward, Inc., 1964).

"Society and Self in Recent American Literature," *The Search for Identity: Essays on the American Character.* Ed. Roger L. Shinn (New York: Harper and Bros., 1964).

"Auden's Subject: 'The Human Clay'—'The Village of the Heart,'" *Four Ways of Modern Poetry.* Ed. Nathan A. Scott, Jr. (Richmond: John Knox Press, 1965).

"The Bias of Comedy and the Narrow Escape Into Faith," *Comedy: Meaning and Form*. Ed. Robert W. Corrigan (San Francisco: Chandler, 1965).

"Foreword," *The Gospel According to Peanuts*, by Robert L. Short (Richmond: John Knox Press, 1965).

"Kafka's Anguish," *Forms of Extremity in the Modern Novel*. Ed. Nathan A. Scott, Jr. (Richmond: John Knox Press, 1965).

"The Theatre of T. S. Eliot," *Man in the Modern Theatre*. Ed. Nathan A. Scott, Jr. (Richmond: John Knox Press, 1965).

"The Broken Center: A Definition of the Crisis of Values in Modern Literature," *A Casebook on Existentialism*. Ed. William V. Spanos (New York: Thomas Y. Crowell Co., 1966).

"The Christian Understanding of Man," *Conflicting Images of Man*. Ed. William Nicholls (New York: Seabury Press, 1966).

"Flannery O'Connor's Testimony: The Pressure of Glory," *The Added Dimension: The Mind and Art of Flannery O'Connor*. Eds. Melvin J. Friedman and Lewis A. Lawson (New York: Fordham University Press, 1966).

"The New Mystique of l'Actuelle," *Man and the Movies*. Ed. W. R. Robinson (Baton Rouge: Louisiana State University Press, 1967).

"Poetic Vision as an Expression of Ultimate Concern," *Religion and Contemporary Western Culture*. Ed. Edward Cell (New York-Nashville: Abingdon Press, 1967).

"Drama," *The Westminster Dictionary of Christian Education*. Ed. Kendig Brubaker Cully (Philadelphia: Westminster Press, 1968).

"Judgment Marked by a Cellar: The American Negro Writer and the Dialectic of Despair," *The Shapeless God*. Eds. Harry J. Mooney and Thomas Staley (Pittsburgh: University of Pittsburgh Press, 1968).

"Introduction: Theology and the Literary Imagination," *Adversity and Grace: Studies in Recent American Literature*. Ed. Nathan A. Scott, Jr. (Chicago: University of Chicago Press, 1968).

"Society and the Self in Recent American Literature," *Dark Symphony: Negro Literature in America*. Eds. James A. Emmanuel and Theodore L. Gross (New York: The Free Press, 1968; London: Collier-Macmillan Ltd., 1968).

"Sola Gratia: The Principle of Bellow's Fiction," *Adversity and Grace: Studies in Recent American Literature*. Ed. Nathan A. Scott, Jr. (Chicago: University of Chicago Press, 1968).

"The Bias of Comedy and the Narrow Escape into Faith," *Holy Laughter*. Ed. M. Conrad Hyers (New York: Seabury Press, 1969).

"The Dark and Haunted Tower of Richard Wright," *Black Expression: Essays by and About Black Americans in the Creative Arts*. Ed. Addison Gayle, Jr. (New York: Weybright and Talley, Inc., 1969).

"The Conscience of the New Literature," *The Shaken Realist: Essays in Modern Literature in Honor of Frederick J. Hoffman*. Eds. Melvin J. Friedman and John B. Vickery (Baton Rouge: Louisiana State University Press, 1970).

"The Dark and Haunted Tower of Richard Wright," *The Black Novelist*. Ed. Robert Hemenway (Columbus: Charles E. Merrill Publishing Co., 1970).

"The Dark and Haunted Tower of Richard Wright," *Five Black Writers: Essays on Wright, Ellison, Baldwin, Hughes, and LeRoi Jones*. Ed. Donald B. Gibson (New York: New York University Press, 1970).

"Judgment Marked by a Cellar: The American Negro Writer and the Dialectic of Despair," *Cavalcade: Negro American Writing From 1760 to the Present*. Eds. Arthur P. Davis and J. Saunders Redding (Boston: Houghton Mifflin Co., 1971).

"Poetry and Prayer," *Literature and Religion*. Ed. Giles B. Gunn (New York: Harper and Row, 1971; London: S. C. M. Press, 1971).

"Criticism and the Religious Horizon," *Humanities, Religion, and the Arts Tomorrow*. Ed. Howard Hunter (New York: Holt, Rinehart, and Winston, Inc., 1972).

"The Dark and Haunted Tower of Richard Wright," *Contemporary Literary Criticism*, Vol. 1. Ed. Carolyn Riley (Detroit: Gale Research Co., 1973).

"The Modern Imagination of Death," *In the End of Life*. Ed. J. Roslansky (London: North Holland Publishing Co., 1973).

"Ernest Hemingway: A Critical Essay," *Ernest Hemingway: Five Decades of Criticism*. Ed. Linda W. Wagner (East Lansing: Michigan State University Press, 1974).

"Faith and Art in a World Awry," *Twentieth Century Criticism: The Major Statements*. Eds. William Handy and Max Westbrook (New York: The Free Press, 1974).

"The Name and Nature of Our Period Style," *Religion and Modern Literature*. Eds. Georg B. Tennyson and Edward Ericson (Grand Rapids: William B. Eerdmans Publishing Co., 1974).

"New Heavens, New Earth—The Landscape of Contemporary Apocalypse," *Philosophy and the Civilizing Arts: Essays Presented to Herbert W. Schneider on His Eightieth Birthday*. Eds. Craig Walton and John P. Anton (Athens: Ohio University Press, 1974).

"Reinhold Niebuhr," *Makers of American Thought*. Ed. Ralph Ross (Minneapolis: University of Minnesota Press, 1974).

"Criticism and the Religious Prospect," *Essays and Studies: 1977*. Ed. W. Moelwyn Merchant (London: John Murray, 1977).

"Burdens and Temptations of the Pulpit," *Preaching on Suffering and a God of Love*. Ed. H. J. Young (Philadelphia: Fortress Press, 1978).

"Criticism and the Religious Prospect," *The Poetics of Faith: Essays Offered to Amos Niven Wilder*. Ed. William A. Beardslee (Missoula, Montana: Scholars Press, 1978).

"Black Literature," *The Harvard Guide to Contemporary American Writing*. Ed. Daniel Hoffman (Cambridge: Harvard University Press, 1979).

"Day by Day," *Theologians in Transition*. Ed. James M. Wall (New York: Crossroad Publishing Co., 1981).

"Ralph Ellison's Vision of Communitas," *American Writing Today*, Vol. 1. Ed. Richard Kostelanetz (Washington, D. C.: International Communications Agency Forum Series, 1982).

"The Rediscovery of Story in Recent Theology and the Refusal of Story in Recent Literature," *Art, Literature, Religion: Life on the Borders*. Ed. Robert Detweiler (Chico: Scholars Press, 1983).

"Santayana's Poetics of Belief," *American Critics at Work: Examinations of Contemporary Literary Theories*. Ed. Victor A. Kramer (Troy: Whitston Publishing Co., 1984).

"Orwell's Legacy," *George Orwell and Nineteen Eighty-Four: The Man and the Book* (Washington, D. C.: The Library of Congress, 1985).

"Tillich's Legacy and the New Scene in Literature," *The Thought of Paul Tillich*. Eds. James Luther Adams, Wilhelm Pauck, and Roger L. Shinn (New York: Harper and Row, Inc., 1985).

"Religious Dimensions of Modern Literature," *The Encyclopedia of Religion*. Ed. Mircea Eliade (New York: Macmillan, 1986).

"The House of Intellect in an Age of Carnival: Some Hermeneutical Reflections," *The Whirlwind in Culture—Frontiers in Theology: Essays in Honor of Langdon Gilkey*. Eds. Donald W. Musser and Joseph L. Price (Bloomington, Ind.: Meyer Stone Books, 1988).

"On the Teaching of Literature in an Age of Carnival," *Teaching Literature: What is Needed Now*. Eds. James Engell and David Perkins, Harvard English Studies: 15 (Cambridge: Harvard University Press, 1988).

ARTICLES

"Neglected Aspects of the Theological Curriculum," *The Journal of Religious Thought* 7.1 (1950): 38-46.

"Lionel Trilling's Critique of the Liberal Mind," *Christianity and Society* 16.2 (1951): 9-18.

"T. E. Hulme: A Reconsideration," *Union Seminary Quarterly Review* 6 (1951): 24-30.

"T. S. Eliot's The Cocktail Party: of Redemption and Vocation," *Religion in Life* 20.2 (1951): 274-285.

"The Testimony of the Novel," *The Intercollegian* 69 (1952): 10- 12.

"The Kingdom Foreseen: An Interim Assessment of Contemporary Literature," *The Intercollegian* 71 (1953): 7-18, 22.

"Poetry and the Crisis of Metaphysics," *The Christian Scholar* 36 (1953): 273-80.

"Poetry, Religion, and the Modern Mind," *The Journal of Religion* 33 (1953): 182-97.

"The Relation of Theology to Literary Criticism," *The Journal of Religion* 33 (1953): 266-77.

"Graham Greene: Christian Tragedian," *Volusia Review* 1 (1954): 29- 42.

"Religious Implications in the Humanities," *The Journal of Human Relations* 2 (1954): 16-24.

"Maritain in His Role as Aesthetician," *The Review of Metaphysics* 8.3 (1955): 480-92.

"The Personal Principle in Recent Literature and its Religious Implication," *motive* 15 (1955): 19-21, 36.

"Prolegomenon to a Christian Poetic," *The Journal of Religion* 35 (1955): 191-206.

"Recent Christian Writing," *Union Seminary Quarterly Review* 10 (1955): 11-18.

"Beneath the Hammer of Truth," *Christianity and Crisis* 16 (1956): 124-26.

"Poetry and Religion: A Relation Reconsidered," *The Chicago Theological Seminary Register* 46.1 (1956): 1-7.

"The Search for Beliefs in the Fiction of Richard Wright," *University of Kansas City Review* 23 (1956): 19-24.

"The Collaboration of Vision in the Poetic Act: Its Establishment of the Religious Dimension," *Cross Currents* 7 (1957): 137-53. [this article also appeared in *The Christian Scholar* 40 (1957): 277-95].

"The Meaning of the Incarnation for Modern Literature," *Christianity and Crisis* 18.21 (1958): 174-84. [this article also appeared in *The Chaplain*, 1958].

"Religion and Literature: A Selected Bibliography," *The Christian Scholar* 41 (1958): 70-76.

"The Broken Center," *The Chicago Review* 13 (1959): 182-202.

"The Example of George Orwell," *Christianity and Crisis* 19.13 (1959): 107-10.

"The Modest Optimism of Albert Camus," *The Christian Scholar* 42.4 (1959): 251-74.

"The Poetry of Auden," *The Chicago Review* 13.4 (1959): 53-75. [this article also appeared in *The London Magazine* January (1961): 44-63].

"Art and the Renewal of Human Sensibility in Mass Society," *motive* 21 (1960): 29-35.

"The Literary Imagination and the Victorian Crisis of Faith: The Example of Thomas Hardy," *The Journal of Religion* 40.4 (1960): 267-81.

"The Bias of Comedy and the Narrow Escape Into Faith," *The Christian Scholar* 44.1 (1961): 9-39.

"Faith and Art in a World Awry," *motive* 22 (1961): 22-28. [This article also appeared in *Student World* 55 (1962): 196-210].

"The Recent Journey Into the Zone of Zero: The Example of Beckett and His Despair of Literature," *The Centennial Review* 6.2 (1962): 144-81.

"Society and Self in Recent American Literature," *Union Seminary Quarterly Review* 18.4 (1963): 377-92.

"The Tragic Vision and the Christian Faith," *Anglican Theological Review* 45 (1963): 23-45.

"The Dark and Haunted Tower of Richard Wright," *Graduate Comment* 7 (1964): 93-99.

"Man in Modern Literature," *Criterion* 4 (1965): 19-22.

"Poetry and Prayer," *Thought* 41 (1966): 61-80.

"Judgment Marked by a Cellar: The American Negro Writer and the Dialectic of Despair," *The Denver Quarterly* 2.2 (1967): 5-35.

"Nathan A. Scott, Jr.," *Criterion* 6 (1967): 29-31.

"Response to Charles Long's Paper," *Criterion* 8 (1967): 8-11.

"On the Fallacies of a 'Close Reader'," *The Journal of the American Academy of Religion* 39 (1971): 76-82.

"History, Hope, and Literature," *Boundary* 2 1.3 (1973): 577-603.

"'New Heav'ns, New Earth,'—The Landscape of Contemporary Apocalypse," *The Journal of Religion* 53 (1973): 1-35.

"Eliot and the Orphic Way," *The Journal of the American Academy of Religion* 42.2 (1974): 203-31.

"The Poetry and Theology of Earth: Reflections on the Testimony of Joseph Sittler and Gerard Manley Hopkins," *The Journal of Religion* 54 (1974): 102-18.

"Criticism and the Religious Prospect," *Semeia* 13 (1978): 225-40.

"Arnold's Version of Transcendence: The Via Poetica," *The Journal of Religion* 59 (1979): 261-84.

"Day by Day: Plotting the Dialogue Between Christian Theology and Modern Literature; How My Mind Has Changed," *The Christian Century* 97 (1980): 962-66.

"Ellison's Vision of Communitas," *The NICM* [National Institute for Campus Ministries] *Journal* 3.4 (1978): 40-49. [This article also appeared in *The Carleton Miscellany: A Review of Literature and the Liberal Arts* 18.3 (1980): 41-50].

"Pater's Imperative—To Dwell Poetically," *New Literary History* 15.1 (1983): 93-118.

"The Rediscovery of Story in Recent Theology and the Refusal of Story in Recent Literature," *The Journal of the American Academy of Religion: Thematic Studies* 49.2 (1983): 139-55.

"Elizabeth Bishop: Poet Without Myth," *Virginia Quarterly Review* 60.2 (1984): 255-75.

"Religion and the Intellectual Life," *Religion and Intellectual Life* 1.4 (1984): 66-73.

"The New Trahision des Clercs—Reflections on the Present Crisis in Humanistic Studies," *Virginia Quarterly Review* 62.3 (1986): 402-21.

"Prayer for Mircea Eliade," *Criterion* 25.3 (1986): 5.

"The House of Intellect in an Age of Carnival—Some Hermeneutical Reflections," *Journal of the American Academy of Religion* 55.1 (1987): 3-19.

"The Poetry of A. R. Ammons," *The Southern Review* 24.4 (1988): 717-43.

"On the Teaching of Literature in an Age of Carnival," *Journal of Literature and Theology* 1.2 (1987): 123-34.

"Romare Bearden," *Callaloo* 11.3 (1988): 420-22.

"Warren's Career in Poetry: Taking Counsel of the Heart Alone," *Centennial Review* 33.2 (1989): 141-86.

"The Poetry of Richard Wilbur—'The Splendor of Mere Being'," *Christianity and Literature* 39.1 (1989): 7-33.

V
Contributors

Contributors

Canon A. M. Allchin was ordained in the Church of England in 1956. He was on the staff of Pusey House in Oxford during the 1960s. After fourteen years as a Canon at Canterbury he returned to Oxford in 1987 as Director of an ecumenical center for the study and promotion of Christian spirituality. A life-long concern for Christian Unity has in recent years been combined with a desire to open up the frontiers between religion and literature, and with a growing involvement in the literary and linguistic tradition of Wales.

J. Robert Barth, S.J., is Dean of the College of Arts and Sciences, Boston College. He has also taught at Canisius College, Harvard University, and the University of Missouri-Columbia. A specialist of English Romanticism, he is a co-editor of the *Marginalia* in the ongoing *Collected Coleridge* (Princeton). His recent publications include *Coleridge and the Power of Love* (1988) and *Coleridge, Keats and the Imagination: Romanticism and Adam's Dream* (1990), the last of which he co-edited with John Mahoney.

Larry D. Bouchard is Associate Professor of Religious Studies at the University of Virginia. He teaches in the area of Religion and Literature, and he has also taught at Eureka College in Illinois and at Regent's College in London. He is the author of *Tragic Method and Tragic Theology: Evil in Contemporary Drama and Religious Thought* (1989). He received his doctorate (in Religion and Literature) from The Divinity School, The University of Chicago.

Frank Burch Brown is Associate Professor of Religion and Humanities at Virginia Polytechnic Institute and State University. His publications include *Transfiguration: Poetic Metaphor and the Languages of Religious Belief* (1983) and *Religious Aesthetics: A Theological Study of Making and Meaning* (1990). Also a composer and musician, he received his doctorate (in Religion and Literature) from The Divinity School, The University of Chicago.

Kimberly Rae Connor received a B.A. from Gettysburg College and an M.A. from the University of Bristol, England. She is a candidate for a Ph.D. in Religion and Literature at the University of Virginia, and is currently completing a dissertation titled: "Conversions and Visions in the Writings of Afro-American Women."

Linda-Marie Delloff, former Managing Editor of the *Christian Century,* is Arts and Books Editor of *The Lutheran,* the magazine of the Evangelical Lutheran Church in America. She received her doctorate (in Religion and Literature) from The Divinity School, The University of Chicago.

John Dillenberger is professor emeritus, Graduate Theological Union, Berkeley, California, which institution he also headed during its formative first decade. He has also held professorial positions at Princeton, Columbia, Harvard, and Drew Universities. Among his recent publications are *A Theology of Artistic Sensibilities and The Visual Arts* and *Christianity in America.* He did his doctoral work at Columbia/Union, where he first met Nathan A. Scott, Jr.

Mary Gerhart received her doctorate (in Religion and Literature) from the University of Chicago and is Professor of Religious Studies at Hobart and William Smith Colleges. Her publications include *The Question of Belief in Literary Criticism: An Introduction to the Hermeneutical Theory of Paul Ricoeur* (1978), *Metaphoric Process: The Creation of Scientic and Religious Understanding* (with A.M. Russell, 1984), *Genre, Narrativity, and Theology* (ed. with J. Williams, 1988), and a forthcoming book on genre. She is a past Editorial Chair of *Religious Studies Review.*

Langdon Gilkey's adult life has found itself strangely interwoven with that of Nathan Scott. He first knew Scott as one of the vastly respected "senior" graduate students at Union-Columbia when Gilkey entered the program as a freshman in 1946. Then in 1963 they became colleagues on the faculty of the Divinity School of The University of Chicago until Scott left for Virginia in 1976. Now Gilkey has recently retired as the Shailer Mathews Professor (of Theology) at the Divinity School, the same chair of which Scott had been its first occupant. Like Scott, Gilkey has been primarily concerned with the relation of Christianity with culture and so with the issues that developments in culture—intellectual, existential and historical—have raised for theology and for faith. His books include *Maker of Heaven and Earth, Naming* and *Reaping the Whirlwind, Message and Existence*, and *Society and the Sacred*. His most recent interests have been issues in religion and science and the new question—or form of the question—of the plurality of religions.

Giles Gunn is Professor of English at the University of California, Santa Barbara, and author most recently of *The Culture of Criticism and the Criticism of Culture* (1987). He has written or edited seven other books, among them *F. O. Matthiessen* (1975), *The Interpretation of Otherness* (1979), *New World Metaphysics* (1981), and *The Bible and American Arts and Letters* (1983), and is currently finishing a new book entitled *Cutting Across the American Grain*. He received his doctorate (in Religion and Literature) from The Divinity School, The University of Chicago.

Ihab Hassan is Vilas Research Professor of English and Comparative Literature at the University of Wisconsin, Milwaukee. He is the author of many books, including *Radical Innocence* (1961), *the Dismemberment of Orpheus* (1971, 1982), *The Postmodern Turn* (1987), and most recently *Selves at Risk* (1990). He has also written an autobiography, *Out of Egypt* (1986).

David H. Hesla is Associate Professor of Literature and the History of Ideas in the Graduate Institute of the Liberal Arts and in the College of Emory University. He received his doctorate (in Religion and literature) from the Divinity School, The University of Chicago. His was the first dissertation Nathan Scott directed at Chicago, and the dissertation eventually was published as *The Shape of Chaos: An Interpretation of the Art of Samuel Beckett* (1971).

David Jasper was trained at Cambridge, Oxford, and Durham and is at present Principal of St. Chad's College in the University of Durham and Director of the Centre for the Study of Literature and Theology. He is the Senior Editor of the Journal Literature and Theology and his books include *The New Testament and the Literary Imagination* and *The Study of*

Literature and Religion: An Introduction. He is at present completing a book on religious rhetoric.

Carolyn M. Jones is Acting Assistant Professor of Religious Studies at Louisiana State University. She is also a doctoral candidate in the Department of Religious Studies, University of Virginia, where under Nathan Scott's direction, she is completing a dissertation entitled "Pilgrimage to the Sun: Marriage in D. H. Lawrence's Major Novels."

Wesley A. Kort received his doctorate (in Religion and Literature) from The Divinity School, The University of Chicago in 1965. He taught for two years at Princeton University before joining the faculty at Duke University where he is now Professor of Religion and Culture in the Department of Religion and the Graduate Religion Program. His published books and articles primarily treat the relations of narrative and belief and of narrative theory and religious thought to one another. His most recent book is entitled *Story, Text and Scripture: Literary Interests in Biblical Narrative.*

J. C. Levenson is the Edgar Allan Poe Professor of English at the University of Virginia. He is editor of *The Letters of Henry Adams* (6 vols., 1983, 1988) and of the Library of America edition of *Stephen Crane: Prose and Poetry* (1983). He is the author of *The Mind and Art of Henry Adams* (1957, 1968) and of articles on American literature from the times of Melville and Mark Twain to the recent past.

Charles H. Long has been the Jeannette K. Watson Professor of Religion and Director of the Humanities Doctoral Program at Syracuse University since 1988. He is past President of the American Academy of Religion (1973) and currently (since 1985) President of the Society for the Study of Black Religion. With Mircea Eliade and Joseph Kitagawa, he was a founding editor of *The Journal of the History of Religions* at the University of Chicago. His most recent publications include *Significations: Signs, Symbols, and Images in the Interpretation of Religion* (1986).

Edward Mendelson is Professor of English and Comparative Literature at Columbia University. He is editing a complete edition of W. H. Auden's writings and preparing the second volume of a critical biography of Auden. He has written extensively on other modern writers.

Anne E. Patrick is Associate Professor and Chair of the Department of Religion at Carleton College, and the immediate past president of the Catholic Theological Society of America. She has also taught at the University of Tulsa, the University of Chicago Divinity School, and at schools in Maryland, New York, and Florida. She is the author of the forthcoming study, *Conscience and Community: Challenges in Catholic Moral Theology*, and editor of the forthcoming volume, *Providence and Responsibility: The Divine and Human in History*. She is also completing a book, *Faith, Ethics, and Fiction: The Case of George Eliot's Last Novels*. She received her doctorate (in Religion and Literature) from The Divinity School, The University of Chicago.

Norman Pittenger was for more than thirty years professor at the General Theological Seminary in New York. He has been senior resident at King's College, Cambridge University in England, and a member of the Divinity Faculty of the University since 1966. He has published eighty-nine books and numerous essays and reviews in the fields of theology, philosophy of religion, and history.

Lynn Poland pursued a degree in Religion and Literature from the University of Chicago while Nathan Scott was a member of the Faculty. Since receiving her doctorate, she has taught Religion and Literature at several institutions, among them Indiana University, The University of Chicago Divinity School, and Bates College. She is currently Associate Professor of Religion at Davidson College. Author of *Literary Criticism and Biblical Hermeneutics: A Critique of Formalist Approaches*, she is interested in the intersecting histories of literary and biblical criticism, in the moments when the Bible becomes a literary as well as a religious classic, and in the affective dimensions of reading sacred and classic texts.

Robert P. Scharlemann is Commonwealth Professor of Religious Studies at the University of Virginia, where he teaches philosophical theology. Among his publications are *Reflection and Doubt in the Thought of Paul Tillich, The Being of God, Inscriptions and Reflections*, and several edited volumes. He has also served as editor of the *Journal of the American Academy of Religion*.

David Tracy is Andrew Thomas Greeley and Grace McNichols Greeley Distinguished Service Professor at The Divinity School, The

University of Chicago, where he is also a professor in The Committee on the Analysis of Ideas and Methods and The Committee on Social Thought. Author of numerous books and articles, he has recently published *Plurality and Ambiguity: Hermeneutics, Religion, Hope* (1987) and with Hans Küng, *Paradigm Change in Theology* (1989). He is a Fellow of the American Academy of Arts and Sciences.

Ralph C. Wood has taught in the Religion Department at Wake Forest University since 1971. He serves as a contributing editor for the *Flannery O'Connor Bulletin*, an editor at large for the *Christian Century*, and as book review editor for *Perspectives in Religious Studies*. In 1988 he published *The Comedy of Redemption: Christian Faith and Comic Vision in Four American Novelists*. He received his doctorate (in Religion and Literature) from the Divinity School, The University of Chicago.

Anthony C. Yu received his doctorate (in Religion and Literature) from The University of Chicago, where he is currently Carl Darling Buck Distinguished Service Professor of Humanities. He holds faculty appointments in The Divinity School, Department of East Asian Languages and Civilizations, Department of English, and the Committee on Social Thought. From 1983 to 1989, he also served as Chair of The Committee on Comparative Studies in Literature. Translator and editor of *The Journey to the West*, published in 4 volumes (1977-83), he is also author of numerous journal articles on religion and comparative literature.

DATE DUE

NOV 5 '91			

HIGHSMITH   # 45220